Dancing at the Yurt

an interfaith spiritual journey

by

Charles W. Pearl

HOLON
PUBLISHING

For permission requests, contact the publisher at:
www.Holon.co

ISBN#: 978-0-9966685-4-5
Library of Congress/Certificate of Copyright
Registration Number: TX 8-902-236

Published by:

Holon Publishing & Collective Press
A Storytelling Company
www.Holon.co

Dedication

To my late mother, Mary Lucy Pearl; my children, Charlsie
Garrett, Kevin Pearl, Kennedy Pearl and Kathryn Pearl; grandchildren,
Toshia and Jordan Garrett; Dawson, Preston and Charles Pearl III;
Kamdyn and Kalleigh Johnson; Lucie and Luke Pearl; and my
12-year-old black Lab, Lily

To my Frankfort Interfaith Council family: Ashiq Zaman,
Aejaz and Afeef Shaik, Mohammad Razavi, Titin Farida, Nathan,
Shannan, David and Julia Rome, Jim Jackson, Reed Rhorer, Avinash
Tope, Nash Cox, Rich Green, Leslie Saunders, Linda Axon, Ruth Scott,
Gayle Bourne, and Stephanie Cramer

To my Glitterbugs family: Sylvia and Don Coffey, Angela
Mitchell, Chris Sparks, Alice Delambre, Marcia Burklow, Jan Fowler,
Arba Kenner, Marie Berberian, Eileen Cackowski, Karen Cosby, Julia
and David Rome, Cary Sudduth and Joseph Fiala

With Love and Gratitude

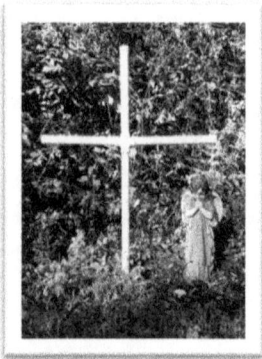

The Yurt -
"Pearl
Center for
World
Peace"

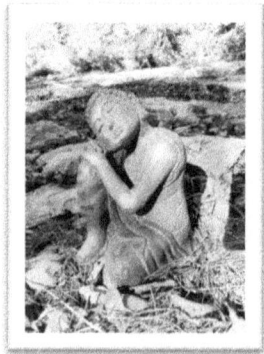

Table of Contents

Acknowledgements

As a former sports editor, managing editor, news editor and associate editor at weekly and semiweekly newspapers in Kentucky, I've been fortunate to get to know a lot of other editors. Unfortunately, many of them are dead now, including my all-time favorite, Carl West, editor of The State Journal in Frankfort, Kentucky, from 1979 to 2013.

Books brought Carl and me together. Not long after meeting him in 1988, he let me serve on his Kentucky Book Fair board and write book reviews. It took another 12 years to talk him into hiring me as a staff writer at the Frankfort newspaper. I'm guessing I was the oldest staff writer he ever hired. I had worked in community journalism since the early 1970s but it wasn't until February 2001 that I found my true home in journalism.

I loved working for Carl. He was the tough older brother I always wanted, and even though he was just six years older, he also was like a father. We argued at times and I disappointed him at times, but I knew he cared about me and everybody in the newsroom.

A lifelong bachelor, Carl once said he was married to journalism. "I think all of Carl's reporters were like the children he never had," said former State Journal reporter Gayle Coulter Deaton, who was with me in Carl's hospital room when he died on February 28, 2016.

Carl was tough on all his children. Compliments were rare. He would yawn in staff meetings, and roll his head on the conference table in mock agony when we pitched a story he hated. He taught us to work hard, develop sources, be persistent and accurate, bend over backwards to be fair, and read much more than we write. After giving me a story assignment, he also spoiled me by saying frequently, "Write the hell out of it, Charlie."

I thought about Carl a lot while working on this book, especially while trying to put the finishing touches to it. I think he would like some of it, and I'm sure some pages would have him yawning. He actually edited several chapters, which started out as State Journal stories.

My main editor for "Dancing at the Yurt" was Don Coffey, a man I had heard about and read about but hadn't met when I began writing the book in 2012. I'm grateful an international dance class in 2016 finally brought us together in our senior years. For decades, Don and his wife, Sylvia, have been involved in traditional music and dance.

After nearly forty years of mostly writing for federal and state governments, Don retired and began writing whatever he pleased. He's the author of "Paul Sawyier, Kentucky Artist," a 2010 book, which received high praise from Frankfort's Richard Taylor, a writing professor, author and former Kentucky Poet Laureate. Taylor said, "Through diligence and careful research Don Coffey has painted the fullest portrait of Kentucky's most celebrated landscape artist we're likely to see."

Don is one of the most brilliant, generous and progressive-thinking persons I have ever known. He spent many hours voluntarily proofing, editing and suggesting changes to improve the book. He did a magnificent job, even better than I imagined, and I already had the highest of expectations when I first handed him the manuscript. Thank you, Mr. Coffey.

Molly Williamson Tate, communications director for the Kentucky Housing Corporation, also volunteered to edit the manuscript. We had worked together a few years at The State Journal before she left to work at Kentucky State University, Northern Kentucky University and the University of Kentucky. We saw each other at a women's suffrage program at the Paul Sawyier Public Library in February 2020, which Sylvia Coffey helped coordinate. I was surprised Molly had moved back to Frankfort and she was surprised I was getting ready to have a book published. She offered to help and quickly handed me a small piece of paper with her contact information, along with a note at the bottom saying "Editor to the Stars." In addition to being an excellent writer, Molly has a wonderful sense of humor. She could always say something off the cuff at The State Journal that would make me laugh, even if it wasn't that funny. It was just the way she said it. Thank you Molly for reading the book, making edits, and making me laugh.

A huge thank you also goes to production manager Angela Mitchell, who has put in countless hours designing the book and its draft cover, editing copy and making all the corrections, offering good suggestions, getting manuscripts printed, doing redesign, and calling and texting me constantly to quit procrastinating and stay on deadline. A creative soul, Angela has a bachelor's degree in computer science from Kentucky State

University and retired from state government in the Commonwealth Office of Technology.

I also thank Angela for riding into my life in the 2006 Grand Autumn Bicycle Ride Across Kentucky (GABRAKY). She said a feature story I wrote on the 2005 ride was what inspired her to participate. On a 90-mile ride the second day of GABRAKY 2006, Angela spent a lot of time listening to me talk about a novel I was writing that focused on environmental pollution and racism. I had 26 chapters done at the time, and I still haven't finished it. In fact, I haven't written another word on it since I met her. It's been an enjoyable 14-year journey now, and I'm thankful to have her in my life.

I want to thank The State Journal, FRANK magazine, and The Lebanon Enterprise for allowing me to reprint articles I wrote for those publications; Hannah Brown, editor of FRANK magazine, for providing file photos I requested from FRANK and The State Journal; Jenny Neat and Leigh Ann Schrader for sharing a photo; friend Jeremy Gotwals, founder/creative director at Geronimo and founder/publisher at Holon Publishing & Collective Press, for publishing this book, and creative coordinators Catherine Valerio and Grace Beck Faile for their assistance; artist Linda Boileau for her illustration; daughter Charlsie Maria Garrett and friends Nancy Osborne, Vicki Pettus and David Rome, for proofing and making suggestions; friends Mary Lynn Collins, Connie Crowe, Normandi Ellis, Gina Morales, Gayle Coulter Deaton, Eric Lynes, Sally Everman, Anna Laura Evans Davenport, Trey Abell and C.C. Long for encouraging me to finish the book.

And a special thank you goes to my main spiritual teachers: Dr. Chuck Queen, senior pastor at Immanuel Baptist Church; Anam Thubten, a Tibetan Buddhist master now living in Richmond, California; and Father Lawman Chibundi, pastor of Rabbouni Catholic Community in Louisville and Lebanon, Kentucky.

Tibetan Buddhist monks create a sand mandala at the
Paul Sawyer Public Library in Frankfort, KY

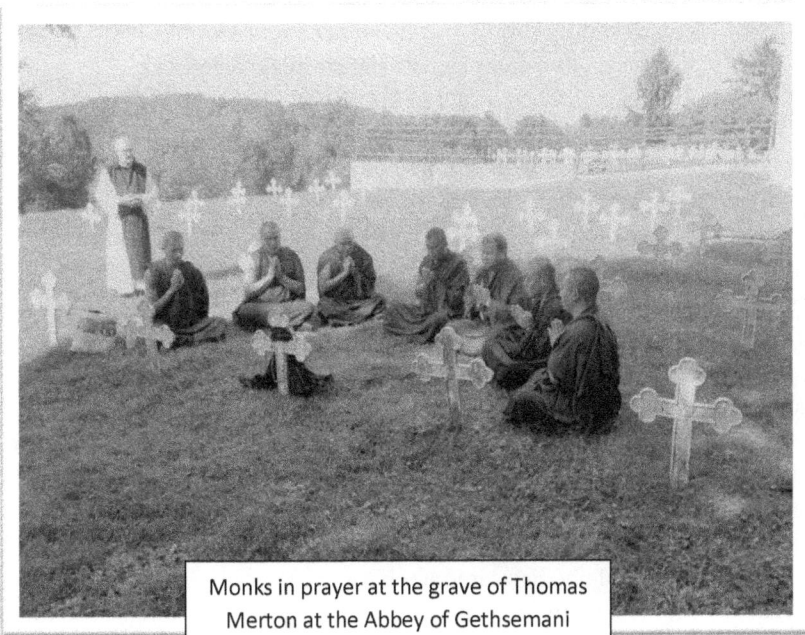

Monks in prayer at the grave of Thomas
Merton at the Abbey of Gethsemani

Preface

My pal, Charlie Pearl, has written a fairly deceptive book.

I knew he was writing it. The giveaway was the several times he mentioned it over the past year, for he seldom mentions anything more than once per month. As completion neared in recent months, I noticed he even waxed a tad intense, most un-Charlie-like, with mutterances about how very *much* he just had to put into it. I perceived he meant content as well as personal energy, though Charlie's really good at the ambiguous one-liner.

Then, too, there was the deceptive part. When he first began mentioning it, I would ask—quite naturally, I thought, "What's the book about?"

"Well, it's kinda like my memoirs... sort of."

"Okay, memoirs, about your life experiences, right?"

"Yeah, well ...and some of the neat people I've known."

You see what I mean—lack of forthcomingness. Ambiguous, at best.

Then, he prevailed upon me to accept the great honor of editing and proofing his manuscript. How could I say no? And that's when the truth began unfolding before me.

Most chapters do indeed tell something—a little—about the life of Charlie Pearl. A very few are even dedicated, mostly, to Charlie himself, his family and his extended family, including the dogs he has loved and who returned unconditional love to him.

But when you get right down to it, most chapters are about other people—the people Charlie has known. People Charlie considers so unique and interesting that he must include them in his memoirs. And Charlie—this old newspaperman, after a full career of interviewing people and writing them into a zillion of his articles—knows a lot of people.

And that's how you get to know the real Charlie Pearl—by meeting so many of the people he has cared about over the years. Imagine: a lifelong journalist, immersed in the skeptical, hard-crusted, jaded, seen-it-all profession of journalistic news reporting, who knows all about people…and still loves them. He finally had to arbitrarily cut himself off, knowing that no publisher would consider a book voluminous enough to contain all the unique, interesting, lovely people Charlie cared for and would like to tell about.

They say a person's values are evident in the things they love, and Charlie loves just about everybody. It clearly pains him to be pressed to say anything unloving, much less negative, about anybody. His book reveals that his default option is love for humankind. The only discernable distinction is how fulsomely he loves the many, many individuals with whom he has crossed paths over his long years as a newspaper reporter interested in basically everything. Some few of the many he has loved over all those years now find their way into his memoirs.

And so, as I edited, I learned how welcomingly Charlie Pearl's memoirs are given over to telling about all those other people he has found interesting, cared for, loved. Many receive a whole chapter unto themselves and their doings, with little mentions here and there about Charlie himself and the ways in which he came to interact with them.

And then, after a while at this level of understanding, I began a slow mind-opening graduation up into Charlie's level. This happened with gradual arrival of realization that the book is really about religion, or—to choose the infinitely broader term—spirituality.

In his time, Charlie Pearl has been, variously, a Baptist, a Catholic, and a Buddhist. And through these years of deeply personal evolutions and emergings, by his own admission, never was he unattached to a spiritual anchor of some nature. A non-material reality of meaning and purpose has ever been a vital, intrinsic part of him. As I slowly grasped the unfolding synthesis of these inner experiences, while reading his calm mentions of them, I wondered what else he has been, what is now and what will yet become?

Charlie's memoirs are a thoughtful reader's welcoming into a Garden of Contemplation where the atmosphere is quiet almost all the time, where delicate fragrances of abundant flowers drift on perpetual soft breezes, and compassionate loving kindness with empathic consideration for the well-being of other human spirits is the perpetual ambiance.

Reading on, I began feeling uplifted. I realized the reader's mind really ought to be kept attuned—alert to notice the unfolding as his chapters are encountered, one by one—each introducing some new person, some new set of circumstances, in which the author's instinctive focus was on the values and worth represented by the circumstances and persons being written about.

At some point, the customary distinctions between Buddhists and Catholics and Baptists seem to fade away, they all flow together—and the reader becomes aware that there really are no distinctions worth mentioning. As the chapters accumulate, the world's religions seem to meld together and become something higher, something broader than religion, something representing a higher plane of love that is—among other things— unconditional. And the reader wonders, when did that happen without me noticing?

Then, pretty far down into the book, comes the ultimate realization—I'm reading a book about God. When did that happen? God is in every one of these people. They are all children of God, and—with the spirit of God in them—they represent God. Their feelings and emotions, their faculties of reasoning—these are "the image of God," are they not?

Mortal, full of failings and shortcomings but still trying, they are all participating in God's great experiment whereby we all come here *to do things*, to dance with each other, so that we may perchance *grow in spirit*, become something a bit *more*, be *risen* to something a bit higher and better— and then one day return that hard-won growth thankfully back to God the Creator of it *all*, every last molecule, photon and quark.

Charlie said all this without saying it. In his choices of which people and stories to include in his book of wonderful rememberings, as in the way he has written about the things included, he reveals his great respect for every person's integral right to be wherever they're at in life. What else but such acceptance should I have expected from this spiritually-minded friend who could say to me, in absolutely innocent candor:

> *I've never thought about being agnostic. I've always felt there has been some type of divine loving power guiding me when I was paying attention, and not just me, but everyone. I feel that everything that happens in life, the good and the bad, is a teaching for us that we need at the time. At this stage of my life, every day, I try to be aware, to see, the divine in every person and thing. Everything is sacred.*

If spiritual teaching is intrinsic in Charlie's way of living, in the way he interacts with the world and his world of friends, the words in his chapters simultaneously convey notice that it is not his way to preach. Certainly, he is no missionary, but the values, the lessons, the options are laid out like a subtle buffet—take whatever you want, keep only that which you feel might be helpful to you. The reader reaches a point of asking: Am I reading a memoir or a subtle teaching on something of great worth to us all?

So it was that, for a while, I imagined I was reading about Charlie Pearl's rich and highly miscellaneous life experiences—each one interesting to read about in its own context even though a tad random, like the trail of that proverbial wandering calf.

But this book is not about calves or randomness, it is about something that is deeper than one man's interesting experiences and the people and dogs he has loved and the religions he has tried on, ever curious to discover how they fit. It is far broader than being a monk or a priest or a Baptist, Buddhist or Catholic or more than these or none of these at all.

It's a book about love. It's a book with values and meanings, and teachings that sneak up on you. And my pal, Charlie Pearl, wrote it. I'm so grateful to him for that.

Don Coffey, March 2020

Charlie, Angela, and Lily at the Yurt in 2008

Walking meditation at the Labyrinth

PART ONE

Learning the Basic Steps

"When you dance, your purpose is not to get to a certain place on the floor. It's to enjoy each step along the way."
--Wayne Dyer

Introduction

I remember the exact moment I first heard of Todd and Leigh Ann Schrader.

Angela Mitchell and I were eating lunch downtown at Capital Cellars café. We were celebrating the reality that our Pacific Yurt – occasionally referred to as the "Pearl Center for World Peace" – was officially on its way to being created.

Just after I placed the order by cell phone, Joel Schrader, then-owner and publisher of Capital Living newspaper, walked in, smiled and asked, "What's new?"

I said, "We just ordered a yurt,"

And Joel asked, "A what?"

That's what just about everybody says here in Kentucky.

"It's a glorified tent – a one-room circular structure with high walls, five windows counting the door, and lots of rafters leading to a domed sky light at the top," I said. "It's going to be a writing and art studio and meditation center.

"It'll be shipped from Oregon in three or four weeks and we need somebody to build the platform and 26-foot-diameter floor. Know anybody that might be interested?"

Joel said, "I think my brother and his wife might like to help you out. They're both retired from state government. Here's Todd's number. Give him a call."

There's no way Angela and I could have known then the gift Joel just handed us. I called Todd the next day. Our conversation was brief. When it ended, Angela asked, "What did he say?"

"They want to do it," I said. "They want to come out tomorrow and look at the site."

Todd's a wise man. Leigh Ann's an angel. And together they're creative geniuses. Honest.

At first we thought it was our accidental good fortune to find them. Now we know it was a part of the Divine Plan.

They have a zillion common sense skills. They're generous. They're intelligent. They're down-to-earth genuine and funny.

Every time we're around them, they lift our spirits. They make us laugh – sometimes so hard we cry.

It's been more than a decade now since the yurt was built. And it's still hard to believe how easily it all came together – thanks to Leigh Ann and Todd. The pine floor is beautiful and smooth.

For their anniversary gift to each other the year after the yurt went up on the Mahoney family farm in Bridgeport, Todd and Leigh Ann took ballroom dancing classes in Lexington. Later when they were showing us what they had learned in class, watching them move smoothly across the yurt floor was enchanting.

We've been to their scenic farm in Bald Knob and tasted their delicious vegetarian spaghetti, made just for us, garlic bread and salad. We've toured Leigh Ann's photography studio and Todd's carpentry shop.

Amateur astronomer Todd has taken us to his miniature planetarium. If he ever decides to build a space ship, we volunteer for the first flight. We're confident he could make it work.

And Leigh Ann, wouldn't that make some incredible photos and stories for the local newspaper?

On snowy evenings when the wood stove is fired up, I love dancing in the yurt.

I love the divine dance of life. The sad moments help us appreciate the beautiful moments.

Accepting and Loving What Is

Sunday, December 29, 2019, was grandson Kamdyn Xavier Johnson's eighth birthday. He's the first child of my youngest of four children, Kathryn Leanne Pearl.

Born on the same day as Kamdyn was Aurelius Xavier Cervantez, a great-nephew from Tucson, Arizona. Aurelius' mother, Kimberly Pearl Cervantez, is a kindred spirit niece. For more than two decades, I've thought of Kimberly as the Great Gift to me from my late father, Charles Wilford Pearl Sr., who I never knew.

When I was very young, my parents divorced and each remarried someone else. If that hadn't happened, Kimberly wouldn't have been in my life. I wish I could have known my father, but I'm elated Kimberly found her way into my life and my four children's lives in the 1990s.

It's what is.

I started writing this book in 2012 while on retreat at the Tibetan Mongolian Buddhist Cultural Center (TMBCC) in Bloomington, Indiana. My black Labrador, Lily, and I stayed in one of the small circular wooden cottages – resembling a yurt – for a little more than a month on our first of four visits that year.

The reason we went to Bloomington was because a Tibetan monk, attending the Kentucky Book Fair in Frankfort in November 2011, invited me to come and stay in one of the yurts when he heard I was planning to do a retreat. When I told him about Lily, he said, "Bring her too."

My first choice had been to go to one of the small retreat cabins at Cedars of Peace on the grounds of the Loretto Motherhouse in Marion County, Kentucky, near Maker's Mark Distillery. Longtime friend, Rich Green, and I did a two-day retreat there a few years earlier. I stayed in the Namaste cabin, and Rich stayed in Simplicity. We loved it. But there's a no-pet rule there, and I wasn't about to do a month's retreat without Lily.

As it turned out, I'm glad that was the rule at the motherhouse. If I could have taken Lily to Cedars of Peace, we wouldn't have gone to Bloomington, and Arjia Rinpoche, the director at TMBCC, probably would have never asked if I would arrange for a group of Tibetan monks from Tashi Kyil Monastery in India to visit Frankfort on their next U.S. tour.

The Tashi Kyil monks came in 2013 and created a beautiful World Peace mandala made of colored sand, which took four days to complete. The monks offered other cultural programs while in Frankfort, including a traditional Tibetan dinner and interfaith gathering at the Church of the Ascension. Dr. Chuck Queen, an open-minded progressive Baptist minister (yes, they do exist) was the keynote speaker at the dinner.

Queen and William Jessee Neat, then-rector at Church of the Ascension who always welcomed the Buddhist monks to have cultural programs at the downtown Episcopal Church, are profiled in this book. So is Neat's wife, Jenny, an iconographer and animal lover who has rescued hundreds of dogs and cats from being killed at animal shelters in eastern Kentucky.

Frankfort has very few Buddhists, but residents of our small capital city quickly fell in love with the Tibetan monks and their artwork. And the monks loved Frankfort – they returned in 2015 and 2019, and hope to come back in 2021.

So in my mind and heart, Lily played a major role in the Love connection between the Tashi Kyil Tibetan monks, refugees in India, and the welcoming Frankfort community, and Kentucky. But I'm dog crazy as you'll find out in this book.

On our 2012 retreat, I met amazing people in Bloomington and started listening to their life stories and writing about them. Then I started thinking about all the fascinating people who have come into my life through the years and have influenced my spiritual journey. The writing was flowing.

A friend said if you want to write a book about interfaith spirituality, you need to include yourself. That's when it became difficult and painful. It's always been a joy to write stories about other people. But telling my story was agonizing. I would procrastinate and give up on it. Then a family member or friend would encourage me to continue, or ask, "When are you going to have your book finished?"

I remember a conversation with Anna Marie Pavlik Rosen, an incredible artist, after I had interviewed her in 2015 for a feature story on her intricate artwork in The State Journal, Frankfort's newspaper. We were sitting at a dining room table in her beautiful mansion on Wapping Street in Frankfort's historic district. The unfinished book was mentioned, and Anna Marie said, "Maybe someone needs to read your book. Maybe it can help someone."

I hope that's true.

In the last few years, most of my closest friends quit asking about the book. They had given up on me finishing it.

But interestingly, while suffering with a terrible case of poison ivy in the summer of 2019, I had an epiphany. Here's an excerpt from a letter I sent to a family member in the middle of the night when I was wide awake from taking a prescribed steroid, prednisone, for the poison ivy that had gotten into my eyes.

"I'm 71, an old man now, and I'm the happiest I've ever been in my life. But I felt a lot of sadness, embarrassment, shame, guilt, fear, anger and insecurity as a child and teenager. I carried it with me as a young adult, a parent, and a man in my 40s and 50s. Even today, I know I still have fears, insecurity and guilt that I've carried into my seventh decade of living.

"During the week of hell, when I wasn't getting more than one or two hours of sleep at night, at some point I managed to surrender to it all and then the major awakening came.

"I realized I've lived much of my life in guilt, and feeling not good enough, not worthy . . . guilt of being abandoned by my biological father, and not being good enough to be loved by my first stepfather; embarrassed at school and everywhere because my parents were divorced and my mother remarried and had a different last name than me; guilt of not making all A's in school like my sister; guilt of being the quarterback on a high school football team that lost most Friday nights . . . not being good enough; guilt of not going to Vietnam when plenty of my friends and classmates did.

"I stayed in college to stay out of Vietnam and received a safe, high number in the draft lottery, 261, to keep me out of war. I wasn't interested in studying when I went to college, except I loved physics and astronomy classes. I felt guilt for getting a divorce after an up-and-down 35-year marriage.

"I resented hurtful, negative comments from some family members, and realize now I was the one who caused the most pain because I didn't laugh it off and let it go. Words really can't hurt you unless you allow that to happen. Carrying along so much useless baggage for years and years is a big waste of time and energy.

"I realized I hadn't finished my interfaith spirituality book I started in 2012 because some parts were going to be too painful to tell and embarrassing (ego).

"But once I set an intention to finish the book, I've been writing like crazy and it's been a joy doing it. It's amazing how the universe is helping me, and it has been written with LOVE."

Divine dance of life

I fasted on grandson Kamdyn Xavier's eighth birthday. I went on a long, slow walk by myself in a drizzling rain through the streets of South Frankfort, downtown Frankfort and River View Park by the Kentucky River.

Many wonderful souls, who have come into my life since 2012, came to mind.

I didn't know Don and Sylvia Coffey when I started writing "Dancing at the Yurt." Now, they're vital family members to spiritual partner Angela Mitchell and me. Don is the wise, older brother I probably always wanted and needed. We met through dancing at the Frankfort Yoga

5

Studio when Angela and her daughter, Sarah Mitchell, briefly owned the small business in the downtown McClure Building. Sylvia taught an international dance class there and we loved it.

Don and Sylvia met through dancing at a dance camp, and they've been dancing ever since. Don, 82, has written and said often that he hopes to die dancing. They host many dances and holiday celebrations at their spacious Dancing Meadow Farm home in Shelby County. Although I am not a person who typically enjoys going to parties now and being in large crowds, I love being with the Coffeys and their friends, and dancing.

In my adult years I've evolved from running 10Ks and marathons to bicycling across Kentucky nine times to dancing. It's great physical and mental therapy.

For three years now, Angela and I have been members of Sylvia's Glitterbugs dance group. We wear glittery vests and bow ties with our clothing that changes from black to blue to white to orange to red and green through the seasons. Don operates our sound system and sometimes jumps in unannounced to join us on the dance floor.

Sometimes I'm the only man in the group. Joe Fiala danced with us for a while until he moved to Athens, Ohio. Cary Sudduth is an excellent dancer and joins us occasionally when he can fit it into his busy schedule. David and Julia Rome are Glitterbugs half of each year when they're not in The Gambia in West Africa during the other half, working as volunteer teachers at Starfish International, an after-school mentorship program for girls.

In the summer of 2018, Angela and I had the good fortune of helping Don and Sylvia relocate and improve their large, beautiful walking meditation labyrinth. It is built using the intricate design of the Labyrinth of Chartres Cathedral, located in the city of Chartres, France.

Helping Sylvia and Don relocate their Jules Delambre Memorial Labyrinth near the entrance to their farm was a three-month workshop in joyful living, laughing, letting go, and loving your neighbors. Any spiritual teaching you can think of was there with us, every day. I knew it was going to be fun and physical, sort of like a wacky boot camp where you smile your way through the sweating, stumbling and suffering.

Minutes and hours sometimes felt like hell. But Don and Sylvia and Angela and I knew heaven was always nearby, just up the winding hill. We ached well and we ate well. Our four-course vegetarian lunches, lovingly prepared in Sylvia's spacious kitchen, were heavenly, healthy and healing.

Often while the chefs got food ready, Don – the all-in-one drill instructor, engineer and professor of all things meaningful and musical – would allow a student to sip a dark Guinness beer with him and relax on the screened-in back porch. Enlightenment felt so close in those moments.

At the construction site, sometimes we would jokingly call Don "God," especially after he would announce "Perfect" after a student placed her brick on the black ground-cloth exactly in the proper spot. Rare three-consecutive Perfects always brought cheers. Several days later, Don stopped the "Perfect" proclamations. He felt it was becoming too much of an ego thing.

Midway into the labyrinth project, Angela gave us important teachings on thankfulness, impermanence and toughness when she suffered multiple fractures in her left collarbone and a severely sprained right arm in a bicycle wreck. We witnessed how our lives can change in a second. Even if we become centenarians, we dance on this beautiful fragile Earth for only an instant.

I didn't know Jules Delambre as well as many of Don and Sylvia's friends. But I was fortunate to get to interview him in 2001 for a State Journal Q & A, shortly after the September 11 terrorist attacks on America.

Born in 1941, Delambre grew up in Baton Rouge, Louisiana. He earned bachelor's degrees in mathematics and anthropology from Louisiana State University, and got a master's in anthropology from LSU after serving two years in the Peace Corps in the mid-1960s. He was assigned to Cameroon in West Africa where he taught algebra.

Those two years gave him a deep appreciation for people who speak different languages and have different customs. All Peace Corps volunteers learn what it's like to be a stranger in another society, Delambre said. When they return home, most of them see things from a new perspective. After returning home to America, Delambre never stopped studying international issues.

After moving to Frankfort, Kentucky in 1974 he became active in the United Nations Association. One of his several jobs in service to humanity was as a systems analyst in the Office of Technology Services for the Kentucky Cabinet for Families and Children.

Jules was a tremendous help to me in 2001 when I heard and felt so much widespread hate toward all Muslims because of the terrorist attacks. I wanted to meet and interview local Muslims and visit the Islamic Center of Frankfort. It was easy to do, thanks to Jules.

Today, I serve on the Frankfort Interfaith Council with four compassionate Muslims, whom I consider my brothers and sister. I always feel at home when I attend services or celebrations at their worship center, thanks to Jules.

Angela and I are also blessed to be in the Glitterbugs dance group with Jules' wife, Alice Delambre. Jules died of cancer in 2007. He was 65. But his passion for peace is alive and well.

Compassionate and generous carpenter

Helping build the new labyrinth at Dancing Meadow Farm led to two more major construction projects. Soon after I purchased a small five-room house near downtown Frankfort in 2015, the living room floor began showing signs of water damage near the glass double doors facing East Main Street.

I received two repair estimates that seemed high, according to good friend Don Coffey. He said we could do the work. I said you're 81 and I don't have any mechanical or construction skills whatsoever. "We can do it," Don insisted. "And I want us to do it. It will be fun." He was right, and it was a joy watching him work and witnessing his patience with me.

First, we installed gutters and downspouts on the front and back of the house, to replace the French drains, "which are worthless," Don said. That was in the fall of 2018. In the spring of 2019, we started the bigger project, repairing the damaged floor.

We worked three to four hours in the morning for 22 days between June 24 and August 19. Don was right. It was fun. And Lily, who doesn't like any kind of strange noises, eventually came out of hiding when the hammering and sawing was under way, and looked forward to Don arriving each day. She became a good supervisor, and now no longer goes into hiding when I run the vacuum cleaner.

Don's brilliant mind, construction skills, strength and generosity saved me thousands of dollars.

Less than two months after the floor repairs were completed, Don suffered a heart attack – on the early Friday morning of October 11. Sylvia drove him in their van to Frankfort Regional Medical Center where he immediately underwent cardiac-catherization surgery in which two stents were inserted into his heart's southern artery.

He was released from the hospital on Saturday afternoon and has made a wonderful recovery.

"I was responsible for causing the blockage by the way I ate and didn't exercise," Don said. "So I was responsible to change the conditions that allowed that heart attack to happen. My state of mind was as good as always. But my diet and exercise needed improvement, so I was determined to make significant changes in both areas, and I have done that. I'm thankful I didn't die from the heart attack and that there was no permanent heart damage."

In late January 2020, Don said he felt much better than he has in at least a year.

"Starting early in 2019, I could feel myself getting tired quicker, not having as much energy, just not being up to par," he said. "New eating habits and more exercise have helped tremendously."

Jewish friend provides interfaith connection

Not long after Angela and I put a Pacific Yurt on her parents' farm in the fall of 2008, I invited longtime friend Vicki Pettus, a woman who happens to be Jewish, to come visit it. I told her I would love for it to be a place where people from diverse faiths could meet occasionally to talk about the common ground they share in wanting peace, respect and understanding.

She didn't forget. Later, Vicki became a member of the Frankfort Interfaith Council. Then in 2014, at her recommendation, I became the first Buddhist member to serve on the local interfaith council.

Vicki talks about her circular interfaith path in one of the chapters in this book. Although she no longer serves on the interfaith council, her compassionate heart and brilliant mind will always focus on inclusion and world peace.

When I started writing this book, FRANK, a monthly magazine at The State Journal didn't exist. When then-editor Brent Schanding asked me to write a feature on the Frankfort Interfaith Council for the first issue in August 2016, I was happy to contribute. But I had no idea how much of a joy it would be writing several stories a year for FRANK. I love all the splendid stories and photos in FRANK and I've put my heart and soul in every story I've written for our capital city magazine. A few of my FRANK stories, especially those relating to interfaith spirituality, are included in this book, usually with added information.

All the people I write about in "Dancing at the Yurt" have helped me tremendously in my spiritual journey through life. None of them, except perhaps our dogs, are saints, yet. But there's still time for some of us. And I'm grateful for each new day.

Namaste!

Chapter 1

Saying goodbye to a father I never knew

The first time I remember seeing my dad *for certain* was the day of his funeral in the summer of 1969 in Louisville. I had just turned 21.

Charles Wilford Pearl Sr. was 46 when he died of cancer. He worked in a chemical factory in Brandenburg, Kentucky, and lived in Louisville where he grew up.

More than 20 years later while working for the Kentucky Department for Environmental Protection (DEP) in Frankfort, I traveled to Brandenburg to do a feature story on Meade County's outstanding solid waste management program for DEP's quarterly magazine "Land, Air and Water."

The solid waste coordinator said he once worked with a Charlie Pearl at Olin Matson, a local chemical company. He said Charlie died of cancer, as did several others who worked in his section. I didn't tell him his friend was my father. I've wished a million times since then I had.

Although I was in my early 40s then, that was still a part of my life I didn't discuss. It was too painful.

The first Earth Day was the year after my father's death, and 1970 was also the year President Richard Nixon signed legislation enacting the U.S. Environmental Protection Agency. If the EPA had existed earlier, perhaps my father would have lived a long life and I would have gotten to know him.

Before his funeral, I had several vague memories of dad but I think perhaps they're just stories I heard from my mother:

• I was lying between my parents in bed and was accidentally burned by dad's cigarette. I cried.

• He took me to a barbershop to get my first haircut and I cried.

• I bumped my head on a Greyhound bus window and cried as my mother, sister and I left him for Lebanon, Kentucky, where mom was born and reared.

• He took dog Teddy and me on a ride in a red wagon in our neighborhood, and I'm sure I didn't cry that time. I've always loved dogs. Dad did too. He brought Teddy home from Italy in a duffel bag after serving in the U.S. Army Air Corps during World War II.

I was born in Clark Memorial Hospital in Jeffersonville, Indiana, just across the Ohio River from Louisville. Mom, dad, sister Beverly, 16 months older than me, and my paternal grandmother, Mary Esther Haynes Pearl, lived in a low-income government housing project in Charlestown, Indiana.

Dad's father, Henry Clay Pearl, died of a heart attack in 1944, and dad, his youngest son, had promised him he would take care of his mother.

Eventually living in the house with her mother-in-law became unbearable for mom and after seven years of marriage, she took her two children back to her hometown of Lebanon in May 1950. Mom thought dad would figure out a way to get his mother in another residence, and would come to Lebanon to take us back with him. He never did. He made one $50 child support payment and that was it.

Mom and my grandparents in Lebanon went with my sister, Beverly, and me to the funeral. When I looked in the coffin, I knew I didn't know the man. He never showed me the love my mother or grandparents had. Mom was sad and hurt and I felt sorry for her. But on a positive note, Beverly and I found out that day that we had a new brother and two sisters: Mary Esther, 17, Mark, 11, and Vickie Pearl, 6. I was elated.

Childhood friends and a love for baseball

Going back to my early childhood, after my parents divorced it didn't take long for each of them to remarry someone else.

Beverly and mom and I lived at 309 North Forest Street in Lebanon – the upstairs of our grandparents' three-bedroom brick home. That's where I had the first memories of which I am certain.

I remember liking Ted Roberts, who would become my first stepfather. When he was dating mom, he would let me sit on his lap on the living room sofa in my grandparents' home.

But after Ted married Mary Lucy Crowdus Pearl and the day they returned from a brief honeymoon, things changed. I was elated to see them

12

again, especially mom. But when I attempted to crawl up into Ted's lap on the sofa, he gently pushed me away, whispering "No."

I was confused, and sad. Beverly and I loved living upstairs with our mother in the home of our grandparents, William Jennings and Julia Irene (Webb) Crowdus, and now we had to move a mile away to a smaller house on Rowntree Court.

It wasn't all bad, though, because lots of children lived on Rowntree Court and played outside in the yards and street. And Ma-Maw Crowdus continued babysitting for us, so we stayed at her house while mom did office work at McDuffee Motor Freight on High School Avenue (now Hood Avenue). Mom would walk to work from her parents' house most days since McDuffee's was less than two blocks away.

Our granddaddy was Marion County Circuit Court clerk for 24 years. Ma-Maw was a homemaker and a full-time baby sitter.

I loved to go to granddaddy's office. The Coca-Cola machine was right outside his office door. Mr. James Phillips, the black janitor, became my special friend. I loved him because he was so kind and polite and would buy me Cokes. Granddaddy's brother-in-law, Charlie Webb, was the county sheriff and his office was right across the hall. Uncle Charlie liked to smoke cigars and listen to the Cincinnati Reds on the radio. One of his sons, Donald, was one of my early friends. His older sister, Sue Ella, was always friendly too.

Donald was my sister's age but ended up in my class at Lebanon Elementary School on College Street.

He was one of our school's best softball hitters. He was a good pitcher and infielder too. I always wanted to be on his team, and was most of the time. He was usually one of the captains and would choose me out of kindness since I was a cousin.

We'd play behind the school building every morning before the first bell rang, at recess, and after school most of the year.

In the summers, we all spent a lot of time in the swimming pool at Graham Memorial Park. There was one baseball field at the park for Little League, Babe Ruth League, high school teams, independent leagues, and church softball leagues.

I tried out for Little League three summers before I finally made a team. That was the year the number of teams expanded from four to six. The Braves and White Sox were the expansion teams and finally, when I went up to the announcement board, I saw the name Charles Pearl typed on a white sheet of paper with Braves at the top.

I was thrilled. And besides getting selected, we had sharp-looking new uniforms, white flannel with blue trim including a light pinstripe. A new Little League field with a home run fence – up the hill from the older one without a fence – also opened about that time.

I started two years and was a decent infielder but never got many hits. In my second year when we won the league championship, I think I got a double once that bounced off the centerfield wall. I was our number-two pitcher that year and won most of my games because we were playing the weaker opponents when I was on the mound.

I remember the only game I lost pitching. One of my good friends then and now, Pat Settles, played for the Yankees and he hit a grand slam home run. That accomplishment earned him a brief write-up in our weekly newspaper, The Lebanon Enterprise. He kept the clipping in his billfold for a long time and enjoyed showing it to me occasionally. He would always add, grinning, "That was the only home run I ever hit."

Pat excelled in academics and earned a law degree at the University of Kentucky before moving to Florida where he practiced for many years. He now lives in Lebanon most of the time in the house on Springfield Road where his late parents lived.

His mother, Geraldine, and my mother, Mary Lucy, were classmates at Lebanon High School, graduating in 1943.

Two of my Braves teammates were Terry Mills, who became a state representative from Marion County; and George Leonard "Bubba" Abell, who went on to play basketball at St. Augustine High School and Morehead State University. Bubba had a grandson, Remy Abell, who played basketball for Indiana University in the first two years of his college career and Xavier University the last two.

Two other little league teammates were Jerry "Tex" Brady, who became a good high school pitcher, and is retired from GE in Louisville and owns B.J.'s Steakhouse in Bardstown where our Lebanon High School Supper Club meets monthly; and Norman "McGoo" McGohon, an all-conference football player at LHS and one of my best friends in high school, who owned a decorative concrete business in Augusta, Georgia, before retiring.

Moving up to Babe Ruth League, I played on the Cubs and we were always competitive. One of the reasons: left-handed pitcher Ronnie Howell who had excellent control and a great curve and fastball. He was one of the best in the state at Lebanon High. Howell and the Yellowjackets lost in the regional playoffs in a close one to eventual state champion Bowling Green. Ronnie then went to Western Kentucky University on a baseball scholarship.

Other Cubs teammates were James "Buffalo" Brady and his brother John, who went to St. Charles High School where another brother, Joe Jess, starred in basketball. Many years later, Buffalo's son, Al Brady, married my daughter, Charlsie Maria.

Their marriage was brief but Al will always be a friend.

My most painful memory, physically, in baseball was a pick-up game on the Babe Ruth field. All three of the Brady brothers were out there. I was playing first base and Joe Jess was on the mound. A runner was on first and Joe Jess fired the ball to me trying to pick him off. It was a great throw but my glove didn't even touch the ball, which pounded my breastbone.

I dropped to the ground unable to breathe, but managed to get up and keep playing after a short delay. The embarrassment hurt almost as bad as my bruised chest.

In Babe Ruth, my best game offensively came against the Tigers in my second year. I had back-to-back triples and several runs batted in as we won easily. The Tigers' pitcher was Donald Webb, my cousin. I also made the All-Star team that year.

Early church life

Before I got involved in sports, my social life centered on church activities.

My grandfather was a deacon at First Baptist Church – later changed to Lebanon Baptist Church when the African-American church rightfully claimed the First Baptist title.

Every week we went to Sunday school and worship service on Sunday morning, training union on Sunday evening, and prayer meeting on Wednesday night. Beverly was in Girls Auxiliary, GAs; I was in Royal Ambassadors, RAs; and we both were in the church's youth choir, under the direction of Winnie Johnston, the organist. Beverly and I also took piano lessons and were in recitals.

Our church had an excellent afternoon summer recreational program with softball, basketball, badminton, shuffleboard and table tennis.

The three pastors I remember at our Baptist church were Fritz Schlaeffer, who moved to Paducah after leaving Lebanon; A.B. Colvin, my favorite, who left for Louisville; and Herman Rowlett who stayed the longest.

Schlaeffer and Colvin earned doctoral degrees later.

15

Not long after Brother Schlaeffer moved his family to western Kentucky, we took our first family vacation that I can remember to Kentucky Lake, an all-day trip on two-lane roads before interstates and state parkways existed.

I loved the lake and beach and a ride in a tour boat. We visited the Schlaeffers while we were there and attended a tent revival several nights.

In Lebanon the church parsonage was at the corner of High School Avenue and Forest Street, just two houses south of my grandparents' home. The parsonage had a two-car garage and since the Colvin family had only one car, my grandfather kept his 1953 light-blue Ford in the vacant spot in winter months.

Brother Colvin and his wife, Irene, had two daughters, Cassandra and Cynthia, who was in my class at Lebanon Elementary. We quickly became best friends at church and in the neighborhood. Cynthia was one of the smartest kids in our class and I learned to memorize a lot of Bible verses with her help.

The song I loved the most was, "Jesus loves the little children, all the children of the world, red and yellow, black and white, they are precious in his sight, Jesus loves the little children of the world."

We're all One. I learned that before I was 10, and I've never forgotten it. I thank the Baptist church for that. It sounds so right, so simple.

Cynthia and I got in trouble once for going down in my grandparents' basement and playing in the coal bin. We were filthy and our clothes were ruined when it was time for Cynthia to go home. Ma-Maw, a disciplinarian, was extremely unhappy with us. But sweet Cynthia being a co-conspirator in the crime saved me from getting a whipping.

Bible school was a big event in the 1950s, and in addition to going there, I went to Cedarmore at Bagdad in Shelby County for RA camp in the summers.

I remember being homesick on the first day there in 1958, but having good friend Bobby Elliott as one of my roommates in one of the new "hotel" cabins helped keep me in the present moment and content.

I think we had six boys in our cabin and many of the campers had to stay in a spacious building with numerous bunk beds. There was a big commotion outside late one night, and we went out to see what was going on. Someone in the big open dorm pooped in his bed and the smell was horrible, a frowning Lebanon friend, Frankie Johnston, told us.

Most of them camped under the stars that night without tents, and with the mosquitos. It was better than the alternative.

At our awards ceremony the last day of camp, besides receiving "Honor Camper" badges, Bobby Elliott and I received "Honor Chapter" pennants for keeping our cabin the cleanest.

Since 1958, I've never been able to keep my living space as neat as it was at camp, but it's still a goal to keep eliminating clutter.

Bobby also was a good athlete, playing baseball, football and basketball in high school. He was in the LHS Class of 1965 with my sister, and like Ronnie Howell, Bobby also played college baseball for the Western Kentucky Hilltoppers.

At camp, I think going to early morning and evening devotionals with campfires in the great outdoors, circled by fragrant cedars, opened a window to my heart and soul, which is one reason I've always felt closest to God in nature – even today at age 71.

Inside the Baptist Church in Lebanon, I don't remember any "awesome" sermons. I do remember Beverly and me being elated once about getting to shake hands with a visiting minister from Cherokee, North Carolina, who was an authentic American Indian. We said we were never going to wash our hands again.

We both had dark skin and I wondered if we could have Indian blood.

I remember a very sad time – when I heard Brother Colvin and his family were moving from Lebanon to Louisville. He was always friendly and had a great sense of humor. He was a good carpenter and mechanic too, because he built Cynthia a small gasoline-powered one-seat car that could run on the driveway and sidewalk. She let me operate it quite a few times.

We also learned how to ride our first bicycles on the sidewalk between their house and my grandparents' residence.

I just didn't understand why they had to leave us.

On his last or next-to-last Sunday as pastor in Lebanon, I "officially" joined the church. Mom and granddaddy had spent some time trying to explain to me what becoming a Christian and a follower of Jesus meant. I think I understood the basics, but don't remember hearing anything about Christianity being the only path to God.

That might have been emphasized frequently in the sermons, but my mind wandered a lot during the preaching. In the first years the Colvins were in town, Cynthia and I did a lot of work in her coloring books between 11 a.m. and noon on Sundays.

Now life was getting more complicated. I was extremely nervous when I worked my way out of the middle of the pew and walked down the aisle to tell Brother Colvin I wanted to join the church. He had tears in his eyes and choked up a little when he told the congregation about my decision.

I always thought he liked me, but I knew *for certain* at that moment that Brother Colvin loved me. Although I didn't have a real father, it felt as if I did, and that was an incredible feeling. The only problem was, he was leaving me.

Sunday evening, I was baptized along with Vickie Johnston, sister of my close friend Frankie Johnston. We had on white robes and Vickie went first, walking slowly down the ramp into the baptismal font. When she reappeared after being immersed and got close to me on the ramp, she burst out laughing, just cackling. I knew then everything was going to be fine. I had no more fear.

And Brother Colvin kept a promise. I could visit them in Louisville, and I did several times, staying almost a whole week each time.

The Colvins took me to my first ever professional baseball game at Crosley Field in Cincinnati. The Reds were playing the Milwaukee Braves in an evening doubleheader. I was for the Braves because I played for the Braves that summer in Lebanon Little League.

But midway through the opening game, I changed my allegiance and started pulling for the Reds. All of the Colvins were Reds' fans, and it was great being there next to Cynthia and Cassandra watching the Reds win both games. However, I was still going to continue to be a Hank Aaron fan.

A new hero was Frank Robinson who starred in both games. In the opener, Robinson and Braves' third baseman Eddie Mathews got in a fight when Robinson attempted to steal third. Mathews was ejected and Robinson was injured and had to be taken out.

Both returned in the second game and Robinson got several hits including a home run.

I still love baseball but rarely go to major league games anymore. I loved watching grandsons, Charles Pearl III and Preston Pearl play baseball for Frankfort High School, as well as football; and I still enjoy watching their younger brother, Dawson Pearl, play goalie for the FHS soccer team. I occasionally go to watch the Louisville Bats, the Reds AAA minor league team, and the Lexington Legends, a single A minor league team affiliated with the Kansas City Royals.

18

Although I went to numerous Reds' games at old Riverfront Stadium, it never had the intimate feeling that Crosley Field had, or that today's Great American Ball Park has.

The most memorable game I saw in Riverfront was on October 15, 1975. My first son, Kevin, was born that morning around 8:30 in Elizabethtown's Hardin Memorial Hospital. The Reds played Boston in the World Series that night. I sat in the upper deck in centerfield and could have seen the game a whole lot better on TV.

The Reds lost their only home loss of the Series, which they won in seven games. When I finally got home around 2 a.m., I heard that my grandfather in Lebanon had died about 12 hours after Kevin was born.

It was the first time I had gone to a World Series game, and the last. I enjoyed the next game much more, carefully holding Kevin in my arms in a hospital room.

The last time I went to a Reds game with a press credential was in 2003 when the late Frank Robinson came back to Cincinnati as manager of the Montreal Expos. A statue of him was unveiled in front of Great American Ball Park that weekend. It was nice getting to briefly talk to him one-on-one in his locker room office before the game.

I told him about the first major league game I went to and he remembered well the doubleheader.

One week after my first visit to Crosley Field, I was upstairs in my bedroom at my grandparents' house. It was terribly hot and the window fan wasn't helping. I was thinking what a wonderful time I had just one week ago. Now I was miserable. I missed my Louisville family. A part of me wanted to go live with them, but I knew that wouldn't happen.

On yearly summer visits to Louisville, Brother Colvin would take us to play miniature golf several evenings. We would also go to a Louisville Colonels minor league baseball game, and to Fountain Ferry Park – where we could drive stylish little cars on a children's turnpike; and then walk and wind our way through a maze of mirrors before going down Angel's Slide and Devil's Slide inside a large fun room.

Years later while Brother Rowlett was pastor, a youth group from church went to a Reds game at Crosley Field when Pete Rose was a sensational rookie. We had seats close to the dugout and another thrill for the night was getting a roundtrip ride in a sporty Thunderbird convertible – with the top down part of the way – driven by a nice young dentist named Dr. John Collins "Sonny" Polk.

19

Later, Dr. Polk's wife, Carolyn, was my typing teacher in high school. When I took her class, I had no idea how much typing was ahead in a career of journalism. In college, I never thought about taking a journalism class.

Mostly what I thought about during one year at the University of Kentucky, one year at St. Catharine Junior College (which later became a four-year college and is now closed) in Springfield, and two years at Western Kentucky University was staying out of Vietnam. I ended up with a degree in business administration from WKU and accomplished my goal of not being drafted.

The Polks became family members because in 1966 my sister, Beverly, married Tommy Harmon, a first cousin to Carolyn Chelf Polk, whose father was U.S. Congressman Frank Chelf of Lebanon.

Tommy's brother, Billy, was one of my best friends in high school and college.

Decades later, Carolyn and her sister, Bonnie Simpson, sat next to me in a Bardstown theater watching "Seven Years in Tibet," the first movie I had seen about Tibetan Buddhism and His Holiness the Dalai Lama.

I had already become interested in Eastern religions and philosophy, but I had no idea then how much Tibetan Buddhism would become a part of my daily life.

For me personally today, this is the most joyful time of my life. And I would have never reached this place without Buddhism.

I may still have a few family members who don't understand why I need something more than Christianity in my life. I didn't drop my love of Jesus and Christianity. But I had to widen my spiritual path and heart to include Buddhism and how it lovingly connects to Islam, Judaism, Hinduism, Sufism, Baha'i, Unitarian Universalist and other religions.

Chapter 2

Loving the Catholic Church

Between being a Baptist and a Buddhist, I was a practicing Catholic from 1968 until 2006.

Growing up in Lebanon and Marion County if you have many friends, some of them are going to be Roman Catholics.

Although I was baptized as an infant in St. Michael's Catholic Church in Charlestown, Indiana, the first time I remember entering a Catholic Church was at St. Augustine in Lebanon at Christmas Midnight Mass in 1962.

I sat in the balcony with neighborhood friend Shermie Richards and his beautiful, smart sister, Anita.

Shermie was an eighth-grader and Anita and I were freshmen, although she went to St. Catharine Academy in Springfield, an all-girls' school. If anyone would have asked me back then to name a living saint, I would have said Anita Richards.

I polished my black shoes and put on my best Sunday clothes and tie and ran across the street in the rain to the Richards' house around 11 p.m. Christmas Eve. I sat down on the living room sofa and waited for everyone to finish getting ready.

When it was time to go, I stood up and looked down and saw a messy black outline of two shoe prints etched in the light carpet. Besides already being nervous about going to the Catholic Church and trying to impress Anita, I was extremely embarrassed about my artwork on the floor.

But I never mentioned it, and neither did anyone else. Mrs. Ruth Richards was a kind, gentle woman, and I'm guessing she forgave me rather quickly. She also was a saint.

Christmas Eve 1962 was the last time I ever used liquid shoe polish.

If there had been any Buddhists in our neighborhood back then, it's possible I could have already learned the custom of taking off my shoes upon entering a home or temple and saved myself a lot of embarrassment.

Midnight Mass was long and I don't remember anything Father Joseph Gettlefinger said. But I loved the smell of incense reaching up into the balcony, and was impressed with all of the rituals and prayers.

Before long there was another thing I liked about the Catholic Church: It was OK to drink alcohol, and that was forbidden in our Baptist church, or was supposed to be.

In the summer of 1963, I found out there was some closet drinking in the Baptist church. I discovered a pint bottle of bourbon whiskey in a brown paper bag on the floor in a back corner of my stepfather Ted Roberts' bedroom closet.

A few days later in the middle of the afternoon, while my parents were at work, Shermie and I sat on my front porch – four houses up from my grandparents' home on Forest Street – and shared a tall glass of bourbon and Coke. It tasted terrible.

Not long after that, two houses down at the Coyle residence – a Catholic family – our young friend Moe Coyle stole a Schlitz beer from their refrigerator and we took turns sipping from the can. It tasted worse than horrible.

At Lebanon High School, I think I had quite a few friends who were girls – Anna Laura Evans, Denise and Donna Gray, Millie Wade, Wanda Tharp, Marian Spragens, Lucille Gabehart, Barbara Rogers, Jane Carol Burris, and others.

But my only "girlfriends" were St. Augustine students and Catholics. I had very few dates in high school because Marilyn Borders, with whom I was in love, was two years younger and couldn't date for a long time. We had our first official date at the 1966 LHS Junior-Senior Prom in our gymnasium, just a few weeks before my high school graduation.

Since she couldn't go to the prom with me when I was junior, Marilyn suggested that I ask Julia Ann Wallace, a St. A sophomore, to be my date. Julia Ann accepted and we had a great time.

Like Marilyn, she was attractive, intelligent and friendly. We had several dates after the prom and I always enjoyed being with her. But when it was time to choose a date for the senior prom, I wanted to go with Marilyn.

At the time, I felt they were both devoted to their Catholic religion and I liked that. Although they never tried to convert me to Catholicism, their devotion to their faith certainly played a part in my later decision to become a Catholic.

22

I remember going to Mass at St. A with Julia Ann several times, sitting at floor level. I was in awe of the artistic beauty of the church – the stained-glass windows, and the statues of Jesus, Mary and Joseph, and the Stations of the Cross on the walls.

Just being there, smelling the aromatic incense, sitting next to a special friend I considered a saint (like Anita and her mother) – I'm sure I had at least five dates with Julia Ann before I received that first small kiss – I felt an inner peace that I had never experienced in the Baptist church.

Many years later, I met Julia Ann's uncle, Victor Wallace, who was named Brother Julian after he became a Trappist monk at the Abbey of Gethsemani in 1949, the year Julia Ann was born. For a long time Brother Julian carefully crafted with compassion the nice wooden gift boxes for the monastery's famous cheese, fruitcakes and fudge.

Chapter 3

A special bus ride with a priest

On a Greyhound bus in the spring of 1968, I met a priest. When I stepped on the bus at Madden Howard's service station in downtown Lebanon, the only vacant seat was next to a 50-year-old man wearing a black suit and white collar.

I had never had a one-on-one conversation with a priest, but I knew the time had arrived. I was nervous. He offered me the window seat and I took it.

The Rev. James Thompson, better known as Father Jim, was president of St. Mary's College, a seminary in Marion County for men studying to be priests.

He was going to Louisville to board a plane to California. I was a 19-year-old student at St. Catharine Junior College heading to Bowling Green to catch a ride to Florida for spring break with Lebanon friends, Carl Crews and Dave Kerr, students at Western Kentucky University.

The only bus route to Bowling Green was through Louisville.

Before the bus arrived in nearby Springfield I knew I liked this ebullient priest. He seemed genuinely interested in all people, regardless of religion, race or age. Father Jim seemed to understand teenagers.

We talked about horses, tennis, basketball, the Beatles, JFK, Bobby Kennedy, my upcoming summer job at a YMCA camp in Michigan, Martin Luther King Jr., civil rights, human rights, sociology, crime and the Vietnam War.

It was a quick trip to Louisville. He invited me to visit him at St. Mary's, and I surprised him one day, arriving unannounced. He gave me a tour of the beautiful campus and chapel. When we went into his office, I told him I was interested in becoming a Catholic and asked where I should go to take instructions.

"Would you like to take them right here?" he asked. "I'll be your instructor if you want."

I was amazed that a busy college president and teacher of sociology and philosophy would take the time to teach me about the Catholic faith, but I accepted his offer.

Before the year was over, I made my first communion in the chapel at St. Mary's College with Father Jim officiating. No family members came and only one friend attended, Beverly Barber from Springfield, whom I had met at St. Catharine College. She and a seminary student were my two official witnesses.

A third baptism wasn't required since Father Jim received an official document that I had been baptized in the Catholic church as an infant in 1948 in Indiana.

Father Jim left St. Mary's for Louisville in 1970 to work as a parish priest until his retirement in 1987. We remained friends until his death in 2006 at the age of 88. I attended his funeral in Louisville.

Our meeting that spring day on the bus was providential, he said. I just knew I always felt better after visiting him, or talking with him by phone.

I also was with Father Jim in Louisville the only time I was ever in the presence of Mother Teresa.

PART TWO

Exploring Different Styles and Steps

"When you dance you can enjoy the luxury of being you."

--Paulo Coelho

Chapter 4

Every day for Rich Green is Earth Day

Rich Green is one of my closest friends. We don't see each other much or talk on the phone much or send email or text messages much. But we're there for each other when needed. Now that we're both serving on the Frankfort Interfaith Council, we do get to see each other at our monthly meetings, most of the time.

We grew up in the same small town, Lebanon, Kentucky. But we didn't know each other then. He was four years older and went to St. Augustine Catholic Church and Catholic schools. I went to Lebanon Baptist Church and public schools.

I went to his house twice a year because his father and uncle had their dental offices in the large home on North Spalding Avenue where Rich and his parents and five older siblings lived. It was never a pleasant experience sitting in a dentist chair in the 1950s and '60s.

We met in 1988 not long after I moved to Frankfort to work in the state Natural Resources and Environmental Protection Cabinet. Rich was a communications and education officer with the Division of Forestry and we both went to the downtown Good Shepherd Catholic Church.

It didn't take long to figure out we were kindred spirits when it came to enjoying and appreciating being in wilderness areas.

After four years in state government, I wanted to return to community journalism. While working as news editor for our hometown weekly newspaper, The Lebanon Enterprise, I wrote a feature story on Rich for our quarterly magazine titled "Montage: A journal of life in Marion County," in the Summer 1997 edition.

Here it is:

Rich Green finds a true friend in nature

He was headed to the Red River Gorge, to die perhaps, from the bite of a rattlesnake. And that was OK.

He had to leave Louisville. He had to find solitude in the mountains, by the streams, to save his sanity.

Walking along a muddy Gorley Trail one rainy spring Saturday, 53-year-old Rich Green is recalling his wandering journeys through life with a St. Augustine classmate, Terry Ward.

Somewhere between tasting the sourwood leaves and examining the ferns, wife Nora Green says, "That first day I was introduced to Rich, I thought he was the weirdest person I'd ever met."

After 25 years of marriage, they both agree her initial assessment of him was accurate.

"The curiosity about what I'm going to do next is what keeps you with me," Rich says, laughing.

In the late 1950s, Rich left St. Augustine School and Lebanon for St. Thomas Seminary and Louisville. He wanted to be a priest.

Then he changed his mind. He wanted to be a Trappist monk at the Abbey of Gethsemani in Nelson County.

The vocational director at Gethsemani met briefly with him. When Rich told him he was interested in pursuing a religious life, the director said, "I don't think so. You need to get out a few years, even get away from the seminary."

As soon as he said that, the vocational director was called away on an emergency, "and that was the end of our conversation," Rich said. That wasn't what Rich expected to hear, "but he was so convincing. I thought he was right."

After a visit to Lebanon to discuss his future with his parents, the late Dr. Spalding and Mahala (Lancaster) Green, Rich headed for Cincinnati and Xavier University where his brother, Ned, was going.

Majoring in world history and minoring in French and English, Rich earned his bachelor's degree in 1966.

"I studied hard," he recalls. "I had to because I wasn't smart enough to get away with anything."

After getting his degree, he had no idea what he wanted to do. So he listened to the silent voice inside and heard, "When it doubt, stay in school."

That sounded reasonable so the next stop was Lexington. After an interview with Dr. Thomas Clark at the University of Kentucky, Green was accepted into graduate school in the history program.

"Then the most fortuitous thing happened," Rich recalls. "It tickled me."

Hugh Spalding, superintendent of Marion County Schools who lived near the Green family on Spalding Avenue, called.

"A teacher had suffered a heart attack and he asked if I would be interested in temporarily replacing her at St. Charles High School," Rich said. "I was thrilled to have some alternative to school. I was sick of school."

He wasn't offered much money because he didn't have a teaching certificate.

"But I was able to buy a car. That's all I cared about. And I was able to go to the Golden Horseshoe (nightclub)."

Several other young teachers and friends, just out of college, had returned to Marion County.

"It was a fun time," he recalled. "We had a ball. I was quite serious about teaching, of course, and I was quite serious about socializing on weekends."

Teaching history and social studies, his temporary job became a permanent one and he stayed at St. Charles High from 1966 through 1969.

"I liked teaching. It was something I needed to do. I was so full of information from college and I wanted to spout it out."

But in 1969 it was time to move on. He was living at home and it was time to try something different. So he moved to Louisville and began teaching at Thomas Jefferson Middle School.

"I absolutely hated it. It was a shock to my system, going from a nice rural school to the city."

On his first day, he saw a boy holding another male student out a third-floor window, threatening to drop him.

Police were constantly in the hallways. Before the first semester ended, an assistant principal was stabbed. Shortly after the second semester started, Rich had had enough.

"Every day was such a headache. In a short period I saw a lot of things I'd never seen before. It was just too hard."

A colleague told him the only way to survive was "to beat the kids till they bleed."

"I couldn't do that," he said. "I loved the kids and I wasn't a disciplinarian. I was a total pushover. Some of the students cried when I left and tried to talk me out of leaving. They said they'd straighten up. But I knew it wouldn't work."

He found a part-time job at Burger Chef on Fourth Street.

"I was flipping hamburgers, frying fries, mopping floors, jumping on trash in dumpsters," he said, laughing.

He moved from St. James Court to Second Street and walked to work. The Burger Chef manager wanted Rich to go into management training. But he declined.

"I wanted a no-brainer job for a while. There were no lessons to prepare. It was nice to take a break from the serious stuff. I worked only four hours a day so I had a lot of free time."

He spent a lot of time on the Ohio River bank and walking across the Second Street Bridge. He'd watch young men shooting rifles at rats by the riverfront where the Galt House is today.

While working at Burger Chef, he met Nora Kasting, a Baptist, at a weekend encounter. She was a student at the Norton Infirmary School of Nursing.

"Encounter groups were popular in the late '60s and early '70s," Nora said. "The sessions focused on increasing awareness, building trust, improving relationships."

Most of the people there were couples. Nora came alone and Lebanon's Bob "Nolan" Myers suggested that she match-up with Rich since he was also alone.

They became friends. He was definitely different. They took a walk through a cow pasture. The thought of a young man with a college degree working at Burger Chef, and liking it, intrigued her.

It wasn't a quick courtship.

"I think I hunted you down," Nora said. "I wrote you a letter. I was studying to be a nurse. I was going to rescue you, straighten you out."

Rich was impressed that she wrote to him.

"We liked to go to the airport and smooch out on the observation deck," Nora recalled, smiling briefly, and then frowning. "Then he left me to hitchhike across the country."

Before he left, Rich introduced Nora to the world of nature. He had always loved the outdoors.

"Even though I was a town boy, I was a country boy too," he said. "Our back yard in Lebanon was near big fields when I was growing up. A lot of friends lived on farms so I was always spending time in the country.

"We'd ride our bicycles out to Sulphur Springs and Cartwright Creek as kids. We thought nothing of walking the railroad tracks to Calvary and hiking all over the hills. That's the way we grew up."

He loved all living creatures, and still has a picture of Ollie, a little pet alligator. Ollie didn't live long so Rich gave him a nice sendoff. He made a tombstone for him and conducted a big funeral.

"All my turtles, everything, got gravestones," he said.

His family belonged to the Lebanon Country Club and Rich caddied a lot.

"I tried to play but never got the hang of it," he said. "Golf is one of those normal things that I was not genetically meant to do. And I wasn't interested in it. The only thing that ever interested me on the golf course was what was in the rough or around the ponds" – the critters and wildflowers.

"Basically where my love for nature came from was Marion County. It's such a beautiful area. It's a good community for being close to nature."

In late spring 1970, Rich knew it was time to get closer to nature, to get out of Louisville, to go live in the woods.

He sold his Plymouth Valiant car and put the money in traveler's checks. He had already drawn out his teacher's retirement and had been living off it.

When he stuck out his thumb to hitchhike to the Red River Gorge in eastern Kentucky, he was scared. He was carrying a backpack and thoughts of dying on the journey crossed his mind. But he knew he would die if he didn't get out of the city.

"I was a seeker. I was trying to figure out what I could do to make a living. I felt I wasn't going to be able to make a living by teaching. I was looking for some way to settle down. And I knew I wasn't going to settle down at Burger Chef."

His first ride took him to the Watterson Expressway. The next car that stopped was driven by a University of Louisville professor going to a conference in Washington, D.C. He invited Rich to ride along as far as he wanted.

"I think he wanted somebody to go along and keep him awake," Rich said.

The Red River Gorge hike was put on hold. Rich was headed to D.C., a bigger city.

Through some hippies, he found a place to stay in Georgetown. Later he called Dick Bowling, who had been a priest in Campbellsville. He left the priesthood and was teaching at a community college in northern Virginia, just outside D.C.

After staying at Bowling's residence a few days, he hitchhiked to Philadelphia to attend a folk festival. While there, he stayed with Lebanon native Jim Thompson and his wife.

"Jim, a social worker, would take me into the city in the mornings. He liked what I was doing. He would go to work and I would bum around. I had a great time."

Rich was never a big eater. He would buy cans of vegetables, sit on street curbs, and eat out of the cans. While sitting there he began thinking about his next move. Rural New York was on his mind.

His Aunt Isabel Green had told him about an Indian swami who had property in New York. "I was thinking about maybe going to visit him."

While visiting a college campus, however, he noticed a note on the travel bulletin board. Someone was looking for riders to California. He called the number and reserved a seat. Then he called his parents – "probably collect" – to let them know he was alive and on his way to California.

"It was an adventure, five of us in a little car. We only stopped once for the night, in Salt Lake City. We slept in a park by the Great Salt Lake. The sunrise was unbelievable. Earlier when we crossed the Rockies, that was a memorable experience too.

"We drove through the Sierra Mountains at night. I remember how impressive the redwoods looked with the headlights shining on them. I'd never seen trees like that."

The other four travelers were going to a small college in Chico, California, north of San Francisco. Rich hitchhiked to San Francisco and made his way to the University of California at Berkeley.

"The obvious place to meet anybody was on a college campus," he said. "I had become aware of the hippie movement and the elaborate system they had to help people find places to stay. They put me in touch with a little old lady who let me camp out in her back yard in Berkeley. Her house was already full and she apologized that I had to stay in the yard. But I thought it was wonderful."

For two weeks, he picked vegetables with migrant workers.

"It was one of those wonderful experiences I wouldn't want to relive. The work was tough."

The migrant workers didn't speak English and Rich didn't know Spanish. He slept in their housing quarters.

"There was a lot of drinking and fighting some nights," he recalled.

A couple of nights, peaceful Rich slept with a two-by-four under his pillow. The migrant workers moved with the crops, up and down the California coast. And soon Rich and his backpack headed for the beautiful hills behind Berkeley. A lean-to, which somebody built and abandoned, became his home for the next month.

He met a couple from Louisville and they told him the rainy season would start soon and he would have to leave the shelter.

Fall arrived. The rains came. And Rich left his shelter. He knew where he was going.

He hitchhiked to Vina, California, where a Trappist monastery, New Clairvaux, waited for him to arrive. He knew he would be welcome. Rich visited the vocational director and told him he wanted to join the monastery.

"It was an experience of a lifetime," Rich recalled. "I had never felt so loved and accepted. They're such sensible people.

"The Trappist life was a life I had been curious about since high school. And this was the time to find out if I wanted to make a commitment or not."

Religion was, and is, a vital part of Rich's life.

"One reason I'm religious is that I couldn't stand the chaos. I meditate a lot on spiritual things. In prayer, you try to bring the grace of God to Earth at the present moment to make order out of the chaos. I think that's what monks do."

Rich and Nora attend Good Shepherd Catholic Church, and a new Good Shepherd Church was under construction away from the downtown area.

A priest saying Mass in an open field would suffice for Rich.

"I don't understand the need for buildings," he said. "But I accept it. And I understand other people's needs for buildings."

He entered the monastery on a temporary basis and started living the life of a monk.

"I was an explorer," he said. "I didn't wear the robes or anything."

The monastery was new and much smaller than Gethsemani in Kentucky. While Rich was there, the monastery's main building burned to the ground.

Rather than viewing the electrical fire as a tragedy, the monks saw it as "an opportunity to establish hermitages and rebuild the monastery the way they wanted it," he said.

In December, the vocational director encouraged Rich to return to Kentucky for Christmas to visit his family. The monks also encouraged him to visit Gethsemani again to see if he would be happier there. They bought him a round-trip plane ticket, drove him to the airport in San Francisco, and sent him back to Kentucky.

In Lebanon, he got together with old friends, and gave away all his possessions – books and records. He called Nora and went to Louisville to see her. They went ice skating.

He also went to Gethsemani to visit a cousin, Brother Julian, Victor Wallace, a monk from Lebanon.

"And since I had a round-trip ticket, I headed back to California and continued living the life of a monk through January. But then I began having second thoughts. The routine became too routine. Boredom set in. And you either work your way through it or you don't."

Nora was on his mind and he talked honestly to the monks about her.

"It was amazing. They were so open to any experience that I needed and wanted."

Telephone calls to Nora became a daily part of his life.

"The monks would do their evening chant, and I would do my long-distance courtship. Nora and I fell in love over the phone."

Soon he told the monks he needed to go back to Louisville and make a life with Nora.

"They thought that was fine, and again, they bought me a plane ticket."

Nora met him at Louisville's Standiford Field in March 1971.

"We sure had a wonderful time dating," Rich said.

They were married on January 15, 1972. He went back to teaching in Louisville and hated it.

"I decided I had to head to the woods," he said. "I had had enough experiences with nature that I knew what I wanted to do."

Rich and Nora packed up and moved to an apartment in Lexington. He was going back to school, at the University of Kentucky, to earn a bachelor's degree in forestry. Nora worked as a nurse and Rich went to college full time for five semesters.

Tornadoes ripped through Kentucky in the spring of 1974 and Rich's first job in forestry was to "assess the damage in the mountains. Tornadoes knocked down a lot of timber."

35

He had several job possibilities with forestry agencies and he accepted a job with the Kentucky Division of Forestry in the Natural Resources and Environmental Protection Cabinet.

They moved to Prestonsburg in Floyd County, "and at the time it was a dusty, coal town," Rich said. Nora broke down and cried when they first arrived.

"I'll live here," Nora said. "But I certainly won't like it. It was such a depressed looking place."

"It looks much better there now," Rich added.

Soon after they arrived, Rich received a call from the Division of Forestry's chief of foresters. Someone had resigned and there was an opening at Pineville in Bell County. The chief said, "I hate to disappoint you, Rich, but would you mind going to our field office in Pineville?"

Trying to act not as thrilled as he was, Rich responded, "Yeah, I believe I can do that."

"That was a wonderful break. We headed to Bell County and loved it. We could sit on our front porch and see the Cumberland Gap area."

Their two daughters, Karen and Jennifer, were born while they were living in Middlesboro. Karen, now 22, is an art education major at Eastern Kentucky University. Jennifer, 20, is a student at UK and is interested in physical therapy.

The Green family stayed in Bell County for six years before moving to Frankfort. That's when Rich became an information and education officer with the Division of Forestry. Since 1980, they've lived in the city of Frankfort on Powhatan Trail in Indian Hills Subdivision.

They had "such a boring yard – a typical suburban subdivision yard," Rich said. "We missed Pine Mountain and Cumberland Gap National Park and the beauty of the woods.

"And I got tired of cutting all the grass. So one day we decided we would let some of it grow wild. We had a private hedge so it wasn't as if we were going to make an eyesore to the neighborhood."

In the summer of 1986, Rich stopped cutting one-third of the back yard. He planted another hedge and cut the grass in front of it. The part behind the hedge grew wild. "That way I got my woods back," he said.

Today, Rich and Nora have a mini-forest in their back yard with a small path that winds through it. They have more than 30 species of trees. "Some we've planted and some have come from seed," Rich said.

They have lots of colorful wildflowers in their forest and in the rest of the yard, front and back. They plan to plant more ferns and shade-bearing plants. If he could pursue another degree today, it would be in botany, he said.

To their delight, their back-yard forest – 100 feet wide by 30 feet deep – has also brought in rabbits, chipmunks, squirrels, raccoons and possums. Some of the neighborhood kids have brought in a few turtles.

Forestry spokesman

For years, whenever forest fires occurred in Kentucky, the statewide or national radio voice explaining the situation was Rich Green's from the state Division of Forestry. Being the forestry division's primary spokesman to the media, Rich's job often involved taking TV reporters to fire scenes.

He loved his work in forestry, especially developing educational programs and materials for school students.

But after 21 years in forestry, Rich decided he "wanted to see how the rest of the Natural Resources and Environmental Protection Cabinet lives."

Two years ago he accepted a job in the recycling section of the Division of Waste Management. He works with local government and community officials interested in expanding their recycling programs. He provides marketing and equipment purchasing information to recycling programs throughout the state.

Rich likes his job.

He bought back his teaching retirement years so he'll have 28 years of employment with the state in October. Not bad for a restless explorer.

Today he and Nora appreciate "more than ever" the gifts of nature. They love to travel through Kentucky and visit the state parks and nature preserves. "I think we've been to every state park," he said. "One of our goals was to stay at every lodge."

Nora said they also enjoy "primitive camping in a tent as long as I can get a hot shower."

Practically all of their time away from work involves outdoor adventures.

"We still get out and hike a lot," Rich said.

They love the Cecil Gorley Trail in his home county, even on a muddy, slippery path.

In late June 1997 they traveled to Banner Elk, North Carolina, visiting Grandfather Mountain and taking a four-hour day hike on the Appalachian Trail.

"We thoroughly enjoyed it but four hours was enough," Rich said. "I thought Grandfather Mountain would be a tourist trap. But it wasn't at all. There's such marvelous scenery and it's so clean."

If you look at Grandfather Mountain in the right way from the back side, it has the appearance of an old man staring up into the sky.

On July 19, 1997 they visited Pilot Knob in the 308-acre protected Spencer-Morton Preserve. Rising to 1,400 feet, Pilot Knob stands almost 730 feet above the surrounding landscape of Powell County and offers splendid views to the south and west.

It's reported that Daniel Boone first saw the flat lands of the Kentucky bluegrass region from Pilot Knob in 1769. The 1.5 mile (round-trip) Pilot Knob Trail to the summit is steep and strenuous.

The Greens have even found a delightful trail in the city of Frankfort, maintained by Boy Scouts. It starts beside the 24-story Capital Plaza Tower and goes up Fort Hill. At the top is a nice view of downtown Frankfort and the Capitol.

Rich sees a lot of himself in daughter Karen, "and it scares the daylights out of me," he said. She has fallen in love with the state of Arizona and is thinking about returning there to live after getting her degree.

"She loves nature and is a wander-lust," he said. "She takes things at face value and is naïve. I hate to see kids learn by hard knocks and that's the way Karen learns."

Daughter Jennifer said she has only one problem with camping and hiking. She hates bugs and bugs love her. It's her sweetness, she said.

Jennifer's friends think her parents are sweet, too.

"Dad is so down to earth," she said. "He's good to everybody and everything. He's funny. He's eccentric. And he's going to be a cute little old man."

Dad laughed, saying, "I'll never be old. Or I've always been old. I don't know which."

Nora said Rich is kind, sensitive, awfully moody, and a worrier.

"He takes it all to heart. He wants to do a good job, but he gets frustrated. He's certainly been a good father and husband. He helps with the housework. He does the grocery shopping. He helps with the laundry. Actually, he ends up doing most of the laundry."

On the hot afternoon of July 15, 1997, Rich spent three hours under their house repairing the condensation pump for the central air conditioner.

"It's pumping and nothing has blown up yet," he said in the early evening. "I'm tickled to death."

When Rich is home and he's not in the back-yard forest, or under the house, or doing laundry, he's usually watching television – nature shows, public broadcasting shows, or old movies.

"That's something I really enjoy, relaxing in front of the TV," he said. "I've never been a serious reader. I wish I was. My reading kind of goes in spurts."

A longtime friend, John Dever, formerly of Lebanon, once told him the reason he didn't read "is because you would rather get out and experience it."

The Green house is uncluttered. It's too confusing, otherwise, Rich said. There's an openness in the rooms, a sense of contentment, like inside the walls of the monastery at Gethsemani.

Their little white poodle, Ginger, stays near Rich most of the time. She likes to hike up Fort Hill too.

Rich has enough years in state government work to retire now. But with two daughters in college, "it seems nearly every penny we can make goes toward their education," Rich said.

Nora has worked as a psychiatric nurse at Comprehensive Care in Frankfort since 1980.

"And I'm her best, most challenging client," Rich said. "I don't try to be weird. There's nothing I'd rather be than normal. But normal just doesn't seem to be in the cards."

Mother Earth would appreciate more weird ones like Rich Green.

Chapter 5

Walk for Tibet

This newspaper column about my first visit to the Tibetan Cultural Center was published in The State Journal on March 23, 2003. It was titled "Dalai Lama's presence felt during walk."

Some friends are in training for the 13.1-mile Kentucky Derby Festival mini-Marathon in Louisville the last Saturday in April. A part of me wants to join them. The other part wants to hand them business cards of two remarkable surgeons.

In a past life, I was addicted to running. Not fast. Just to finish. I loved the runner's high, and getting into that mind space where the road carries you. After a lot of 10Ks, and Derby minis, I moved up to marathons, running four in Louisville, the Boston Marathon in 1981 (although I didn't qualify; in the old days, thousands of runners without qualifying numbers could start from the back of the pack and participate), and the 1982 U.S. Marine Corps Marathon in Washington, D.C.

For some ludicrous reason, I also did a 50-mile ultramarathon in 1981, starting in the dark on U.S. 60 in Louisville one December Saturday morning and finishing 9 hours and 57 minutes later in Frankfort in front of the Capitol as the sun was setting.

Seventeen years later, I learned what it's like to not be able to walk one minute without severe pain. I had spondylolisthesis, where one vertebra slips on another, causing spinal nerves to be pinched as the vertebrae slipped forward. It was probably caused by jogging, 20 years of pounding the pavement.

For a year and a half, I tried all the conservative measures: physical therapy, chiropractic treatments, craniosacral treatments, acupuncture, Zen meditation, and a series of cortisone injections. I read books and listened to tapes about mentally defeating the pain, believing that healing without surgery was possible.

It didn't work. I underwent surgery at Norton Hospital in Louisville in June 1999. I have two rods and four screws in my lower back. Things have worked out well. I choose not to run anymore. Walking works wonderfully.

Two weekends ago I went on the most enjoyable walk of my life, thanks to a niece in Indianapolis, Kimberly Pearl, who invited me to join her.

The five-day event in my native state was a walk from Bloomington to Indianapolis called March for Tibet's Independence. The march was inspired by Thubten Jigme Norbu, the oldest brother of His Holiness the Dalai Lama. He's a retired professor of Tibetan studies at Indiana University and founder of the Tibetan Cultural Center (TCC) in Bloomington.

The Dalai Lama is the head of state and spiritual leader of the Tibetan people. Born to a peasant family, he was recognized at the age of two, in accordance with Tibetan tradition, as the reincarnation of his predecessor, the 13th Dalai Lama, and thus an incarnation of Avalokiteshvara, the Buddha of Compassion.

In 1959, nine years after China invaded Tibet, the Dalai Lama fled to Dharamshala, India, where he lives today as leader to the Tibetan government in exile. He travels throughout the world teaching Tibetan Buddhism's central tenet of compassion. He won the Nobel Peace Prize in 1989.

Two 12-mile days of walking were over when I arrived Friday evening at the cultural center, where walkers returned each evening to shower, eat, sleep, talk, laugh, play games, stretch, pray, meditate, read, listen to music and watch TV.

From 9:30 p.m. Friday until 2 p.m. Monday, I was among many Tibetan people. I've never met such compassionate, kind, polite, peace-loving people with a great sense of humor. The whole weekend, I never saw anyone complain about anything, argue or even frown, except maybe at Monday's 5:30 a.m. wake-up bell.

About 30 of us slept on the floor in sleeping bags in one spacious room. A large picture of the Dalai Lama watched over us.

"We're sleeping where the Dalai Lama has walked," niece Kimberly reminded me each evening. He *is* here with us. His presence brings the tranquility we feel right now."

A large group came from Minnesota. Others were from Michigan and Indiana. Kentucky was well-represented. Ten students from Berea College, most of them from other countries, arrived late Friday night and stayed through lunch at the side of the highway on Sunday.

Tibetan monks and a few Indiana University students, including one from Louisville, also participated in the walk and weekend activities. We covered 14 miles Saturday on a warm, blue-sky day. Then we returned to the cultural center, relaxed and attended a big Tibetan New Year's dinner and party. The food was incredible. Young people, and a few not so young, sang, played musical instruments and danced late into the night.

We walked in breezy, 24-degree weather Sunday and Monday, covering 10 miles Sunday and 7.5 miles Monday.

Jigme Norbu, a nephew of the Dalai Lama, led the walk all five days and set a brisk pace. He kept reminding us the soreness, blisters or temporary pain we experienced along the way was nothing compared to the pain the people of Tibet have suffered for decades under Communist China's rule.

Many were slaughtered, and many escaped Tibet without shoes, clothing or food, he said.

"Tibet was once an independent country, and we have been illegally occupied," Jigme said.

Sunday morning, I walked alongside 24-year-old Kalden Norbu, a Tibetan native and Berea College senior majoring in accounting. His parents and many siblings still live in Tibet. He left Tibet in 1985 and hasn't seen or talked to his parents in five years. One brother lives in India.

He can't return to his homeland because of the dangers involved. He has frequent dreams about being in Tibet with his mother and father and brothers. Then he wakes up and tears always come.

"My biggest hope is that I will someday be reunited with my family," he said. "I have no idea how that's going to happen, but I try to be positive about it. I hope someday the Chinese let us get our country back."

Kalden is president of Berea College Students for a Free Tibet.

At the conclusion of the five-day walk, the Dalai Lama's nephew spoke at a rally at Monument Circle in Indianapolis. That Monday commemorated the 44th anniversary of the Tibetan Uprising in Lhasa, Tibet.

Along the route, many people in vehicles expressed support for the walkers.

"For those few who gave us the finger or tried to run us off the road, I hope one day they will wake up and understand the true issue," said Jigme, a handsome young man who owns and manages a Tibetan restaurant, Snow Lion, in Bloomington. "Tibet belongs to Tibetans. We cannot let the Tibetan culture die. It's up to us, the young people, to make sure that doesn't happen.

"This experience has made me much stronger. It will stay in my heart for many years to come, and I hope it stays in yours as well."

Another Tibetan person read a statement from the Dalai Lama. The concluding part said, "The reality today is that we are all interdependent and have to co-exist on this small planet. Therefore, the only sensible and intelligent way of resolving differences, whether between individuals, peoples or nations, is through a political culture of nonviolence and dialogue."

One of Kimberly's friends, who coordinated the walk, said the Tibetan people believe in and understand the power of compassion and the interconnectedness of all beings.

"It is their mindfulness, the peace within that they put into action, which gives me hope for the future of our world," she said.

I don't want to ever forget the pain I felt before spinal surgery. I don't want to ever forget that walking pain-free is a gift, like breathing.

I won't ever forget the Tibetan people I met this month in Indiana who simply want to return to their beautiful homeland and families in peace. I sense our connections will remain ever strong in ways we cannot even begin to imagine.

Chapter 6

TMBCC Temple Dedication

This column was published in The State Journal *on September 21, 2003, the United Nations-designated International Day of Peace. Two weeks earlier, I had been in the presence of the Dalai Lama for the first time.*

I don't like to be in large crowds anymore, and it has nothing to do with fear following 9/11. I think, in a way, I've always been a seeker of silent places.

Meeting celebrities and writing about them doesn't excite me anymore.

But earlier this month, I chose to put myself in a large crowd with a couple of world-famous celebrities.

His Holiness the Dalai Lama was in Bloomington, Indiana. So was Louisville native Muhammad Ali.

They were there for the dedication of the Chamtse Ling Temple on the grounds of the Tibetan Cultural Center (TCC), which was renamed the Tibetan Mongolian Buddhist Cultural Center (TMBCC). Chamtse Ling, meaning "field of compassion," is an interfaith temple dedicated to the promotion of world peace and harmony.

"The temple "will be a place where people of all faiths and all cultures can gather to plan deeds of compassion and wisdom rather than acts of violence and war," said Thubten J. Norbu, 81, the cultural center's founder and the Dalai Lama's oldest brother. "It will be a safe haven for all those who wish to conduct workshops, seminars, and perform religious services and rituals to promote world peace and harmony.

"All persons of all beliefs are welcome here. We open our hearts and arms to all."

I knew I wanted to attend the temple dedication on September 7.

In the lobby of the Travel Lodge Saturday afternoon was a stack of free newspapers: the Indiana Daily Student. A front-page story, headlined

"A Gathering For World Peace," was written by Indiana University senior Michelle Perry, an intern at The State Journal this summer. Nice photos of the Dalai Lama and his sister-in-law, Kunyang Norbu and two of her sons, Jigme and Kunga, accompanied Perry's story.

The first people I met in the motel lobby were Richard Farkas, design and production manager for The University Press of Kentucky, and his wife, Julie. They also were in Bloomington to attend the temple dedication on Sunday. Richard, a Buddhist, works in Lexington with friends of mine who are actively involved with the Kentucky Book Fair in Frankfort. Julie is Episcopalian.

Small world.

In his books and speeches, the Dalai Lama always talks about the world getting smaller and smaller. In a recent book, "An Open Heart: Practicing Compassion in Everyday Life," he says, "When we look closely at the many problems facing humanity today, we can see they have been created by us. . . . Conflicts, bloodshed, problems arising out of nationalism and national boundaries, are all man-made.

"If we looked down at the world from space, we would not see any demarcations of national boundaries. We would simply see one small planet, just one. Once we draw a line in the sand, we develop the feeling of 'us' and 'them.'"

In today's world, he said at the temple dedication, somebody winning a war and somebody else losing it "isn't normal reality." Instead, "destruction of your enemy, destruction of your neighbor, is actually destruction of yourself," he said.

In the afternoon session, the Dalai Lama said he believes the younger generation around the world is more committed to peace today than older people are.

When the war in Iraq began, "many people showed disappointment," he said. "I think this is a clear sign. It seems a genuine desire for peace is growing."

The present generation, particularly the younger generation, has an extremely important role in the future of humanity, he said. Prosperity, development and growth without peace "cannot be achieved."

To solve problems peacefully, he encouraged people to use dialogue instead of force.

"Fighting is the wrong way," he said.

A long-term goal to work toward, "and it may take 100 years," he said, "is, the whole planet should be demilitarized."

Small world.

Louisville cellist Michael Fitzpatrick, whom I interviewed for a Q & A in The State Journal in December 2001, was on stage with the Dalai Lama and Muhammad Ali. For them and 3,000 others, Fitzpatrick played music from the "Compassion" CD he produced in honor of the Dalai Lama's visit to the Abbey of Gethsemani in rural Nelson County, Kentucky, where the late Christian monk Thomas Merton, a peace activist, writer and poet, lived.

Merton and the Dalai Lama met in India in 1968 in hopes of working together to bring the world together in peace. Three weeks later, however, Merton died accidentally in Bangkok, Thailand. Then the Dalai Lama pledged to commit the rest of his life to fulfilling Merton's wish to bring East and West together in peace, harmony and compassion.

Small world.

I grew up 25 miles from the serene Abbey of Gethsemani and have visited there often. The white and black robes of the Trappist monks are as familiar to me as the Tibetan monks' maroon and saffron robes.

The man in a white and black robe on the TMBCC grounds early Sunday morning was the Rev. Damien Thompson, abbot of Gethsemani. He had met the Dalai Lama on several occasions but it was his first visit to TMBCC in Bloomington. He said the intentions of Thomas Merton brought him to the cultural center platform.

The Dalai Lama "bringing all these people, all these religious leaders, together for peace is wonderful," Thompson said. Leaders of 16 religions and denominations participated in the outdoor dedication. Gathering on one platform "expresses a unity of our search as a human family for the fullness of life," Thompson said.

"Our differences in the past led to violence, caused by the smallness of who we are. The violence indicated a need in us for the search of a common identity." Rather than excluding others who don't share the same beliefs, "the new era we are entering is an inclusive one that is beyond all our individual beliefs," Thompson said.

Offering a prayer, he said, "We are children surviving in a world torn by violence, division, poverty and ignorance. . . . I recognize violence exists in the world because of my own incapacity to manage the violence in my own heart. I can't change others, (but) I can change myself. . . . Use me as an instrument of your peace."

Small world.

In the huge crowd, I saw Michelle Perry, the recent State Journal intern. She said she was enjoying the day, but was tired "because I didn't get to bed until 5:30 this morning."

"I got up before you went to bed, at 4:15, and was here before 6," I said, laughing.

Then she gave me her best "why?" expression.

I feel at home at the cultural center. Knowing Michelle volunteered to cover the dedication for the IU newspaper, and spent a great deal of energy and her weekend doing it, made me happy, and gives me hope.

I was elated that my niece, Kimberly Pearl, an active member of the International Tibetan Independence Movement in Indianapolis, was invited inside the temple for a special meeting with the Dalai Lama. She was in New York City this past week attending several days of teachings by the 68-year-old Dalai Lama.

The September trip to Bloomington was a two-day family reunion, being with many people I had met in March of this year on a walk for Tibet's independence from Bloomington to Indianapolis.

On a warm Saturday afternoon in March, after a 14-mile walk, I sat on the deck floor outside the main TCC building and was served Tibetan tea. After drinking it, I lay down, looked up and watched thick, cottony clouds move quickly across a blue sky. Tall trees swayed and bent way over in the breeze. Tree branches clacking in the wind created an outdoor symphony, and I knew I was experiencing one of those moments of inner peace you never forget.

Shortly thereafter, I walked into the kitchen and several friendly Tibetan monks and women were preparing food for the Tibetan New Year's dinner and celebration that night.

Then Sunday morning, just before beginning a 10-mile walk in breezy, 24-degree weather, I realized one of the attractive women preparing our New Year's dinner was the Dalai Lama's sister-in-law, Kunyang Norbu.

Her husband, the retired IU professor, had suffered a major stroke in 2002 and was quite ill. But when he heard how successful the walk was going, he wanted to meet the walkers and thank them. So on Sunday morning, more than 30 walkers gathered inside the small Norbu family residence at the TCC.

He sat in a chair in the living room, with his wife by his side, and asked all of us to say our names and towns of residence. After the introductions, he gave each of us a small Buddhist pin as a token of his appreciation.

The Norbus' son, Jigme, led the walkers each day and set a brisk pace. I walked beside him for two hours that frigid Sunday morning and listened as he answered questions about his famous uncle, known around the globe for his compassion and work for world peace in a nonviolent way.

In a book, "Architects of Peace," the Dalai Lama, Tenzin Gyatso, says, "We tend to forget that despite the diversity of race, religion, ideology, and so forth, people are equal in their basic wish for peace and happiness. . .

"I believe the very purpose of life is to be happy. From the very core of our being, we desire contentment. In my own limited experience I have found the more we care for the happiness of others, the greater is our own sense of well-being. Cultivating a close, warm-hearted feeling for others automatically puts the mind at ease. It helps remove whatever fears or insecurities we may have and gives us the strength to cope with any obstacles we encounter. . .

"Since we are not solely material creatures, it is a mistake to place all our hopes for happiness on external development alone. The key is to develop inner peace."

Preaching peace doesn't bring peace. Developing inner peace takes daily practice – slowing down, pausing, finding silent places. Sitting meditation helps. Walking meditation helps.

"Genuine compassion is irrespective of others' attitude towards you," the Dalai Lama says.

I've found this year when you surround yourself with people of compassion, people of peace who exude loving-kindness, it's contagious. The positive energy you feel when you're with them stays with you when you leave. It's real and it's up to us to practice peace with every breath, every step, and pass it on.

Chapter 7

Thai monk lives a simple life in Franklin County

This story first appeared in The State Journal on September 14, 2009. Since then Charus Changchit, a Buddhist monk originally from Thailand, has moved from Bridgeport to a residence with a temple and more land in the Choateville community, at the edge of Frankfort.

Charus Changchit knows about change.

He grew up in northern Thailand in a province of more than a million people.

Now he lives in tiny Bridgeport, Kentucky, where gentle ripples of Benson Creek can be heard from his back yard on summer afternoons. The water speaks to him daily as he walks a straight and narrow meditation path beside the creek.

His simple clothing – an almond-colored robe – would stand out in a crowd. But Charus tries to avoid crowds.

Before moving from Bowling Green, Kentucky, to Franklin County, he ate at Thai Smile restaurant in Frankfort's Century Plaza shopping center, just ahead of the lunchtime crowd.

Now as an act of kindness and generosity, the Thai Smile owners, formerly of Thailand, deliver Charus his daily meal – the only one he's allowed.

It must be eaten before noon. He is not allowed to cook, and he can't ask for food – or anything.

As a Buddhist monk, Charus is called Phra Abhijoto. He has 227 rules to follow. But it's obvious he enjoys the spiritual path he's chosen. His perpetual smile mirrors his contentment and happiness.

One of the many teachings in Buddhism is about impermanence.

"Our lives change all the time, every moment," he says, sitting in his living room on a platform padded with brown carpet. "Everything is changing all the time."

When he goes to the platform or leaves it, he bows deeply to the five small Buddha images surrounded by vases of roses and other colorful flowers on a table by a window. The prostrations express humility, reverence and gratitude.

On a September 2009 afternoon, three Franklin County visitors sit in front of him on a soft, beige-and-maroon rug, looking up slightly and listening to him talk about his life.

The simple life of a monk was not so simple at first, he says, smiling.

He came to America 30 years ago, living in Lexington, Kentucky, where he earned a master's degree in nutrition from the University of Kentucky.

His bachelor's from a university in Bangkok was in agricultural science and he had worked "in industrial research and development."

Charus also lived in Los Angeles two years and "worked a little bit helping my brother, a medical doctor, in his office."

Later he moved back to Lexington to work on a Ph.D. in toxicology at UK. Then his father, who had been a goldsmith, became ill with cancer while living in California. One of 14 children, Charus "was the one most available" to take care of his father for two years, he says.

Charus returned to Thailand with his father before he died at 73.

"It's a tradition in Thailand when a parent passes away that one of the members of the family – the more the better but at least one – go to become a monk. I was the only one available."

He says more than 90 percent of the people in Thailand are Buddhists, including 700,000 monks.

Charus, who will be 60 on Nov. 1, 2009, has been a monk for 20 years.

His only possessions are his clothes and glasses. He has seven brothers and six sisters. About half of them live in the U.S. A sister from Lexington, who works at UK, owns the small yellow house where Charus lives.

His 90-year-old mother lives in Texas.

He moved to Franklin County from Bowling Green in the summer of 2009.

"I like Frankfort," he says. "There are a lot of trees. It's beautiful, peaceful and good weather."

He says his next-door neighbors are friendly and have given him tomatoes.

Before becoming a monk, Charus lived in the mainstream and ate three meals a day.

It was difficult at first eating only one meal, he says. He would get hungry and "a little bit weak sometimes, but not now. After a while you get used to it."

Since Thai monks can't cook, "they have to depend on others," he says. "And it would be inconvenient for people, who have to go to work, to come back to prepare more than one meal for the monk."

One meal a day is also "good for meditation. That's the most important thing."

He usually gets up about 5 a.m. and goes to bed around midnight.

He sleeps on a "mat, not a mattress," he says.

After chanting for 30 minutes at 6 a.m., he does a silent meditation for about two hours. He says his longest meditation at one sitting has been nine hours.

Why is meditation important?

"To purify the mind," he says. "The world is full of suffering and stress and meditation is the only thing you can do to escape from the world. There is no other way."

A humble man, Charus says his meditation practice isn't perfect.

"Not yet," he says, laughing.

Random thoughts still enter his mind and when they do, "I just let them go."

He says he never feels lonely, sad or depressed. He practices living in the present moment.

"The future has not come yet, so don't worry about it," he says. "And the past has already passed, so we should be in the present."

He usually eats around 10:30 a.m. and can have coffee and tea – without milk – throughout the day and evening.

In the afternoon he can drink apple juice or other liquids, "but not all."

If the fruit is bigger than the palm of his hand, "such as a pineapple or coconut, it's too big," and he can't have the juice.

Alcohol is forbidden.

Although he's not vegetarian, Thai monks can't hunt, fish or kill any animal for food or accept meat from anyone who killed an animal specifically for them.

Also, he says, monks can't eat these meats: human, dog, horse, bear, elephant, lion, tiger, cheetah, cougar and snake.

51

On September 9, 2009, Charus' Thai Smile meal was shrimp and vegetables.

"It's something different every day," he says. "We take what we are given."

He says he doesn't have any favorite foods.

After his meal he often goes outside for a slow walking meditation on a tiled-brick pathway that Thai and other friends in the area built for him.

The path is supposed to be 25 to 40 steps in length, "so it's not too short or long," he says.

He also does a two-hour sitting meditation in the evenings.

He isn't allowed to cut trees or use a lawn mower, but he can gather grass clippings after it's cut.

He can't drive a car or watch TV, but he can read a newspaper and listen to a radio as long as it's not for entertainment.

Books are limited to those that help with his spiritual path.

He's allowed a telephone and a computer with Internet access to stay connected to his Buddhist order in the U.S.

He can do his laundry and wash his food bowl, and do housecleaning and repairs. Another form of daily meditation is "sweeping the floor in mindfulness."

While at UK, he used to enjoy jogging about 5 miles but running and swimming are prohibited now. However, he can go on short walks.

As a child he says he never thought about being a monk.

"Like everybody, I thought about getting an education, making money and having a good life and entertainment."

As an adult, he drove a small Datsun and says he never had a desire to make a lot of money – just enough to live comfortably.

He had a girlfriend but he never married. He also enjoyed drinking an occasional beer at home.

Now as a monk he must remain single and abstain from sex and alcohol.

In the monastery he was taught meditation by a Buddhist master, and says he must "practice a lot more" before becoming a master. "My master was in the first group of Thai monks to come to the West."

He's lived in Bridgeport since early July 2009 and said he has no idea how long he will stay there.

"We don't look at the future too much."

But one goal is to "attain enlightenment in this life, where my mind is absolutely pure."

While on his spiritual journey here, Charus says he wants to help others as much as possible by providing guidance to Thai and Asian people in the area and anyone else interested in Buddhism.

Bob McClain, a retired state government employee who enjoys studying philosophy and spirituality, says Charus' presence in the community is a gift.

"He lives in a calmer world than the hectic, materialistic one many of us seem to be caught in," McClain says.

"Whether or not one would be interested in Buddhism, there are certainly some fresh perspectives to consider learning from this man who aspires to live in tranquility in a higher consciousness."

Chapter 8

Dalai Lama in Bloomington and Indianapolis

This column is similar to one published in The State Journal on June 4, 2010 after a two-day trip to Indiana to see the Dalai Lama.

I just returned from Indianapolis – or so it seems.

Instead of going to the 500, I went two weeks early to be with a world famous spiritual leader for two days.

And when His Holiness the Dalai Lama and I meet in Indiana, I always lose sleep. But it's worth it.

There are no expectations of one-on-one interviews. Just the excitement of being in his presence is overwhelming.

And if he read this, he would laugh and say, "why? I am just a simple Buddhist monk – no more, no less."

He says he has no special healing powers and offers proof by saying he doesn't think his gall bladder surgery would have been necessary if he did. And it's the same story with his eyeglasses, he says, laughing.

Being near the Dalai Lama requires getting up before daylight. That's no problem. I never use an alarm clock, and I'm always awake by 4:30 a.m.

Franklin County friend Angela Mitchell accompanied me to a May 13 teaching and press conference in Bloomington and a public speaking the next day in Indianapolis.

The two-hour teaching began at 9:15 a.m. and we had to be at the Indiana University Auditorium media entrance no later than 7 a.m.

All rooms were booked in Bloomington so we stayed in a Martinsville motel, 20 miles away.

The motel walls seemed paper thin, and the first night I heard endless talking and laughing and TVs and toilets flushing and snoring and someone on the second floor walking all night.

Angela slept through it all. I tried to fall asleep meditating but don't ever remember dropping off.

When Angela heard about the marathon walker upstairs, she laughed, saying, "It was probably a Tibetan monk – just as excited as we are about seeing the Dalai Lama – doing a walking meditation."

At 6:15 in Bloomington, one reporter was in front of us at the locked media door – Ronald Hawkins, a Louisville native and University of Kentucky graduate.

Shortly after 7, the line was long and when the door opened to go through the first-round of security scanning, we felt we'd known Ronald forever.

He writes for The Reporter-Times in Martinsville and was eager to see the Dalai Lama.

Tenzin Gyatso, the 14th Dalai Lama, 74, is the head of state and spiritual leader of the Tibetan people. The Dalai Lama honorary title means "Teacher Whose Wisdom Is As Great As the Ocean."

In 1959 he fled his homeland after China's takeover of Tibet and now lives in Dharamsala, India, where he established the Tibetan government in exile.

He's a tireless worker for peace, and every year travels throughout the world giving talks about wisdom and compassion.

He was awarded the Nobel Peace Prize in 1989, and in 2007 was presented the Congressional Gold Medal of Honor.

We gathered on a stairway and were told if we wanted to attend an afternoon press conference at the Tibetan Mongolian Buddhist Cultural Center – several miles from the auditorium – we would need to leave the teaching early to go through security again two hours before the Dalai Lama arrived.

Before the teaching began, one reporter fainted on the stairs and had to be taken to a hospital for treatment. Later we all had to line up cameras and recording gear in a hallway for canine inspections.

The dog inspections were repeated at the cultural center. The Dalai Lama called the afternoon session "Meet the Press." We lined up as he walked into the Great Hall and Angela and I shook his hand as he walked to the front table.

The room was adorned with paintings of Buddhas and Tibetan wax-butter sculptures.

Our seats were in the second row. As he sat down, he opened a bottle of spring water, took a drink and a deep breath.

He seemed to make eye contact with everyone in the room.

"Media people have a responsibility to inform people," he said. "You should have long noses, as long as elephant noses...People have a right to know."

He believes journalists should report the good news and the bad, in an unbiased manner.

The visit to the cultural center was the Dalai Lama's first since the 2008 death of his brother, Thubten Norbu, who founded the 108-acre center in 1979.

Norbu was a retired professor of Tibetan studies at IU.

The last time I saw Thubten Norbu was September 7, 2003, when the Dalai Lama and Louisville native Muhammad Ali were in Bloomington to dedicate the interfaith Chamtse Ling Temple on the grounds of the cultural center.

This time on his sixth visit to Indiana, the Dalai Lama said in the Great Hall, "Spirituality is very much alive here. That means my late brother's spirit very much still exists here."

The rain began as we departed the cultural center in late afternoon and it was pouring by the time we reached our car. Although we knew 4 a.m. tomorrow would arrive too soon and we'd go through security checks again, we were energized.

Hawkins, the Martinsville reporter, summarized it well in his newspaper column the next day. He wrote: "It's not every day a journalist can say after he was drenched by a torrential downpour, scanned multiple times for security, forced to wait hours for scheduled events, and got his car stuck in mud, that he'd had an exhilarating day.

"That's what this reporter experienced Thursday, from his early arrival on the Indiana University campus until he drove his mud-splattered car home. The cause for the exhilaration was the first-hand experience of shaking the hand and speaking briefly to the Dalai Lama, listening to his wit and wisdom."

What I remember most about being with the Dalai Lama in 2003 and again this year is the positive energy I felt for weeks afterward. The kind Tibetan people – and those working to help them gain their independence – have become my friends, my family.

I asked several what draws them to the Dalai Lama.

Valerie Purvin, an eye surgeon and clinical professor in Indianapolis who grew up in a Jewish family in New York, says, "The thing I appreciate most about him is his lack of religious chauvinism. So many religious leaders, whatever their message is, have a position that this is the one and only path with capital letters.

"He does not do that. Often when he speaks, there is a pause and he will say, 'In any case that is what I think. If you find that useful, fine. And if you don't, then never mind, just drop it.'"

Purvin says she loves his intellectual curiosity.

"I'm appreciating as I get older how hard it is to hold onto that kind of curiosity over time, to not want early closure," she says. "I don't want to keep wondering about it. I just want to learn it and act on it.

"The fact that he is still exploring and open to Western science and neurology with Tibetan Eastern philosophy is very appealing.

"I think he gets more pleasure out of doing his job than anybody I know."

Lexington's Richard Farkas, the official photographer for the Dalai Lama's visit, says he's met His Holiness four times, and has visited Tibet twice and Dharamsala, India, once.

"Anytime you hear the Dalai Lama is a special time." he says. "I feel good whenever I see his picture, and especially when I'm near him.

"He seems very genuine, very open. He's got a good sense of humor. He's serious, funny, gentle and compassionate."

Julie Farkas, Richard's wife, says the best part of her week was "the Dalai Lama coming by and taking my hand. And to hear him laugh does something to me.

"You know everything he's been through and what he goes through on a daily basis, and he just gets such joy out of life."

Lynn Jackson was among 10,000 who gathered at the Conseco Fieldhouse, a basketball arena in downtown Indianapolis, to hear the Tibetan leader speak May 14.

Persons of all faiths attending included 500 school children.

"I feel the Dalai Lama is a message for the world," Jackson said, after his 90-minute talk titled Facing Challenges with Compassion and Wisdom. "He's a prophet. He transcends any specific religion."

Jackson says the Dalai Lama's message is always so clear and understandable "you can put it in your heart."

She says she belongs to a "spiritual oneness group" at St. Luke's United Methodist Church in Indianapolis, made up of a Baha'i, Hindu, Tibetan Buddhist nun, Muslim, Jew, Unitarian Universalist, Christian Scientist, Wicca and American Indian.

"We invite people who might have a different spiritual approach and see if we can find our sameness, our difference and see if we can develop programs for the entire community."

In the arena, the Dalai Lama talked about the importance of establishing a compassionate approach to living, and assisting those in need regardless of their religious, economic, political, ethnic or social background.

The event began with an "Invocation for World Peace" cello performance by Michael Fitzpatrick, formerly of Louisville now living in California.

Frankfort's Mary West says she heard about the Dalai Lama coming to Indianapolis after she "flippantly put on Facebook" that the Dalai Lama was her boyfriend.

"I figured he was the only good boy breathing on the planet," West said. "And one of my girlfriends sent a message back saying, 'Your boyfriend is going to be in my town if you would like to come see him.'"

West said she had met Nobel Peace Prize winners Mother Teresa, Archbishop Desmund Tutu, Al Gore and Jimmy Carter, "and the Dalai Lama would be the crowd jewel of any Nobel collection, so I jumped at the opportunity."

West says she admires him for "his pursuit of peace in a very hostile world, and how he has approached adversity without hostility or animosity.

"Being there I was greatly encouraged by seeing the broad mix, the ecumenical community. It gave me a great sense of hope – especially as polarized as our country has become – that people are out there striving to unite us, not drive us apart."

Chapter 9

Baptist minister with an open mind and heart

When I was contemplating making the long jump from Christianity to Buddhism in 2010, God tossed me a Baptist minister in Frankfort. My mother was elated. While a staff writer for The State Journal, I wrote this feature story on Dr. Chuck Queen for the August 1, 2010 issue.

Chuck Queen's words from the heart – in his sermons and State Journal newspaper writings through a paid column – have sparked plenty of controversy in the Bible belt.

The 51-year-old minister has been called a "messenger of Satan," a "false teacher," and other derogatory names in letters to the editor sent to The State Journal.

The letter writers don't offend or surprise Queen. He understands their thinking, he says, because he felt the same way at one point on his spiritual journey.

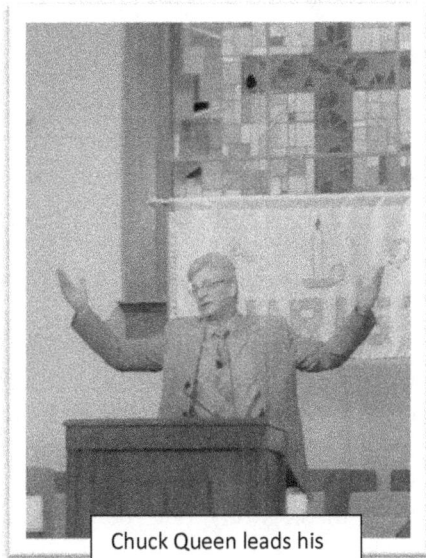

Chuck Queen leads his congregation in prayer

And be believes the negative letters will actually help bring change.

Change is the theme of his 2009 paperback book, "The Good News According to Jesus: A New Kind of Christianity for a New Kind of Christian."

Queen, pastor of Immanuel Baptist Church on Collins Lane in Frankfort, has changed a lot since he was first ordained a Baptist minister while going to Fairview High School in Boyd County.

He was a starting guard on the basketball team when his small school won the region his sophomore year, "which was the first and only time Fairview has ever been to the Sweet 16 state tournament," he says.

Queen went to Campbellsville College (now University) on a basketball scholarship in 1977, but stayed only one year. There was turmoil in the basketball program because of a coaching change.

He missed his girlfriend, Melissa – back home in Boyd County – who is now his wife and mother of their three children, Hollie, 27, Julie, 25, and Jordan, 19.

'Way too liberal'

And he felt his religion professors at the Baptist college in Taylor County were "way too liberal."

So he transferred to "a very conservative" Tri State Bible College in South Point, Ohio – "and felt very comfortable there."

"The college was very grounded in biblical inerrancy, meaning the Bible is without error. It's the word of God."

After getting his bachelor's in religious education at Tri State, he earned a master's of divinity at Grace Theological Seminary in Winona Lake, Indiana, and a doctorate of ministry in 1993 at Southern Baptist Theological Seminary in Louisville.

"One thing I value about my undergraduate education at Tri State is that I learned the Bible, which has been very helpful," said Queen in his office at Immanuel Baptist on a Monday morning in July 2010.

"They didn't teach me theology but they taught me the Bible. In a lot of moderate and liberal seminaries today they may teach you how to think theologically, but you don't really learn scripture, the content of the Bible."

While taking a textual criticism class at Grace Seminary, another conservative school, Queen began to challenge things.

"Even though professors were bound with a system of faith that was pretty rigid, they began to give me the tools I needed to think critically," Queen says.

"The very process of that thinking exposes the weaknesses of the real rigid, conservative position on the scripture.

60

"You realize there are hundreds of manuscripts and they claim the text is inerrant. Yet we don't even have an original manuscript. All we have are copies and all the copies have discrepancies.

"If God was concerned about an inerrant text, wouldn't God have preserved an original manuscript that is inerrant?"

He mentions the debate over the age of the Earth.

"If you contend the Earth is only a few thousand years old, that means God must have created the world with the appearance of age, which seems kind of crazy," Queen says, laughing.

"All of science seems to point that the Earth, the universe, is billions of years old. So why go against common understandings to try to maintain a position? It's just not necessary."

Queen says he loves to write and teach.

He now (in 2013) has three more books published: "A Faith Worth Living: The Dynamics of an Inclusive Gospel," "Shimmers of Light: Spiritual Reflections for the Christmas Season," and "Why Call Friday Good?: Spiritual Reflections for Lent and Holy Week."

He says his sermons are teachings.

Inclusive Christianity

"I'm trying to present a kind of Christianity that is inclusive, gracious, credible, and one that is transformational – that can lead to real positive spiritual, personal, emotional, social growth and development.

"To do that you have to challenge dualistic and exclusivistic versions of Christianity."

In a June 6, 2010 sermon, Queen said, "At an earlier time in my spiritual journey I divided humanity between 'the lost' and 'the found,' obviously putting myself in the category of 'the found.'

"I believed those who were found or saved were children of God, but everyone else was not."

He said he believed the only way one became a child of God was by making a profession of faith in Jesus.

The others were "doomed, damned, condemned," he said. "And as much as it pains me to admit this, I even called such folks 'children of the devil.'

"Similar phrases have been used to describe me recently."

Queen says it's a "waste of good energy getting angry at folks who say these things.

"Whenever I find myself getting upset because someone has called me a false teacher or messenger of Satan, I remind myself of the things I used to believe and say. And then I can't get too angry."

His critics respond out of fear, Queen said.

"Deep down they are afraid, they feel threatened and they lash out. Their sense of identity and security is connected to their particular belief system, so when their beliefs are threatened they become defensive, angry, and they react."

Evolving spiritual pilgrimage

He said as he reflects on his evolving spiritual pilgrimage he feels hope for others to grow beyond a dualistic religion.

Regarding letters to the editor criticizing him, Queen says, "Only angry, malicious people like angry, malicious letters.

"Those on the borderline, who are starting to question or think about their faith, if they look at a letter that lacks civility and they have an open heart and mind, they're going to say if this kind of Christianity produces this kind of results, that's not what I want.

"So I look at it from the perspective that it really helps my cause when they write things like that."

He says the letters don't upset his wife, Melissa, either.

"She's used to it," he says, laughing. "Trouble has sort of followed me around in the sense that I've always pushed the edges a bit wherever I've been."

Queen says the whole Jesus movement was about Jewish reform.

"He never abandoned his heritage," Queen says. "He was trying to renew it and revitalize it.

"The very people the religious community rejected, excluded and condemned are the very ones that Jesus received and welcomed, and made heroes of in his stories.

"Jesus' acceptance of traitors and sinners scandalized the religious leaders. No wonder they rejected Jesus and were determined to be rid of him.

"Don't you think if we sought to actually formulate church policy and practice to model Jesus we would be shunned and condemned by most of the Christian establishment of Frankfort?"

"Christianity was diverse from its inception," Queen says.

"There are some very dualistic passages in the gospels, and some very harsh passages.

"The Bible didn't come down from heaven on wings of angels. They were human beings who wrote scripture. They were inspired but they were fallible, imperfect human beings and you see their flaws. They're everywhere."

Before Immanuel

Before coming to Immanuel Baptist in August 2002, Queen was pastor of Trinity Baptist Church in Waldorf, Maryland, near Washington, D.C.

"They were a fairly conservative congregation but moderate in some respects. It was one of the few Baptist congregations in the area that had women deacons and valued women's contributions to ministry and social activities."

He says he left Trinity on good terms to return to Kentucky.

At the start of his ministry after finishing his master's, Queen taught at Rose Hill Christian School in Ashland, Kentucky, and pastored a Rose Hill Baptist Church mission, Fellowship Baptist Church, in South Shore, Kentucky, for three years.

"I was still pretty conservative at the time but not conservative enough.

"At the school, my goodness, they wanted me to use the Bob Jones curriculum, real conservative stuff. I just couldn't. I had to branch out, and that got me in trouble.

"Instead of them firing me, I took a severance package. They paid my salary for six months."

His next church was First Baptist in Greenup, Kentucky, while he was going to Southern Baptist Theological Seminary in Louisville.

As part of his doctoral work, "I did a teaching plan to try to move the congregation toward a more egalitarian understanding of women in ministry.

"Our church in Greenup had a woman choir director. She could direct the choir but couldn't turn and direct the congregation because it would be usurping the authority of the male leadership.

"Even then I thought it was ludicrous."

Queen said he wasn't fired at Greenup, "but I could see the handwriting on the wall."

Queen says it's a joy being at Immanuel Baptist Church.

The church has women deacons, an ordained woman music minister, Dr. Naomi Walker, and an ordained pastor to youth and children, Lisa Wood.

"The church has given me a lot of freedom here," Queen says. "I think it probably would be a struggle if I had all kinds of pressure from the people here not to say what I'm saying."

The church also is paying for the advertising space for Queen to write his newspaper column.

"I can't imagine a single other Baptist church in Frankfort giving me the freedom to say and write and teach the things I've been saying, writing and teaching. That says a lot about the congregation.

"Not everybody agrees, especially some of the older folks. But I've noticed even now, there's a respect there.

"I'm fortunate this church has given me the freedom to grow and to challenge them to grow. A lot of folks here have walked this journey with me."

And where does this evolving spiritual voyage end?

"It doesn't end," Queen says. "That's the beauty of it. When you're open to grow, you don't have a problem saying, 'This is where I am right now. I could be wrong. I'm sure I am about some things.'

"I'm sure five years from now I'm not going to be the same person I am now because when you have an openness to change and grow, you're open to considering the truth wherever the truth is found."

Queen says the more he studies and the deeper he delves into his own faith, "the more inclusive I become of other faiths. God works through all faiths.

"God meets us where we are."

Chapter 10

The Light Clinic brings new way of healing

This story is similar to one published in The State Journal in 2011, a few months after The Light Clinic opened for business.

Emaline Gray earned a few state track medals for Frankfort High School, including a first in the 1,600-meter relay in 1997, her senior year.

She also suffered knee injuries in high school soccer, underwent surgery twice, and no longer has an anterior cruciate ligament (ACL) in her left knee.

Emaline knows firsthand the difficulties of living with chronic pain and feels fortunate to have found effective relief and healing through Classical Chinese Medicine.

She and her husband, Joseph Fiala, also from Frankfort, are practitioners of Classical Chinese Medicine (CCM) and opened The Light Clinic in 2010 on the sixth floor of the downtown McClure Building on the corner of West Main and St. Clair.

Their mission – through acupuncture, herbal medicine and health and exercise classes – is to "alleviate needless suffering and disease," Joseph says.

After getting their bachelor's degrees, they studied four years under CCM masters at the National College of Natural Medicine in Portland, Oregon, and graduated in 2010.

"It was full-time for four years with lots of clinics and classes," Emaline says. "And like any medical practice, you have to keep up your educational requirements, national certification and licensure.

"We loved Portland and it would have been very easy to stay there. It was tempting. All our teachers were there," along with good opportunities in a state where acupuncture treatments and natural medicine are covered by most insurance companies.

When asked if their teachers encouraged them to stay in Portland, Emaline smiled, saying, "They're good teachers. They allow us to fall from the nest and fly where we should. They support that.

"But in our hearts we always wanted to come back to Frankfort. If you really embody the medicine, there's no way you wouldn't give back to your roots."

However, their hometown does "feel like an oasis, and that has its glory and hardship," Emaline said in 2011, a few months after opening The Light Clinic. "We're back in the community of our hearts but not in the community of Chinese medicine."

Joseph said, "We have to do a lot of extra work to stay in touch with our teachers. We have very close relationships with our teachers so we talk on the phone regularly."

In 2010 they moved back to Frankfort in July, married October 10 and opened The Light Clinic in November.

A heavenly suite

Suite 609 in the McClure Building "is heaven," Emaline said. It has two treatment rooms and a larger room for various classes – all with splendid views of downtown – and a spacious lobby.

They knew their office had to be downtown in a place where windows would open, "and knew this was it the first moment we saw it," Joseph said.

It's a space that "helps your internal state," Emaline says. "So many times when people walk through the door they say, 'Oh, I'm so glad to be here. This space is so great.'"

Joseph said Chinese medicine, like its Western counterpart, was developed to save lives.

"It has been a very powerful and effective way to treat various diseases of all different levels, including people on the brink of death, for thousands of years, and it still has that power today."

Classical acupuncturists are trained to work on the body's structure and energy.

According to their brochure, "acupuncture is an incredibly helpful therapeutic tool with a wide range of application. Whether it's the common cold, the flu, chronic illness or musculoskeletal issues, there are appropriate and effective techniques available in Chinese medicine."

When working on the tissues of the body, the acupuncture needle "is beyond compare for its versatility," Joseph says. "It can create pathways for circulation and microcirculation, break up scar tissue and regulate fluids.

"Then if you're working on energy (the breath of the body and how all the tissues breathe and move on an energetic level), again the needle is beyond compare."

When the body works in an organized manner, it is healthy, Joseph says. When there's disruption, illness arises and acupuncture attends to the organization.

Emaline and Joseph are also trained in classical herbal prescriptions. Chinese herbal medicine can be used internally to influence the body's immune response and externally for strains, sprains, broken bones or rashes, they say.

They've offered qigong and tai chi exercise classes for beginners and advanced students at the clinic; courses such as "Eating for Health and Longevity"; and free lectures.

Joseph's father, Joe Fiala, who has a Ph.D. in social psychology, taught meditation classes at the clinic in its first years. "We're always trying to offer a variety of courses for our community," Joseph said. "They're designed to try to fill a need we're seeing in the treatment room."

They also started group acupuncture, setting up tables in the big room to help keep rates low for many who need medical help but don't have a lot of money.

Emaline's mother, Mary Frank Slaughter, offers craniosacral therapy, which helps release tension and enhances healing.

Finding the path

Emaline earned her bachelor's degree at Beloit College in Wisconsin, majoring in religious and Asian studies.

Joseph was the head of the drum line in band at Western Hills High School in Frankfort and landed a lead role in the school play, "A Few Good Men." He was the Navy attorney played by Tom Cruise in the movie.

Joseph received his bachelor's in business economics from the University of Tennessee.

Emaline and Joseph began seeing each other often in separate booths at Farmers Kitchen and started dating in 2001.

"That was our coffee shop before the downtown Kentucky Coffeetree Café existed," she said.

After graduating from Beloit, Emaline worked for Habitat for Humanity for two years in Raleigh, North Carolina. The job was "all about giving," she said.

"It was so enriching to see that a day-to-day job could really be fulfilling to you and other people. I would sit in coffee shops and think about what I wanted my life's path to be, and spent half a year thinking of a million different things.

"I had tons of background in Chinese philosophy, so I decided to deepen it," and study Classical Chinese Medicine.

Joseph said, "For me, Chinese medicine was in the back of my mind because of Emaline. But I was still finishing college and my main focus had turned toward Buddhist practice."

He went on a four-month trip to India, staying at a monastery in Bodh Gaya. "I even took monastic vows and became a monk for a brief time but not with any intention of staying for a lifetime. It was a great place to study for sure."

While there he contemplated how he could apply his Buddhist practice of serving others in the mainstream world.

"With that in mind Chinese medicine seemed perfect because it's got Eastern philosophy, which I already felt synced with, and the self-cultivation and meditation aspects. And the more you work your way up the better skill level, the more vision you have for treating and helping people."

It's been a joyful journey, they said in the opening months of their clinic. "We feel really supported so far," Joseph said. "We knew things would work here. If you're trained well enough, people recognize that. It's easy to spot.

"The response couldn't be better. It seems there's a lot of people here whose issues or concerns with their health are not being properly heard. They need another option and we feel we can bring light to a lot of those people."

Chapter 11

Arjia Rinpoche's story of torture and escape

This column on Arjia Rinpoche is similar to one published in The State Journal on November 11, 2011, the same day Angela Mitchell and I had a dedication ceremony for the prayer and walking meditation labyrinth that we built next to our yurt. The next day, after he attended the Kentucky Book Fair at the Frankfort Convention Center, author Rinpoche and his assistant, Chunpay Jiumei, blessed the yurt and labyrinth, and had dinner at Angela's house before heading back to Bloomington, Indiana.

Since retiring from fulltime journalism this spring, I've spent most of my time reading books on spirituality and the environment.

The one that has touched my heart the most is "Surviving The Dragon: A Tibetan Lama's Account of 40 Years Under Chinese Rule" by Arjia Rinpoche.

It's a story of Rinpoche's torture and daring escape from a repressive government that eventually led him to Bloomington, Indiana, where he is director of the Tibetan Mongolian Buddhist Cultural Center (TMBCC).

I met Rinpoche several years ago in Bloomington and knew he was a kind, compassionate, intelligent man. But until reading his book, I had no idea what an enchanting and horrifying life he's experienced.

Born to a nomadic family in Mongolia in 1950 (the ninth of 11 children), he was recognized as a reincarnate lama at age 2 and moved to Kumbum Monastery in Tibet, where the Dalai Lama began his monastic life.

For six years, Rinpoche was treated with great care and honor as a living Buddha – until one day Chinese authorities abruptly arrived and systematically rounded up the monks for arrest and torture. With his caretakers and teachers gone, Rinpoche was left alone in his home now populated by strangers.

In the next decade, Rinpoche managed to stay safe from physical harm, but was forced into a life of harsh manual labor.

After the 1976 death of Mao Zedong, chairman of the Chinese Communist Party and leader of the People's Republic of China, Rinpoche rose to prominence within the Chinese Buddhist bureaucracy with the help of the Panchen Lama. (The Dalai Lama and Panchen Lama are the top two spiritual leaders of Tibet.)

In doing so, Rinpoche was coerced into supporting China's increasingly aggressive anti-Tibet agenda, including taking part in carefully orchestrated rituals engineered to undermine the authority of the Dalai Lama, who fled Tibet in 1959.

Spiritually and morally depleted, Rinpoche longed to escape the repressive climate and eventually found the opportunity to do so. In February 1998, Rinpoche and his attendants fled China by disguising themselves as tourists – trading in their saffron robes for jeans, T-shirts and sunglasses – and boarding a plane for Guatemala and then the United States.

Not long after he arrived as an exile in the U.S., Rinpoche met with the Dalai Lama in New York.

Rinpoche settled in California and started the Tibetan Center for Compassion and Wisdom in Mill Valley. He loved California and had no desire to leave. But the Dalai Lama needed him to take over management of the TMBCC in Indiana.

The Dalai Lama's oldest brother, Thubten Norbu, who taught Tibetan studies at Indiana University for 22 years, built the center for the preservation of Tibetan culture on 108 acres of rolling meadows and thick forest. He had suffered a series of strokes and could no longer oversee the center.

On the third request, Arjia Rinpoche agreed to move to Indiana as director of the center. Norbu died in 2008.

In March of this year in Bloomington, Rinpoche welcomed me to his residence where we talked about his book project. He said he spent four years writing it, and it took another six years to find a publisher.

The Dalai Lama wrote the foreword to Rinpoche's "Surviving The Dragon."

The Dalai Lama says, "To understand what is really happening in a country where the press is neither open nor free and people live in a state of constant fear and suspicion, we must rely on the reports of individuals like Arjia Rinpoche, who can now write without restraint about what he has seen, heard and experienced in Tibet.

"I believe what he has to say will be of great interest to the many people in the world who have the compassion to find common cause with fellow humans like the peoples of Tibet, Inner Mongolia and East Turkestan who are currently living under such critical circumstances."

After the interview, Rinpoche invited me to the interfaith temple at the cultural center for a prayer service and fundraiser for victims and survivors of the earthquake and tsunami in Japan. The mayor of Bloomington spoke as did leaders of Christian, Jewish, Islamic, Hindu and Buddhist religions.

In a telephone conversation this week, Rinpoche said he was "very excited" about making his first visit to Frankfort this weekend. He said part of the proceeds from his book sales will benefit Cancer Care Hospital in Mongolia. He's hoping to see a few historic sites before leaving the capital.

He's lectured at many universities including Harvard, Yale, Stanford, University of Wisconsin, Columbia in New York and Oxford in England.

Twice he's met with movie star Richard Gere, a Tibetan Buddhist, including last year in Mongolia, Rinpoche's home country. Next week Rinpoche is traveling to India for a conference.

Coming to the book fair with Rinpoche are Chunpay Jiumei, a young monk who fled China on the same flight as Rinpoche; Lisa Morrison, communications director for TMBCC in Bloomington; and Mary Pattison, Rinpoche's secretary.

Morrison says Rinpoche often appears to be very simple, "but at the same time still waters run deep and he is incredibly intelligent and talented. He's an architect, an artist, a writer, a businessman and even a politician at times.

"If he were not a reincarnated lama, I think he could very easily administer a very large company and be a CEO. He's very organized. He also has a good sense of humor and is very light-hearted."

Chapter 12

Baptist woman's surprise: She's Jewish

Frankfort's Vicki Pettus says she goes to bed with Thomas Merton every night . . . listening to tapes of his talks to the monks at the Abbey of Gethsemani.

Merton was a deep thinker, "and that's why I listen to his tapes over and over again. I like his voice and I love the way he talks to the monks – the humor and that laugh of his.

"Of course I often fall asleep before I get through a tape. So I have to re-listen to it and every time I re-listen I find something different. He's incredible."

Vicki was 31 and living in Lexington, Kentucky, when she found out she's Jewish.

She grew up in northern Virginia near Washington, D.C., and was raised in a Southern Baptist and Primitive Baptist home.

"My father was Primitive Baptist meaning you had all-day meetings and no musical instruments," Vicki says. "You sing all your hymns acapella. You would meet for a couple of hours in the morning for worship with a lot of singing. Then you would have a lunch break with a big meal.

"If somebody had to be baptized we would go down to the river. Then adults would go back inside the church for afternoon services and children could stay outside and play.

"They didn't get into speaking in tongues or snake-handling. But, oh God yes, they were conservative in that it was very simplistic worship, no frills. There were a lot of scripture readings and sermons but they only met once a month."

Vicki's mother was baptized in a Southern Baptist church, "so I was basically raised Southern Baptist. I went to Sunday school every week and had perfect attendance. Instead of going to camps in the summer, we went to Bible school. We did the Bible drills, learning all the books of the Bible and memorizing a lot of verses. I can still quickly find the books of the Bible.

"I went through all the motions but never felt connected to Christianity growing up. I was told I was going to be baptized. I never went forward on my own."

Vicki made straight A's until high school and that's when the C's started. "That's when the boys came in," she said, laughing.

She said she had a chance to get partial college scholarships. But her father told her she wasn't smart enough for college. She believed him and her high school teachers were livid that he would say that.

"It caused a lot of conflict in our family. He was blue collar and basically said I wasn't college material because he couldn't afford to pay for me to go. So he got me a job at the State Department."

She left home at 17, worked four years for the federal government, and went into an agnostic phase.

"I was very disdainful of Christianity. I was sick of the fact that every time I went to church, they had numbers posted about how much money they had collected the week before, and what the attendance was. I didn't like anything the organized Christian church stood for."

She lived in Arlington, Virginia, and it took almost an hour to drive five miles into D.C. One morning while observing the bumper-to-bumper traffic she was in, with people darting in and out of lanes, she stopped her car in the middle of it all.

A truck driver behind her got out and put out a flare. Then he walked up to her car window and asked if she was all right.

"No," I said. "This is crazy."

She was 21 and wanted a different life. She managed to drive on to work, and went in and announced, "'I'm quitting. It's time for me to leave.' I can't believe I did that. I think I was still stoned from the night before."

She cashed in her $2,000 pension money and enrolled at Virginia Commonwealth University in Richmond.

A professor helped get her a scholarship and Vicki put herself through college.

She found an apartment, partitioned off rooms and sublet spaces to other students to pay her rent. Bill, her boyfriend, whom she later married, transferred from Virginia Tech to VCU to be with her.

"We had about 60 roommates in four years because each semester there would be a turnover of students staying with us," she said.

She majored in journalism and political science and earned a bachelor's degree with a 4.0 GPA.

Her father "was the proudest of all at my graduation. I'm sure he regretted saying I wasn't college material." And he did help her go to Russia for a study program while she was at VCU.

"I had an opportunity to go there to study Russian language and history, and I needed $600 for the plane ticket and 10 days there. That was a massive amount back then. I had some saved up and Dad came through and loaned me part of the money, and I paid it back."

After completing their undergraduate work and working for several years, Vicki and Bill married and moved to Lexington so Bill could go to law school at the University of Kentucky. Just before leaving for Kentucky, Vicki suffered a serious injury.

"I had gone running and then we went swimming. Bill picked me up and tossed me in the pool. I landed wrong and tore all the ligaments in my hip. So when we first got to Kentucky I was hobbled and couldn't work for a while."

And something else was going on. "It was like a wave washed over me. For some reason I felt a spiritual vacancy. All of a sudden when I got to Lexington, I had a lot of time on my hands and I really missed being connected with something divine."

She went to the Lexington Library and got books on Buddhism, Hinduism, Judaism and all the major religions except Christianity and brought them home. She read them all and Judaism was the one that touched her heart. She returned to the library and checked out more books on Judaism. She read them quickly and thought, "Oh my God, this is it. This is me. I feel it in my bones. It was more than intuition and I had to act on it." So she called a rabbi.

Rabbi William J. Leffler of Temple Adath Israel invited Vicki to come talk to him. He gave her two books and she finished reading them by the next day, and called him back, saying she wanted to study under him.

Not long after her study sessions began, Rabbi Leffler asked her if she has any Jewish background.

"I don't think so," she said. "And he said, 'tell me about your family. What was your grandmother's maiden name?' I said Schwab and he started laughing. He said, 'Go back and do some checking.'"

She went home and immediately called her mother and grandmother and asked if they were Jewish.

Her grandmother said "yes" and her mother "totally denied ever having anything to do with Judaism," Vicki said. "She said, 'Christ is the way.'

"My grandmother told me honestly, 'Vicki, it was not a welcoming environment around where we lived and we felt it was better to raise Bernice (Vicki's mother) as Christian. So I converted.' My grandfather was not Jewish. He was agnostic and never went to church. My grandmother went to the Episcopal church but my mother got baptized Southern Baptist."

When Vicki told her grandmother she was interested in practicing Judaism, "she was thrilled and so happy for me."

Vicki went back to tell Rabbi Leffler what she had discovered, and continued her studies with him. When she told him she wanted to learn some Hebrew so she could better understand the Jewish services, he connected her with Rabbi Bernard Schwab.

"He was blind and was kind of a sage of the Jewish community in Lexington. He lived near me, so I would walk to his house every day. He knew the prayer books by heart. If I would read, he would know if I made an error. He had it all memorized. He was fantastic.

"Grandma sent me our family tree and I took it to Rabbi Leffler. He said, 'You don't have to convert. You're already Jewish.' And I said, 'But I want to. I want a Jewish name.' So we did the whole naming ceremony, Hannah Vered, on Palm Sunday, and totally immersed myself into Judaism. I taught religious school. I've read every bit of the five books of the Torah and I have a notebook with all my notes in it. I loved studying Judaism and for 20 years I was a very happy Jew."

She and Bill moved to Frankfort in 1983 and they divorced in 1999. A year or so after her divorce, Vicki went with a female friend to a weekend Native American gathering in Asheville, North Carolina. There was a sweat lodge and many lectures. She wasn't in a good mood when she went to one lecture, and it got worse when a man started talking about Jesus.

"I was in the back of the group and didn't want to be there. He recognized that and stopped and said to me, 'You look very troubled today. I can feel hurt in your heart.' Then he had everybody turn around and put their hands toward me and they prayed for me in Jesus' name. I was livid and I got up and left. I thought, 'I didn't come here for any of this nonsense.'"

When she returned home to Frankfort, she was shocked to find a framed picture of Jesus – which had been stored in the back of a walk-in closet – moved to the front of the closet and was face up.

"It blew my mind. I put it up on the wall because I knew there had to be some kind of connection to what happened in Asheville. It was a picture I bought when I was a teenager working at the State Department in D.C.

"Actually it's Jeffrey Hunter from the 1961 'King of Kings' movie. An Indian woman painted it. I thought it was so beautiful."

Another powerful mystical experience followed.

"I awoke one morning and at the foot of my bed was a vision of a royal presence. It was not a dream. He was robed and he looked royal. Without saying words, he spoke to me, saying, 'Get your house in order.' It sounds unbelievable but it was real. That was the turning point. I paid attention after that."

She started studying the Bible again, "but really I was studying it for the first time because I didn't have my heart in it when I was a kid. One thing led to another and I found out about the Abbey of Gethsemani. I started going there and that's when everything changed."

Several members of her book club at the Kentucky Coffeetree Café in downtown Frankfort heard about a lecture on Thomas Merton at Gethsemani and decided to attend.

"I loved it there and started going back. Then I did a retreat there. That's how I got deeply into Christianity, just being around the Catholic monks. After several years, I immersed myself in Christianity."

At first she started attending South Frankfort Presbyterian Church and loved singing in the choir. But Catholicism keeps speaking to her through the Gethsemani experience. In 2014, she joined Good Shepherd Catholic Church in Frankfort and made her first communion.

Not long after becoming Catholic, Vicki talked about her spiritual journey and her love for Judaism and Christianity.

"I don't feel I've left Judaism. I'm just building upon it. I'm still a Jew. Jesus was a Jew. In part of the Catholic liturgy – when I'm on my knees and the priest is blessing the bread and the bells ring – I incorporate my Jewish prayers into the bread and wine. I go to Mass on Saturday evening because it's the end of Sabbath.

"When I do dinners in my home, we bless the candles and do all the Jewish rituals. They're so close to the Catholic rituals. Every day I'm finding a different parallel. Catholicism to me is the beginning of Christianity, and it sprung out of Judaism."

Like so many spiritual seekers, Vicki feels an intimate connection to Merton, a Roman Catholic convert, writer, theologian and mystic. A Trappist monk at the Abbey of Gethsemani, he was a poet, social activist and student of comparative religion.

Born in France in 1915, he graduated from Columbia University in New York City in 1938. He entered the Gethsemani monastery on December 10, 1941. On May 26, 1949, he was ordained a priest and given the name Father Louis.

Merton authored more than 60 books, mostly on spirituality, social justice and a quiet pacifism, as well as hundreds of poems and articles on topics ranging from monastic spirituality to civil rights, nonviolence and the nuclear arms race. His autobiography, "The Seven Storey Mountain", published in 1948, has sold more than one million copies and has been translated into at least 15 languages.

He was an avid proponent of interfaith understanding and pioneered dialogue with prominent Asian spiritual leaders, including the Dalai Lama and Vietnamese monk, author and poet Thich Nhat Hanh.

After several meetings with Merton during the American monk's trip to the Far East in 1968, the Dalai Lama praised him as having a more profound understanding of Buddhism than any other Christian he had known, said Dr. Paul Pearson, in a Louisville Festival of Faiths "Sacred Journeys" book. It was during this trip to a conference on East-West monastic dialogue that Merton died in Bangkok, Thailand, on December 10, 1968, the victim of an accidental electrocution. He was 53. The date marked the 27th anniversary of his entrance to Gethsemani.

Vicki Pettus says, "Merton getting into the Catholic church was not this big lightning strike and fall on your knees type of thing. It was kind of a natural evolution. I feel I can identify with him. Most of us don't have the luxury of having a lightning bolt hit us in the head and say, 'This is what you should do.'

"We kind of have to pay attention to the signs and get there. If you don't listen, you're not going to hear, and a lot of people don't listen. They can't recognize the sound because they're not opening themselves. I'm sure a lot of people would be called one way or another, but they don't allow themselves to pause enough to listen."

She says Merton was critical of himself and so conflicted.

"He wanted to be a monastic while at the same time he's getting letters from all over the world and answering them. He goes from the monastery to Louisville to be with friends and drink and party. If he had been in the age of computers, I'm sure he would have been on the computer with Internet, and what a conflict that would have been with his soul. He agonized over the conflicts and embraced them at the same time."

Besides loving the writings and the voice of Merton, Vicki is a huge fan of Richard Rohr, a Franciscan monk and priest, inspirational speaker and author of numerous spirituality books.

"I went to see him in Cleveland several years ago and he was mesmerizing. He never used a note. He talked extemporaneously for four hours with one break. His theme is always inclusion."

She also saw and heard Rohr in Louisville in 2013 when he was onstage with many spiritual leaders when the Dalai Lama spoke on compassion in the downtown Yum! Center.

On her spiritual journey today, Vicki feels that Catholicism "is my last stop. But who knows? I'm very content being where I am. I've always been happy where I was. I was happy as a kid growing up. I was happy being an agnostic. I was happy being a Jew. And I'm happy being a Catholic-Jew.

"I think this is probably where I will stay because to me, it's the whole picture. It meshes the old covenant and the new covenant so beautifully. It all makes sense. If I didn't like carnal pleasures and other things so much in this life, I would be a monk, a hermit. I would be very happy in an austere, simple existence with just one room, a desk and a bed. That's why I feel so comfortable on retreat at Gethsemani."

She travels to Gethsemani at least once a month to participate in contemplative living group discussions.

"We don't talk about church things. We talk about what Christ said, not who he is. It's fascinating. To me, the biggest joy is when I'm engaged in talks of philosophy and religion. That's when I feel most comfortable, where my whole being just comes alive. Time doesn't exist when I'm there doing that."

She also loves visiting St. Meinreid Archabbey Monastery in southern Indiana, and "I still go to sleep with Thomas Merton every night."

Chapter 13

Catholicism leads Joe Fiala to Buddhism

Seven months after turning 62, I retired from The State Journal, a small daily newspaper in Frankfort, Kentucky. One of the first things I did in retirement was take a two-hour meditation class for five weeks from Joe Fiala at The Light Clinic.

Joe's son and daughter-in-law, Joseph Fiala and Emaline Gray, are doctors of Classical Chinese Medicine and own The Light Clinic.

On the way to my first meditation class, I saw a great egret – a large white heron – flying over the Kentucky River. I've seen a great blue heron many times in Frankfort and I've had a spiritual connection to it since 1968. But this was the first time I had seen a great egret on the Kentucky River. My Tibetan Buddhist monk friends, a few years later, would say that's an auspicious sign.

Yes, I knew the meditation class was where I was supposed to be that evening. Joe was a wonderful teacher, and still is. He keeps it simple. He's friendly, intelligent, wise, adventuresome, and has a calming presence and great sense of humor.

We've become close friends, especially since the Tashi Kyil Tibetan monks have started coming to Frankfort on their biannual tour. Joe, Joseph and Emaline always help me coordinate the tour.

Joe grew up in Lorain, Ohio, and has lived in Frankfort since 1985. He earned his bachelor's degree from the University of Dayton, majoring in psychology, philosophy and English. He obtained a master's and Ph.D. in social psychology from the University of Kentucky.

He retired in 2003 from the Kentucky Legislative Research Commission where he worked in program review and investigations. He started as a senior project manager; then served 14 years as committee administrator and office director. He spent 25 years as a government watchdog, ensuring that government spent money in the best interest of citizens. He also worked as a research and analysis consultant in LRC's

Office of Information Technology; and was an associate professor at Kentucky State University from 2000-2005, teaching management information systems, policy analysis and evaluation.

He is co-owner of Bourbon on Main in downtown Frankfort. In 2015, the Tashi Kyil monks created their World Peace sand painting in a vacant downtown building Joe owned. He installed new carpet in the building just before the monks arrived.

He was director of Lexington Shambhala Meditation Center from 2007-2010; and since 2003 has been a personal development trainer and meditation instructor.

He has a daughter, Michele Fiala, an oboist and professor of music at Ohio University in Athens. He also has two grandchildren, Olivia Grayce and Scott.

Joe went to St. Edward High School in Lakewood, Ohio. It was in that all-boys Catholic school where Joe decided he would abandon the Catholic church as soon as possible.

"The rigidity turned me off. They would call it discipline. But it was control. The final straw was in my junior year when a friend and I did a major paper for theology class. It was about the Jesuits and the church's wealth and its approach to working with poverty.

"We really got into it and thought it was quite fascinating once we began finding out about the Jesuits and all their money and businesses. Basically it wasn't the compassionate, empathetic, kind church on one hand; just the accumulation of massive wealth.

"We did this great paper and had slides and all sorts of stuff. When we presented it we were just beaming, and the brother (teacher) looked at us, called us blasphemous and gave us an 'F' on the spot."

At school, the brothers' way of discipline was "smacking rulers over your knuckles or having you work in the school basement, digging a sub-basement, Joe recalls. "That was the brothers' notion of punishment. They were very sadistic in many ways."

He says he basically saw the church's God as a crutch for people, something they prayed to and depended upon.

His father, a railroad supervisor, was injured in an on-the-job accident when Joe was a college freshman. His mother, a cosmetologist and "very devout Polish Catholic, thought for years God was going to save him." They went to shrines known for miraculous healings.

"Nothing ever helped from that standpoint so she began to lose her faith because his problems became more and more severe," Joe said. "He was a good guy but he got poor medical treatment and his problems got worse and he eventually couldn't get out of bed. He had ulcers on his legs, which meant continuous care.

"My mother said, 'We've spent our whole lives trying to be good and do the right things and this is where we're ending up.'"

At the University of Dayton, a private Roman Catholic university, Joe became interested in Buddhism while taking comparative religions and philosophy classes.

"Probably half of the theological faculty were former brothers and priests who had dropped out, so my religion and philosophy classes were being taught by people who were in the midst of exploration into existentialism, humanism, Buddhism. It was great. I had a lot of exposure to a lot of things.

"But Tibetan Buddhism – for a long time, even after connecting with Shambhala – was to me just another kind of rigid sort of approach, very similar to Roman Catholicism in many ways. Since I've begun to connect with Buddhism and understand practices in some ways, my whole connection has been from a psychology and philosophy standpoint, not from a religious standpoint. I'm not very good on the religious end."

"The Shambhala teachings are founded on the premise that there is basic human wisdom that can help to solve the world's problems. This wisdom does not belong to any one culture or religion, nor does it come only from the West or the East. Rather, it is a tradition of human warriorship that has existed in many cultures at many times throughout history.

'The sacred warrior conquers the world not through violence or aggression, but through gentleness, courage, and self-knowledge. The warrior discovers the basic goodness of human life and radiates that goodness out into the world for the peace and sanity of others." -- Chogyam Trungpa, Shambhala founder

In the fall of 2016, not long before the U.S. presidential election, I visited Joe at his home on Paul Sawyier Drive, across the street from the Kentucky River. I asked him a lot of questions because I suspected he knows as much about Buddhism, perhaps more, than anyone in our little state capital.

Would you say you got into Buddhism because of suffering?

"Sure. Why else would you get into Buddhism?" (He laughs.)

Was it because of your dad's suffering?

"No. For me, Buddhism made sense in terms of the world. It made a lot more sense than a religion that depends upon a God that was doing things. Buddhism says it's all up to you. The world is what you make of it. So that's what appealed to me.

"And then the enlightenment, of course, was a carrot. Wow, I get enlightened and I'll be something great or special and the world suddenly will be totally different, and I'll understand it and know why," he said, sarcastically. "So the suffering was more in terms of the angst that we probably all have, in terms of what is this all about? Why am I here? What's going on? Is there a God? Isn't there a God? Whatever."

Do you think there's some type of higher intelligence?

"Well, intelligence, if you're implying something with a vision and a rational plan to what's happening, no. I think we're all part of a greater aspect of energy or whatever, which includes awareness. But I don't believe there's really intelligence in terms of a God-like figure that's directing what happens. No. But there could be."

Do you pray?

"I don't call it praying. I do aspirational chants."

Is our collective karma guiding things?

"Collective karma would guide things because it's a force, it's a direction, it's a vector of some form. But it can be changed and it's not an intelligence. It's just a law of action that begets reaction."

Joe believes in reincarnation.

"I believe when I die I'm going to move into something else because there's an energy that doesn't disappear."

And is there a choice of what you move into, what you become in your next life?

"You move into the bardo (in Tibetan Buddhism, a state of existence between death and rebirth, varying in length according to a person's conduct in life and manner of, or age at, death). The bardo is a totally confusing and fearful situation if you don't have good mental stability."

So certain meditation practices are about working with your ability to deal with the bardo when you die, "which is essentially the loss of connection to your physical being. You're basically just relying upon your awareness that exists at that point. Meditation practices are meant to stabilize your awareness so when you hit the bardo, you might have half a chance of not panicking."

Could the awareness be your soul?

"Yeah, I guess so. Whatever it is, it's that life force that is present when we exist, after the body disintegrates. That life force, whether it merges or remains separate is also a part of the practice. So when everyone becomes enlightened, I suppose we all just merge together."

For those who don't practice Buddhism or mind-training, Joe says they continue along the path of samsara – the cycle of existence in which a being must continually be reborn due to the accumulated negative karma of previous lifetimes.

Joe says he tries to do sitting meditation every day, in the early morning, for an hour to 90 minutes. He has different meditation practices. One, called samatha, is aimed at calming you down, settling your mind, bringing you to the present.

Another, called tong-len, helps cultivate loving-kindness, compassion and empathy. The aim is to meditatively send good fortune and happiness out to others, and receive any misfortune and negativity others may be experiencing.

"Compassion and empathy are basic characteristics that we're born with. We're not born fearful. We're basically confident and ready to handle the world, although not necessarily physically. We all have the same potential to deal with the world in whatever way it's presented to us.

"But then fear arises and learning, and the karma we bring from past lives – all of that influences how we deal with the world. And the collective karma, of course, has an impact as well."

The Shambhala path is not about becoming a recluse and sitting on a cushion and meditating for years and years – in a cave, or on a mountain – for self-improvement.

"It's basically emphasizing the notion of warriorship and social action by dealing with fear, lack of confidence, hesitancy – the things people have which prevents them from getting engaged in the world and connecting to the world."

Donald Trump, the Republican candidate for president, came to mind. At that point, I don't believe either of us thought he would win. But as a Buddhist did Joe think it was important and fair to take a stand against Trump?

"Discriminating awareness is something Buddhists very highly cherish," Joe said. "Discriminating awareness comes out of your ability to recognize obstacles and understand your mind so you can recognize the difference between making a judgment in the real world as to what the impact of that something is going to be; and having the basic Buddhist notion to not harm.

"If you recognize something harmful and you don't take action, then you're not following your principles. If you recognize Trump as being harmful and you vote for him, or you say what the hell it won't make any difference either way, then you're not taking responsibility.

"It's all about awareness and responsibility in the end and there's no way of getting around it. So that's what makes it a tough path."

One mindful-awareness practice, Joe said, could be sitting down and looking at Donald Trump's picture.

"You can begin to see the thoughts that are going through your mind, which are making up your reaction to that (picture), and then you can choose behavior. You can understand the world when you understand how your mind is visualizing and seeing and organizing the world.

"That really is in one sense what enlightenment is because you're cutting through all the illusion and you're seeing directly. All the practices are trying to get you to where that becomes a basic part of your connection to the world."

In his late 60s now, Joe balances sitting still with being active. He loves babysitting his grandchildren – Scott in Ohio and Olivia in Frankfort. He also enjoys motorcycling, bicycling, kayaking, scuba diving, traveling, hiking, camping, beekeeping, gardening, contemplative photography and dancing.

"Happiness goes from moment to moment," he says. "I think I'm pretty content and have a lot of joy within my life, which is more than momentary. I feel a lot more settled and peaceful with myself."

Prayer flags fly over the grounds at the Tibetan Mongolian Buddhist Cultural Center

PART THREE

Choosing What Dance Feels Best

"To dance is to be out of yourself. Larger, more beautiful, more powerful... This is power, it is glory on earth and it is yours for the taking."
--Agnes de Mille

Chapter 14

Retreat Part 1: Practicing peace and awareness

In early 2012, I spent a little more than a month in retreat at the Tibetan Mongolian Buddhist Cultural Center in Bloomington, Indiana. Before the year ended, my black Lab, Lily, and I had done four retreats at the cultural center. On December 26 and 27, I wrote a two-part series on the experience in The State Journal. Part 2 follows in Chapter 15.

The more I study Buddhism and visit Buddhist friends, the closer I feel to Jesus.

Sandwiched between attending two family baptisms in Catholic churches in Frankfort and Danville this year, I stayed 35 days – most of the Lenten season – at a Buddhist retreat center in Bloomington, Indiana.

When Arjia Rinpoche came to the Kentucky Book Fair in November 2011, I knew I would visit him at his Indiana home before spring. The deal was sealed at a lunch break in the bleachers at the Frankfort Convention Center shortly after Rinpoche's assistant, Chunpay Jiumei, a Tibetan monk, handed me a sandwich from a small cooler.

It was the best egg sandwich I had ever eaten – with sautéed chopped onions, pickle relish, mustard, mayonnaise, and thinly-sliced carrots on wheat bread. Chunpay said he would teach me how to make it the next time I returned to the Tibetan Mongolian Buddhist Cultural Center.

On brief visits in the past I was always drawn to the small yurt cottages, I told him.

"Then come and stay in one," Chunpay said.

"I would love to," I answered. "But I have an attachment, a black Lab named Lily."

"Bring her," Chunpay said.

I did, and Lily thinks the 108-acre retreat center is heaven.

We stayed in Yurt 4, the one nearest the lotus pond with large koi, close to a hut made of cattails. We had one circular room with a sky light plus a small bathroom with a shower. Lily spent a lot of time on the deck watching deer, squirrels and wild turkeys in the woods and listening to woodpeckers and songbirds.

She loved our next-door neighbor, Michael Massey, a young mechanical engineer who was born in Brazil to Christian missionaries. His father, a longtime nondenominational minister, is now a professor at Indiana Wesleyan University.

Michael, also a Reike healer, arrived one day after us and stayed a month. It became almost a nightly ritual for our trio to hike after dark to a fire pit in the middle of the woods. It always felt as if the tall trees and wind appreciated us being there and listened to our conversations.

One night when I asked Michael if he thought humanity's collective karma could have something to do with tornadoes, earthquakes, hurricanes, tsunamis and other natural disasters, before he could answer, the wind picked up and treetops swayed.

Cold chills came when Michael said, "I think the forest just answered your question."

After midnight one breezy evening when we were almost back to our cottages, it seemed strange that a tea light remained lit in front of a Buddha statue by the lotus pond. We paused, waiting for the wind to blow it out, but the small flame kept dancing in the wind. Early the next morning I went back to examine the candle and it was just an ordinary burned-out tea light that could be extinguished with a breath of air.

Around 11 one night, the crackling of the fire was suddenly silenced by a violent ground-shaking crash that seemed to continue for a minute. My first thought was a horrible car wreck.

After the silence returned, Michael said, "That was a massive tree falling and then sliding down the hillside into a creek bed." We had witnessed the awesome power of nature.

At one of our last campfires, I reminisced about our month at the cultural center. "I know there's no utopia, Michael, but this is as close to it as I've ever experienced. We've been here four weeks and I've yet to hear an argument, disagreement, complaint, rumor or somebody gossiping. I know everybody here has problems but I haven't felt any negativity. The energy is incredible. Leaving this place won't be easy."

Michael agreed.

Before going to Bloomington, I had sort of a daily schedule in mind for the retreat. There were no required group meetings to attend. I knew I wanted to spend a great deal of time reading, and would do journal writing, sitting meditation/centering prayer each morning and evening in the yurt, two 45 minute walks with Lily, and focus on eating healthy.

My partner, Angela Mitchell, made a variety of vegetarian soups for me to take and to share with Rinpoche and Chunpay. They had enjoyed her cornbread and white bean and onion soup at her Bridgeport home after Rinpoche spoke at the Book Fair and signed his autobiography, "Surviving the Dragon: A Tibetan Lama's Account of 40 Years Under Chinese Rule."

They had initially stopped at Angela's parents' adjoining farm to bless our yurt and labyrinth, which had been dedicated the day before on 11-11-11 at 11:11 a.m.

At the cultural center, I also wanted to attend group meditations in the interfaith temple and attend teachings there on Sundays.

Meditation is to calm the mind and focus on the present moment, improving awareness. And I forgot to bring my meditation cushion. The temple had plenty of extra ones and I took two to the yurt the first afternoon I arrived. But mine was more comfortable and I missed it.

So I figured out a way to get it. Angela was going to meet me in Indianapolis four days later to attend a "Playing for Change" concert, so I rounded up an excellent relay team. A lifelong friend in Lebanon, Anna Laura Davenport, went to my 86-year-old mother's house to get the cushion. Anna Laura and mom are Baptists. Anna Laura took it to Republican state Sen. Jimmy Higdon's residence. Higdon, a Catholic, delivered it to my longtime friend Sally Everman, who works at the Legislative Research Commission office in Frankfort. Angela went to the Capital Annex to pick it up for the final stretch. Sally, Angela and I belong to the Cathedral of the Great Outdoors.

What I didn't forget to take to Bloomington were books. Angela recommended limiting it to 15. "Realistically, you're only going to be there a month and that's finishing one every other day," she said. She was right and I spent two hours trying to narrow it down. I called kindred spirit friend Bob McClain, explaining the difficult task.

His suggestion: "Don't take any. Man has a hard time just being with himself, doesn't he?" He laughed.

I actually considered that too, knowing the cultural center has an excellent library and plenty of books for sale. Then an empty banana box from Bryant's Pic-Pac was filled with books. Thirty-five made the final cut.

Chapter 15

Retreat Part 2: Some surprising stories

When you enter the temple, you remove your shoes. In the dining room, vegetarian meals are served every Sunday following the teachings for a suggested $5 donation. A sign at the serving table says, "We have ants. Many, many ants. We don't kill ants, but let's not feed them. Please leave food covered and sealed."

Every Monday evening I went to a two-hour group meditation session in the temple and returned on Thursday nights for an hour.

The best gifts of the retreat were meeting new friends, who shared with me parts of their spiritual journeys.

The biggest surprise in Bloomington came one afternoon when I asked Trish Ellis, office manager at the cultural center, how she met her husband, Russ Ellis, facilities and grounds manager.

"In prison," she said, laughing, after seeing my look of disbelief.

They met at a federal prison in Los Angeles in 1991. Russ was serving a 10-year sentence for cultivating marijuana, and Trish was teaching a spiritual healing class.

"I was really there for having a giant ego and a big mouth," Russ says. "I'm embarrassed to talk about it in a way because I was so ridiculous."

He was living in Hawaii, "and my buddies and I would grow a few plants so we'd have something to smoke. So I get busted with this tray of cuttings and in Hawaii it was going to be a $1,500 fine."

Although he was wealthy, Russ fought the charge in court and "went up to the lead detective on the case to tell him how stupid he was. So he had to show me who was stupid.

"He went back to his office and called the feds. They ran my name and said, 'Oh yeah, we want this guy. He's got this business plus he has a prior' (drug conviction in California)."

After spending 14 months in prison for the first offense, Russ was released, and for a while "I was a different person," and stayed out of trouble. "Then I got back into my old ways because I got tired of being broke," he says, laughing.

"I started the first mail-order business on indoor grow lights, the good ones, and became really successful. It was legal, but was a borderline thing. I made a lot of money. I had several million dollars-worth of material things.

"That was the most addictive thing I've ever been through – money and power. People would call me Mr. Ellis." He laughs. "If I saw something I wanted, I could have it. I can't tell you how addictive that is. I'd see a nice Jag (car) and love it and I'd buy it. I wasted so much money."

Then it all ended.

He was playing Frisbee with his children in the yard of his beautiful home in Hawaii when the federal agents rolled in, handcuffed him and took him away.

"I had one of those moments riding down the driveway -- looking at my kids who were stunned -- when I realized, wow, that person who had all that property, business and money just died."

It was eight years before he saw his kids again. His second wife divorced him. But going to prison was a blessing – both times, Russ says.

Prison was where he got serious about practicing Buddhism, forgetting the past and future and living mindfully in the present moment. It's also where he learned his incredible artwork, which is on display in prominent places today.

The first time he was incarcerated, he worked at the prison dairy, mostly with Native Americans, and two Indians he admired taught him how to do intricate bead work. "They were master beaders," Russ says.

Tibetan Buddhism is known for its large colorful, mysterious and mystical banners (thangkas), and Russ decided to use tiny beads to make thangkas. Creating them was, and still is, a major part of his daily meditation practice.

"Each thangka has at least 400,000 beads, 108,000 stitches, and took 2,000 hours to make," Russ says. Each one is a teacher of patience and slowing down.

"I had never done art before," says Russ. "But when I decided I was going to do a thangka, I just drew it. It seems intimidating to look at one. But you just look at a picture, take measurements and get the proportions.

"If you want to get it done in five minutes, it's really hard. But if you have years to work on it and not worry about it, it's not hard. If I can do it, anybody can."

Two of the banners now hang on the front wall by the altar of the interfaith temple in Bloomington.

In 2003 Russ and Trish, along with Arjia Rinpoche and Chunpay Jiumei, traveled to India to present a third thangka to His Holiness the Dalai Lama. And the newest one, which he has been working on this year in the Bloomington temple in his spare time, is 90 percent complete.

Trish, 65, grew up in a Catholic family in Albuquerque, New Mexico, and is the oldest of nine children. Her father had an office equipment business and she worked for him off and on through the years, learning computer technology.

She attended a Catholic college in Dallas, Texas, and became friends with a novice nun who had been to the Congo.

Trish planned to go to Africa in 1969 and teach French in the schools but uprisings in the Congo prevented her from going.

"I was at loose ends at that point and went back home to Albuquerque, enrolled at the University of New Mexico, and got into drugs, sex and rock-and-roll for a few years."

In Albuquerque, Trish got married in 1969 and was majoring in education but dropped out after her junior year not long after she was kidnapped and taken into the mountains and raped, she said.

"I was walking home from campus and got picked up off the street and thought I was going to be killed," she says.

At the time, she was involved in a Religious Science Church, "and had a world view that nothing happens to you by accident," Trish says. "So I believed that I had some role in all that was happening but I didn't know what."

After being raped "the guy was just driving and I didn't know what was going to happen. I started saying in my mind, 'I don't know what this means but I know there's some bigger picture that I don't see and I forgive you.'

"And as I was saying that in my mind, not out loud, he started sobbing and telling me about all these women in his life that had been abusive to him, and when he came out that night he was wanting to get back at somebody for all that abuse.

"He started saying, 'I'm really sorry I picked you because you're not who I wanted to harm.' He ended up driving me back to a block from my house and dropping me off."

She reported the crime, had a medical exam, "and went through all the police stuff," but no arrest was ever made, she said.

"It took a long time for me to get over that trauma. But because I had this view that was different, I didn't have the same kind of suffering or animosity that many others seem to experience. I didn't feel like a victim. So I think I got over it much quicker and it hasn't had a lasting impact on my life. I'm grateful for that."

In 1974, Trish had her first and only child, a daughter, Jennifer. When Jennifer was 11 months old she started having serious seizures, and she's been ill and on medication her whole life, Trish says.

"From 11 months until six-years old she was in intensive care three times a year, and that whole thing really took a toll on our marriage. My husband was a really good man but we were immature and didn't know how to hold things together."

They moved to California and divorced in 1981.

Later Jennifer was diagnosed as being bipolar.

"She is the most resilient person I've ever met," Trish says. "It took her 10 years to graduate from college because she would get to exams and couldn't finish because she would get too stressed, and would have to start over.

"But she graduated with a linguistics degree from UCLA with great grades and has a master's in speech."

Trish had a good business background working with her father but in the mid-1980s decided she wanted to work in "something more heartfelt" and service-related. She found a job at the Center for Attitudinal Healing, an organization started by a psychiatrist doing support groups for kids with cancer.

The center also had spiritual healing support groups in prisons, which was how she met Russ in 1991. Four years later Russ was transferred to a Colorado prison. He knew he was going to miss Trish, the support group coordinator.

"We knew each other well because when you sit in an Attitudinal Healing group, you talk about how you feel," Russ said. "Everything is kept in the group and you feel safe. In time you get to know who people really are as opposed to what's their front."

He asked if he could write to her, "and once he left (the prison where she was working) it was OK for me to communicate with him outside the group," Trish said.

Russ said, "A lot of guys in prison scam on women and I didn't want her to think any of that. All I wanted to talk about was the spiritual path."

They exchanged letters a few times over the next year and a half, but didn't see each other or talk by phone, she said. Then the day her boyfriend told her their relationship wasn't going to work, Trish got a letter from Russ.

"It said I know you're in a relationship and I don't want to interfere but I want you to know I really care about you and if you ever need me for anything, my door's open to you."

Russ was released from prison in 1996 and they married in 1998 and lived in Hawaii. Her job promotion with International Attitudinal Healing eventually took them back to California, although they still have a residence in Hawaii, which they rent.

Saving the cultural center

In Mill Valley, California, they met Arjia Rinpoche not long after he fled Tibet and came out of hiding. They found out he and Chunpay were living just down the street from them, and that Rinpoche is an artist who does beadwork and knows Tibetan art well.

"It was amazing," Russ said.

They became members of the sangha where Rinpoche was doing Buddhist teachings and not long after that Rinpoche asked them to go to India with him. That's when Russ presented one of his thangkas to the Dalai Lama.

When Rinpoche asked the Ellises in the summer of 2009 if they would be interested in moving to Bloomington, Trish had just finished chemotherapy treatments following breast cancer surgery.

The Dalai Lama was coming to visit Bloomington and Indianapolis in 2010, "and Rinpoche wanted us to come and help prepare for that," Trish says. "I think if I had not just gone through that (breast cancer) experience, I would have thought I had to cling to some kind of security, which I didn't.

"When he asked, both of us had already been through a big upheaval, financial uncertainty, all kinds of uncertainty. We just decided it didn't make rational sense." She laughs, and adds, "But we would take the leap, assuming we could rent our house in Hawaii. That was the determining thing to cover our expenses on that end."

Their love and respect for Rinpoche was the only thing that could take them away from Hawaii and California for uncertainty in Indiana.

"We obviously have some kind of karmic connections with him," Trish says. "He's not a teacher for me in terms of a philosophical teacher. But his presence and the way he lives is the teaching.

"And I love Chunpay. He's like a brother. There's something special about him for sure. He's a bodhisattva (an enlightened person who pledges to continually be reborn to help all others attain enlightenment), so devoted and consistent."

Russ and Trish originally thought they would stay in Indiana a year.

"Now we laugh at plans," Russ says. "We're in our third year now. We like it here because we feel we're doing something worthy. In my life I've done so much that was just so I-oriented, completely about me, and this is very refreshing.

"We meet these amazing people. You never know who's coming through the door. It might be the prime minister of Mongolia."

"He's been here," Trish adds, smiling.

"It's an amazing place," Russ says. "I feel I'm doing something worthwhile even if it is just making beds."

Trish says she wouldn't have chosen to do full-time administrative work again. She was enjoying doing social work, with a whole different kind of stress.

"The main stress here is having too many things going on at one time and having to deal with it," she says. "When there's conflicting needs, that's when I get stressed, and I don't see how to meet them all harmoniously."

Buddhist centers attract people with needs, Russ says.

"Sometimes that's hard because needs are heavy," he says. "But this place also attracts open-hearted people who want to help. You never know what you're going to get – every day."

Russ was born in Murfreesboro, Tennessee. His father was a career serviceman, first serving in the Army Air Corps and then the Air Force.

"He died when I was fairly young and my Mom remarried another guy in the Air Force. We lived all across the northern U.S. – North Dakota, Montana, Idaho and Washington.

"It was kind of interesting moving around a lot. I liked it. My brother hated it. I felt comfortable with the changes.

"I was raised the All-American boy. I was captain of the football and basketball teams, and in baseball I was scouted by the Yankees, Pirates and Cardinals. That was my thing – team sports. Give up yourself for the team, and discipline. You have to practice. That's Buddhism."

He played on good teams. His high school basketball coach was Judd Heathcoat, who later coached Magic Johnson and won an NCAA championship at Michigan State.

"When we lived in Spokane, Washington, Los Angeles Dodgers great Maury Wills was our next-door neighbor, and I played baseball with Bump Wills, his son," Russ says. "I knew all these old Dodgers like Tommy and Willie Davis. Maury Wills was really humble. He was in the minor league for nine years before he made it to the majors."

Russ was a good student academically and an outstanding pitcher.

"I was confident that nobody was going to hit me," he says. "I had perfect games and no-hitters often. I thought I was some kind of hotshot, but then I broke my wrist and that went away."

Russ grew up Mormon

"I'm grateful I was raised in the Mormon church," he says. "When I left – after turning 16 and getting my first car – I didn't want to hear anything about it.

"Later I became a Buddhist as kind of a reaction against Christianity. It didn't mean I was burned out on spirituality. It was a part of my life. I knew there was something going on, but I didn't think it was what I'd been told. None of it made a lot of sense to me.

"I had a big library and studied every religion, and Buddhism spoke to me, made the most sense. I'm a member of the psychedelic generation and I knew from those experiences we make choices. That was a very powerful thing to me, and in Buddhism that's one of the basic things.

"From thought moment to thought moment in our life, we can make the choice. We can either bring all of our past stuff with us into the next thought moment or we can leave some of it behind, and that's kind of what (Buddhist) practices are all about. I didn't understand it all, but it just felt right."

After being a Buddhist for decades, Russ says he realizes now he "could go back and be a real good Mormon. It's all about your heart and heart-mind (connection), and service. The Mormon church is very much into that.

"On the mystical level, the heart level, (all religions) say the same thing. There's no disagreement. The common ground is 99 percent and the disagreement is 1 percent, and that's what causes all the trouble.

"To me that's kind of silly. But that doesn't mean I'm right, either."

Something valuable he learned in the Mormon church was to treat your body as a temple.

"All of that has been proven scientifically to be extremely valid," Russ says. "Don't smoke or drink alcohol. Don't take caffeine. If you eat meat, eat it sparingly and well cooked. Take care of each other as brothers and sisters. I think that's pretty common to any spiritual path."

A cradle Catholic, Trish says a priest teaching theology at the Catholic college she attended in Texas opened her mind and heart to other religions and traditions.

"He talked about all the different religions and what they had in common, and how stories were all the same," she says. "At that point I started thinking whatever is common to every religion must be the closest to the truth.

"My experience in the Catholic church was that it was very open-minded. The real rigid views weren't my experience at all.

"I did a lot of reading and was really drawn to Eastern religions and philosophy. It made a lot more sense to me."

But she didn't start practicing Buddhism until much later when she was a spiritual healing teacher at Terminal Island prison in California. There, she was invited to attend Shambhala Training, an international network of centers offering secular meditation programs designed for the general public.

Then she started reading books by Shambhala's founder, Chogyam Trungpa.

In her Christian life, "I used to always pray for a personal connection with Jesus but I never had one," Trish says. Later through spiritual and religious studies she says she could relate to him as a wise brother but not as a savior.

"I relate to Jesus at this point as a bodhisattva from the Buddhist perspective, an enlightened being."

Born of a Virgin Mary?

"No, I think that's the mythology of many traditions you hear over and over," Trish says.

She says she knows Christians and Buddhists who believe Jesus was in India studying with the masters, and that he was a Buddhist master.

"A priest I used to hang out with in southern California went to school in Rome and he said in their archives are all kinds of stories like that. I think Jesus was aware of all those different philosophies."

Trish says her parents have accepted her Buddhism path.

"With nine kids there's a lot of variety in the directions we've gone. I've got one sister who is a born-again fundamentalist. When I had cancer, she came to be with me.

"My mom used to be really upset that all of us weren't Catholic. I think only one of my brothers and one of my sisters still go to the Catholic church. The rest are doing different things.

"Mom was always praying for us. She said one day, 'Please bless my children wherever they are' – we were spread all over – and she said she had this awakening that it didn't mean geographically, but spiritually.

"She got that we all carried the spiritual essence she was trying to give us, but we took it in different directions, so she could stop feeling guilty."

Her parents also accepted their oldest daughter falling in love with a former inmate.

"Russ and my mom are so amazing," Trish says. "She's so far to the right and he's so far to the left they meet on the other side."

"We can talk about anything without it being a battle," Russ says.

Trish has brought wonderful speakers to the cultural center for seminars and teachings, making the Dalai Lama's goal of a "true interfaith temple of peace" a reality.

In February at my first Sunday teaching in the temple, Steve Ballaban, a Bloomington rabbi, spoke on the value of compassion. He gave a personal example, telling how a simple act of compassion saved his father's life after he was released from a Soviet labor camp at age 21, weighing 83 pounds.

His father was wandering through a Siberian forest in a blizzard trying to get out of Russia.

"An elderly woman, who was illiterate and had lived a very hard life in a sod hut in the forest, found him on the verge of death," the rabbi said. "She brought him into her hut and gave him soup and bread. That act of compassion allowed my father to survive and come to the U.S.

"My sister is a pediatric neurologist who treats thousands of children. She has three children and I have five.

"That one woman in Siberia, by all standards, did not have very much merit. And yet she is probably the most meritorious person that ever came along in my family's history."

Returning for retreats

In 2012, Lily and I made four retreats to a yurt in Bloomington – the most recent one in late November and early December.

In June, Frankfort friend Rich Green shared a yurt with us for four days to participate in an "interfaith retreat" led by Father Francis Tiso, a Catholic priest and scholar of Asian religions. Tiso lives in Italy and is on the faculty of Gregorian University in Rome.

After the first day I was so enthusiastic about Father Tiso's brilliance and down-to-earth genuineness, I called Bob McClain in Frankfort and encouraged him to join us for the rest of the session. He came and was glad he did.

Before the retreat ended Tiso, upon request, held the first-ever Catholic Mass inside the Buddhist temple.

Several weeks later I returned for a two-night seminar taught by a gentle, kind Hindu master from India.

In our last week at the cultural center this year, Lily and I arrived at dusk on the Sunday after Thanksgiving. Russ and Trish Ellis were in New Mexico caring for her elderly mother who is ill. Michael Massey was in Sedona, Arizona, where he has been doing earth-energy healing work most of the year.

None of the other yurts were occupied. The cultural center building was empty.

Several hours later I walked around the lotus pond and across the grounds, seeing two deer behind the temple. A sense of Oneness was in the cold air. I stopped briefly by the prayer wheels and then circled the stupas, chanting prayers for the universe and all beings who have touched my life, and those who still will.

They're all teachers and I still have many lessons to learn. That gave me immense joy and contentment on the quietest night of my life.

Chapter 16

Winnie Edgerton has listening perfected

Winnie Edgerton is one of those rare humans who listens completely when someone talks to her. You can feel her sincerity, compassion, gentleness and concern for you and the world.

She says she's also stubborn.

She and her husband were Peace Corps workers in Afghanistan in the 1960s. In late November 2012 Winnie said it was a mistake for the U.S. to go to war there, and that President Obama shouldn't delay in bringing troops home.

"He should do it today … no yesterday," she says. "You can't defeat the Afghans. History has shown that for a long time."

Winnie, with a slight patchouli fragrance, had just finished leading a two-hour group meditation session in the temple of the Tibetan Mongolian Buddhist Cultural Center in Bloomington, Indiana.

She's studied Buddhism for many years, "but I'm always a beginner," she says, smiling. "I'm a very stupid beginner. And it's not that I haven't put in the time."

In Indianapolis where she grew up, Winnie started out Methodist, and then attended a Presbyterian church, and went back to being Methodist.

She recalls a Sunday morning when she was about 13 and everyone in the house was getting dressed for church.

"I went in my bedroom and closed the doors as if I were getting ready, and I didn't get ready. And when everybody said, 'Come on, come on, it's time for church,' I said I'm not going anymore."

"And it was so amazing. The whole family stopped going to church that day. It wasn't that we lost our spirituality. I just think we never found a place that fit us as a family.

"My mother had gone to Unity Church and she read her Daily Word and did a lot of contemplation and prayer. My dad was dad and he loved trees. He would take walks and commune with the trees. My brother was a kid and he didn't care. He indeed is an atheist now but a very good man."

After that significant Sunday encounter, Winnie immediately started searching to try to find what meant something to her.

"I probably fell into magical thinking. I loved to use the Bible and open it up and put my finger on the page and find my message for the day. Whenever I felt unsteady I would do that.

"It actually turned out to be a pretty good daily practice for a long time. I opened the book anywhere and it was always perfect, exactly right."

So there are no coincidences?

"I think there are a lot of circumstances that affect coincidences," Winnie says. "And I think karma in some sense or another probably does control coincidences, circumstances.

"But I was very young then and it gave me something that I could regard as outside of myself that was helping me and guiding me.

"As a Buddhist I don't go there anymore. But that came much, much later."

After two years in Afghanistan where Winnie taught English as a second language, she and her husband, Dave, traveled for a year in India, Pakistan, back across Afghanistan and through Iran and Turkey to Europe.

"I got very sick then with pneumonia and by the time we got to Germany I was coughing up blood and was pretty sure I would die. I was ready to die. Of course I was nowhere near dying," she says, laughing.

Then they lived in Puerto Rico for five years, teaching at a university.

"I discovered yoga at that point and became a yoga teacher," which she loved. Today she's still a yoga instructor.

The Edgertons have two daughters – both grew up overseas – and five grandchildren.

After becoming a yogi, Winnie became a philosophical Buddhist, "which means nothing of course except that you're reading books about Buddhism," Winnie says. "And that was too hard. I couldn't do it by myself.

"We moved all over (for more than 25 years) and I didn't find a teacher."

When they came back to the United States, Winnie was teaching yoga wherever they went, and had basically given up on finding a Buddhist teacher.

"I had yoga students all over the world, and had completely devoted myself to spirit and trying to awaken my mind and find enlightenment," she says.

Did she feel close to reaching those goals?

"No," she says. "I felt I was a wonderful teacher to a lot of students that I knew very well. But I was totally involved in my selfhood, my teacherhood, my Winniehood. And I knew as long as I was so full of self, I would never awaken.

"But I couldn't find a teacher to help me. I tried but it was like trying to claw myself out of myself, or claw myself into myself. I was a very humble teacher always because I knew I wasn't there."

Then in 2004, a boyfriend of one of her daughters suggested that Winnie "go to Colorado to listen to a wonderful teacher," - Sakyong Mipham, son of the late Chogyam Trungpa, and the living holder of the Shambhala Buddhist tradition, which emphasizes the basic goodness of all beings and teaches the art of courageous warriorship based on wisdom and compassion.

"He published a book, 'Turning the Mind into an Ally,' and is going to introduce and teach that method of meditation," the boyfriend told her.

Winnie says she didn't like the boyfriend.

"I thought he was very arrogant. But I decided to show him I have an open mind. So I took one of my daughters and we went to Colorado to take this workshop, and it was a perfect weekend.

"It wasn't that I had found nirvana. We sat all weekend and contemplated and I knew I had finally found my teacher."

Around 300 gathered in a huge tent and Sakyong was with them all the time.

"At the end of the weekend he gave the most generous teaching. Then he asked for questions and this tall, kind of gawky kid asked, 'How will we know if we're ready to take refuge?'

"Sakyong stopped and looked through the whole audience, and looked back at the kid and said, 'You'll know if you're ready.' Then he looked right at me and pointed his finger and said, 'But if you've waited for 30 years, you've waited long enough.'

"So I went running to the coordinator and said, 'I have to take refuge right now.' And she said, 'It's not being offered.' So I couldn't do it. But I knew I had found my teacher."

The next spring Winnie went to a month-long meditation retreat in Vermont.

"It was all in silence and eating in the shrine room, Japanese style," Winnie says. "This is a program people usually do after at least five levels of Shambhala training. It's an intense, wonderful program, but pretty tough for someone who is a yogi and has basically no endurance as far as sitting is concerned. I'm all over the place.

"But I wanted to do it because I assumed I could take refuge afterwards. So at the end of the program, I said I wanted to take refuge, and they said it's not being offered. I said, 'I just sat for a month so I can take refuge,' and again I was told it's not being offered.

"I said, 'OK,' and I realized in my heart I had become a Buddhist and had taken refuge. But when I got home I found out Sakyong himself was doing another month-long program starting right before Christmas. So I told my family I can't be home for Christmas this year. I'm going to sit this month in meditation.

"To make matters worse with my family, I took my daughter again. My husband is such a good man. We've been married since 1965 and we've always given each other all the space needed. We've been through so much together, doing yoga and meditation together.

"At one point, however, he said he needed his Christian faith. He respects me and I respect his path. What I feel is there's a basic purity and equality that is the essence of everything. That's where I go. I don't go to a creator. To me that's where Buddhism draws the line. The whole creation doesn't really matter to me."

But she does feel there is some kind of divine wisdom, power, in all the interconnections of everything.

"Absolutely," she says. "Shambhala calls it basic goodness. Purity perfection."

Chapter 17

The Ebbinhouses: An odd couple still in love

He has a long bushy-gray beard and combs his hair back into a long tightly-braided ponytail. He wears multiple earrings and lots of beads and bracelets. He's 6-foot-4 and lean, and carries a knife in a leather holder on his belt and a large leather pouch strapped on a shoulder.

The first time I saw David Ebbinhouse walk into the temple, I wanted to get to know him better. He seemed very comfortable being his authentic eccentric self. At Monday and Thursday group meditation sessions, David is usually the one who lights incense by the altar.

I was surprised when I heard David was an Eagle Scout, and when I learned he's married to Marilyn, the extremely friendly volunteer in the temple office on Thursdays who used to make chocolate-topped rum cream pies for the Little Tibet restaurant in downtown Bloomington; and crochets berets for women cancer survivors who've lost their hair.

Originally from Richmond, Indiana, David went to Indiana University planning to be a doctor like his father.

"Later I got scared when I realized what it's really about and that I would have to work all night without sleep as a resident. I thought I can't go without sleeping – I'll kill somebody."

His parents "freaked out," David says, when they heard he wasn't interested in studying medicine. "I betrayed all their values.

"I flunked out my freshman year at IU because I wasn't going to class and I wasn't happy."

Then he met Marilyn, "and I thought new life, new rules."

"He embraced art," Marilyn says.

David says he used art "as a cover." He wanted to avoid the draft and stay out of Vietnam. He needed to get back into school "to have an excuse to not live at home.

"Art was great because I was smart enough, and I could read a lot of art history and understand what it was about," David says. "My professors realized I was self-motivated."

After earning a bachelor's in art from IU, he worked as a studio assistant for one of his art professors.

"He was a rebel, one who didn't follow rules very well. He told me not to go to graduate school. He always encouraged me to do unusual things. He would say, 'I don't understand what you're doing. That's great. Keep doing it.'

"In some ways he betrayed me by the conventional notions because he didn't get me connected to a graduate school and an eventual job, where I would have sunk like a stone in academia.

"What I decided early on was I need freedom and I'll pay anything to get it. So I made up my own job, my own life and rules, my own art."

David decided he was going to leave Bloomington "and be a big-deal artist in New York City. But when I visited friends in New York who had the same idea, I saw the baby-boom demographics meant that statistically I was highly unlikely to win the lottery."

Shortly after returning to Bloomington, he met the Dalai Lama's oldest brother, Thubten Jigme Norbu, a professor of Tibetan studies at IU. At the end of a semester, a friend invited David to a class party, which Norbu attended.

"He was dressed in a very conservative chuba (satiny Tibetan jacket) with his wooden prayer beads on his wrist. I sat down next to him and started talking and he was really elegant and charming. I just loved him. Later he showed me how to work the prayer beads.

"When I look back on it with many years perspective, I realize this was so auspicious. The first time I met him he gave me dharma: simple, hidden, not ostentatious. This all turned into me going with him to Dharamshala, India in 1978."

Then in 1979, David and Marilyn "got an audience with the Dalai Lama in his living room in India." Tibetan friends of theirs encouraged the meeting, saying the Dalai Lama likes to hear Westerners' points of view.

One friend said, "You'll be doing him a favor because he likes to find out how to make Buddhism more understandable to Westerners."

But David didn't have high expectations.

When the screener, the interviewer for audiences with His Holiness, asked David why he wanted to meet with the Dalai Lama, he said, "Because

Tibetans told me to. If I don't get an audience, I don't care. In fact, I don't expect to get it.

"I'm not Buddhist. I don't have any question to ask him. He's got a big job to do, trying to save his country. I know he has important people to see, people who can help the Tibetan cause. I don't have any money, any influence."

But knowing Professor Norbu probably helped them get a private meeting with the Tibetan leader.

When the Dalai Lama asked David if he was a Buddhist, David said, "I haven't taken refuge so I can't say I'm Buddhist. If I have to believe something like reincarnation, then I have a really hard time because as an empiricist in the West we don't understand the mechanism. We don't believe in it by tradition."

Perhaps you'll change your mind someday, said the Dalai Lama, "but if you don't, that's OK." He laughed, and added, "If you're a good person, that's the main thing. Keep an open mind."

He suggested that David learn the Tibetan language, "if you really want to understand Tibetan culture."

And David said, "I don't think I'm going to be able to take that advice. Every time I try to talk Tibetan with Tibetans, I end up teaching them English, and I'm not good with languages.

"We went way over our time limit and had good discussions."

David and Marilyn knew they would probably never have another private audience with the Dalai Lama. However, getting to spend a great deal of time with his brother in Bloomington, a small town in Indiana with an international essence, was a blessing they recognized decades ago and today, more than five years after Mr. Norbu's death in September 2008.

Although David and Marilyn have had a lot of Shambhala training in recent years, David says he never had "an affinity to Chogyam Trungpa (Shambhala's founder who was instrumental in popularizing Tibetan Buddhism in the West) because I had already been blinded by Norbu's elegance, his grace, his lightness of touch.

"Norbu didn't have that big burning charisma of Trungpa that everybody loved so much."

Marilyn says, "Mr. Norbu's teachings were subtle and every time you were with him you would get an insight."

"If you paid attention to what was going on," David adds. "He didn't talk about the stuff. He embodied it. That didn't mean he didn't get mad at people if they were just stupid and causing problems. He was a human being. He wasn't perfect."

At Indiana University, Norbu simultaneously taught four levels of Milarepa (1040-1123) in one class. Milarepa was one of the most famous yogis and poets of Tibet. It is said that Milarepa, through his teachings and other accomplishments, achieved the ultimate goal of enlightenment in one lifetime.

"One level was for grad students," says David. "Another was for people needing credits and they were studying Tibetan (language). One was for jocks who wanted an easy 'A'. The other was for us dharma bums who wanted to get dharma from Norbu. And if he's teaching Milarepa, it's dharma.

"He would make some particular point and he's looking at you. And you realize that's the very fault that you have and you kind of hoped he would never notice. And not only has he noticed, now he's giving you the example from the teachings of Milarepa's life story. And your ears turn red.

"If you were really on the wave length, he was a peerless teacher."

"And he was so kind," Marilyn says. "I'd see him in Kroger and he would always ask about our family. Some college professors would hardly notice you. He made a point of not only noticing you, but making you feel special."

David says he liked to "hang out with Norbu, but not too close because the moth can get its wings burnt in the flame; and not too far away because you don't get any warmth from the fire. You have to know where your orbit is.

"That's one of my big things: get in and get out. You have to be a moving target. If you stand still you get mowed down. You have to keep moving. That's how I live."

Marilyn says David's a warrior.

He says he decided he was a bodhisattva warrior 30 years ago, long before finding out Trungpa created the metaphor.

"But I was coming from the martial arts and American Indian idea of warrior, of someone who is brave and unwavering in their commitment," David says. "I was already on the Buddhist path. I didn't want to call myself a Buddhist, though, because I didn't want to say I believe in anything."

David grew up Methodist, and Marilyn, from Greensburg, Indiana, was raised Catholic. They met through mutual friends at a musical concert January 28, 1968 when Marilyn was a high school senior at Oldenburg Academy. David was an IU freshman.

"Oldenburg was an old German settlement with a seminary on one side of Main Street and a convent on the other side," Marilyn says. "I went to the girls' school with the wall around it. We stayed all week and went home on weekends because Greensburg was only a half-hour away."

After playing a piano solo on stage, Marilyn was walking up the aisle and saw David "in a cool leather jacket," he says. "My hair is longish and I had horn-rimmed glasses like a Beatle, and no beard. Nobody had ever looked at me like she did right there.

"So we went to her place for dinner and she sat across from me. I don't remember anything we ate. I just looked in her eyes the whole time."

After dinner he taught her how to pick a folk song on a guitar, "and I loved that," she says.

"I tricked her," David says. "I didn't really know anything about music. I just had this one little trick I could do to get her attention, and that was it."

He also recalls his friend, Michael Winston, saying on the ride back to Bloomington, "I think you're going to marry that girl."

And David said, "Wait a minute, I think that's a little premature, but I think she's fascinating and I want to see her again as soon as possible."

"He came back to see me the next weekend on a borrowed motorcycle," Marilyn says.

Marilyn was 19 and David 20 when they married on August, 16, 1969 at St. Paul's Catholic Center in Bloomington.

"It was Woodstock weekend," Marilyn says. "And now we'll be married 44 years this year. My dad was a farmer all his life. We raised chickens and sold the eggs, and we helped plow and bale hay. I have four sisters and none of us married farmers because we knew how much work it was."

At IU they lived with several others in a farmhouse, "which was like our own little hippie fraternity," David says.

"Some would call it a commune," Marilyn adds. "We had a big garden and we took turns cooking and cleaning."

"I used all my Eagle Scout training to organize them, just like a campout," David says. "We had a duty roster and I made people clean their rooms. It wasn't like the Marines, but I knew how to do all of that stuff because of my training.

"Our marriage at first was the hippie, flower-child perfect romance," David says. "Then reality set in. It wasn't easy. People aren't always who you think they are.

"We didn't know what we were going to do in life. We didn't know how to make money."

They were still working on getting college degrees at IU, and Marilyn switched her major from music to art.

"I went into weaving and textiles and loved that, but I didn't know how to market my weaving," she says.

They were going to a lot of art fairs, "and we hated it," says David. "They're horrible and humiliating."

On visits to India, David started researching and collecting ancient gzi beads, which are expensive and revered by Tibetans.

"I was learning a lot about ancient beads and did get lucky and find a few important antiques and sold them for good money," David says. "Then I started to realize this is all gambling every time I do it. I got hepatitis in 1979 and almost died. I realized there's no future in this."

A job requiring frequent travel to Asia brought the Ebbinhouse couple "a lot of money at times, then no money, and then some money, and then a lot of money, and then no money, no money, no money," says David. "It was nerve-wracking, especially for Marilyn. She needs security."

They didn't own a home. They didn't have health insurance. They wanted to have a family. Something had to change.

Marilyn heard about a one-year licensed practical nurse program at Ivy Tech in Bloomington and told David she was serious about enrolling. And she wanted David to be the stay-at-home father.

And David said, "OK, if you really think you can do this, I'll give up going to Asia and give up any ambitions I have for being a big-shot artist. I'll be a dad. When the kids are old enough I'll take them to learn karate and Scouts. Until then we'll go hunt fossils in the creek and go camping."

David gave up smoking and when their children arrived his Buddhist meditation practice increased.

"I knew if I didn't practice every day, I wouldn't be a good father to our kids because I'd get pissed off and yell at them. I knew I had to reorder my whole life to make it work, even if it meant giving up some friends, or going to rock-and-roll concerts, or whatever."

Meditation practice has helped him in his artwork.

"It's helped everything," he says. "Mind training is supreme. The practice is nonnegotiable. No matter what, I have to do it. It sounds easy and it's hard to do."

David says he normally doesn't sell much art.

"I just do it. If you need hype for your art to be important, then your art isn't important. Hype is important. What makes it important? You're making money for somebody, or some critic gets a reputation and makes money, because we're a capitalist society and everything is gauged by money.

"But I thought there's no reason why I couldn't stay in Bloomington and do serious, cutting-edge art, pushing the limits, not for money, but as a part of my spiritual practice."

Marilyn says David has a real affinity to ancient sensibilities.

"He has that shaman sensibility in his art. He's done performance pieces with sculptures and head dresses he's made. It's very personal."

As a part of his art and spiritual practice at the Tibetan Mongolian Buddhist Cultural Center, David has built a shaman meditation hut made of cattails in the woods near the lotus pond. One of the themes of the hut and a tenet of Buddhism is impermanence.

He and Marilyn also have done much of the sculpturing and landscaping around the lotus pond. Three of his shamanistic paintings are framed and displayed on the walls of the yurt in which Lily and I stayed, and more of his artwork is in the dining room of the cultural center building.

Before retiring in 2010, Marilyn worked 22 years as a hospital nurse and loved caring for patients. Occasionally, however, she envied her husband for going on Buddhist retreats while she went to work.

And David would say, "Marilyn, you're the Buddhist because you have compassion. I'm trying to get some of your compassion and you're trying to get some of my understanding."

"He pointed out that when I'm approaching patients and families, I'm showing compassion every day on the job," Marilyn says.

The Ebbinhouses have two sons, Adam 22, a senior at IU majoring in biochemistry, and Alex, 19, an IU freshman (in Spring 2013), hadn't declared a major.

Marilyn has an uncle who is a Catholic Franciscan priest in New Orleans. He often returns to Greensburg at Christmas and says Mass at Marilyn's family home.

"He's traveled all over and worked with the Navajo Indians in his first assignment in New Mexico, and learned the Navajo language," Marilyn says.

"He's a sweet guy," David says. "They all have the Christmas Mass and he gives a sermon, and that's it. And then I go up and talk to him about his sermon. And he says, 'You've got a really interesting point of view on this stuff. I really like talking to you.' So I actually give him more feedback from the religion than his own family."

Although Marilyn loves exploring Buddhism now, she says she still goes to a Catholic church sometimes.

"I've never forgotten my Catholic prayers and my Catholic upbringing," she says. "It's still a big part of me."

David adds, "Whether you like it or not, it's your karma."

In the Spring 2012 issue of *Buddhadharma* magazine, a quarterly for serious practitioners, a headline on the cover asked: Can you be a Christian-Buddhist?

David's answer to the question is, "Why not?"

Marilyn says, "I would say so. Jesus taught 'Love one another.' That's the essence of it. The Dalai Lama says 'My religion is kindness, compassion.' It's the same thing."

In those lost years of Jesus' life, which aren't mentioned in the Bible's New Testament, was he hanging out with Buddhists?

"Who knows?" says David. "I can't say. I don't care. In his message, there's no contradiction to me, but that's just my personal take on it.

"I think if you would study the Buddhist attitude and go back and look at Christian teachings again, then when you see things like 'turn the other cheek,' that's mind training. So if this person is mean to me, I'm not going to lose my temper. I'm not going to judge them. 'Judge not, lest ye be judged.'

"If you look at it from a different perspective, you see that all the tenets are there. It's the same thing. It's compassion. Forget all the rules. Forget all the categories and all the intellectual part of it. Just look at what Jesus is doing, what he's saying."

David says he was "terribly bored" growing up in the Methodist church but he found John Wesley's story interesting.

"Wesley thought by faith alone ye are not saved. By works ye shall be saved. You need to do something. You can't just say, 'OK, I believe in the Trinity. So now I'm saved. I go to church on Sunday, and OK, that's it.'

"You're getting down on your knees every morning and you're saying you can't dance and you can't play cards. It's not because those are sinful activities but because they take energy away from getting the job done. And I understood basically what they were talking about.

"Many people think those are sinful things, and that's too extreme. That's not what (Wesley) was saying. Our church, once a year, handed out a pledge card to not drink. And everybody treated it like here's the boring card again. It wasn't important.

"I'd go over with friends to their Protestant churches and it was exactly the same -- the hymns and boring sermon. It was hard to understand. I saw it as lofty ideals and poor performance. And everyone there was wearing their nice clothes and being social. But there was no real feeling of spirituality.

"Then one day it struck me: Dharma is Method. That's what they're talking about. They (Buddhists) have the means to do this stuff. If John Wesley could have known, he would have gone to dharma immediately because they had the method. And they had the holiness and he wasn't getting it and he wanted it.

"That's why he went around and tried to organize all these people because he felt this isn't getting it. It's all bogged down in all the other stuff.

"I'm still a Methodist really, but it's a different method," David says.

Marilyn laughs, saying his Methodist parents still wonder about him.

"His father is always asking, 'What is Buddhism? What do Buddhists believe?'"

In his travels through the years, authentic David has always attracted people of other faiths to him. It's the long hair, the full beard, the prayer beads and something else.

In India he met friendly Muslims and Jains and Hindus, "and there was no way I could go home with everybody who wanted to feed me dinner. It was amazing. I didn't know what it was, but they saw something they liked.

"I think they saw me as some kind of a spiritual seeker – a sincere, wise holy person. They always want to tell me their life story and ask for my advice."

He tried to assure them he wasn't any spiritual master, and was no different than them.

"Then they would tell me these amazing stories. I learned so much about human nature from them. I also realized I can give them something. I don't know where it comes from. I just say whatever comes into my head.

"It's like, OK, I listened to your story, and it seems to me you're telling me this. And then they go, 'Oh, thank you for your wonderful sage advice.'"

Marilyn suggests, "You just put the mirror up to them and they can see more clearly."

At the Tibetan Mongolian Buddhist Cultural Center, Marilyn and David help plant a vegetable garden for the monks each spring near the prayer wheels.

"We've been a part of this center since the beginning," Marilyn says. "We helped plant all these trees here when they were seedlings."

"I climbed up in the trees and hung the first prayer flags that went all the way around," David says.

The place is special to them. They still feel Professor Norbu's presence.

David recalls Norbu telling him a Tibetan monument called a chorten was going to be built on the property with a pathway around it for Buddhists to walk and chant and pray. Then a center would be built.

David said, 'Why don't you build the center first and get a dharma teacher to come because people want dharma? I don't see how you're going to have a success if you just built the chorten.

"And he says, 'Don't worry. We'll take it one step at a time and change our mind a thousand times.' He said, 'You don't need a plan, you need a vision. If you have a vision, the plan can change accordingly.'

"I told him I guess you know a lot of people so maybe it will work. And he just laughed saying, 'Don't worry. There's no need to worry.'"

Marilyn said laughing, "Mr. Norbu wasn't going to be frustrated if the timetable went astray because there was no timetable."

"We loved Mr. Norbu and I feel obligated to make sure this center continues to work out here," David says.

More landscaping needs to be done around the lotus pond, "but if I get struck by lightning tomorrow there's enough completed to make a lasting difference," David said in March 2012. "I know Mr. Norbu would have loved it. He loved people taking initiative.

"What I've found out as I've gotten older (he's 64) is there's only so much energy that you have. And to do any kind of liberation thing, striving for enlightenment or whatever you want to call it, you need a lot of energy, more than we really have available, especially since the modern world saps off so much of it.

"So the only place to get extra energy is to steal it from something, like from habits you don't need."

What they give in volunteer work at the center always comes back to them in abundant inner contentment. You can feel that deep joy by

114

reading David's book of poems, haikus, titled "The Lotus Pond," or listening to Marilyn's kind voice and perpetual enthusiasm in the temple.

Chapter 18

Jeremy Gotwals has a happy magical energy

When you're on a narrow hallway stairs with a crowd of journalists and photographers in the early morning, waiting to see the Dalai Lama, it's hard to be in the present moment.

Jeremy Gotwals seemed to be. I guessed he was an Indiana University student who knew something about Buddhism. He had this magical energy about him. Most of us were probably happy to be there. But I had the feeling Jeremy was happy to be *here* – wherever – everyday.

His thick dark hair was spiked about an inch high. He looked like he could be a competitive swimmer. He was charming, friendly to everyone around him. I saw him frequently the next two days: at Indiana University Auditorium and the Tibetan Mongolian Buddhist Cultural Center in Bloomington; and in Conseco Fieldhouse in Indianapolis.

His joyful countenance and enthusiasm never faded. That was in May 2010.

It was a year later before I realized Jeremy is the son of Lisa Morrison, director of media and public relations for the Buddhist Cultural Center in Bloomington. I had known Lisa since 2003 when I obtained a press pass to attend the Dalai Lama's dedication of the interfaith temple – to promote world peace and harmony – at the cultural center.

Jeremy attended that ceremony too, although he didn't grab my attention that time.

I got to know him better March 24, 2012 at Snow Lion Restaurant in Bloomington. It was a fundraising dinner to promote Walk For Tibet and Ambassadors For World Peace. I sat at a table with Jeremy, 22 then, and his mother.

Ambassadors for World Peace is a nonprofit organization started by the late Jigme Norbu, a nephew of the Dalai Lama.

Lisa Morrison, who also owns Morrison Marketing & Media in Bloomington, was one of the sponsors for the dinner. She's a busy, compassionate woman who considers herself a Christian-Buddhist.

After listening to Jeremy at the dinner table for 30 minutes, it was obvious he inherited his kindness and nonstop energy from his mother.

When he first heard the Dalai Lama speak in 2003, Jeremy was 13.

"But I was blown away, touched in a very profound way," he recalls. "That catalyzed a tremendous transformation and planted some really powerful seeds. Within a year and a half I began volunteering at the Tibetan Mongolian Cultural Center, and began my meditation practice and studies of Buddhism. I also started my music."

In his early teens, Jeremy weighed over 300 pounds.

"I was sucked into a lifestyle many teenagers are sucked into involving video games," he says. "I turned away from that (and junk food) and became very serious about music and meditation, and very dedicated to my work for the Tibetan Center and for the Dalai Lama's campaign (for Tibet's independence from Communist China).

"But I was even more dedicated to the transformation of my own mind and body. So I lost 150 pounds."

He had started practicing Kundalini Yoga, and Reike at 16.

"That was a profound practice that transformed my life and brought everything into focus. I knew there was some way to externalize this subtle energy that I was finding, and use it practically. Through Reike, I discovered energy healing was the way to go."

Then MTV came to Jeremy's high school to film his involvement with music and spirituality. He was featured in an episode called MTV's Made, which debuted in 2007.

"It was a season premier, a special, and I was the Reike Rocker," he says. "During that same time I was writing for the local newspaper, The Herald Times, and I had a radio show called Well Spring, which was a spiritual, philosophical talk show."

He was so passionate about spirituality in high school that he seriously considered becoming a Buddhist monk.

"I had a dilemma between pursuing a practical life or a spiritual life. I came to realize I didn't need to become a monk, but I did need to utilize all this energy and passion I have to directly influence my generation.

"MTV was sort of the beginning for me. I started classes at IU when I was a senior in high school. Then after my freshman year at IU I did another MTV miniseries, The Truth Campaign, on the West Coast. I had all

117

these ideas percolating like doing a world music travel show, and multimedia shows about meditation."

He was on American Idol in 2011 in the season launch episode.

He's traveled with a children's author, Fairy Queen Flutterby (Robin Borakove), working with his mother, Lisa, her publicist, "basically directing her PR campaign on the West Coast while singing and performing with her. It was creating a lot of power for her as a newly self-published author.

"I didn't know anything about the publishing world at the time, but I knew how to make someone like an author successful in building her platform, and reaching out to the community and public.

"One thing led to another and I realized I could work for all authors. I had something to give to authors and clients."

He started working for a publishing company, "sort of designing campaigns for authors," but the company went out of business in 2011.

Now he has his own business, Holon Publishing, based in Cincinnati, Ohio.

"I realized this can be so much more than authors and books because I immediately had a client base and a means of promoting and distributing for that client base. It can be a gateway to all my other multimedia exploits.

"On the horizon some big things are hopefully coming to fruition as a result of many years of hard work. The real secret is to create a buzz. I believe that's something I've learned how to do. So the goal is to create a buzz about all sorts of things and raise the awareness of the masses."

Jeremy says he meditates every day.

"I was doing an hour a day for a while, but now it's 15 to 30 minutes. I haven't been on par these last few months because of my work schedule, which is greatly unfortunate.

"I consider myself a Tibetan Buddhist but I'm very much a nonsectarian Buddhist student. I'd like to call myself sort of a scholar on Buddhism and Eastern thought."

After his two years at IU and Ivy Tech College, he left college to pursue his career.

"I came to the conclusion I learn by doing. College wasn't giving me the resources I needed to succeed, and it wasn't giving me the challenges I needed. At the same time the costs were outweighing the benefits.

"I realized the issue was discovering how I was going to do what I wanted to do. The issue wasn't learning what I wanted to do or learning how to do what I wanted to do. I've been unraveling that for a long time."

He says he's learned people with master's degrees "aren't necessarily any more employable.

"I intend eventually to get a master's degree and Ph.D., but later when the time is appropriate when I know precisely what it is that I'm going to do that for."

Through his spiritual studies and meditation, Jeremy says he's learned a beautiful little paradox.

"There are no ordinary moments," he says. "There is something profound and blissful happening in each experience.

"Yet on the flip side of this coin, even our most outrageous and divine experiences simultaneous are completely ordinary – ordinary magic."

He smiled, the same way he did that morning on the stairway of IU Auditorium while waiting to see the Dalai Lama.

Chapter 19

Joby Copenhaver's spiritual path

The first time I met Joby Copenhaver we shared a book at a conference table in the temple of the Tibetan Mongolian Buddhist Cultural Center. Arjia Rinpoche sat across from us, teaching from the "Great Treatise on the Stages of the Path to Enlightenment," by Tsong-kha-pa.

After the teaching, Joby told me she was a retired educator and had last taught at Indiana University. All three of her children live in California and she was headed there soon. Her younger son, Garth, had invited her to ride with him on his sailboat in a competitive race in treacherous waters off the Pacific Coast. Joby was apprehensive about going.

That was March 2012.

The next time I saw her in Bloomington, she was moving slowly inside the temple with a metal walker in front of her. I wondered if she had been injured in the sailboat race in which, I found out later, one person had drowned.

"No," she said in June 2012 while getting ready to attend a three-day retreat led by Father Francis Tiso, a Catholic priest who lives in Italy and is a scholar on Tibetan Buddhism and other Asian religions.

Her son felt it would be too dangerous for her to participate and she was relieved. But her hips were deteriorating and she needed surgery.

Our next meeting was the week after Thanksgiving 2012, and Joby no longer needed the walker. She had undergone successful hip replacement surgery in California, and had just returned to Bloomington two weeks earlier. She felt much better.

I told her I was writing a feature story on my visits to TMBCC in 2012 for my hometown newspaper, The State Journal in Frankfort, Kentucky, where I was a staff writer for 11 years before retiring in 2011. I also was working on a book that would profile some of the interesting people I had met on my spiritual path – and the Bloomington connection would be a big part of it.

She agreed to have dinner with me at Taste of India restaurant in downtown Bloomington, and would share some of her life stories.

I was wondering what led her to Buddhism after she grew up Episcopalian in upstate New York. She still attends Episcopal church services.

"I had some questions as a child in Sunday school, like what the relationship was between the dinosaurs and Adam and Eve," she says. "The minister laughed at me as if I were so cute to ask a question like that. Another question I asked was did the Episcopal church begin so King Henry could have a divorce?

"When they said only Christians could be saved, I could not stand that because I didn't want to leave everybody else out. That made me uncomfortable but I didn't know what to do about it.

"I didn't want that to be. That wouldn't be really the way I would want the world."

Later she was in a women's group, and they were talking about the 10 Commandments.

"I had taken catechism and was really interested in it, and we had read, Love thy God with all thy heart and with all thy soul and with all thy mind. And the second is likened to it: Love they neighbor as thyself.

"I brought the question up at the discussion group: If you love your neighbor as yourself, you have to love yourself. The ladies told me I was in the wrong church because I sounded like a humanist, and that was not a good question.

"So I stopped going because it didn't fit.

"I wished I could *see* Jesus. It would help, I thought."

Once at a camp with her children, Joby met a meditation instructor who told her about Muktananda, a living saint.

"Later while studying in India, Joby saw Muktananda.

"He had a divine presence," she recalls. "He was powerful. That's what I had wanted – to see a god incarnate. The more I learned about that, the more it changed me."

Joby has been interested in Eastern religions since 1976, when she was studying Hinduism and involved with Siddha Yoga.

In 1997 while teaching in upstate New York she met a Tibetan Buddhist lama.

"The minute I met Garchen Rinpoche I was hooked," Joby recalls. "I heard he was coming to town, I saw his picture, and I was so excited. I went to the public talk at the Universal Church."

She talked about the good fortunate of arriving early.

"I'm not usually on time and I got there a little early. I saw him on the other side of the parking lot with his prayer wheel, and I waved to him and he waved to me.

"I ran to open the door, and it was a double door and the part I tried to open was locked, and one of his attendants opened the other door and he went in, and the attendant told me to go in. So I walked into the hall following him. I was so happy to meet him. He was so kind. He touched my face and hugged me."

She says Garchen Rinpoche has been her friend since that day.

"I wanted so badly to have some really personal relationship, and I do with Garchen Rinpoche. He had been tortured for 20 years in a Chinese labor camp and learned from it. And now we have Arjia Rinpoche living here in Bloomington with us. I really do appreciate having human teachers. That's the thing I love. We can be so close to these beings, and learn with them and each other."

So now, is she content where she is on her spiritual path?

"My gut reaction would be to say 'yes.' But that sounds complacent. But I'm not looking for another path because I know this path is very broad."

She pauses, and says, "Contented isn't quite the word. I know I'm very earnest, that's true. My discipline, however, is not very good. I'm easily distracted, and I procrastinate."

When I asked her if her spiritual path is sort of her top priority now, she said, "Yes, but not sort of. It *is* my top priority. I can't function if it isn't. I've come to that."

Sometimes, she says, she wakes up at night and feels depressed.

"And all I have to do is talk to Garchen Rinpoche." Even though he's not there with her, she can feel his presence and his goodness. "I also can talk to Jesus. It so happens I tend to talk to Garchen Rinpoche."

"I used to ask Garchen Rinpoche what kind of practice I should do. He said, 'Teaching is your practice. Do your teaching.' I thought oh my God, I'd like to do 2,400 prostrations. But my practice is to be in the world."

She was asked if she considered herself a Buddhist-Christian, or a Christian-Buddhist?

"I don't know. I guess I would say I'm a Christian-Buddhist because I started out as a Christian, and it's not that I've left."

She said she planned to attend an Episcopal church service early Sunday morning, and then go the Buddhist temple for a teaching.

Christianity is still important to her. She says she's always had a sense of connection not necessarily with the church, "but with Jesus and Mary, even though Episcopalians don't do much with Mary."

Joby said both of her parents came to New York City from Germany.

"My mother was Catholic, my father was Lutheran, so they thought they'd compromise and become Episcopalians," she says, laughing.

So she doesn't want Buddhism without Christianity, or vice versa?

"In a way it's just another aspect of the same thing," she says. "One informs the other. It's pretty easy to figure out how Buddhism can inform Christianity. But there are aspects of Christianity that inform me, I think. There's the compassion and the devotion. Christ's life. He gave his life because he loved us so much. That was his sacrifice."

Do you think he wants everybody to worship him?, I asked.

"I don't think so. I don't think Buddha wants everybody to worship him, either. I used to think God looked like what Michelangelo had painted. Buddhism helped me to kind of get over that."

In 1961 while living in California, Joby married Matt Copenhaver, an architect who had gone to the University of California at Berkley. They lived in Mill Valley, next to San Francisco, and had three children. Jonathan, the oldest, is a chef, a music producer and event planner. Katherine is a photographer, a bookkeeper at a church, and plays in a rock band. Garth, the youngest, is a psychotherapist and Buddhist.

"Jonathan and Katherine came to India when I was in Siddha Yoga and that was wonderful to be there at the ashram with them. Katherine says the community church she works for is very ethical about money. There's no corner-cutting. She's very happy at such an ethical place."

Joby's husband was 15 years older than her, grew up in California, and wasn't interested in spirituality at all, Joby says.

"He had been an Episcopalian but I think he had been abused by one of the clergy, the choir master. So he was very, very negative (toward religion). I wanted us to grow up as a family, believing what I had heard earlier that the family that prays together stays together."

Joby grew up in Rochester, New York, "and our lives revolved around church community," she says. "That's what I thought should happen to us, but of course it didn't.

"I still tried to go to church. I'd take the kids and it would take forever to get their clothes and shoes on and look nice. It was very difficult. But I did it. They'd cry sometimes and I would leave early."

Her one marriage ended after 13 years and she moved with the children to Sebastopol, California, not far from Mill Valley and quickly found a teaching job.

"We continued to bring the kids back and forth, and Matt would come up for birthdays and visit and have dinner. We maintained a relationship and it became a pretty good relationship in fact toward the end. I had always loved him."

He suffered a stroke and died in 2010 at age 90.

"Toward the end I was with him a lot. I went to California and wanted to be with him. We ended up really loving each other."

In 2002, Matt had gone with son Garth to Rochester, New York – where Joby was living and teaching at the time – "and actually took refuge (in Buddhism) with Garchen Rinpoche and got the White Tara empowerment," Joby said.

An empowerment is a ceremony that enables a person to make a closer connection with a particular diety or Buddha. Tara, the most popular meditational female deity in Tibetan Buddhism, is the goddess of universal compassion. There are 21 Taras and White Tara grants long life and wisdom, according to the book "Elements of Tibetan Buddhism" by Lexington, Kentucky's Richard E. Farkas.

"It didn't mean too much to him but he was searching," Joby said. "He told Garth he wanted to know where Buddhists go when they die. He was worried about it."

As an educator, Joby taught and was a reading specialist and a principal. She earned a scholarship to Indiana University and planned to only be in Bloomington a year. But after returning to California to help teachers in her district with a writing program, she loved IU so much she returned to start work on her doctorate.

"I was here at IU for 3½ years, but then my father died. So I got a job teaching in upstate New York to be with my mother."

She was on the faculty of State University of New York, teaching two graduate classes and two undergraduate classes, "plus I was trying to write my dissertation, prepare for conference presentations, and take care of my mother. I was really, really rung out."

After her mother's death, Joby returned to Bloomington. She owns two nice homes in California, has another home in New York, and rents a two-bedroom residence in Bloomington. For now this is where she is supposed to be.

"This is my time to study, to really look seriously at the dharma, and it's working out. I really appreciate having these opportunities to study."

When Buddhists take refuge in the Buddha, dharma and sangha, the sangha is more than the group of practitioners Joby gathers with in the temple.

"It doesn't have to be just this community here," Joby says. She thinks of it "as the whole community of angels, and archangels and all the company of heaven – all those lineages that are there with us. And it's quite effective."

Garchen Rinpoche told her that teaching is her practice. And although she's a retired faculty member at IU, she did a great job of teaching the night we had dinner at the Taste of India.

Chapter 20

Ambassadors for World Peace dinner

Kunga Norbu, thanking 60 people for attending a 2012 fundraising dinner for Ambassadors for World Peace and Walk for Tibet, said the situation in Tibet is really bad today.

"Young people are setting themselves on fire. We want independence for Tibet. My father wanted that, and I want to carry on the legacy of my father and brother. And please do not forget about our brothers and sisters in Tibet."

His father was the late Thubten J. Norbu, a professor of Tibetan studies at Indiana University, founder of what is now the Tibetan Mongolian Buddhist Cultural Center in Bloomington, and oldest brother of His Holiness the Dalai Lama.

Kunga's younger brother, Jigme Norbu, died tragically February 14, 2011 when he was struck by a vehicle in Florida while doing a Walk for Tibet through the Sunshine State. Jigme also founded Ambassadors for World Peace in 2009 and opened Snow Lion, a Tibetan restaurant in downtown Bloomington in 1987 when he was 21 years old.

Kunga recalled driving Jigme to the airport in Indianapolis when he was leaving for Florida.

"He never dressed up. He had on jeans that were kind of ripped at the bottom, a leather jacket and black shoes. I got his bags out of the car and we looked at each other. We're not real huggy but I gave him a hug. I told him I hoped the walk would be successful and I'd meet him in a couple of weeks.

"I watched him as he went through the departure door with two bags. Twenty minutes later he was texting me saying he was sorry he had missed my birthday (the day before on Feb. 12)."

Jigme had called Kunga on Feb. 11 reminding him to pick him up to go to the airport on Sunday.

"He said, 'Why don't you come by tomorrow on your birthday and I'll make you a nice Tibetan dinner.' I said, 'Why don't we wait until you get back,' because I usually go to Ocean Air, my favorite seafood restaurant in Indianapolis on my birthday. I love seafood.

"Until I die I'll never forget that phone call from my sister-in-law telling me of Jigme's death. He was averaging 20 miles a day and was almost finished for the day but he wanted to put in a couple more miles. He was supposed to meet with Voice of America or some media, but unfortunately he was taken."

Kunga had originally planned to join his brother in Florida about five days into the Walk for Tibet to finish with him.

Not long after Jigme's death, Kunga, 49, traveled to Florida and completed Jigme's final Walk for Tibet journey. Many others who had heard about the tragedy joined Kunga on the walk.

At a press conference in Florida, Kunga said he would "carry on the tradition and legacy of what my brother was doing."

Kunga said it was "like a whirl at first after Jigme's death, finishing his walk in Florida. Since it's slowed down a little bit it's kind of hitting me. It's tough. But you have to move forward. I know my younger brother would be telling me to keep moving, look ahead, don't look behind, keep going. That's how he would want it."

Although he has a world famous uncle, Kunga said, "we're just us, Jigme and Kunga. We're very fortunate our uncle is the Dalai Lama and my dad was a lama, an abbot. We come from hierarchy. But we grew up here. We're downright Hoosiers."

But when the Dalai Lama comes to Bloomington, Kunga gets to spend a little time with him.

"Well, yeah, but even that isn't easy. You have to jump through loopholes (and security)."

If necessary, Kunga said he could talk by phone to the Dalai Lama tonight.

"I couldn't call him directly. I'd have to call a cousin who is a press secretary. You have to go through channels."

Another Walk for Tibet

March 10, 2013, Kunga began a historical 228-mile Walk for Tibet from Washington, D.C. to New York City. It began on the anniversary of Tibetan Uprising Day.

The five participants – four walkers and one driver in a support vehicle – started at the Chinese Embassy, and then continued to the White House gate for remarks, prayers and a peace rally.

They had planned to walk 14 days but completed the journey in 10.

Kunga got back to Bloomington in time for the second annual Ambassadors for World Peace dinner held March 23 at Café Django, once owned by Kunga's mother, Kunyang Norbu. He was walking with a slight limp and shared pictures from his iPhone with several friends, showing his severely swollen feet after the walk.

But he said his discomfort was nothing compared to the pain the people of Tibet have suffered for more than 50 years under Communist China's rule.

Kunga said he did the walk in memory and honor of his late father and brother Jigme, and he wanted to start it "in D.C. on the anniversary date of the Tibetan Uprising 54 years ago." Kunga says he's for "total independence for Tibet," as were his father and brother.

"When we were walking through Philadelphia, we went through one of the lowest poverty areas ever. But we saw a lot. We're walking through this really run-down neighborhood, which they're trying to revitalize.

"There was a three- or four-story brick building, and I looked up and all the windows had been broken out. It said Phase 1 development for apartments and condos. They were using this huge ply-board to cover up seven broken windows, and it said 'Tibet, Tibet, Tibet….' We left a Tibetan flag and scarf. It was very auspicious."

Besides Kunga, the other Tibetans participating were from D.C., California, Ohio and New York.

After completing each day's walk they would get in the car to go to the place where they were staying for the night.

"And I would think there's another person (here), and when I said that in Tibetan, all the others thought the same thing. You know who that other person was? Probably my brother Jigme. That's so very, very auspicious."

When Professor Norbu died, "Tibetans didn't know who would be the leader," Kunga said. "Then it was Jigme and he has passed. Now the Tibetans are depending on me and they're really happy. Everywhere we went there was so much support.

"And I said, 'I'm just one person. We have to stand up and work together. What we need to do with the Chinese government – not the Chinese people, they're good people, but the regime – is keep pricking them in the ass and eventually it's going to burst. The Tibetan issue needs to be constantly out there.'

"We have 108 Tibetans right now who have set themselves on fire. They're that desperate for people to know what's going on. We don't want violence. Three things they're saying: 'Long live the Dalai Lama. Come back to Tibet. Free Tibet'."

"You don't hear them saying Free Tibet and Middle Way Approach (as the Dalai Lama has proposed after many years of not being able to solve the issue). The Tibetans within Tibet are asking for *total independence.*"

Kunga said, "I'm the nephew. I'll say and do whatever I want. His Holiness will never look at me and say, 'You're doing wrong.' I'll say, 'I'm standing up for what my late father stood for and what my brother stood for – total independence.'

"People don't know this. When my father passed away, on his altar when we were taking it down, underneath a Buddha statue was a letter from the Dalai Lama.

"When my father started the Tibetan movement from Bloomington to Indianapolis, His Holiness wrote a letter to his brother stating how proud and happy he was that he started that. My mother has the original letter, I'm going to get a copy, and that letter is going to be published all over the world.

"His Holiness and my father had different views. They respected each other. I love my uncle, but you know what, Charlie, 54 years and nothing has happened.

"We all want the Dalai Lama to live a long life. He's 76 years old and if he passes away, what do you think is going to happen if they are already burning themselves up. There's going to be a lot of bloodshed in Tibet. Nobody talks about that."

Sitting at a dinner table with Kunga at Café Django was his older brother Lhundrup, 51, who can't do the Walk for Tibet because of diabetes.

Lhundrup said all three sons were born in Manhattan, New York.

"I've always been intrigued with history," Lhundrup said. "Writing books about Tibetan history, civilization, religion favors to a certain crowd of people. I told my father he needs to write down what he did with the American government, the CIA, OSS, what his experiences were.

"My father told me how he trained Tibet guerrillas on the Pacific Islands with the CIA, but said he couldn't talk or write much about that right now."

Lhundrup said he would get a tape recorder and ask him questions, "and when the time is right I can transcribe all of it. But then he had a stroke and lost the ability to talk."

His father was one of the "forefront Tibetan freedom fighters," Lhundrup said. "The thing that's unique about my father was, he would always talk straight. He never wavered, never played both sides. That's something very commendable."

He said when he was younger he traveled extensively with his father.

"In the '70s we would go to India. I got to sit in on a lot of conversations with guerrilla leaders that filtered down into India."

I asked Lhundrup if he has had a lot of one-on-one conversations with the Dalai Lama.

"No," he said. "I'm here. He's there (all over the world). I wouldn't even begin to know what to say to him. He's not on my plane."

He laughs, and then turns serious again.

"Tibetans, from what I've seen, if you look at other groups of people who have lost their country, people go into exile and forget their differences. You forget the differences and work for a common goal. Unfortunately, I told my father, we Tibetans we're putting the cart in front of the horse. We should forget all our differences and gain our country back. Once we have our own country we can get those policies and things like that."

I asked him if he thinks Tibetans will regain their country in his lifetime.

"It's really scary," he said. "I have this really bad feeling. His Holiness is getting up in his years. If the Chinese don't come to terms with him and allow him to go back to Tibet – and that's a real scary proposition – and he dies outside of Tibet, I have a feeling Tibetans in exile are going to up their game a little bit. There's going to be a lot more sacrifice and burnings. It's going to be ugly."

Lhundrup said he once mentioned to his father that "maybe Tibetans, one time in history, did something really bad, and this is why we are where we are today, (karma). My father told me there is some truth to that, I forget what century, but something bad happened."

When he listens to Tibetans speak, Lhundrup understands most of it.

"Vocalizing becomes a little more difficult because I don't have a chance to speak it all the time. But when I speak to Tibetans generally they get the gist of what I'm saying."

Donna Kim-Brand came from West Palm Beach to attend the fundraising dinner.

She spoke briefly to the crowd, saying, "Most of us bumble our way through our lives trying to find out what we're here for. I had the great pleasure of meeting Jigme in 2009. We became friends and I helped him develop his strategy, and it turned out differently than what we had planned. Part of what he wanted to do was develop leadership, not only amongst young people but all people. He wanted to invite everyone with their unique talents and gifts to be an Ambassador for World Peace.

"Each of you can do that just by being yourself, being kind and reaching and supporting people who are doing good work. The legacy the Norbu family has created in Bloomington will continue to ripple out. It is huge, supported by all of you here. Thank you for doing your part."

Chapter 21

Q & A With Father Francis Tiso

I first met Lisa Morrison on a Saturday afternoon in September 2003 when I picked up press credentials for the next day's dedication of the Chamtse Ling Temple for World Peace on the grounds of the Tibetan Cultural Center in Bloomington, Indiana. She was director of media and public relations for the center. It was the first time I would get to see the Dalai Lama in person.

Lisa was so pleasant and kind and helpful – the perfect Buddhist, I was thinking. After that amazing weekend, we stayed in touch by phone or email mostly, and she was always encouraging me to return to Bloomington for various events at the center. She was a very busy woman but always took time to help me in any way she could.

Seven years after our first meeting, I learned something new about Lisa while reading Evan Osnos' excellent profile on the Dalai Lama and Tibet's future in the October 4, 2010 issue of The New Yorker magazine. In the middle of the 14-page story was a comment by Lisa Morrison saying, "There's a whole group of us out there who consider ourselves Christian Buddhists. I believe in Jesus Christ – that he lived is not a question, it is a fact – but I have also been touched so deeply by His Holiness."

So have I. But I think it was the first time I had heard the term Christian Buddhist. I liked it and I felt a closer connection to Lisa after that. We talked about it a lot.

In the summer of 2012, Frankfort's Rich Green and I traveled to Bloomington to attend a three-day interfaith retreat led by Father Francis Tiso, a Catholic priest and scholar of Asian religions, who lived in Italy. In the early evening of the second day, Tiso, upon request, held the first-ever Catholic Mass inside the interfaith temple at the Tibetan Mongolian Buddhist Cultural Center. Near the end of the retreat the next day, I did a Q

& A interview with Father Tiso. He warned me at the start that his answers would not be sound bites. An excerpt from the interview follows:

Q: Is it possible to be a Christian-Buddhist?

A: Well, it's the old problem of getting past labels. My sense here is that if you're going to follow a spiritual path, you have to follow it as much as you possibly can within its own parameters – its framework, guidance and content.

However, what we've discovered in the past few decades is not only that there's been a meeting of world religions, but there's also been the sharing of spiritual experiences, such as in retreats like this one all over the world.

And folks have found that sometimes your Buddhism is enriched by a deep encounter with Christianity, and vice versa. There are a lot of people who use terms like 'dual practitioner.' There are even experimental communities in which Christians and Buddhists share practice together.

In Japan there's a friend of mine, a Catholic priest, who has founded a Christian community with a Pure Land Buddhist community together in the same building. They live together, share together, practice together as well. It's clearly a response to a sense of recognition.

Let me give you my idea about what it means to recognize. When people write about religion, let's say they're writing a textbook for a college course, and they describe a religion, and it happens to be my religion, let's say. When I'm reading it, do I recognize myself in that college textbook? Sometimes I don't. Sometimes I do, because it sounds like that author understood the faith that I practice, the faith to which I adhere.

Similarly when I hear a Buddhist speak as an authentic Buddhist deeply rooted in tradition, and I hear a lot of things that sound very familiar to me, I recognize myself in that. And so that shared recognition opens up the possibility that a Christian could recognize Buddhism as having not just apparent things in common, but have some deep continuity – some kind of deep connection between the best of Buddhism and the best of Christianity.

It doesn't mean the systems are the same. But it means there's a recognition process that occurs through dialogue, through encounter.

There are going to be times when some of us discover that when our practice is challenged – when we're going through a difficult time – we get some support and help and clarity through returning to, and sharing with, and reflecting with the other tradition.

That has happened with me a number of times, I know that for sure. And it's almost as if, especially in the area of contemplative spirituality of Buddhism and Christianity, that there's a lot of mutual support.

To know and to practice that kind of Buddhism helps me as a Christian contemplative.

So does that take it then to the next level to be able to use labels, such as the hyphenated Christian-Buddhist or Buddhist-Christian, or dual practitioner?

I think people use labels for convenience, and if it's convenient that means it's helpful to others. But if it's not helpful to others, we won't use it. A lot of times folks find these kinds of labels troubling. So it would be better for them to be looking at why people encounter, and learn from, and share spiritual practices, rather than to get all balled up with the problem of using words and labels.

Q: What in Buddhism strengthens your Christian path?

A: I think one of the most important things in Buddhism is the teaching about how to work with your mind, because Christianity depends on a contemplative system which takes you beyond your mind. We are also built on a dogmatic system that is profoundly committed to the life of the mind. So intellectual discipline, study, scholasticism and concepts raise the level of dogmatic truth.

The Christian faith is very strongly verbal. We have a verbal revelation alongside the personal revelation in Jesus Christ.

So it's very important for us every once in a while to touch base with a tradition that has a critical view of concepts, dogmas, words, and even experiences, because it kind of sharpens the focus.

What are you really talking about when you say Jesus Christ is our Savior? What are we really talking about when we talk about grace? The holy spirit guides us?

When you talk to people who do not have those concepts and that language in their religious traditions, and yet have a profound spiritual and contemplative life, it makes it more insistent and compelling, the need to clarify with greater depth and precision what we have been saying, which is one of the historic things down through the centuries that has sharpened the edges of Christian thought time and time again.

Books recommended

Not long after getting back to Kentucky, I visited Elaine Prevallet, a sister at the Loretto Motherhouse and author. She told me I might like to read Paul F. Knitter's book titled "Without Buddha I Could not be a Christian." I loved the book.

Then I noticed in the Spring 2012 issue of *Buddhadharma*, a quarterly magazine, a review of a new book titled "Buddhist and Christian? – An Exploration of Dual Belonging." The reviewer was Paul F. Knitter, the Paul Tillich professor of Theology, World Religions, and Culture at Union Theological Seminary in New York City.

I read the review but didn't buy the book because it cost $140 then and was listed on Amazon for $165 in February 2020.

"The Zen Teachings of Jesus" by Kenneth S. Leong is another book I've enjoyed reading on my interfaith path, and there are many more – way too many to get through in this lifetime.

Chapter 22

15,000 see Dalai Lama in Louisville

Frankfort's Vicki Pettus, a woman who embraces both Judaism and Christianity, loved being in Louisville's KFC Yum! Center Sunday with the Dalai Lama, probably the most famous Buddhist on the planet.

On May 19, 2013, plenty of Frankfort residents including Mayor Bill May were in the crowd of 15,000 listening to the Tibetan spiritual leader's message of compassion and forgiveness.

"What struck me that was so profound is the simplicity of his message," Pettus said. "It's so pure and simple, and yet so deep and complex. That's the beauty of him.

"I thoroughly enjoyed listening to him although he was a little bit hard to understand. American audiences can be so rude. Cell phones were going off and kids were screaming. I was in a nosebleed section but we could see him on the big screen, and I got about 80 percent of what he said.

"On the face of it, his message seems naïve. But if you listen to him it's not naïve. It's simple, basic human decency that we forget all about. We're so caught up in our strategies and trying to do this and that, and he just breaks through all of that and makes it a very simple task of just respecting each human, and respecting all life."

The Dalai Lama, 77, was the main attraction but many religious leaders from other faiths joined him on stage and spoke briefly, including Franciscan priest and author Richard Rohr, founder of the Center for Action and Contemplation in Albuquerque, New Mexico.

That was a pleasant surprise for Pettus, who participates twice a month in contemplative living and prayer groups at the Abbey of Gethsemani near Bardstown where the late Catholic monk and author Thomas Merton – a friend of the Dalai Lama – lived until his accidental death in 1968 in Thailand.

Mark Roberts, a retired state Legislative Research Commission employee from the Peaks Mill area, said the excitement of being in the presence of the Dalai Lama for the first time was "the spiritual equivalent of seeing the Beatles reunited."

He arrived early in Louisville and missed the long lines of people waiting to go through tight security to enter the arena.

"It was grand because when the doors first opened I walked right in," Roberts said. "It was interesting watching the line form outside. It probably went three-quarters of the way across the Ohio River at one time."

He said the Dalai Lama's "English was difficult, but not so difficult I couldn't understand him. He had the kind of message I expected, just a very simple message of compassion for everyone, even those who were allegedly responsible for the recent bombings in Boston."

Getting to see and listen to the Dalai Lama three consecutive days in Louisville was one of the greatest spiritual experiences of my life.

What made it even more special was to get to meet for the first time seven Tibetan Buddhist monks from Tashi Kyil Monastery in India. After leaving Louisville, the monks were headed to Frankfort for the first time on their U.S. tour and it was definitely a Memorial Day weekend to remember.

Attendance was outstanding at every cultural program and we were all elated and surprised at how successful fundraising had gone. (See Chapter 22.)

At a pizza party in Ev and Mike Claffy's home (the monks' host family) on the night before they left Frankfort, I broke down crying while trying to explain how amazing their seven-day visit to our capital had been.

The tears came unexpectedly. It was OK. I was with friends.

A group of volunteers in the dining room had just devoured two humongous pizzas from Buddy's that barely fit in a mini-van.

It was a happy cry because the monks in their maroon robes had bought so much joy and amazing energy to our community.

One day after the monks left Frankfort, heading to Indiana, I made a spur-of-the-moment trip to the Tibetan Mongolian Buddhist Cultural Center (TMBCC) in Bloomington. Lily accompanied me and we stayed one night in the same circular cottage we had stayed in on our first retreat there in 2012.

Before getting to Bloomington, however, I stopped in Columbus, Indiana, in the early afternoon to make a surprise visit to the Tashi Kyil monks, who were creating a World Peace mandala, in a Unitarian Universalist Church.

The monks seemed elated to see me and I was thrilled to see them again. Lily stayed on the back patio in the shade with a bowl of water. The monks and I visited her often during the 90 minutes I was there.

I told them I was on the way to Bloomington to take Refuge Vows tomorrow morning, Friday, May 31, from Arjia Rinpoche. Being with the Tashi Kyil monks for a week made me realize it was time to commit to the Buddhist path.

When we arrived at TMBCC, Lily and I felt at home. I saw Trish Ellis and Marilyn Ebbinhouse in the front office of the temple.

They reminded me that group meditation was at 6:30 p.m. in the temple. I said I may not make it because I'm exhausted. But I changed my mind after getting settled in the cottage. Before going back to the temple, Lily growled. I looked out the front door and saw a tiny deer with its white spots slowly following its mother across the yard. It looked so fragile and I said a prayer for them.

I struggled during the hour of meditation with David Ebbinhouse leading. A brief walking meditation is done between two sitting sessions, and I thought about leaving before the second silent sitting began, but chose to stay.

I sat next to Trish and she told me later she also struggled to stay awake. My head bobbed a lot but she said she hadn't noticed. My biggest fear was snoring, which I guess I didn't do.

Afterward, I walked around the Kalachakra Stupa in front of the temple while chanting the "Om Mani Padme Hum" Mantra of Chenrezig 108 times. Then I went to the nearby prayer wheels and turned them several times before getting a phone call from Arjia Rinpoche's assistant, Chunpay Jiumei. He wanted me to come to their house to pick up a plate of momos and Brussel sprouts for dinner with a spicy sauce on the side.

I happily walked there to get the food, and was invited to return for breakfast with Rinpoche and Chunpay tomorrow morning at 8:30.

Veggie momos (dumplings) are my favorite Tibetan food so I was in heaven when I got back to the cottage with Lily.

I went to bed at 10 p.m., two hours earlier than usual, and woke up about 3 a.m. It was raining and thundering a little and nervous Lily had moved into the small bathroom.

After a 22-minute sitting meditation, I managed to go back to sleep for almost two hours.

Breakfast at Rinpoche and Chunpay's residence included cereal and fruits, tsampa and other baked Tibetan breads, and warm salted almond milk, and green tea later.

They were aware of how successful the Tashi Kyil monks' tour had been in Frankfort and said the monks would be happy to return to Kentucky before their 2013 tour ended if I would want to coordinate another trip.

Rinpoche also recommended that I not put Tibetan people up on a pedestal. "Most are good people, but not all. They are human."

We moved into another room for the refuge ceremony.

When you "take refuge," you are committing yourself to the Buddhist path and to the Three Gems: The Buddha (teacher), The Dharma (teachings of the Buddha), and The Sangha (community of Buddhist practitioners).

I had read one week earlier in a new book, "Elements of Tibetan Buddhism" by Lexington friend and author Richard Farkas, that "it is not necessary to give up the religion you were raised in in order to take refuge vows."

I had read that sentence to my elderly mother, who was concerned that I was giving up the Christian path. It seemed to ease her mind.

At the ceremony, I did three prostrations. Rinpoche chanted a little and then asked me to repeat several phrases after him. He spoke slowly in Tibetan and made it easy for me to follow him. Then I did three more prostrations.

Rinpoche then gave me a light blue Mongolian khata (a prayer scarf), prayer flags, a bracelet he had made, and a nice writing pen with Arjia Rinpoche Charities on it.

Later, Chunpay made me two of his delicious egg sandwiches for the road trip back to Kentucky.

No family members attended my Roman Catholic first communion in 1968 at St. Mary's College chapel in Marion County, Kentucky. And it was the same way 45 years later when I took refuge vows at TMBCC in Bloomington. I liked it that way and felt joy both times.

Working on another monks' tour

I drove from Bloomington to Lebanon, and early the next morning I started planning for the second 2013 Tashi Kyil Tibetan monks' tour in Kentucky.

I called longtime friend Georgianna "Jody" Mattingly, a nurse, and asked her if she could go walking with me. She said "yes" so we went to the

Loretto Motherhouse and walked the mulched trail around Mary Lake and then walked to Joseph Lake by way of Cedars of Peace cabins. Then we went to the nearby Abbey of Gethsemani and attended the 12:15 p.m. Sext service, which lasted only 15 minutes.

I told Jody I wanted to organize another tour for the Tashi Kyil monks and that Lebanon was where I wanted it to happen.

My mind said Lexington would be the ideal place for them to go because of the larger population and a Tibetan Buddhist Center is there. But my heart said Lebanon and Marion County where I grew up.

Jody, who followed the monks' tour in Frankfort through Facebook, was enthusiastic about it and wanted to help. She works at Spring View Hospital in Lebanon and believed several doctors there would contribute to help fund the World Peace mandala.

She also mentioned that her friend, Mary Batt, a nurse and massage therapist who lives on the same street as my mother, would be excited to help. Mary had gone to see the Dalai Lama in Louisville.

Jody and Mary organized wonderful cultural programs for the monks, and Mary and her husband, Jay, welcomed the monks into their home for seven days and nights in October. The Batts were also their host family in 2016 and 2019.

The weekly Lebanon Enterprise newspaper staff gave tremendous coverage to the monks' visit, the best I had ever seen.

The World Peace mandala was created at the Marion County Public Library and the staff and library board's hospitality was wonderful. An interfaith dinner for the monks and Lebanon clergy was held at Republican state Senator Jimmy Higdon and wife Jane's beautiful historic home.

The monks toured the Loretto Motherhouse and had lunch there, and then attended a service at the Abbey of Gethsemani. After the service they hiked with several Trappist monks to the small Hermitage in the woods where spiritual writer Thomas Merton lived in the last years of his life.

Daughter Charlsie Garrett and Anna Laura Davenport organized a successful Picnic in the Park on a beautiful autumn Sunday afternoon.

We were hoping to raise $2,000, the suggested donation for the monks to build the intricate World Peace mandala over four days. So we were surprised and elated when we raised $9,538 for the monks' refugee monastery in Dehra Dun, India.

More important than the fundraising, we planted little seeds of compassion during their visit. Now all our community garden needs is a sprinkling of love and little acts of kindness every day.

Fundraising from Lebanon continued after the monks' visit too. In her home while the monks visited, Mary Batt and Ngargo Rinpoche, a Tibetan Buddhist lama, combined their artistic talents to create an interfaith painting depicting Mother Teresa holding a baby Buddha. The painting was done in late evenings after public events.

Shortly after the monks left, 200 limited-edition prints of the "Compassionate Mother" painting were released as a fundraiser for the monks' monastery.

Buddhist, Christian and Catholic symbols can be found throughout the painting.

Rinpoche painted the Buddha and eight auspicious symbols of Tibetan Buddhism – Umbrella, Golden Fish, Treasure Vase, Lotus Flower, Right-coiled Conch Shell, Endless Knot, Victory Banner and Dharma Wheel.

A smaller gold fish was painted by Mary, a Catholic.

"We said, 'two fish, one ocean,' and laughed constantly while working on that part," Mary said. "The eye of Rinpoche's larger fish reflects the Tibetan flag."

The main key to the painting is the mermaid named Transcendence, Mary says.

"Next to the mermaid is a yellow circle," she says. "In the words of St. Augustine, 'God is a circle whose center is everywhere, whose circumference is nowhere.'"

Joseph's coat of many colors contains lots of quotes from Mother Teresa and Buddha. Three crosses and five drops of blood represent the wounds of Christ.

The 16-by-22-inch prints have been signed and numbered by the artists and are $50 each. Twenty percent of proceeds goes to the Tibetan Mongolian Buddhist Cultural Center in Bloomington, Indiana, while the Tashi Kyil Monastery gets 80 percent.

PART FOUR

Mixing it Up and Dancing Together

"With boundless love toward all beings, we dance each and every moment in the sea of god, in the sea of truth."
--Anam Thubten

Chapter 23

United by their faiths

This feature story appeared in the August 2016 premier issue of FRANK magazine, a monthly publication of The State Journal newspaper.

A Buddhist visitor to the Islamic Center of Frankfort had a question for his Muslim friends following a Friday service: What's the toughest thing you've experienced?

Ashiq Zaman, president of the local center, said being unable to attend his mother's funeral in his native country of Bangladesh in 2013 tops his list.

"We enjoy many, many things here. However, we miss family. My mother passed and I wasn't there. Seven brothers and sisters got married and I was present only for one.

"My father is sick. He's 83 and has had two heart attacks and I see him once every two years."

Three days later Ashiq's father died. Again, he couldn't go to the funeral.

Taking a scary ride

Mohammad Razavi, a native of Iran, remembers a frightening day when he was 16 and walking with two friends on one of the busiest streets in Tehran.

"These patrolmen, the Guardians, saw us and quickly made a U-turn and came back to us.

"They blindfolded us and put us in the back of the vehicle. The driver was speeding. Then he would slam on the brake and turn around. I don't know where we went, but they took us out of the car and separated us."

Still blindfolded, Mohammad was asked if he prays, what kind of books he reads, and what his parents do for a living. He heard a clicking noise, perhaps a gun.

Mohammad gets car sick easily and felt nauseated from the erratic driving.

"They finished questioning us, threw us back in the car and started driving crazy again. After a while I told the driver I'm about to throw up in your car. He pulled over and threw us out, and that was the end of it."

Mohammad, 49, still doesn't know why the patrolmen stopped them.

"I probably looked like a punk, wearing a black coat and tight jeans," he says, smiling. "They may have suspected I was anti-government or communist."

The 1983 incident occurred four years after the Iranian Revolution.

A year after his frightening ride, Mohammad was living in Pennsylvania with a cousin.

"Iran was a scary place," he says. "It's chaotic for a long time after any revolution. The first chance I had to leave the country, I took it."

Today, he's an environmental engineer for the state Division of Waste Management.

Mohammad, Ashiq and another Muslim, Aejaz Shaik from India, are on the Frankfort Interfaith Council, a group promoting respect and understanding of all religions.

In its three year history, the council has had two Baptists, four Baha'is, three Muslims, a Jew, Hindu, Buddhist, Catholic, Methodist, Christian Scientist and a Unitarian Universalist. Council members aren't religious scholars or clergy.

Finally finding her faith

Religion wasn't a big part of Shannan Rome's life growing up in Berea.

She went occasionally to the Berea College church at Easter or to other Christian churches with a friend or her grandmother, a Sunday school teacher. She recalls a "defining moment as a teenager" – a discussion on religion with a friend's mother.

145

"I asked, 'What if you were a devout Muslim and lived a virtuous life and upheld your morals and did everything you were supposed to do, and you died. What would happen to you?'

"The mother said, 'You would go to hell.' And I said, 'How is that fair in any kind of supreme being sort of way?'"

Shannan then asked, "What if you had never heard of Christ but were a good person and lived your life the way I mentioned? Her answer was the same, 'You'd go to hell.'"

Shannan couldn't accept that. She believed in God but felt she would never belong to an organized religion.

"I liked certain things about all the places I checked out. But something always came up that didn't sit right. If I was going to align myself with a religion, it had to be a meaningful guide to my everyday life."

Shortly after that, however, she met a Berea College student from Frankfort, Nathan Rome, who grew up as a Baha'i. When she heard about his religion, she was shocked and wanted to know more.

"He was not pushy at all," she recalls.

"I was an obstacle in her path," Nathan says. "I wanted to make sure if she wanted to be a Baha'i, she was doing it for her, not me."

Shannan thought, "Oh my, there's a religion saying men and women are equal, everybody deserves an education, and all races are from the same human family . . . all these things I believed in my heart."

Soon she met more Baha'is and they were "talking about social and economic development projects, working for race unity and having friends from different cultures.

"It wasn't just a nice idea. They were walking the walk, and committed to practicing their beliefs every day – not just one day a week."

Interfaith journeys

Nathan and Shannan Rome, husband and wife for 19 years, came to the Islamic Center of Frankfort May 10 for an interfaith council meeting.

After touring the center, council members ate vegetarian pizza and talked about their spiritual journeys.

Jim Jackson, a Methodist and retired school superintendent, says there's a distinction between respect and agreement. "I can respect someone but that doesn't mean I agree with them. Our agreements can be very different, but I'm still going to respect their journey.

"I love being around people who are comfortable in their faith because they're so open. They're not threatened. God is love and he wants us to love one another."

Nash Cox, a Christian Scientist who has an interfaith "Simple Gifts" church service in her home on Sundays, says Franklin County has "remarkable diversity compared to the community I knew growing up. Religious diversity has enriched the community.

"Interfaith activities are a way of enriching our lives . . . not being threatened by differences but embracing them while maintaining our own beliefs."

Ruby Layson, a Unitarian Universalist and a retired journalist and educator, participates in Lexington's Christian-Muslim Dialogue. But she feels a closer relationship with the Frankfort Interfaith Council "because we're a smaller, more intimate group."

Aejaz Shaik says Muslims and Christians together make up well over half the world's population.

"It's critical for these two religions, along with other religions, to come together to promote peace and justice. This council has given me a platform to connect with people of other faiths to build mutual respect and understanding."

The newest council member, Linda Axon, is a Methodist and president of Kentucky Church Women United.

In CWU, "we say we agree to differ, resolve to love, and unite to serve," Linda says. "We're all people of worth."

Kentucky State University professor Avinash Tope, a Hindu, says growing up in India he was taught "all religions sit on the circumference of a circle. They're all equidistant from God in the center, where they're all trying to get.

"Scratch the surface a little bit and deep down, all religions are going to teach you the same thing."

In India, you don't have to be on a council to experience interfaith action, Avinash says. "You step out your door and you're with almost every faith on the globe. Unless you have tolerance and learn respect, you're not going to make it through the day."

With a heavy heart from his father's death one day earlier, Ashiq Zaman came to the interfaith meeting because of his love for council members. They felt his pain.

Shannan Rome said losing her father in 2011 was tougher than finding out she had cancer at age 37 three years ago.

147

"My dad dying was harder because that was final. There was no getting him back."

Shannan believes suffering opens our hearts and makes us more compassionate, altruistic and grateful for the things that matter.

"When you experience hardship, that's the forest fire that seems awful, but creates new growth. Right here, this is such a beautiful breath of fresh air to have a group like this from different faiths who just love you and support you."

Frankfort Interfaith Council visiting local
Islamic Center

Chapter 24

Muslims speak out against backlashes

This lead front-page story was in the January 18, 2016 issue of The State Journal. The headline said, 'Our Islamic Neighbors: A time to heal.'

Islamic terrorism.

Ashiq Mohammad Zaman has seen and heard those two words thousands of times since Sept. 11, 2001. It hurts every time.

He's president of the Islamic Center of Frankfort and loves his religion.

Zaman believes with all his heart and soul that Islam is a religion of peace. Islam is an Arabic word that means peace and submission to God.

A native of Bangladesh, Zaman also loves the U.S. and small-town life in Frankfort, where he has lived since 1994.

He has a bachelor's in civil engineering from Bangladesh University of Engineering and Technology, a master's in civil engineering from Louisiana Tech University, and is a branch manager for the state Commonwealth Office of Technology.

He also serves on the Frankfort Interfaith Council – a group of 12 local residents representing eight different religions – working to promote respect and understanding of all religions.

"I enjoy serving because it gives me an opportunity to learn about other religions and the diversity among the world community," Zaman says. "It's a platform for me to make a little contribution in clearing up misunderstandings about Islam, and make friends with others in Frankfort with common values."

At the interfaith council's December 2015 meeting, Zaman and Aejaz Shaik, also a Muslim on the council, talked about terrorism and religious extremism in the world today and the Muslim position and responsibilities.

They also expressed sadness over recent terrorism in Paris that killed 130 and wounded 368; and in San Bernardino, California, that killed 14 and seriously injured 22.

Zaman said he felt compelled to speak about terrorism after his wife, Saika Aktar, a medical school graduate from Bangladesh, asked him "if there was any truth in the militant Islam," he said.

"I knew she had very limited knowledge in Islam like the majority of Muslims around the world. The news about the heinous activities of ISIL and propaganda efforts by some media equating those with Islamist activities even convinced *her* to ask that question.

"I realized then I have to do something about this."

Zaman and Shaik also realized since the twin towers crumbled in New York City in 2001, suspicion of all Muslim people and disrespect of mosques and the sacred scripture of Qur'an has grown exponentially in America.

Shaik, originally from India, told how all the recent Muslim-bashing in the news has hurt one of his young American-born sons. While driving him to school one morning, his son heard an NPR radio reporter say presidential candidate Donald Trump wants to ban Muslims from coming into America.

"I understand what's going on politically and told him that's just what one candidate is proposing and he may not get elected or be able to do that," Shaik said. "But this is the first time my son is hearing this. He panicked and started asking so many questions why Muslims are being banned. He was worried that his grandparents wouldn't be able to visit him, which they traditionally do every three years."

Then his son started hearing similar reports on TV over several days, and woke up in the middle of the night worried again about not being able to ever see his grandparents again.

To help the interfaith council better understand Islam and its condemnation of terrorism, Zaman presented a detailed analysis based upon a 2005 religious ruling by the Fiqh Council of North America, an Islamic juristic body.

The ruling states that "Islam strictly condemns religious extremism and the use of violence against innocent lives. There is no justification in Islam for extremism or terrorism."

Interfaith council member Jim Jackson – a Methodist, retired public school superintendent and international traveler – asked Zaman and Shaik why there doesn't seem to be more of an organized worldwide effort by peace-loving, highly-educated Muslims to speak out against the small percentage of extremists who "highjack the Islam religion."

Islam is the second-largest religion in the world and Muslims are in 56 countries. They said unlike the Roman Catholic Church with a "Pope-type structure," there is no one central figure of authority who can claim to speak on behalf of the entire Muslim community.

While the religion itself unifies all, individual Muslims tend to reflect the culture of their country, which creates a huge mixture of people – socially and politically, they said.

After the meeting, Jackson thanked them for their presentation, saying, "As a Christian, I could never appreciate or fully understand these challenges, since I practice my faith in a majority culture. I don't think any of us can appreciate what you and your families must deal with, unless we had personally experienced practicing our faith, as a small minority in a culture with another faith as the majority."

Zaman and Shaik invited the interfaith council to their Friday afternoon, December 18, jummah service at the Islamic Center on Schenkel Lane. Several attended, listening to Zaman give an Islamic teaching against terrorism.

He chose that subject, Zaman said, "In the light of recent terrorist incidents in California and Paris, and the aftermath of those incidents. We live today in an interdependent and interconnected world where peaceful and fair interaction is imperative.

"A grave threat to all of us nowadays is the danger of religious and political extremism that manifests itself in various forms of violence, including terrorism.

"As Muslims we must face up to our responsibility to understand, clarify and advocate a faith-based, righteous and moral position with regard to this problem, especially when terrorist acts are committed in the name of Islam. We need to do that not because of external pressures or for the sake of political correctness, but out of our sincere conviction of what Islam stands for."

Zaman said "jihad" is not to be equated with terrorism. "The word doesn't mean 'Holy War' or war that is justified by differences in religious convictions. The Arabic equivalent of 'Holy War" is never mentioned in the

151

Qur'an. There is nothing holy about war, and it is described in the Qur'an as a hated act."

He said Muslims are part of the universal human family, and are committed to co-existing in peace and justice.

Zaman said he hopes neighbors and friends from other faiths will understand the true teachings of Islam and "speak out against the recent backlash and widespread demonization of Islam and Muslims.

"Islamophobic statements and actions punish and victimize the entire global community of Muslims for the actions of a few, and hinder our efforts to provide a moderate voice, and promote mutual understanding and peace.

"The vicious cycle of violence in our interconnected world has to be broken, and we must work together to do so through mutual understanding and constructive dialogue, rather than allowing those who would divide us through hate to achieve their goals. It is the only hope for bringing about real and genuine mutual respect, justice and peace."

A diverse congregation of Muslims attended the December 18 service in Frankfort. Besides the U.S., their native countries included Jordan, Syria, Palestine, Iran, Iraq, India, Pakistan, Bangladesh, Morocco, Nigeria, Tunisia, The Gambia, Canada and Bosnia.

President Obama, in his final State of the Union address last week, said Americans need to reject any politics that targets people because of race or religion.

"This is not a matter of political correctness," Obama said. "This is a matter of understanding just what it is that makes us strong. The world respects us not just for our arsenal; it respects us for our diversity and our openness and the way we respect every faith. . .

"When politicians insult Muslims, whether abroad or our fellow citizens, when a mosque is vandalized or a kid is called names, that doesn't make us safer. That's not telling it like it is. It's just wrong. It diminishes us in the eyes of the world. It makes it harder to achieve our goals. It betrays who we are as a country."

Chapter 25

What would Martin Luther King say today?

This is the unedited version of a newspaper column that was published in the January 18, 2016 edition of The State Journal in honor of Dr. Martin Luther King Jr.'s birthday.

D
r. Martin Luther King Jr., the 1964 Nobel Peace Prize winner, was only 39 when he was assassinated in Memphis, Tennessee, on April 4, 1968 by hate and ignorance.

Imagine if the young, energetic, intelligent, articulate Baptist minister and peace activist – who was inspired by a Hindu, Mahatma Gandhi's nonviolent activism – could have lived to have reached his 87th birthday Friday.

I think he would have said, "I just want to sit down now for an hour and be still ... let go of thoughts for a bit."

I think he would have told his assassin, James Earl Ray, "I forgive you," like Jesus said at his death on the cross, "Father, forgive them, for they do not know what they are doing."

I think Dr. King would have smiled and said, "Oh my, we have lots of work to do. We have evolved, but we haven't reached the Promised Land. The key is love ... none of this 'us vs. them' stuff."

As Mirabai Starr says in her beautiful book, *God of Love: A Guide to the Heart of Judaism, Christianity and Islam*, "The sacred scriptures of all faiths call us to love as we have never loved before. This requires effort, vigilance, and radical humility.

"Violence is easier than nonviolence, yet hate only perpetuates hate. The wisdom teachings remind us that love – active, engaged, fearless love – is the only way to save ourselves and each other from the firestorm of war that rages around us."

Dr. King wasn't just speaking out for African Americans in his famous dream speech. He was standing up for all Americans, all beings.

Today Dr. King would be speaking out, and hugging, and walking arm-in-arm with his Muslim brothers and sisters, his gay brothers and sisters, his homeless brothers and sisters, and everyone else who feels hated and misunderstood and defeated.

I think Dr. King would say, "We need to do better. But we also need to slow down. Turn off the TV for a while. Park the car. Go to a place of silence, and sit. Don't just do something, sit there . . . for 20 minutes. Let go of thoughts. They're like clouds. They pass. Just sit with the Devine.

"Attend the 5:15 p.m. Tuesday Silent Service at the downtown Church of the Ascension."

After King traveled to India in 1959 as a guest of the Gandhi Peace Foundation, he returned to America determined to devote one day a week of his busy schedule to fasting and meditation.

As the late Christian monk M. Basil Pennington says, "One of the surprises of centering prayer is that we discover God can manage the world for 20 minutes without us – and not mess it up too much.

"In centering prayer we get in touch with God at the very center of our being, the ground of our being, as the source. We come to know our true self as that beautiful person who at each moment comes forth from his creative love."

The poem accompanying this column about my visit to a mosque was written September 9, 1998. I didn't title it until this month.

In 1998 I was in New Mexico visiting Barney Bush, a Shawnee friend and writing coach. He had taught creative writing and journalism at the Institute of American Indian Arts in Santa Fe a few years earlier and I had spoken to his journalism students and worked with them for a week.

On my return visit he gave me a large book of blank pages and told me to fill it up with poems.

"You need to do more than newspaper writing," he said. "Start putting your heart on paper. It will help in whatever writing you decide to do."

I wandered into the adobe mosque that evokes both Native American heritage of the American Southwest and the architectural design of many buildings in North Africa.

But I don't believe in coincidences. Divine guidance led me there.

The mosque and educational center was run by Dar al Islam, a non-profit group dedicated to helping non-Muslims understand Islam and to deepening the practice of Islam among Muslims.

Soon after the September 11, 2001 terrorist attacks when it seemed on TV as if the majority of Americans were mad at all Muslims, I knew I had to meet Muslim residents in Frankfort. The peace I felt inside the little mosque in the desert three years earlier helped me appreciate the Islamic faith and understand our oneness with the Divine.

It was easy to find local Muslims. The first one I met was Alauddin A. Alauddin.

A civil engineer, he was a branch manager in the state Division for Air Quality and was at a training session in Austin, Texas, when the September 11 tragedy happened.

I interviewed him for a lengthy Q & A in The State Journal.

Regarding the September 11 tragedy, Alauddin said, "I feared for my family right away. The first thought was: oh, my God, this is horrible. The second thought was: oh, God, let this not be the work of anybody related to Islam or Muslims."

Speaking about Islam and Christianity, he said, "Islamic values are in many ways similar to Christian values. So people who are trying to revive Christian values – and by that let me be clear, I'm talking about values as opposed to imposing religious practices on anybody – will find Islam and Muslims to be your strongest allies."

A resident of the U.S. since 1992, Alauddin's feelings about America were, "We have looked at other countries, other societies, and have had a chance to live in other places. We have made the conscious decision to settle here because we feel America is already the best country in the world."

We became friends and he invited me into his home to meet his wife and young son and daughter, and to enjoy wonderful meals. I also attended prayer services and celebrations with him at the Islamic Center of Frankfort and in Lexington at the end of Ramadan.

He and his family moved to Columbus, Ohio, a few years later but we have remained good friends.

One of my main spiritual teachers is His Holiness The Dalai Lama. In his 2010 book, "Toward A True Kinship of Faiths: How The World's Religions Can Come Together," the Dalai Lama said when he grew up as a child in Lhasa, Tibet, he had personal contacts with local Tibetan Muslims. When he fled into exile in 1959, "a number of Muslims came after me – being no less loyal to the cause of a free Tibet than other Tibetans. Several have served in the Tibetan government in exile for a long period, and continue to do so."

One thing immediately recognizable in Islam is the sheer dedication to the observance of regular daily prayer, which is undertaken five times a day, the Dalai Lama said.

His book says, "Right next to Buddhism's most holy place, the stupa at Bodh Gaya that commemorates the site of the Buddha's enlightenment more than 2,500 years ago, there is a mosque that issues the typical Islamic call for prayer, 'Allahu Akbar,' literally, 'God is Great,' at dawn every morning, which you can hear as you walk around the stupa.

"These calls for prayer are sung in a beautiful cascading chant that conjures up the image of a voice traveling across the Middle Eastern desert and helps connect the faithful with the awareness of the Divine."

When the Dalai Lama had the opportunity in 2005 to visit Jordan, an Islamic country in the Middle East, and heard the calls for prayer from the mosques in Amman, "it was most impressive," he said. "The thought that right then, at that very moment, millions of people were collectively taking a pause, however brief, from their lives, to turn their thoughts toward God, moved me deeply."

In India, a country with one of the largest Islamic populations in the world, the Dalai Lama has had longstanding personal friendships with several devout Muslims, including an imam. In their discussions, the Dalai Lama was told that any person who causes bloodshed to his fellow human beings is not a true Muslim.

"Another stated that a true Muslim must love God's creatures as much as he loves Allah," says the Dalai Lama in his book. "This is beautiful. Of course, the language used in Islam to articulate its vision of universal compassion is different from that of Buddhism, but the concept and its spiritual effect on an individual's ethical life are not different here from the fundamental Buddhist tenet of compassion for all sentient beings."

The Dalai Lama says, "The perception of Islam as narrow, intolerant, and even open to terrorism is a false one and a very unfortunate consequence of 9/11. To take the insane acts of a misguided handful as representative of anything but their own depravity is to make a generalization that simply has no basis.

"In the religious community worldwide we must work unceasingly to reverse this wrong image, and in Islam itself leaders must make clear to Muslims that the extremists' interpretation of their faith is not only damaging to the tradition but in fact does no justice to the richness and beauty of what Islam stands for."

One of my greatest joys and blessings today is serving on the Frankfort Interfaith Council with 11 other local residents representing many different faiths. Three of our members – Mohammad Razavi, Aejaz Shaik and Ashiq Zaman – are Muslim.

We've walked together the last two Thanksgiving mornings to help support the ACCESS Soup Kitchen and Men's Shelter. We've supported the building of a World Peace sand painting by Tibetan Buddhist monks, who are refugees in India.

We've held a Celebration of Diverse Faiths in Franklin County at the Paul Sawyier Public Library. We invite many diverse spiritual leaders to speak at our monthly meetings to help us continue to open our hearts and minds to our community, state, nation and world.

I think Dr. Martin Luther King Jr. would smile and say, "Good job my brothers and sisters. Stop to rest and pray, and then keep going. Keep the love going."

Three years before 9/11 --- Charles Pearl

Wandering down dirt roads to silent places
Alone, but not lonely, in the red rocks
Chimney Top Trail at Ghost Ranch,
Christ in the Desert Monastery
Thinking of Georgia O'Keeffe and Thomas Merton …
Then in the white rocks a jewel:
adobe mosque in the New Mexico desert
Inside alone, I quietly remove shoes and socks
Sit on a shining tiled seat,
under a row of faucets I wash my feet
drying them on a soft beige towel …
A prayer mat waits for me under the dome
Thinking of Muhammad Ali and Kareem Abdul-Jabbar
I don't know any Muslims personally
Still I feel at home in this sacred place of peace
As sitting meditation begins
I feel intimate connection
to all beings, all things in this mosque
built on a juniper-dotted mesa …
No appointments, no deadlines
no worries, no sense of time
no us and them, no coincidences
Just One with the Universe

Chapter 26

Romes have life-changing year in The Gambia

This feature story was in the October 2016 issue of FRANK magazine.

Less is More.

For Frankfort's Julia and David Rome, that philosophy has danced in their minds most of their adult lives.

Now it's planted firmly in their hearts . . . after living almost a year in The Gambia in West Africa, near the Atlantic Ocean.

"We've spent most of our lives accumulating things, and now it's time to let go of stuff," says David, 67, a retired technical writer for a Louisville engineering company.

Their beautiful 50-acre Leeland Valley farm, off Pea Ridge Road on the west side of Franklin County, is for sale. They're downsizing, and letting-go of many material possessions has become a daily meditation for Julia.

From September 2015 through July of this year, they worked primarily as volunteer English teachers at Starfish International, a mentorship program for girls attending high school in Lamin, a village of 25,000 where a third of the population lives below the international poverty line of $1.25 a day.

English is the official language in The Gambia, which has 1.8 million people living in a geographical area twice the size of Delaware.

Starfish co-directors are Yassin Sarr and her husband, David Fox, who met in Kentucky.

Yassin, a native of The Gambia, went to Berea College in Kentucky and met the Romes' son, Nathan, when he was a student there in the 1990s. Yassin and Nathan became friends and that's how Julia and David Rome met her.

Nathan, a South Frankfort resident, says Yassin "was raised in a strong Muslim family and was very outspoken. While at Berea, she had the vision of returning to her home country and starting an after-school program for girls."

The Romes belong to the Baha'i faith, a monotheistic religion which emphasizes the spiritual unity of all humankind. Yassin and her husband also are Baha'is now, but Starfish welcomes girls of all faiths.

The goal is to instill girls with five core values: nobility, independence, courtesy, knowledge and service. Ultimately, each student learns she is responsible for helping to raise her community around her.

Julia, longtime owner and teacher at the Frankfort Yoga Studio, becomes emotional when thinking about Starfish and its founder.

"Yassin is like a Mother Teresa," Julia says. "She's so dedicated. She's a genius, a dynamic speaker, and has such high energy she hardly sleeps. Her husband doesn't think she's human."

Although the school opened to provide advanced education to 100 girls, about 30 boys now attend as well.

"Girls typically can be high-risk of dropping out of school because of family pressure and financial situations," Julia says. "They're doing well in school and learning good leadership qualities.

"These young women, even 14 year olds, can get up and speak to a large group. They have so much confidence. It's amazing to listen to them recite poetry and they're incredible writers. You have to experience it to realize how powerful this program is."

In addition to teaching English, yoga, and social and environmental studies, Julia taught a journaling class, "and they loved it," says David, who was co-editor of the academy's magazine.

"A Baha'i teaching says if you have to choose between educating a boy or girl, you educate the girl because she's the primary educator of a child," Julia says. "There's another saying when you educate a boy, you're educating an individual, and when you educate a girl, you're educating a nation because girls are going to teach children."

The majority of students at Starfish are Muslim.

Lifetime of service to others

Julia served in the Peace Corps in Palau in the South Pacific from 1977 to 1979.

One of the things that lured her to The Gambia at age 62 was the opportunity "to live in a predominantly (90 percent) Muslim culture. I wanted that experience. I wanted to know for myself what it's like. It was wonderful. I have a much greater appreciation for Islam now."

They loved listening to the beautiful Islamic call-to-prayer chant five times each day, beginning at dawn. They appreciated that faithful Muslims – like Baha'is – don't drink alcohol.

"That eliminates so many problems," Julia says.

David says, "You can get alcohol in The Gambia, especially in tourist areas. But you never see public intoxication."

The Romes rented a three-bedroom concrete house – a mansion compared to most residences in Lamin – for $250 a month. They had electricity, indoor plumbing, a gas stove, refrigerator and TV. They either walked or used a taxi or public transportation – a 14-passenger van – to get wherever they needed to go.

The two main roads in the village are paved, and other roads are sandy soil.

It was a 15-minute walk from their house to Starfish.

"We were close to public transportation," David Rome says. "We could get anywhere within the urban area in an hour. The farthest place away is the capital, Banjul, and we could be there in less than an hour by public transportation."

Julia and David both lost 15 pounds while living there, by walking a lot and eating healthier. They ate mostly fish, chicken, sweet potatoes, rice, cabbage, eggplant, mangoes and peanuts.

Extremes of two cultures

Since they've returned to Frankfort, the Romes have thought a great deal about the extremes of the two cultures.

"America has way too much and The Gambia has way too little," Julia says. "They're happy without very much and we're so very possessive. They share food, clothing and money. Anything they have they share.

"The people are so kind and generous and loving. They accepted us as their family."

David says when you go there, "you first look at things as an American by our standards of needs and wants. We look at them as being really poor. They know their life can be hard as far as making ends meet.

"But I don't think they think of it in terms of poverty because most people are like that. A lot of them now, however, do want smart phones. That's the thing.

"And there are a lot of TVs. Really modest compounds have TVs in them. There's no escape from materialism because of the media and the Internet – that double-edged sword. It creates desires that used to not be there.

"Beyond that they don't seem to want much."

Julia believes The Gambia is a safe country in terms of "personal safety."

"You don't have 911 to call," she says. "But if something happens to you and you yell, people will be there in seconds to assist you. That's what they do if someone is in need."

But David says the village does have a theft problem.

"I feel a little more vulnerable to theft there than here. That's why we pay a little for a night watchman, and we have bars on our windows and a wall around our compound. The watchman's presence is a real deterrent."

There's another deterrent, Julia says.

"Gambians are strong believers in God. They believe if they steal something, they'll have to pay for it and go to hell.

"Nobody has guns except police, the military and hunters.

"I think because it's such a communal culture there are no homeless people. Everybody is taken care of. You don't have a lot of mental problems because people are loved so much and cared for."

David and Julia feel they are a part of three families in The Gambia: Starfish, the Baha'i community of about 50, and their neighborhood.

Life outside is like a U.S. 127 yard sale

They say most Gambians live in extended-family compounds with grandmothers and aunts living with children and their parents.

"Most of the time people are outside except when they're sleeping or it's raining," Julia says. "Or when they're watching TV," adds David.

"They get up early in the morning and start sweeping the dirt smooth outside," Julia says. "Laundry is a big to-do because it's all done by hand."

David says, "Gambia and the neighborhoods smell good. The pleasant smell of cooking fires and food is just everywhere. I miss those smells."

"It's like we're all in one big campground," Julia says. "There's hardly a time when you can't walk out on the street and see goats, children playing soccer, and venders selling produce and stuff. It's almost like New York City.

"Almost everybody has a little stall. Somehow they get shipping containers of second-hand stuff, mostly from Europe. They're selling shoes and clothes and dishes and mattresses. It looks like a U.S. 127 yard sale."

Farming, fishing and tourism drive the economy in The Gambia.

Agriculture accounts for 30 percent of the gross domestic product and employs 70 percent of the labor force.

Birdwatching brings many tourists to The Gambia. Julia kept a bird log and saw 121 of the nearly 500 species there.

The Gambia, the smallest country on mainland Africa, is mostly surrounded by Senegal with a 50-mile strip of Atlantic coastline at its western end.

It has a sub-tropical climate with plenty of sunshine throughout the year and average temperature highs between 84 and 93 degrees. June to October is the hot, rainy season, and the cooler, dry season is from November through May. The upper 50s is as low as it usually gets.

The Romes visited the coast two or three times a month.

"Their beaches are nice," David says. "I wouldn't call them dazzling. Sometimes you get beautiful sunsets. Waves aren't usually big enough for surfing. When there are rip tides, making it dangerous for swimmers, Gambians will say, 'The ocean is getting ugly.'"

The Gambia River flows through the center of the country, emptying into the Atlantic at Banjul, the capital.

Although 40 snake species – including the venomous cobras and mambas – are in The Gambia, David saw only one snake while there and it wasn't poisonous.

They saw green monkeys and the endangered western red colobus monkey.

The Gambia also is land of the hippopotamus, crocodiles, leopards, hyenas and numerous other animals. They saw many species of African wildlife at national parks and nature preserves.

The late American author Alex Haley won a Pulitzer Prize in 1977 for his book, "Roots," the story of a black family from its origins in The Gambia, Africa, through seven generations to the present day in America. The same year, "Roots: The Saga of an American Family" was adapted as a popular TV miniseries.

Back home and homesick

Now David and Julia Rome are back home in Franklin County with their four sons, one daughter, nine grandchildren and one great-grandchild. They feel fortunate to have friends and such a loving, supportive family here.

And they feel homesick for Africa. It's hard to explain, Julia says.

"I'm still trying to figure out what's going on. As Baha'is, we believe in the oneness of humanity. We feel at home there and it makes me want to cry just thinking about it, because how can that be? Frankfort is where our family is. This is where we've grown. ... Yet we miss The Gambia and we love those people with all our heart and soul.

"I've been in the Peace Corps, but this is so different from anything I've ever experienced."

Spiritually, Julia and David recognize Gambian people as part of their world family.

"I think that's why it brings me to tears," Julia says. "That's the way it's supposed to be."

"That's right," says David. "That's what we've evolved into. This is the time to recognize that. A lot of people are still fighting it. But it's reality."

They've fulfilled their dream of going to The Gambia, but more volunteer work needs to be done there.

"We love Starfish and want to continue helping anyway we can," Julia says. "Financially, we can live there cheaper than here. A little money there goes a long, long way. So we can help in assisting our growing Gambian family members, who are so kind, generous and loving."

The first chapter is history. Only time will tell how many Rome chapters – years – remain in Africa.

Chapter 27

An officer and a clergyman: Jessee Neat

This story, titled "A different kind of service," was published in the December 2016 issue of FRANK magazine. The Rev. William Jessee Neat retired as rector of the Church of the Ascension in downtown Frankfort in 2019. One addition to this story is what two women, who were married by Father Jessee, had to say about him on his farewell Sunday at Church of the Ascension. Neat is also a retired U.S. Army officer.

On the morning of the 2016 presidential election, Jessee Neat sits in his downtown office and talks about war and peace and voting and vacationing.

Since 2011, the Rev. William Jessee Neat has been rector of the Church of the Ascension on Washington Street. Before becoming an Episcopal priest, Neat served 21 years as a commissioned officer in the U.S. Army Military Police Corps and retired as a lieutenant colonel in 1996.

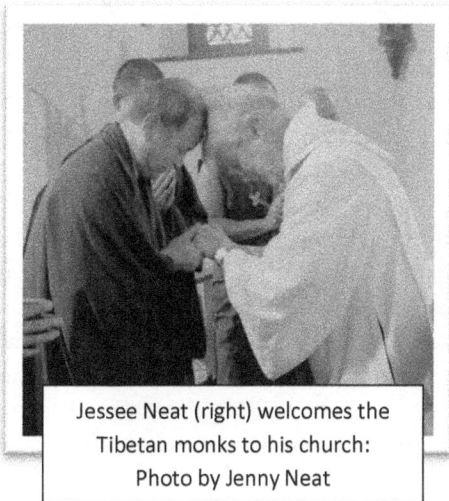

Jessee Neat (right) welcomes the Tibetan monks to his church: Photo by Jenny Neat

He always seems to have a calm presence but Neat admits he's anxious about the election.

"A large segment of the population has been ignored or overlooked and this election process has exposed that. It's like opening up a wound and maybe some folks didn't even know it was there.

"I'm anxious, regardless of which one wins, how this will be addressed. Clearly at no time since the Roaring '20s, when we had robber barons going full blast," has the chasm between the poor and the rich been so massive. It's created a tremendous sense of unease and inequality."

"Whether intentionally or unintentionally, over several decades the way in which our elected officials and our economic and political systems have functioned has robbed people of their personal dignity and their ability to rise up."

As a parish priest, he often gets asked for election advice. This year Neat advised Episcopalians to read their baptismal covenant.

"I told them to take seriously that which they have promised, especially the last two items of the covenant, and then prayerfully vote their conscience."

The last two items say, "Seek and serve Christ in all persons, loving your neighbor as yourself," and "Strive for justice and peace among all people, and respect the dignity of every human being."

Neat is asked if he will respect the presidential winner, whether it's Hillary Clinton or Donald Trump.

After a pause, he answers, "With God's help, I will endeavor to do so. While I'm a priest, I'm still an Army officer. I did not resign my commission. I'm a retired Army officer subject to recall. Therefore, regardless of who occupies the office of president, I have to be mindful of that.

"That's not necessarily an easy thing to do, but I have sworn to uphold the Constitution and I have not revoked that."

In addition to upholding his baptismal covenant, Neat says he had to decide which candidate "would best represent us as president, who is the face of our nation to the world," and which one would have the best temperament and disposition to act as commander-in-chief.

"The military doesn't get to vote on whether they want to agree with a decision the commander-in-chief makes."

His thoughts on war

In the Army from 1975 until 1996, Neat served two tours of duty in South Korea, in 1986-1988 and 1995-1996. While he was never in war, he witnessed riots and plenty of violence and crimes while spending almost seven years in the Army's criminal investigations division.

"In a perfect universe there wouldn't be war," Neat says. "And from a religious perspective, war surely makes God weep. War is evil, bottom line . . . and sometimes war becomes the lesser of evils.

"Perhaps because of having a law enforcement and military police background, I see the military on a continuum from the police on the street.

"I wish we lived in a world where the police weren't necessary. But we know better than that. Somebody has to be there to keep order. Sometimes as a result of that, deadly force ends up having to be employed through self-defense, or in stopping someone from harming others."

Using that analogy, the armed forces preserve and defend the peace of the nation on the global stage, Neat says. He believes in going to war only "when all else has failed, and there is a clear or present eminent danger.

"I've often said I wish we put as many resources in our department of state – and were willing to go the extra mile to create the circumstances where war was not used – as we are willing to throw into our department of defense."

Neat says most of the old soldiers he knows aren't war hawks.

"I know a few hawks but I don't know many officers that are. I wish politicians and hawks had to see the human carnage and damage and suffering they cause. If you took the time to look at a body that had been blown into smithereens, and to deal with the sadness and tragedy of killing, and you had to bear responsibility for decisions you make, I suspect there would be less conflict.

"I know it's not possible but I've often said no commander-in-chief should employ the forces unless they're prepared to be on the front line."

The day after the November 8 election, Neat and his wife, Jenny, left on a week's vacation to rustic Fryemont Inn in Bryson City, North Carolina, in the Great Smoky Mountains. Although they didn't intentionally schedule it right after the election, he said it was good timing to be away from TV.

Jenny is a stained-glass artist and iconographer. She's also an animal angel. For almost four years, she's been a volunteer transporter and coordinator for The Way Home Rescue Alliance in Midway.

The Neats have a son, Will, and two granddaughters living in Morgantown, West Virginia.

Jessee met Jenny in law enforcement classes at Eastern Kentucky University. She was from Lexington and he grew up in rural Adair County.

Band program taught him discipline

He played in the Adair County High School band in Columbia from the sixth grade through his senior year.

"My principal instrument was the B-flat cornet. I would pinch-hit on the baritone. I was not a percussionist but we lost our base drummer and I got stuck in there to play it in August 1970 at the State Fair.

"Year after year we would come in second or third, and that was the first year in recent memory we won first place in our class."

Neat says he knew about hard work from growing up on a farm – raising tobacco and milking cows.

"But being in band instilled a great deal of discipline. Our band director was retired Army warrant officer Walter Tooley. He played Army shows with Benny Goodman, Glenn Miller and Dick Powell.

"If you read Jesse Stuart's book, 'Mr. Gallion's School,' I was told there's a character named Shan Hanigan who was modeled off of Tooley. After he got out of the military Tooley finished his degree work at Morehead State University and got somehow in the loop with Jesse Stuart in Greenup County.

"I credit Mr. Tooley's coaching and mentorship in the band for giving me the discipline and the encouragement and a sense that I could do something. I think that's also what got me interested in the military."

Neat says he was an above-average student, academically, "but certainly not a straight-A student."

He enrolled at EKU in 1971, "and I was able to see that getting a degree in law enforcement and being affiliated with ROTC worked really well. There was a cadet military police company there and I became a part of that. To this day, many of us still hang out together."

Neat earned his bachelor's from EKU in 1975. While in the Army, he received a master's in administration of justice from Wichita State University in 1981. Then in 1999, he got his master of divinity degree from The General Theological Seminary of the Episcopal Church in New York City.

God and religion were always important

Growing up on Neat Hollow Road in Adair County, near Neatsville and the Green River, Neat "for the most part went to my mother's people's Evangelical United Brethren Church. In 1968 the EUBs and Methodists merged and became United Methodists."

He says he enjoyed going to church as a child.

"I can never remember a time when I wasn't drawn to God, to religion," he says. "Sometimes if my parents weren't going to church on Sunday, I would end up riding my bicycle down to a Christian church not far from our house."

Jenny Neat says her father was Southern Baptist and her mother was Presbyterian.

"I grew up in a Southern Baptist church basically but when I was a teenager I started going to Mom's Presbyterian Church," she says. "In college when Jesse and I started dating, we began looking for a place we could agree on and that's how we ended up in the Episcopal church."

She says they were still quite conservative when they met at EKU.

In the military, the Neats moved about every two-and-a-half years. Besides Korea, they lived in nine states in America.

"The church provided a sense of a stable community," Jessee Neat says. "Regardless of where we went, we would almost always run into somebody who knew somebody we knew – either an Episcopal priest, chaplain or somebody in the service who was Episcopalian."

Life experiences, especially in the military, helped open their minds and hearts.

Experiencing the greater mix of humanity

"Just being able to see people from around the country – different religions, different races, different belief systems, Republicans, Democrats, Socialists, the greater mix of humanity – expanded my life view, my world view," Jessee Neat says.

"My sense of humanity evolved through experiences in military law enforcement. Seeing people I normally would not have had any reason to be up close to and studying their lives and what they did – that caused me to have to think an awful lot about what it meant to be a human being.

"We end up in the law enforcement business essentially defining the totality of someone's life oftentimes by an isolated incident of poor judgment or a horrible act. That something may have lasted for a brief 30 seconds and that becomes a definition of who a person is."

His first two-year tour in Korea probably made the greatest impact on Neat's way of thinking.

As a criminal investigations division commander, he was responsible for the southern two-thirds of South Korea as far as enforcing military justice as well as the U.S. criminal code as it pertained to soldiers and Army interests.

"All Western concepts are plopped down into an Oriental, Eastern society that in many respects is the complete opposite of what Western ideals and cultures embody. As Westerners, we focus on the individual and it's embodied in our Constitution. It's also very much embodied in our responsibility within most of Christianity."

In Daegu, Korea, population 2.5 million now, he was working with a culture and people who were largely defined by a Confucian understanding of society – "with the emphasis on the great whole more so than the individual. For example, bribery, or the accepted way of paying a share to your supervisor – those things don't work well with Western law."

He also was in a place where "you see children for sale. Some would say life was very cheap. But life is cheap where people are trying to survive.

"Living and working in that environment caused me to have to plumb the depths of everything I believed about Western philosophy and ideals and religion. It was an opportunity where life was sort of turned inside out to take a look at. Through all of that, I found that my faith grew deeper, but at the same time much broader."

An enchanting place to be

On Apsan Mountain above their house in Korea was a very old Buddhist temple and monastery. He loved listening to the chanting in the morning and evening.

"I would often hike up to Eunjeok Temple on weekends. Being there in that place and having always had some attraction to the mystical element of religion, I found the draw even much greater.

"So that began my quest for going much deeper inside. Through different practices of meditation, I learned about the rich tradition that Christianity had for centuries – contemplative prayer and the use of mantras."

South Korea was where Jessee first started feeling called to the seminary," Jenny Neat says. "I didn't know it was going on. It was later in Virginia he told me he thought he was supposed to go to the seminary. I was shocked.

"I wouldn't have been surprised if he had said a deacon because he had been so active in the church. But when he said priest, that surprised me.

I was OK with it but it came out of the blue. Obviously it hadn't come out of the blue for him."

For the last 25 years, Jessee Neat has been an associate of the Order of the Holy Cross, an Anglican Benedictine Community of Men. Twice a day – in the early morning and evening – Neat prays the Psalms, reads scripture and sits in silence for about 30 minutes.

"It keeps him grounded and open to listening to God," Jenny says. "I think he has a really good way with people, and talking to them about grief and so forth.

"He's thoughtful and he thinks before he answers questions. A lot of times people consider that to be an unsure thing. But it's him being more careful about his responses."

David Hurt, a vestry member at Church of the Ascension, says "Father Jessee is pretty much the same yesterday as he is today and will be tomorrow. Oftentimes in priests you find kind of mercurial personalities. It's reassuring to me in a lot of ways that we have somebody that's very stable. It's good for the finances and fundraising and business aspect of the church."

Neat has excellent organizational skills from his military career, Hurt says.

"Our vestry meetings used to be mass chaos. Once he showed up and got the committee structure set up, all the arguing got done in committee, and vestry meetings turned into quiet, short, business-like meetings. You didn't have to plan on staying all night."

Hurt also likes that Neat is "heavily into the meditative side of Christianity. I had never experienced that before he made me aware of it. I doubt I would still be in the church if it wasn't for being able to share meditation, contemplation, praying the Psalms regularly."

Hurt usually attends 9:15 daily morning prayers at the church, and the 5:15 p.m. silent service each Tuesday.

"Sunday service now is the least important part of the week for me," Hurt says.

Scott Kimbel, who rarely ever misses the one-hour silent service, says he likes Neat because "he's so inclusive. He accepts and embraces diversity. He's open and nonjudgmental about things like sexual orientation or one's station in life. He has a strong social justice point of view without being self-righteous.

"He's an excellent facilitator in terms of teaching, discussion, and allowing people to open up and feel free to say what's on their mind."

Opening the church to the world

About seven months after the U.S. Supreme Court ruled in June 2015 that the Constitution guarantees a right to same-sex marriage, Neat officiated at the Saturday, January 23, 2016 wedding of two women, Kristi Ann Buffenmyer and Laura Kathleen Napier, before a large crowd in Church of the Ascension.

When Father Jessee retired as rector in 2019, Laura and Kristi spoke at his farewell Sunday at Church of the Ascension. Laura said, "On September 13, 2012, our hearts were broken. The church we had attended, where we had hoped to raise the girls to know and serve God, basically told us that we could not participate in classes as a family because Kristi and I were in a relationship.

"I was upset and ready to give up hope of finding a church. But Kristi acted. It became her mission to find a church that loved us, welcomed our family, and would help us raise the girls to know and love Christ."

After Kristi read about the Episcopal Church, she sent an email explaining their situation to Church of the Ascension, Laura said. "Less than two hours later, Father Jessee replied, saying, 'Dear Kristi and Laura: I am so sorry to learn of your deep and painful hurt. I pray that you may find solace in knowing that the love of Christ is for all God's children for we are all Christ's sisters and brothers. Please know that you and your children are most welcome to worship here at Ascension.'

"We took a leap of faith and started attending the next Sunday," Laura said. "Father Jessee was right. The church welcomed us and much to our surprise we were invited to receive Holy Communion.

"We started attending regularly and eventually we brought the girls with us. From the beginning the girls have felt comfortable with Father Jessee. He took the time to know them and to let them know at 13 years of age they are important to the church. He has always had time to speak with us, to guide us through decisions, to laugh with us, and give us advice, even when it wasn't something we wanted to hear. He would remind us to pay attention to what and where the Lord was calling us."

Kristi said, "Father Jessee has been with our family every step of the way in our journey to a new faith, a new way and a new path. He baptized the girls, and confirmed our faith as Episcopalians and the girls. Our family

172

is a product of his guidance. He has been more than a priest. He is our mentor, our confidant, and our counselor.

"Father Jessee has taught us about social justice. Believe it or not, we had lived in our own world hoping no one would bother us or pay attention to us. He has fought for us to be like everyone else. Imagine our surprise attending our first-ever Lexington Pride event and running into our priest. Father Jessee made us feel like we weren't any different from any other family and quite honestly, we never felt that way before. He gave us a voice and let us know we truly are loved by Christ and all of us are sisters and brothers."

Neat organized a communitywide prayer service at Church of the Ascension following the June 17, 2015 massacre at Emanuel African Methodist Episcopal Church in which nine were shot and killed during a prayer service in Charleston, South Carolina.

He held another ecumenical prayer service in June of this year after 49 were killed and 53 wounded in a popular gay nightclub in Orlando, Florida, in the worst mass shooting in American history. Neat was elated that the Roman Catholic bishop of Lexington and the Episcopal bishop of Louisville shared the pulpit and liturgy with him.

Neat also was involved in advocating for the Fairness Ordinance, which was approved by the Frankfort City Commission.

In 2013 and again in 2015, Neat invited a group of Tibetan Buddhist monks – refugees living in Tashi Kyil monastery in India and touring the U.S. – to have cultural programs and a traditional Tibetan Dinner at Church of the Ascension to help raise funds for their monastery.

"As Anglicans we've always been open to the community around us," Neat said. "The walls and doors have been very permeable. God created the world and all that's in it, and said it was good, according to our scripture.

"For me and our congregation, we think it's important to have that kind of up-close and personal relationship with those not always like us. We can learn from them and contrast in a good way. We certainly realize we're all in this world together, and are committed to many of the same things like reconciliation, peace and harmony."

Christians are to be hospitable, Neat said, and welcoming the monks "is a logical thing to do because we have the space and a good location. Like Christian monks and nuns, the Tibetan monks are dedicated to a way of life that sets them apart.

"They're at peace with who they are and it radiates. People can see and sense holiness, even if they can't name it. That's one of the things that makes them so enjoyable to be around."

Peace on Earth season?

The election is over. The people of the 50 states are not united.

Although Hillary Clinton won the popular vote by more than 2.8 million, Donald Trump outscored her 304-227 in electoral votes and will be sworn in as the 45th president on January 20, 2017.

Thanksgiving is over. Christmas is almost here . . . that hopeful season of Peace on Earth.

The Episcopal rector in Frankfort feels a deep inner peace and joy at Christmas, despite all the violence, hatred and injustice throughout the world.

"Through the mystery of the incarnation, God became and walked around as one of us – both fully human and fully divine. God got actively involved and we believe God is still actively involved. Jesus taught us a way to hold together and not destroy each other, similar to what the Buddha taught and similar to the tenets of all the major religions.

"The Christmas message is that God chose to go through the experience of being a human, ultimately into its most cruel manner. So God understands and feels a child being pounded and ultimately killed in Aleppo, Syria.

"God feels and suffers for that child, that person who has been sold into sexual slavery, wherever that may be. God feels and suffers with that junkie . . . and with that person who is trying to get into a country that has so much and so much opportunity. God understands through Jesus what it's like to be a refugee . . . what's it's like to be a murder victim.

"God understands what it's like to be crying out for justice and mercy and to have the political establishment turn on them. God understands what it's like to be tempted in every way as we are.

"The message of Christmas is one of the divine coming down and touching humanity and pulling up the human to the divine. The marriage of the human and the divine is there for us all to grasp and accept."

Most days, Neat's job as a parish priest is uplifting. He says he likes being a spiritual leader, a teacher and encouraging people.

"I enjoy sharing with them what I've learned along the way, and what has and hasn't worked, and let them figure out what works for them.

It's very rewarding to be a coach for people on a spiritual quest, to sort of walk that journey with them, to see how people can be changed and will be changed in their faith journey."

On the other hand, there's the death part of his job.

"I've lost count of how many people I've buried." But it's never easy experiencing grief with families.

"There's usually no answer for why. Sometimes there is. You get old, you get worn out and you die. None of us are going to get out of this alive. But when a 15 year old dies because a doctor wrote the wrong prescription and it was administered by a parent and it killed him, where's the answer for a parent?

"I just have to go back to scripture, chant the Psalms and sit in silence to turn over to God that which I can't understand. Let God be God."

That's the way it was in 1993 when Jessee and Jenny Neat's best friends in Adair County, veterinarian Joe Wellnitz, his wife Beth, and their son, Dennis, were brutally murdered in their home.

When it's Jessee Neat's time to die, he says the highest compliment that could be etched on his tombstone would be the words, "He did his best."

So far, the 63-year-old priest has seemed to live his life the way Mahatma Gandhi suggested: "We must be the change we wish to see."

Chapter 28

Q & A with Dr. Chuck Queen

Several years after interviewing Dr. Chuck Queen, senior pastor at Immanuel Baptist Church, for a feature story in The State Journal's Sunday Spectrum section, I returned to his church office in February 2016 for a question-and-answer session.

Q: I was reading last night a belief that the miracle of the loaves and fishes in the Bible could have actually been the crowd taking what they had been given and sharing it with others.

A: Parker Palmer, a writer I like, a Quaker, he kind of takes that (view) on it, where it probably wasn't a real miracle where Jesus was multiplying the bread and loaves. Maybe the miracle story kind of emerged out of that experience where people shared their food with each other. And maybe that's the greater miracle, people sharing what they have with others.

Q: That could be a miracle today.

A: Oh yeah, we don't want to share much of anything. And with Trump, it's all about winning. (Laughter)

Q: Is that scary to you, Trump winning?

A: As a president, yes. That ought to be scary to anybody with common sense. I can't even imagine the possibility. To even suggest the possibility that he could be president is really a sad reflection on where we are as a country.

Q: What are your thoughts on the miracle of the loaves and fishes?

A: I read the miracle stories in the Gospels first and foremost as parables, metaphors, symbols, as poetry ... religious language that is intended to convey spiritual and theological meaning. Some of the miracles are simply the good news in parable, I think. Now having said that, I would also say the historical Jesus was most likely recognized in his time as a miracle worker. What does that mean? I don't know fully what that means.

He was known as a healer. Did he heal people? I think he did. How did he heal people? I don't know.

Q: Do you think there are healers today?

A: I do and I think there's more to it than just chemical interactions. I think there is a real spiritual dimension to it that's even more than a psychological dimension. Again, I can't explain how that works but I do believe there is a spiritual aspect and dimension to healing. I'm not a healer.

Q: Do you wish you were?

A: Well, I wish I could make people whole, sure. I think that anybody with goodwill towards others, with any compassion for others, would love to be able to do that. And I think that applies to our own self. There are times I wish I could make myself whole. There are times I'm as broken and in need of healing as anyone else.

The late Henri Nouwen had a wonderful book called "The Wounded Healer" in which he said, how can we be spiritual healers of others if we haven't experienced that brokenness in our own soul and appropriated the healing grace and love of God? A Catholic, he's one of my favorite spiritual writers.

Q: Do you still read a lot?

A: Not as much as I used to. But I don't know how you grow if you don't read and expose yourself to new ideas. I try to as much as I can.

Healing, to me, it's a mystery. I think faith is a big part of healing, trust in the process ... in a source greater than ourselves ... trust that the Divine in us is capable of healing us, liberating us, freeing us from a lot of stuff. There are more kinds of healing than just physical healing. And I think it's all intricately connected – the physical and the spiritual – and connected in different ways with different people. That's why there's no formula, no prescription for healing. There are no seven steps or four spiritual laws. Every person is unique in their makeup – physically, biologically, genetically, spiritually, psychologically. I think healing has to be unique to each person, but I certainly believe there is that spiritual dimension to it.

Q: Who are your main spiritual teachers?

A: I've learned from a lot of people. I mentioned Henri Nouwen as one. If I had to narrow it down, I would say there are two people who have mentored me in the spiritual life more than anybody else through their writings, Richard Rohr and Marcus Borg, and I don't know them personally. However, I did have some correspondence with Richard and he endorsed one of my books. I recommend their writings.

(On the back cover of Queen's 2011 book, "A Faith Worth Living: The Dynamics of an Inclusive Gospel," Rohr says, "Why are there not hundreds of teachers and pastors saying what this book is saying? Chuck Queen is faith-filled, intelligent, and honest, and does not let theory get in the way of Christian good sense and Christian good love. Read and be fed!")

There have been many others. I've recently discovered J. Philip Newell, who is in the Celtic Christian tradition. John Dominic Crossan and Hans Kung are others.

Q: Marcus Borg, did he write "Meeting Jesus Again for the First Time?"

A: Yes, and that was one of the first books that really set me on the path that I'm on now. That little book made a huge difference in my life when I first read it.

Q: Have you read a lot of Thomas Merton?

A: I haven't. I've read some. For some reason I find Merton hard to read. I think he's deep and I respect him. But in that same kind of tradition, I've gravitated more toward Richard Rohr and Henri Nouwen.

Q: Do you believe certain humans can communicate with people in the spirit world?

A: I think it's a real possibility. That's about as far as I can go with it. I don't know any people who can, but I don't deny that there may be people who can. I just think there's more to this world than what we can reduce to the materialistic. I think there are dimensions and aspects to the world, the universe, that are beyond us. I'm perfectly comfortable living within that mystery.

Let's take a simple thing as prayer. I can't explain prayer and don't even attempt to. I don't know how it works. I don't believe God is intervening into the world in direct ways. Yet, at the same time, I think that somehow in the intricacies and intimacies of the spirit world and the physical world, there are powers and forces at work where prayer affects things.

Q: Do you think a silent prayer is just as effective as a vocal prayer?

A: Absolutely. You're speaking mentally, you're just not saying the words. So you are projecting these thoughts, these images, out of yourself, and how those affect the world and people and things around you – there is where the mystery is. But there's no question that it does.

A simple experiment of a person walking into a room, who reflects a particular demeanor, affects that room, impacts that room. There's the energy. I think it's the same way with prayer – there's energy that is projected that impacts the world around us.

There's a transforming power of love because love is such a powerful, positive force that really has the power to deeply change and transform people.

Q: Do you love Donald Trump?

(Laughter)

A: I can't say that I do. Let me put it this way. It's a good question, how do you respond to people like that, to Donald Trump or total jerks? Do I feel love for that person? I wish I did, and I would pray that I would. But I'm not there yet. But maybe I can be.

I try to recognize when I look at people like that, I try to see beyond all that stuff and realize in spite of all that, there's a real person there who is infinitely loved by God as much as I am loved by God … who is a child of God, just the way I'm a child of God.

I'm a universalist in the sense that I believe eventually, everyone, Donald Trump included, and Hitler, is going to be redeemed. Part of that process of redemption is shedding all that stuff – love for power, egotism, being consumed by greed, whatever it is – and recognizing who one really is as a child of God, and being receptive to Divine love and being changed by Divine love. That is a real difficult process. None of us have completely arrived.

Q: What do you think happens when we die?

A: (He pauses.) I used to be able to tell you real quick. But honestly, I don't know. I hope that what will happen is what I just talked about. My hope is we go on, the spirit goes on, that the core and substance and heart of who we are continues. I believe that's the case, but I don't know that.

My Christian tradition teaches that there is vindication and there is more to come. And if not, then life really is unfair. There are people who really get shafted in life. So you hope there is more to life than this life. I'm living my life on the basis of that faith that there is more to come. I hope there is because I love life.

Q: Of all that you've read and studied, do you think that Jesus felt that he was the only son of God?

A: No. I think he believed himself to be not the one and only son of God, but I believe he understood himself to be a son of God. Personally, I don't think he would have regarded himself as God in flesh. I look to Jesus as the Incarnation of the Divine in a very complete sense. So for me, Jesus is a definitive revelation of God. Is he the only revelation of God? No. Do I believe there are other mediators? Yes I do. For me personally, Jesus is my definitive mediator and revelation of God. But I can't say that's true for everybody.

I don't believe he felt himself the only revelation of God. I think he felt himself intimately related and connected to God. I think out of that experience of God that he spoke of God, and affected how he read his Scriptures, how he interpreted his tradition, why he took on the religious establishment, why the open table became a symbol of the good news that he proclaimed – this inclusive welcome and acceptance of all different kinds of people, because I think that's how he experienced God. I think out of this experience of God, he became the person he was and how he lived his life, and why he taught love your neighbor as yourself; why he said love your enemies and pray for them. In that particular teaching, he bases his teaching on the character of God. He says love your enemies, pray for them, do good by them because this is how God treats all people. He healed all kinds of people, welcomed all to the table, broke down boundaries, extended God's compassion and grace to all people. It was his experience of the Divine, I have no doubt, that led him to be the kind of person he was.

I would say he knew himself to be son of God. That has evolved in the Christian tradition. Jesus was a Jew. He never saw himself other than a Jew. He looked upon himself as a Jewish reformer. He was trying to reform his tradition.

Son of God in the Hebrew tradition could have meant several things. Israel was called son of God. The nation was called son of God. Heavenly messengers were called sons of God. Son of God simply referred to a representative of God, someone who was acting on behalf of God.

He experienced God in such a way that he felt compelled to speak of God and reflect the God that he knew. I think a part of his mission was to reform his tradition, to help bring this aspect of welcome and acceptance and grace so it was at the forefront of his own tradition. So I see him as a Jewish reformer and of course it got him into all kinds of trouble. It got him killed.

The establishment, the gatekeepers, saw him as a threat, not a violent threat, but a threat. I believe it was his nonviolence that was a threat to the establishment. He wasn't afraid to take on religious laws and religious institutions, practices that he felt were detrimental to human need, which were life-diminishing rather than life-enhancing. He could see the negative aspects of religion, and I think he wanted to change that, and it got him in lots of trouble.

Q: Would you talk about the gap, why the Bible leaves out many years of Jesus' life?

A: We have this episode in Luke when he was a boy, when he went into the temple where his parents were looking for him. And that's all we have. We begin with his baptism by John, which, by the way, that's where you had this experience, all three synoptic Gospels have it, Matthew, Mark and Luke, where Jesus is baptized, the heavens open, the dove descends, the heavenly voice says, 'You are my son in whom I am well pleased.'

Again, I don't take that literally, but I take it seriously. What I think it points to is some sort of experience that he had that he realized his true identity as a son of God. He experienced being loved by God. He experienced God's favor. I think out of that experience, which in some sense was an ongoing experience, he drew power for his work and ministry. So that's where the story starts. The Gospels are not history books.

Q: What does your mind say that Jesus was doing in those years where there's a gap?

A: He was growing up, learning, working, maturing, developing.

Q: Do you think he was doing a lot of meditating, centering prayer?

A: Yeah, I do. I think he cultivated a prayer life.

Q: The 40 days in the desert?

A: I think the 40 days and 40 nights is the connection with Israel, with his people. That whole wilderness story of being in the desert, to track through the wilderness, through the desert for 40 years. The symbolism of that is that the desert is a time of solitude, of testing, a time of trying to discern the will of God, the purpose of God. That's how I read it. This was a time in his life where he was figuring it out.

Q: Like the Buddha sitting under the Bodhi tree?

A: Yeah, I think so, trying to discern the voice of God in the midst of all the other voices. Luke and Matthew have those three temptations. Probably the symbolism of that is here are these other voices, compelling interests trying to pull him away from what he senses his mission to be. Competing for attention. I think that's true of all of us. That's what Nouwen and Merton and Thomas Keating and others emphasize: centering prayer and solitude. The significance of all that is, you're trying to pull yourself away from all that noise and commotion and the clutter and all the competing interests and kind of discern what is the true voice. Call it your true self. Call it God. Call it the Holy Spirit, whatever terminology you feel

181

comfortable with. But you're trying to hear that deeper, larger self that is calling you to something more, something larger.

Q: And it's tough. There are all sorts of voices.

A: Yeah, it is. Nouwen compares it, when you first start to withdraw into solitude, to monkeys jumping around in a banana tree. But what he says is you just keep doing it even though nothing happens. It's the discipline of doing it, training your mind … and eventually, the monkeys start to quiet down.

Q: Do you do centering prayer?

A: I do periods of solitude. I don't have a particular time or way, but I have to have solitude. I cannot live a spiritual life without some solitude. Sometimes it's in the morning when I wake up, and it drives me crazy sometimes if the TV is on because I need solitude, the quiet. I need to have everything be still so I can focus and center and listen. There's a listening to that deeper self. It can be here in my office, home in my bedroom, in a car, or out on the lake.

If I go for any period of time and I haven't had a time of solitude, I can tell. I get irritable and feel myself losing control. Most people go through life totally unaware of that. We're driven by circumstances, by those voices … whether it's to meet a deadline, whether it's to get a promotion. You feel these voices tearing at you, talking to you, all this chatter. You feel this tug, and a lot of people simply go through life being driven by those types of things and they never pause to ask who am I really? What do we really need? What is really best for us? So we're driven from one thing to another thing. It's true in my profession, ministers who are simply driven by the institution, growing the institution, being successful as a minister, building the institution.

Q: I feel really blessed I got on this path. But I don't know how it happened.

A: Me either. All we can say is it is grace.

Q: How does pro football connect with love?

(Laughter)

A: The only thing I can say is I love to root for the Cincinnati Bengals. It's a violent sport. Geez. I think it's going to be around for a long time. The whole phenomena of sports teams are interesting. There's a sense in which it's no different than life in general. Everything in our world, the world that we know and function in, is competition and comparison. We have to function in that world to a certain extent. Now I think a big part of the spiritual life is withdrawing from that world, stepping out of that world and living in a different world. You could say that's the kingdom of God.

Q: Giving it up?

A: Just living in an alternative world. Could you imagine a society not based on competition or comparison? What would it look like? It's hard to imagine. I think Jesus, when he talked about the kingdom of God – and I think he uses that term simply because it was subversive – what he meant by kingdom was totally different than what Rome meant by kingdom.

Q: And his kingdom was?

A: The kingdom of love, the kingdom of grace, of reconciliation.

Q: So get rid of all competition?

A: Yeah. Think about it. The disciples are debating about who's going to be greatest when Jesus comes into his kingdom. James and John say can we sit on your left and right? They're thinking power, glory, position, prestige. That's how kingdoms of the world function. What does Jesus say to them? 'No, if you want to be the greatest, you have to be the servant of all.' What he was really saying is you have to give up the idea of being great at all because that's not what my kingdom is about. He's saying who gets in first will be last and the last will be first. It's a total reversal of the way the world functions. When Jesus says 'blessed are the poor. . .,' that's crazy, radical stuff; and how in the world are the poor blessed? 'Blessed are you who mourn, for you will be comforted. Blessed are the peacemakers, for yours is the kingdom of God. Blessed are you when you are persecuted for my name's sake.' That's crazy stuff.

Q: Would that be some of your favorite Scriptures?

A: Well, it's some that drives me crazy because I realize I've got a long way to go to experience life that way. I still have a lot of growing to do.

Q: So maybe that's why we have to come back?

A: A big part of the spiritual life is about letting go. When Jesus talked about repenting, that's really what he's talking about. Surrendering, letting go, relinquishing. Letting go of the ego stuff, this need for power and position, and need to accumulate and be successful. That's deeply embedded in us and saying goodbye to that is the work of the spiritual life. You have to just keep working at it. It's really hard to do. But that's a big part of what love is, letting go of that kind of stuff where your focus and attention is on your true self and on the good and wellbeing of others, rather than your own needs.

Of course the paradox is, you have to have a strong ego to let go of one, because self-loathing is just as egotistic as self-inflating. If I'm going

183

around saying, 'woe is me, I'm terrible, I'm a nobody,' what good is that going to do anybody? I'm just as focused on myself in an ego-deflated mode as an ego-inflated mode. I'm still focused on self. Letting go of the ego is where the focus goes off of the self and on to a larger reality, a greater story than just my own little self. Now I have to love myself to love others. If I'm going to love somebody, I'm only going to love them as much as I love myself. So there's the paradox.

Q: How do you feel you've grown spiritually since 2010 when I wrote the "Evolution of Faith" story about you in The State Journal newspaper?

A: I'm not sure I can answer that. The spiritual life is three steps forward and two steps back. Sometimes it's three steps forward and four steps back. Sometimes we regress rather than progress. That's the winding nature of the journey. I measure spirituality in terms of attentiveness to the larger story and the greater reality – God and the world. Am I more attuned to that? Am I more in touch with that? Do I have a greater sense of who I am in God? I hope so. But I can't tell you whether I do or not.

Q: The sexual-orientation issue has come up more since then, and you took a stand and supported gay marriage.

A: It was the right thing to do. Would I have done that had I been in a different situation, if I had really feared for my job? I don't know. I hope I would have.

Q: In the 2010 story you said the evolving spiritual voyage doesn't end and "that's the beauty of it."

A: I don't think we ever fully arrive. I think it's all about the journey. So we're always evolving. I'm not sure the early Christians envisioned it that way. I think probably in their thinking there was some sort of perfection, and that's where we get images of heaven and that sort of thing. But I don't sense that. I don't believe we ever fully arrive, that we reach that absolute point. It's just a part of who we are, what we are. It's the nature of the universe, to evolve, to change. Death and rebirth.

Q: So did Jesus talk about eternal life?

A: Did he or didn't he? One thing that scholars are pretty certain about, he talked about the kingdom of God. Yeah, there are passages where Jesus mentions eternal life. In the Gospel of John, life is one of the dominant images. Jesus talks about eternal life frequently. Now was that the early community's take on Jesus or was that really the historical Jesus? Who knows? Did the historical Jesus actually talk about eternal life? Or did he talk about the kingdom of God and the early Christians read that as eternal life. I don't know.

Q: **In those lost years of Jesus' life, do you think he was with people who were talking about meditation or centering prayer or mindfulness?**

A: Prayer was a rich part of his tradition. He was a Jew. Mostly vocal prayer, but I think silent prayer was a part of the Jewish spiritual tradition. I think he knew that.

Q: **How did he learn the practice of quietening his mind?**

A: It was probably more from his own experience than anything. Silent prayer, solitude, has always been a part of the mystical tradition of all great religions – Islam, Judaism, Buddhism. He didn't invent it. Why did he gravitate toward it? I don't know. But I don't think it was unique to him in Judaism. I think you can argue that Jesus was a really, really good Jew. He had no intention of starting a new religion. He was about reforming his own tradition.

Q: **Do you think Jesus was married?**

A: No. I think it's a real stretch to try to argue from the little bits and pieces that we have that he was married.

Q: **Do you still read the Bible a lot?**

A: Oh yeah.

Q: **Do you gain new insight all the time?**

A: Yeah, I think so. Growing up as a conservative, I had a deep respect for the Bible, even worshipping the Bible, the Bible was God. For many Christians, the Bible is God. But I never lost my love for the text, and my interest in the text. The way I read the text and the way I appropriate the text has truly changed 180 degrees. But my love for the text hasn't changed.

Q: **Do you love it all?**

A: I do. What I love about the Bible is the humanness of it. You have some wonderful, high-level, spiritually enlightened, potentially transformative passages and texts in the Bible, and at the same time, often in the same book, there are low-level, petty, punitive, regressive, life-diminishing texts as well. But what you have in the Bible are people on a journey. So it's three steps forward and two steps back. The beauty of those texts is their ability to self-correct and self-critique, which you have in scripture. That's why the Bible can be used for good and evil. An unenlightened person will use the Bible in unenlightened ways and vice versa. An enlightened person, a changed person, a converted person will use the Bible – the same texts – in an enlightened way, and a transformative way.

185

Q: What are some of your favorite chapters in the Bible?

A: I love the Sermon on the Mount, Matthew 5-7; First Corinthians 13, that love passage is a great text; Romans 8 is a wonderful passage. I love the little book of Jonah. It's protest literature. It challenges the popular theology of the day. I like Job too. It's a great one. It's protest literature. Ecclesiastes – literature like that. Some of the passages of the prophets have the capacity to challenge conventional religion and the popular theology of the day. That's where you get both, and that's the ability of the texts to correct itself.

Those challenging parts were not edited out. They were allowed to stand. That's a unique thing. You can have conflicting, contradictory teachings, sayings, theology in the same book. Apparently in those communities, the final editor or editors let it stand. I think they were much more comfortable living with inconsistency and contradiction and differences of perspective than we are today.

Q: So we haven't evolved much?

A: No. I often say we can't be past the adolescent stage in our spiritual evolution when you look at society as a whole. We've got a long way to go.

Chapter 29

Pilgrimage to Mecca

I haven't done any international traveling in my lifetime. But I feel an intimate connection to numerous places around the world because of friends I've met through the years who have lived in other countries or traveled internationally. I love listening to their stories. I met Ashiq Mohammad Zaman in 2001 and interviewed him several times for stories in The State Journal. When I was invited to serve on the Frankfort Interfaith Council in 2014, I got to know Ashiq much better. The diversity on our council is what makes it special. In the fall of 2016, not long after Ashiq and his wife, Saika Aktar, returned from their pilgrimage to Mecca, Ashiq spoke to the interfaith council about their special journey. His talk inspired me to write about Ashiq and Saika's experience, which became the cover story for the January 2017 FRANK magazine.

Muslims usually prepare for hajj – their pilgrimage to Mecca – as if they're not coming back.

For Ashiq Zaman, president of the Islamic Center of Frankfort, that included in 2016 "making a will, cleaning up as much as possible all un-Islamic practices in life, saying goodbyes to loved ones and promising to remember them in prayers during hajj," the annual Islamic pilgrimage to Mecca in Saudi Arabia.

"We prepared in such a way that hajj was our final journey and we were not coming back home. If I come back, so be it. If I don't, so be it. That's the mentality and it was not an easy task."

For the past 1,500 years, all Muslims making the trip have left their homes with the understanding death is a possibility, Zaman said.

In 1990 a pilgrimage ended in tragedy when the ventilation system failed in a crowded pedestrian tunnel and 1,426 people were either suffocated or trampled to death in a stampede.

On September 24, 2015, 769 pilgrims were killed in a stampede at Mina as they made their way to Jamarat for the symbolic stoning of the devil ritual, according to Saudi officials. A construction crane fell over the mosque during a storm and killed around 130 in 2015 as well.

"However, according to the count of countries who lost their citizens, the death toll was as high as 1,200," Zaman said. "Similar incidences in 2006 killed 350 people."

Two million Muslims participated

Hajj is the largest annual gathering of people in the world. In 2016, when Zaman and his wife, Saika Aktar, successfully completed the pilgrimage, two million Muslims participated. In 2010 through 2012, almost three million pilgrims were there.

Zaman, who has a master's in civil engineering, is a branch manager for the state Department of Revenue. Aktar is a medical school graduate. Natives of Bangladesh, Zaman has lived in Frankfort since 1994 and Aktar since 1995.

Hajj is one of the five pillars of Islam. It's a mandatory religious duty that must be carried out at least once in a lifetime by all adult Muslims who are physically and financially capable of undertaking the journey.

"My wife and I considered ourselves in that category and felt hajj was an obligation on us," Zaman said. "We had been thinking of doing the pilgrimage the last few years. But the means seemed always a little bit out of our reach as the expense was going up every year. In 2016, however, we managed to arrange the money and decided to go."

Zaman said the entire 20-day trip in September cost $20,000.

"The minimum would have been $15,000, but we decided to go for a little longer so we could visit other historic sites and see my younger sister and her husband, who live in Saudi Arabia. I had seen my sister a few times over the years including last May in Bangladesh after our father died. But I hadn't seen her husband in 15 years.

"They made the trip to Mecca from Riyadh, an 11-hour bus ride, to meet us. We spent a couple of good days with them after the hajj rituals."

Zaman, 52, said hajj is "extremely physically challenging. We have to walk a lot and sleep very little. I played basketball and soccer so I thought I was physically prepared. I was wrong. It requires miles and miles of walking . . . some days 10 miles."

He said he lost 10 pounds on the trip.

Pilgrims have to complete tawaf three times as part of hajj.

"Tawaf means circling the Kaaba seven times, counterclockwise," Zaman said. "The Kaaba was the first house on the earth and the circling symbolizes our love for Allah (God), and demonstrates the unity among Muslims as we move together in harmony while praying to Allah.

"Completing a tawaf may take an hour to an hour-and-a-half, depending on the distance of the person from the Kaaba. The area closer to the Kaaba is not shaded and is the most crowded. We were close to the Kaaba, but not close enough to touch it.

"It is not part of hajj or even recommended to touch the Kaaba during circling. But people out of their respect do touch it. It's recommended to kiss the black stone located on one corner of the Kaaba. We could not and did not even try to go there because of the crowd."

Muslims also have to complete sa'ay twice in the trip, which is walking seven times between the hills of Safa and Marwah, located near the Kaaba. The total distance is a little more than two miles.

"But this place is now entirely enclosed and this ritual can be completed through an air-conditioned tunnel," Zaman said.

Since returning to Frankfort Zaman has spoken to several groups about his pilgrimage, including the Frankfort Interfaith Council and a Kentucky State University "cultural responsiveness" education class. He also was recently invited to speak about the Islam religion at South Frankfort Presbyterian Church's Counterpoints Sunday school class.

Giving a brief history about sa'ay, Zaman said according to Islamic tradition, Allah commanded Abraham to leave his wife Hagar and their infant son alone in the desert between the hills of Safa and Marwah. Hagar went in search of water when her provisions were exhausted.

"She went alone, leaving the infant Ishmael on the ground," Zaman said. "She first climbed the nearest hill, Safa, to look over the surrounding area. When she saw nothing, she went to the other hill, Marwah, to look around.

"She was able to see Ishmael while she was on either hillside and knew he was safe. However, when she was in the valley between the hills she was unable to see her son, and would thus run while in the valley and walk on the hillsides."

Hagar traveled back and forth between the hills seven times in the scorching heat before returning to her son, Zaman said.

"When she arrived she found that a spring had broken forth near her son's feet. This spring is now known as the Zamzam Well. Muslims imitate her during sa'ay by walking and running between the mountains."

He said water is the source of life and the city of Mecca grew because of the Zamzam Well.

Mecca is Islam's holiest city

As the birthplace of Prophet Muhammad ibn Abdallah and the site of his first revelation of the Quran, Mecca is regarded as the holiest city in the Islam religion.

Mecca houses the largest mosque in the world, the Masjid al-Haram. The mosque surrounds the Kaaba, the cube-shaped shrine in the heart of Mecca which Muslims around the world turn toward while offering daily prayers.

The Kaaba is granite masonry, covered with silk curtain and calligraphy in gold and silver-wrapped thread. The mosque covers 99 acres, including outdoor and indoor praying spaces, and can accommodate up to four million people.

There are around 112 grand gates for entrance, with 78 gates on the ground floor alone. The prayer hall has domes decorated with gilded calligraphy on the inside. The columns have marble panels. The floor of the prayer area is made of marble tiles. The area around the Kaaba is covered with colored marble tiles. The prayer area also extends to numerous plazas outside the mosque.

"The Masjid al-Haram campus is huge and moving from one point to another, walking is the only option. We have to move from place to place as part of hajj," Zaman said.

In modern times, Mecca has seen tremendous expansion in size and infrastructure. One of its amazing structures is the Abraj Al Bait, also known as the Makkah Royal Clock Tower Hotel, the world's fourth tallest building with the third largest amount of floor area.

Mecca has a resident population of about 2 million and more than 15 million Muslims visit Mecca annually, including several million during the few days of hajj. As a result, Mecca has become one of the most cosmopolitan cities in the Muslim world, despite the fact that non-Muslims are prohibited from entering the city.

Zaman and Aktar started their trip on September 1, flying from Cincinnati to Paris to Amman, Jordan, and then to Medina, Saudi Arabia.

Medina, a city of 1.2 million, is not a part of the pilgrimage.

"But we spent the first five days there, visiting Prophet Muhammad's mosque; graves of the prophet and many of his renowned companions; Kuba Mosque, the first mosque in Medina; the second battlefield in the history of Islam; and many other historic places. It was a very emotional time – yet peaceful and exciting time – as we had learned about those places in history lessons.

"I had prepared in my mind what I wanted to say at Prophet Muhammad's grave. But when I got there I was completely overwhelmed with emotion and forgot pretty much everything I wanted to say. After talking to other people I found out that's a common experience."

The prophet's two-tiered mosque has a floor area of more than four million square feet.

Their five-day stay in Medina also helped them "get rid of jet lag and adjust to the 110 to 114 degree weather," Zaman said. "Sleep deprivation is a major problem during hajj. The jet lag kept us awake the first few nights in Medina. The acclimation period to hot weather in Saudi Arabia also impacted our sleep.

"I didn't get any feeling that I was in a foreign country when we were in Medina, except for the weather temperature. It was an urban area like any modern city – with 5-Star hotels surrounding Prophet Muhammad's mosque – because millions of tourists visit there."

Then they traveled 280 miles by bus to Mecca.

"That's when we got a glimpse of real Saudi Arabia," he said. "It was complete barren land – nothing other than sand, desert and stone mountains. The blackish-colored mountains give a scary impression. It's unbelievable how people walked through that land 1,500 years ago, or traveled by camel."

They arrived at their hotel at Aziziah, a suburb of Mecca, about five miles from the Kaaba, at 2 a.m.

"We stayed in a single room with two semi-strangers and shared a bathroom for two days at Aziziah."

While there, they completed a "lesser pilgrimage called umrah," before doing hajj since it's permissible to combine both pilgrimages in the same trip.

During umrah, "when we saw the Kaaba for the first time, we were almost speechless because we've prayed toward that building five times a day all of our lives. We had seen so many pictures of the Kaaba numerous times. It was very emotional.

"The crowd was unbelievable and we completed one tawaf and one sa'ay during that two-day period. Then we moved from hotel living to staying in tents at Mina, a five mile bus trip that took 90 minutes because of the crowd. That was the beginning of the actual hajj rituals."

Staying in a tent city

There were 100,000 air-conditioned tents available with 50 people per tent. Thin, folding mattresses were separated by inches, Zaman said. Although men and women were in separate tents, Zaman and Aktar's tents were close.

Instead of port-a-potties, there were regular bathroom facilities, but because of long lines, it's best to "go there a half-hour or hour earlier than necessary," Zaman said.

"Three box meals a day were delivered to us. We spent the whole day resting in preparation for what comes on the second day of hajj, the most intense day."

Early the next morning, their group rode a bus nine miles to the plains of Mount Arafat, arriving about 8 a.m. They were required to be there, standing in vigil from noon through sunset, "praying, offering supplications, repenting for our sins, asking for forgiveness, seeking the mercy of God and listening to sermons from Islamic scholars," Zaman said. "Muhammad delivered his last sermon in Arafat.

"Millions of people were standing and I didn't see a dry eye. Everybody cried that day."

After sunset they left for Muzdalifah, six miles away, where they slept under the stars on sleeping bags in an open field, "inches from strangers." Zaman collected pebbles from under his sleeping bag for the next day's stoning of the devil ritual.

That night, Zaman and Aktar were permitted to sleep near each other.

"She was about five feet away from me," Zaman recalled.

Aktar said during the entire pilgrimage, she slept very little.

"There were just too many people in the desert. The night we slept outside, I slept no more than an hour."

She said while they were moving from place to place during the days of the pilgrimage, she had a fear she would get lost from her husband and never find him again in the massive crowd, even though they both had phones in their backpacks.

She tried to always keep one hand on his backpack.

192

They were allowed to take photographs during the five days of hajj, but decided not to because we didn't want our concentration to be distracted," Zaman said. The two sheets of clothing he wore could not have pockets, "so I would have had to always hold the phone in my hand."

"If you dropped the phone and just tried to pick it up, it could cause a stampede," Aktar said.

Besides their phones, they kept water, snack bars, clothing, prayer mats and emergency medications in their backpacks.

Stoning of the devil ritual

On day three of hajj, they traveled three miles back to Mina, and then moved back and forth from Mina to Jamarat for the symbolic stoning of the devil – "throwing seven pebbles at the largest of three walls (formerly pillars) from sunrise to sunset." One round-trip walk is about 3.5 miles.

The walls or pillars represent Satan. The first and largest wall represents the devil's temptation of Abraham against sacrificing Ishmael; the second represents the temptation of Abraham's wife, Hagar, to induce her to stop him; and the third represents the devil's temptation of Ishmael to avoid being sacrificed. The devil was rebuked each time and the throwing of the stones symbolizes those rebukes.

Remembering that more than 700 pilgrims were killed in a stampede at Mina the previous year, Zaman said he was "a little nervous but more cautious than nervous" as the stoning ritual got underway.

As a part of hajj rituals, an animal was sacrificed on Zaman and Aktar's behalf on the third day – a camel, cow, lamb or goat. The meat from animals is processed and much of it is sent to poor countries where people need food, Zaman said. "No part of the animal is wasted," he said.

It was also the day in which Zaman shaved his head and Aktar cut the tips of her hair.

The fourth day was again spent throwing seven pebbles at each of the three pillars, from noon until sunset.

On the fifth day, they left Mina for Mecca before sunset, and then in the night they again threw seven pebbles at each of the three pillars. They also did tawaf again, circling the Kaaba, to complete the hajj rituals.

Then they stayed four more days in Mecca, residing in a luxury hotel with their own private space, and "very close to the Kaaba.

"I don't have the words to describe how wonderful it felt. We were back to our American way of life, breakfast and dinner buffets. It's amazing how many kinds of food there are in the world. They cater to an international audience for a few days so it's line after line after line of food buffets and you eat whatever you want.

"That was supposed to be the fun time for me."

However, while he was overwhelmed with emotion and joy of the pilgrimage experience, the physical exhaustion and lack of sleep took its toll on Zaman.

"I fell sick," he said, and it took several weeks after returning to Frankfort to fully recover.

Just before leaving Mecca to return to Kentucky, they did their farewell tawaf, circling the Kaaba seven more times.

Back home in Frankfort

Before going to Mecca, Zaman had heard plenty of hajj stories from family members and friends. He had read about the trip and seen videos.

"But in reality this experience was completely incomparable. It was a sea of people representing the whole humanity. Millions came from all over the world – different races, color, belonging to different countries and speaking different languages.

"They all came to perform hajj and followed the rituals in the same manner to exhibit that there is no difference in Islam among human beings on the basis of wealth, race, creed, language and region. Everybody is mindful of others' needs and comfort."

The pilgrimage gave them a broader perspective of humanity and an increased understanding of diverse cultures, Zaman said.

"It united us with others in mutual respect and harmony. It made us leave our biases and accommodate others. We experienced life away from worldly affairs, wearing unstitched clothes, using no means of adornment and beautification. We embraced our true identity as a creature of Allah."

All men wore two sheets of seamless white cloth or towel. Women could wear regular clothing within Islamic guidelines.

Unforgettable experience

While the trip is over, Zaman believes the September 2016 pilgrimage to Mecca will always be with him in his everyday religious life.

"Spiritually, hajj was a self-renewal opportunity for us," he said. "Hajj rituals were the most vivid manifestation of our belief in monotheism (one God).

"From a historical perspective, we were on the same journey that people from all corners of the world have been making from the time of Prophet Abraham."

While her first trip to Mecca was physically challenging, incredibly spiritual and unforgettable, Zaman's wife, Saika Aktar, said she wouldn't want to live in Mecca or Saudi Arabia. She prefers the green grass of Kentucky.

The 2016 trip to Mecca will probably be her last, she said.

If he had the money, Zaman said he would love to go back again this year for hajj.

"But that's easy to say when I know I don't have the money," he said, laughing. "Hajj is a major physical and financial challenge. Still millions of Muslims undertake the journey every year to obey one of the mandatory commandments of Allah with the unparalleled reward being the forgiveness of entire past sins."

Being in the beautiful city of Mecca during hajj was "the closest I've ever felt to Allah on the face of the earth," Zaman said.

Chapter 30

Ghetto Prince: From hoodlum to CEO

This feature on hatmaker Eric Lynes was the cover story in the January 2018 issue of FRANK magazine. I liked Eric before I ever officially met him. I thought of him as the best dressed man in Frankfort. I heard through friend Mark Roberts at Poor Richard's Books that Eric had written an autobiography. Not long after hearing that, I saw Eric in "Nature's Way" health food store, and asked him, "Are you the hatmaker who is writing a book?" He smiled and said "yes," and we had a delightful conversation. He told me to drop by his office in the downtown McClure Building and he would show me his book. I did and we had a long conversation. We've been friends ever since. And I'm still trying to recruit him to serve on our Frankfort Interfaith Council.

As a Louisville teenager, he tried it all: marijuana, mescaline, LSD, cocaine, heroin and angel dust. He sold drugs and at 15 was arrested for armed robbery and locked up in the city's juvenile delinquent center.

In 2018, Eric Lynes, 61, hopes to talk about his roller-coaster life story at churches, schools, community meetings and bookstores. He also wants to sign and sell his new book. He's been alcohol and drug-free for many years, and won't even take aspirin.

On the back cover of his autobiography titled "Ghetto Prince: A journey from hoodlum to CEO," Penny Estes Wheeler, bestselling author of "The Appearing," says Lynes' book has "more twists and turns than an Agatha Christie mystery."

The back cover also says, "From the hood to the Andes Mountains of South America, this is the riveting true story of a young black man who had the vision to become a hat designer and manufacturer. It is the story of a man who single-handedly resurrected hats to the forefront of fashion.

"As a young man Eric was determined not to be destroyed by the 'project culture' of urban America. He prayerfully and methodically worked his way up from drugs and crime in the hood to realize his dream and to seize the reins as president of the world-renowned Biltmore Hats of Canada. Biltmore is the maker of the world's most famous hat – The Royal Canadian Mounted Police Hat."

Lynes acquired Biltmore Hats in 2005 and sold the company to Dorfman Pacific in 2010. After selling it, Lynes ran the Biltmore brand division for six years in Dallas, Texas.

Today Lynes is president of Prowess Uniform Solutions Inc. His office is in the McClure Building in downtown Frankfort.

The website says Prowess is a small business "that aspires to be the most successful comprehensive uniform supplier in North America. Our core competency is providing specialized uniform garments, headwear, footwear and accessories required by commercial industries, law enforcement, medical, military and educational institutions.

"Eric has a passion for quality, service and style, whether it is with the foods he eats (he's been a vegetarian for decades) or the garments he wears and manufactures. These attributes are uniquely woven into the fabric of his being. While working in the headwear industry, Eric was known as the walking-talking billboard of the highest quality hats in the industry."

One of his Prowess customers is Popz Topz hat designer Ron Stephens, father of award-winning singer John Legend.

Background

Lynes was born in Springfield, Ohio, in 1956 but grew up in Louisville. He hardly knew his father, who served 10 years in the Indiana State Penitentiary for armed robbery.

"He was an alcoholic," Lynes said. "I heard he was a good person but when he drank, he was like someone possessed with demons."

After his release from prison, "I was always hoping he would get his act together and come home to my mom and our family (six children), and be the father of my dreams," Lynes says in his book.

It didn't happen. His father was shot to death in a domestic dispute shortly after being released.

Later, Eric was expelled from Louisville Central High School in his sophomore year after "mouthing off" to the principal.

"Then I went to Kentucky's first ever alternative high school in Louisville," Lynes said. "My mom, who went to Kentucky State University three years and was a substitute teacher at some schools I attended, got me enrolled. But I got kicked out of there when I got busted for selling marijuana.

"Mom then somehow found Hope Academy, where teenage mothers were working on getting their GEDs, and I got my GED there."

His mother died October 27, 2017 in Phoenix, Arizona where she lived with a daughter. She was 90.

In his book, Eric said his mother, Frances Louise Smith Lynes, "is one of the true saints to walk this earth. That's not to say she didn't have her problems, because a saint is a sinner saved by grace. Her tenacious attitude for excellence, her courage in danger and discouraging circumstances, her hope and faith in God to deliver and rescue in the time of adversity and need, was instilled and woven throughout every fiber of our being.

"She's responsible for our spirit to fight back, our 'put family first' mentality, and the never-give-up attitude that enabled us to make it out of the hood and through the tough times of life."

After earning his GED, "passing the exam with flying colors," he was offered a full scholarship to Jefferson Community College.

"I felt grateful but I wanted to travel the world and Louisville was not the world," he said.

He followed in the footsteps of his older brother Percy and joined the U.S. Navy.

On the USS Forrestal Naval aircraft carrier, Lynes was caught smoking pot and spent 28 days in jail on the ship. One week after his release, he got in a fight that erupted into a "full-blown" race riot involving about 60 men.

He was upset about going to jail, "after being framed on a drug-possession charge by a crooked naval police officer." He also was angry after hearing two black sailors were "brutally beaten by a group of white guys, and nothing was done about it."

After the brawl, Lynes was flown back to the U.S. to stand trial for inciting the riot. He was never convicted, and eventually received an honorable discharge.

In his book he says, "In 1975, racial tensions ran high on board the USS Forrestal. One reason was the war-alert situation of our being at sea for extended periods because the Turkey and Cyprus dispute was still ongoing in the Mediterranean. This dispute had an adverse effect on young black and white sailors who seemed to get along fine as long as we were passing the peace pipe – the social weed and hashish, which was so prevalent in the Mediterranean coastal areas. Our 6,000-man naval operations in the Med depleted the hashish and marijuana stashes on board and around the local coastal towns," and that's when racial tensions increased.

A retired Navy chaplain told Lynes the Taranto, Italy Incident (riot) was instrumental in creating awareness, which helped bring about a positive change of culture concerning race relations in the Navy.

After serving in the Navy, Lynes attended Oakwood College, now a historically black Seventh-day Adventist university in Huntsville, Alabama.

Lynes paternal grandfather, Carlos Alexander Lynes, was pastor of Magazine Street Seventh-day Adventist Church in Louisville. During all of Eric's "foolishness" growing up, he had many prayers coming his way and knew he was "Bilt 4 More," as he puts it repeatedly in his autobiography.

Through genealogy research, Lynes learned his great-grandfather was a "royal ruler from South America," . . . thus the book title "Ghetto Prince." It's a story of how, "against all odds, I broke the cycle of circumstances in my life . . . because of my faith in God and His plan for my life. . . I know my life is the result of providence and divine intervention.

"I also believe this same God is willing to lead and guide any other willing soul. That's the sole reason I'm telling my story."

A lifetime love of hats

Eric's wife, Tezeta Gabriel, an Ethiopian woman he met in 1983 at the Seventh-day Adventist Church in Frankfort, gave him a book, "The Panama Hat Trail" by Tom Miller. A retired librarian who worked at KSU and the state Department for Libraries and Archives, Tezeta "has been my 'rock in a hard place' and has supported me every step of the way, through thick and thin, for richer or poorer.

"She was the one who vicariously opened the door to my research, traveling and exploring Ecuador."

Eric and Tezeta have a daughter, Rahel Danielle, who was a National Merit Scholar at Western Hills High School and has a master's in environmental health. Their second daughter, Astaire Birhan, was a "very special child who taught me many lessons of love and determination as she struggled with Down Syndrome and a defective heart from birth." She died of heart failure "at the tender age of two."

Lynes came to Frankfort in 1983 and studied accounting at KSU. He worked in the electronic data processing section of state Auditor Bob Babbage's office. He also worked as gift shop manager at Ancient Age Distillery, and at Toyota in Georgetown.

"The pain of assembly line work at Toyota is the real deal," Eric says. He eventually had to undergo spinal surgery from a work-related injury. "Toyota was my last steppingstone en route to Biltmore Hats. After surgery and extended time away from work, I decided I would pursue my dream to manufacture specialty caps."

While healing from surgery, Eric made his third trip to Ecuador. In the Andes Mountains he awoke early one morning with the vision "to scrap the idea of making specialty premium Panama caps for the fresh new idea of breaking into the hat industry with the small-brimmed hats known as stingy brims (anything under two inches wide).

"The stingy brim was what I was wearing at that time. It was my preferred style and choice of hats. That morning God made it crystal clear that the stingy brim was our new product. Never before had I had such conviction of the path I should pursue."

As soon as he returned home, he started exploring how to make the small brimmed hats. He worked on creating styles that would sell online and began looking for a manufacturer to make his designs. In 2002 he formed the Stingy Brim Hat Company. He went to Florence, Italy to get sample molds, and then delivered the molds to the Biltmore factory in Guelph, Ontario, Canada. The master hatters at Biltmore created beautiful samples.

In 2004, Eric found out Biltmore was in bankruptcy, and told his partner, "We're going to buy that company." Initially, they put in an unsuccessful bid, but after a long, difficult process, Lynes took all of his savings and managed to buy the company in 2005, he said.

What was his fascination with hats?

"I've always worn hats," Lynes says. "It was in my blood from Louisville – the Kentucky Derby, and my uncles, my mother and aunts always wore beautiful hats to church. An aunt bought me a dress hat when I was eight. I wanted to look sharp like my uncle, and he wore a stingy."

W. Nick Taliaferro, a Philadelphia radio broadcaster, wrote the foreword to Eric's book. They met at Oakwood College. On campus, "there was something about the way Eric carried himself – almost regal-like – that suggested he might be cut out for an embassy, or a boardroom," Taliaferro writes.

". . . And then there was the look. Eric Lynes seemed custom-ordered from Central Casting's leading man division. Tall, athletically lean, and with a glowing complexion that suggested health and exuberance, he looked like a model . . . Added to that was the bonus of likability. Eric was, and is, a nice guy."

Today, if there was a category for best-dressed adult man in Frankfort, Eric Lynes would be a top competitor any day of the year.

When asked recently if he's wealthy, he responded, "I'm wealthy in happiness. I'm happier than I've ever been. My wife underwent successful ovarian cancer surgery in 2017, and I'm so thankful she's doing well. I have a loving family and a few good friends.

"When I owned Biltmore Hats, my net assets were over $1 million. Now I don't have much disposable income but I'm comfortable. I have less stress. I'm very content and blessed. I hope my book will help young people understand there's a better way than what I went through. My goal is to turn the book into a film."

And Eric Lynes is living proof that anything is possible.

Chapter 31

Tashi Kyil monks create World Peace mandala

This story was published in the May 2019 edition of FRANK, a monthly magazine of The State Journal newspaper.

Impermanence is always one of the teachings when the Tibetan Buddhist monks from Tashi Kyil Monastery in India come to Frankfort.

They visited Kentucky's capital around Memorial Day in 2013, during Christmas Candlelight Tour in 2015 and Valentine's week in 2019. Each time, they've taken four days to create a beautiful, intricate World Peace mandala made of colored sand, and then they tear it up and pour the sand into the Kentucky River to show us that everything is impermanent. Enjoy the moment.

On all three visits here, the Tibetan monks will tell you they've witnessed teachings of loving kindness, compassion, generosity, joy and gratefulness from the Frankfort and Franklin County community.

In 2013 when I was asked by Arjia Rinpoche, director of the Tibetan Mongolian Buddhist Cultural Center in Bloomington, Indiana (the U.S. sponsor for the Tashi Kyil monks), if I would arrange programs for the touring monks in Frankfort, I said "yes." But truthfully, I didn't know how successful we would be.

There aren't a lot of Buddhists in Franklin County. However, I thought it would be a great opportunity to promote interfaith cooperation.

Bloomington's Mary Pattison, the overall tour coordinator, eased my mind that first year when she said, "Don't worry, Charlie. Just raise what you can and the monks will be happy to be there. You will thoroughly enjoy having them in your community."

Mary, 85, died this year in January. But I've never forgotten her comforting and prophetic words.

From August 2018 until April 2019, the monks were on a U.S. tour to educate the public about the Buddhist culture and religion; to raise funds for their small refugee monastery in Dehra Dun, India; and to promote peace, compassion and interfaith understanding. Donations from previous tours helped build a classroom for young student monks, and a library.

Generous community

Each time the monks visited Frankfort, our goal was to raise at least $2,000 to cover their suggested donation for building the World Peace mandala. But thanks to the generosity of the community, we've managed all three times to raise more than $12,000 – counting overall donations, ticket sales from the Tibetan dinner and interfaith gathering, and the purchase of Tibetan merchandise such as prayer flags, prayer beads, singing bowls, clothing, books, book bags and jewelry.

Major sponsors for the World Peace sand painting this year were Simple Gifts Spiritual Community, The Light Clinic, Libby Marshall and Prentice Harvey, Joe Fiala Sr., Jim and Pam Jackson, Frankfort Interfaith Council, Angela Mitchell, Mary Hunter Purdy, Mary Frank Slaughter, Gene Burch Photography, Gina Morales, Nancy Rose Osborne, Nash Cox, Brad Marston, Don and Sylvia Coffey, Mohammad Razavi, several anonymous donors, and myself.

Donna Gibson, director of Paul Sawyier Public Library, and the library board helped tremendously in allowing the monks to create the World Peace sand painting in the new, spacious River Room. It's the perfect place for the mandala to be built. The entire staff, especially Michael McIntosh, in charge of security, were so accommodating and friendly.

Ev and Mike Claffy were the hosts for the monks and their van driver, welcoming them into their home on Wapping Street for the second time. Brent Sweger provided a house in South Frankfort for them in 2015.

The Rev. Jessee Neat, rector at Church of the Ascension, and his parishioners, welcomed the monks into their downtown Episcopal church for the third consecutive time for the Tibetan dinner and cultural programs. And we've always had more than 100 to attend the dinners.

Shari Thompson opened her doors at My Old Kentucky Om Yoga Center on Second Street for a monk to teach four yoga classes through the week with all proceeds going to the monks.

Joseph Fiala and wife Emaline Gray welcomed youngsters to The Light Clinic for a children's art workshop with the monks.

Providing food for the Tibetan dinner or for the monks through the week were Stephanie Cramer, Gina Morales, Angela Mitchell, Nancy Osborne, Annie Metcalf, Anne Bourgeat, Connie Lemley, Trina Peiffer, Sandy Wilson, Veronica Gayle, Diana Hogan, Jane Mize, Thai Smile, Rick's White Light Diner, Casa Fiesta, Buddy's Pizza, Joe Fiala Sr., and Ev and Mike Claffy.

Participating in the cooking class for the Tibetan dinner were Betty Beshoar, Debbie Israel, and Angela and Reed Wilbers. Other volunteers for the Tibetan dinner were David Gierlach, Gene Coverston and Patricia Griffith; and Lizz Taylor sold tickets for the dinner at Poor Richard's Books.

Muslim student speaks at Tibetan dinner

A highlight of the Tibetan dinner and interfaith gathering this year was the keynote address by Afeef Shaik, a 16-year-old junior at Franklin County High School. He's a Muslim and a second-generation immigrant. His father, Aejaz Shaik, is a Frankfort Interfaith Council member and Afeef has attended several interfaith events through the years.

He's on the FCHS yearbook staff and bought an ad for the yearbook on behalf of the Frankfort Interfaith Council, to help bring awareness to his classmates about the local organization that promotes cooperation and understanding among all religions.

And that sparked another idea: the creation of a youth interfaith council, "which would bring together a group of high school students to openly discuss religion in a relaxed setting," Afeef said.

"It does not matter if you are an immigrant or were born here. It does not matter whether you are in the majority or minority. It doesn't matter if you are Republican or Democrat. All that matters is that you are open to learn."

The interfaith council unanimously approved Afeef's proposal of a youth council.

"I was overwhelmed by the support I received," he said. "I am now actively finding members of various backgrounds and faiths to commence a new tradition in Frankfort. Coming together and understanding what our community holds is something integral that I would like everyone – including my generation and the ones to come – to understand.

"The only way we as a community can grow is by first seeking what is in the community. Once we understand everyone's backgrounds, we can adjust to the needs of everyone and share an appreciation for one another.

My goal with youth interfaith is to create a circle for young minds to learn the truth behind religions and openly share any thoughts, ideas and concerns in a relaxed and fun setting."

Afeef received a standing ovation.

Monks bring beautiful art and calming presence

Dave "Tuck" Kerr – a retired corporate accountant who moved to Frankfort several years ago from Spirit Lake, Iowa – attended almost every Tibetan program through the week. He said when he's in the presence of the monks, he feels "a dramatic sense of positive energy. Peace and calmness begin to flow through me.

"Those feelings continue to grow deeper as the monks exude a genuine sense of compassion and love for the simple, uncomplicated experience of life. Their joy for life is contagious, overwhelming, and exactly what we are all searching to experience in our lives."

Kerr said conversation with the monks is "simple, open, honest, with absolutely no hidden agenda, and no sense of the social anxiety we might feel when engaged in conversation with people we have just met. To be in their presence is a humbling experience. I absorb their harmonic love and joy through some sort of spiritual osmosis. I take it with me when I leave them, and it lasts indefinitely."

He said the monks and the Buddhist teachings have influenced him to want to live a simpler, more peaceful life with love and respect for all beings.

Ev Claffy loves hosting the monks when they're in Frankfort.

"It's absolutely amazing having them in our house," she said. "One of the first nights they were here, they were in the living room chanting and the whole house gently vibrated. It was the most calming feeling to hear the beautiful sound they make when they chant together."

Ev said she's a night owl and would be downstairs late, in a chair reading a book. "They would be upstairs in one of the bedrooms and I could hear them talking. There was such joy in their voices. They are so kind to each other and everybody. I loved listening to them laugh."

She said it seems odd to have seven visitors in your home for a week, and not have any work to do, "because they take care of themselves and don't expect you to wait on them."

Nancy Osborne, one of the main organizers, said, "The joy of helping our monk friends three times over the last six years in our welcoming and generous community fills me with gratitude. The monks' artwork reminds me of our human tapestry, colored and strengthened by our diversity. With compassion, love and art as our guides, no matter our situation, we can promote peace and diminish suffering."

Impermanence

A child brought a teaching of impermanence to the library's River Room one day before the closing ceremony for the World Peace mandala. It was the third day for creating the sand painting, and the monks had taken a lunch break.

A barrier was placed around the mandala on the carpeted floor and a sign attached to the front rope said, "Please Don't Touch The Sand Mandala!"

But the little boy, unable to read, broke loose from his mother's hand and walked under the barrier, onto the mandala. After about two steps into the sand painting, one of our volunteers, Angela Mitchell, grabbed his hand and kept him from destroying the artwork.

The few adults in the room felt nauseated. Soon monk Lobsang Manjushri returned from lunch. When he heard the news, he laughed, saying, "It happens all the time." Well, not all the time. But he said it had happened several times on the current U.S. tour, and this was the "fourth worst mishap. One in New York happened on the final day and couldn't be corrected."

Our mandala was salvageable. Five monks were scheduled to work in the Episcopal church kitchen all afternoon with the cooking class to prepare the Tibetan dinner for that night. But Lobsang needed assistance in repairing the damage so the youngest monk, Tenzin Gyatso, returned quickly to the library to help rescue the mandala.

They smiled and remained calm and focused their minds on their artwork. Four hours later, the sacred mandala looked perfect – again.

Anam Thubten, my main Buddhist teacher, says, "True happiness comes from a very strange reality, from loving uncertainty, from falling in love with the lack of security. Once you know how to love this truth, you are going to feel true happiness. You're going to know what true joy is. This bliss is literally going to dance in your heart. . . The truth is that we are going to lose everything in the end. It is just a matter of time."

Since his last visit to Frankfort, Lobsang's mother died tragically in India in 2017.

"She was a good person and very innocent," Lobsang said. "She never went to school and only spoke our local dialect. She was about 45 and very loving. She had gone out in the early morning to cut grass for the animals – cows, goats and sheep. She was on a high mountain and fell 100 feet to her death. For me, that was the most suffering I have felt."

On Valentine's Day 2019, the day after the mandala mishap in Frankfort, with more than 150 people watching, the Tibetans monks ritually dismantled the beautiful mandala by artistically brushing the colorful grains of sand into the center of the blue board. Spectators received samples of the sand in tiny plastic bags and the remainder went into an ornamental container.

Then the monks – with their horns, cymbals, bells and drum, and in their ceremonial yellow hats and robes – led the crowd on a short walk to the Singing Bridge, where the sand, with its healing energies, was poured into the high and muddy Kentucky River.

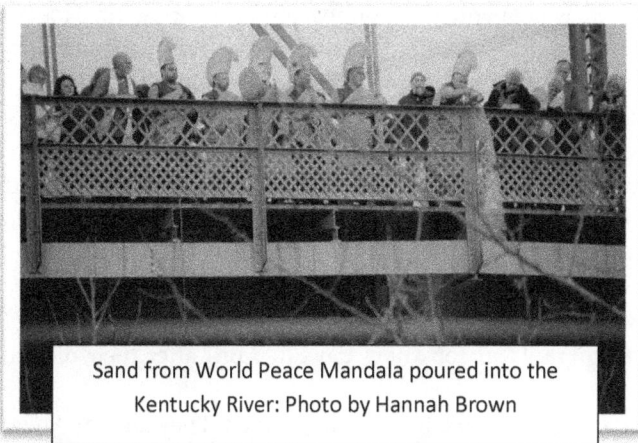

Sand from World Peace Mandala poured into the Kentucky River: Photo by Hannah Brown

Later the monks told local volunteers if the Frankfort community would like to preserve a World Peace mandala one time for an educational display, it can be done, and there would still be a closing ceremony. We have at least two years to decide.

Chapter 32

Tibetan monk recovers from critical injuries

In 2019 Frankfort and Franklin County were fortunate in getting to have the Tashi Kyil Tibetan monks visit for an additional four days at the end of their U.S. tour. They had an extra two weeks in the United States before they would depart on a plane from Chicago and fly back to their refugee monastery in India.

The first week was spent in Bloomington, Indiana at the Tibetan Mongolian Buddhist Cultural Center – their U.S. tour sponsor. In Bloomington they had to complete financial reports, participate in prayers and ceremonies at the interfaith temple, and help with whatever chores were needed doing at the center.

Earlier in the year, after leaving Frankfort in mid-February, the next two stops on their Kentucky schedule were in Berea and Lebanon. Joe Fiala and I decided to visit them on a Sunday afternoon in the Berea College library where they were creating a World Peace mandala. It was there where Lobsang Manjushri and Yeshi Rabgyal told us about the good possibility of being able to return to Frankfort for a few days in April after their official tour ended.

They asked if we would like to have them again. They already knew the answer. Of course we would love to have them again.

So it happened. We ended up having to share them with Lebanon but that was OK. Lebanon – a little more than an hour's drive from Frankfort – was my hometown and my black Lab, Lily, and I had family and friends we could stay with there.

However, one thing was different about their extra visit to Frankfort and Lebanon. We wanted them to relax and not work so hard. Fundraising was over for the most part.

We decided to have a thank-you dinner for major sponsors of their February visit to Frankfort. Don and Sylvia Coffey were happy to host the dinner at their lovely Dancing Meadow Farm home. A donation basket was placed by the food line for anyone voluntarily wanting to help pay for their roundtrip gasoline expense from Bloomington to Frankfort.

Sylvia and Don have had numerous dinners, celebrations and dances in their spacious home over the years. And Sylvia said the Tibetan dinner was one of the easiest for her because the monks did the entire cooking and kitchen cleanup afterward.

Right before the dinner prayer of thanks, the monks performed a Tibetan dance, "Tashi Sholpa," the Traditional Good Luck Dance, in the large dining room. After dinner, Sylvia's Glitterbugs group performed several dances for the monks and other guests including their version of "New York, New York," and "Fly," a popular contemporary Tibetan song, which the monks loved.

The monks also loved the huge, 7-foot tall wooden rocking horse in the living room, which was a Christmas gift from Sylvia to both of them in the mid-1990s. The monks took turns climbing up on the horse and having their pictures taken while laughing and smiling.

Mary Batt – a nurse, massage therapist and the monks' host in Lebanon – attended the dinner and told them she would take them to a farm in Marion County tomorrow where they could ride a real horse.

They were leaving Angela Mitchell's farm home in Franklin County the next morning, heading for Marion County and Lebanon. At Angela's residence it had been a joyful four days filled with conversations, laughter, chanting, Tibetan prayers, delicious meals prepared by the monks at their insistence, and relaxing walks to the yurt and prayer labyrinth for solitude and inner peace.

Kalsang Gyatso said the short walk from Angela's house to the yurt and labyrinth reminds him of his homeland in Tibet, which he fled when he was 20, so he could freely practice the Buddhist religion he loves so deeply.

While visiting Franklin County for four days in April, the monks also enjoyed short trips to Buddhaland in Carroll County (see Chapter 46) and Good Acres Sanctuary for rescued animals in Anderson County (Chapter 37).

After preparing a big, delicious farewell breakfast at Angela's house on Thursday morning, April 18, the monks said goodbye to Angela. She told them she looked forward to seeing them again in two years on their next U.S. tour. Nancy Osborne and I decided to spend another day with them.

They were meeting Mary Batt and Scott Garrett from Springfield in mid-morning at Shaker Village of Pleasant Hill in Mercer County. Nancy drove her car and we followed the long silver van to what is often called Shakertown.

I had been there several times, primarily for hiking, and the two-hour educational visit with the monks in their maroon robes on a sunny, blue-sky Holy Thursday made it a day of pure joy.

Our excellent tour guide gave us a brief history of the Shakers in The Meeting House, where they worshiped by ecstatic dancing or shaking. Then we sang "Simple Gifts" and our guide demonstrated a shaking dance.

The Shakers were known for their beliefs about equality – man or woman, black or white, no one brother or sister was considered more or less important than another. Each leadership position had male and female counterparts.

Ann Lee (1736-1784), the founder of Shakerism, was beloved and respected by her followers. But a woman speaking out in public, and especially about religion, in the 18th century was a major breach of social norms, and Ann often suffered at the hands of non-believers because of it.

Lucy Wright (1760-1821), another leader of the Shaker ministry, was responsible for creating the rigid uniformity in dancing or "shaking" that has come to define Shaker worship.

In 2019, the only active community remaining was Sabbathday Lake Shaker Village in Maine, which had three members.

After leaving The Meeting House, we went outside and saw farm animals and organic vegetable gardens. At lunchtime, while waiting for a dining room table, the monks enjoyed trying on straw hats and sunglasses in a gift shop and having their picture taken on a spiral staircase.

Of course I had to buy a book: Thomas Merton's "Seeking Paradise – The Spirit of the Shakers." I already had Merton's "Mystics and Zen Masters" book, in which he devoted a chapter to "Pleasant Hill: A Shaker Village in Kentucky." He admired their approach to work as a form of worship, their simplicity and rejection of violence, their architecture, extraordinary craftsmanship and furniture, their clean, uncluttered living spaces.

The United Society of Believers in Christ's Second Appearing, more commonly known as the Shakers, came to Kentucky and established themselves at Pleasant Hill in 1806. The Shakers were devout, orderly, and practiced celibacy.

At its height, there were 500 members, 5,000 acres of land with 25 miles of rock fence at Pleasant Hill. Sister Mary Settles, a native of Louisville, was the last Shaker in Mercer County. She died there in 1923.

During a 105-year span, the Pleasant Hill Shakers built more than 260 structures on the property. Today, there are 34 surviving buildings, most located along the mile-long gravel turnpike that runs through the heart of the village.

In the 1960s a group of local citizens founded Shaker Village of Pleasant Hill, a private, nonprofit organization, dedicated to restoring the historic property and interpreting its rich history.

After leaving Shaker Village, we headed to downtown Danville and briefly visited Elmwood Inn Fine Teas store. I bought two cans of herbal tea: "Cup of Serenity" and "Labyrinth Blend." I also purchased a small book, "Looking Deeply into Tea: Thoughts and Prayers," containing poems and photos from tea lands of India and Sri Lanka by Shelley and Bruce Richardson, the store owners.

Our next stop was at Mary and Jay Batt's residence in Lebanon, where the Tibetan monks stayed in 2013, 2016 and 2019. One of Mary's mottos is: "Life is all about the food," so of course we had some snacks in mid-afternoon before our 45-minute naps.

Then it was time for some of the monks to go horseback riding. I was ready to head back to Frankfort, but Nancy, the driver, wanted a little more time with the monks. I'm thankful now she chose to stay longer, even though a day filled with fun was about to change drastically.

We went to a large farm in the beautiful knobs of Marion County, between Gravel Switch and Bradfordsville. To get to the horse stable, we had to walk a swinging bridge over the Rolling Fork River and the monks were laughing and playing like little children. Nancy, Mary and I loved every second of it too.

After everybody made it across safely, we had another short hike down a rocky path. I received permission to take as many small geodes as I could carry back to our prayer labyrinth in Franklin County. Four were enough.

The first two riders on the beautiful light and dark brown horse were Tibetan natives Kalsang Gyatso and Kalsang Jinpa. Both had plenty of horseback riding experience in Tibet, before they fled to India. Kalsang Gyatso, first up on the horse, smiled and waved to everybody as he and the horse moved smoothly down the path for about five minutes. He was immensely enjoying the moment. Next, it was Jinpa's turn. Everything seemed fine at first. Nancy and I were taking pictures. Then all of us became witnesses to what I thought was surely going to be Jinpa's death.

211

Suddenly the horse reared three times, and on the third time fell backwards on top of Jinpa. It felt like a slow-motion scene. We rushed over to try to help. The owner helped the horse up, and took it away. We heard later it hadn't sustained any injuries.

Jinpa somehow managed to stand up. He had a laceration on his swollen right eye. He briefly sat down in a chair and the farm owner quickly got his pickup truck and transported him to Ephraim McDowell Regional Hospital emergency room in Danville. We didn't want to wait for an ambulance to arrive. Mary and Kalsang also rode in the pickup, and Lobsang and I rode with Nancy to the hospital.

The other monks rode in their van back to Lebanon.

A series of tests, scans and medical examinations revealed Kalsang Jinpa suffered two anterior and two posterior pelvic fractures; seven fractures in his front rib cage, and eight fractures in his back rib cage, on his right side; and a displaced right clavicle.

Around midnight Thursday, Jinpa was transferred by ambulance to University of Kentucky's Trauma Center in Lexington and admitted. Friday he underwent surgery at UK to repair an eye-lid laceration.

Nancy and I stayed at the Danville hospital about four hours, mostly in a waiting room. But we did get to see him briefly a couple of times before we headed for Frankfort. Jinpa was in a lot of pain but was awake and remained calm. Mary and Lobsang, who speaks English well and served as Jinpa's translator, stayed in the emergency room with him most of the time.

On the ride back to Frankfort, besides feeling nauseated because of Kalsang Jinpa suffering critical injuries, Nancy and I also learned from Lobsang at the Danville hospital that night that Jinpa had no medical insurance.

The monks traveled throughout the U.S. for nine months, working extremely hard to raise money for their monastery in Dehra Dun, India. The tour had been a huge success. But now, would the costs of this one unfortunate accident, wipe out everything the monks had earned on this tour and even previous tours to America?

Everything weighed heavily on our minds and hearts that night. Sleep did not come easy.

In mid-afternoon of Good Friday, I drove to Lexington to see Jinpa and ended up staying all night in his room, along with Yeshi Rabgyal.

Before the accident, Mary Batt had planned a fundraising dinner for the Tashi Kyil Monastery at two of her friends' home in Jessamine County, near Lexington. I assumed the event would be cancelled but I was wrong.

212

The five other monks unanimously agreed to go on and have the dinner. Cooking Tibetan food, being with compassionate people who care about Tibetan refugees and Tibet, and staying busy seemed like the right thing to do on Good Friday in the Bluegrass region of Central Kentucky.

The monks were scheduled to be in Bloomington, Indiana, by Sunday evening and their flights to India were set for the middle of the next week. We all knew Jinpa would still be in Kentucky when the plane left Chicago. And Saturday, the day before Easter, we all knew Lobsang, the best translator, would be staying with Jinpa in Kentucky and the United States as long as Jinpa remained here.

Late Friday night, Yeshi brought vegetarian momos from the dinner to the hospital room and I enjoyed a late night snack. He said the fundraiser went well. Yeshi insisted that I sleep on the comfortable sofa and he slept in a recliner. About the only thing I did to help Jinpa through the night was to push a few buttons on his bed a couple of times to make him more comfortable when I couldn't get Yeshi to wake up. He was too exhausted from all the work he had done in the last 36 hours, and from everything that had happened.

I stayed with them through mid-afternoon Saturday, and was in the room with physical therapists when Jinpa got out of bed and walked for the first time. It was painful watching it happen, and inspirational. He remained calm and silent, and never moaned or complained. I felt the therapists were in awe of Jinpa's quiet, unemotional determination almost as much as I was.

He was at UK Trauma Center five days before being released and transferred to Cardinal Hill Rehabilitation Hospital in Lexington. I visited him four times during his 16 days at Cardinal Hill. Every visit at both places, I received spiritual teachings from Jinpa on calmness, surrendering to what is, the power of positive thinking and prayers, inner strength and physical strength, gratefulness, and the art of smiling through pain.

It also was fun being with Lobsang, who was frequently watching cricket tournaments on his phone, when he wasn't needed by Jinpa or the medical staff.

One afternoon at Cardinal Hill, in his last week there, I asked Jinpa if the thought of dying entered his mind when the horse fell on top of him. Lobsang translated for us.

"He said he didn't really think about dying. But he thought maybe in the future he could be handicapped. At first when he tried to talk, words wouldn't come out. His nose was bleeding and it was hard to breathe. But he said he didn't suffer horrible pain."

In the Danville hospital emergency room shortly after the accident, Jinpa had described his pain level as 7 on a 1 to 10 scale with 10 being the severest. "Today, his pain level is a 3," Lobsang said.

When asked if the horseback riding accident was the toughest thing that's happened to him, he said "No," through Lobsang. "This is nothing compared to when he was in Tibet. This is a very small, temporary problem."

When he was trying to escape from Tibet, Lobsang explained, whenever you go against Chinese rule, you know there's a good chance you will die. And it's not a temporary problem, he explained. It can go on for one or two years.

Jinpa said if he ever returns to Tibet, there's a good possibility he would ride a horse again because some of the rough roads aren't suitable for a car or motorcycle. He was from a nomad family, and was riding horses and yaks when he was eight years old.

Does he really feel he might return to Tibet someday?

"If Tibet and China ever have a good relationship and try to understand each other, then he could go back," Lobsang said. "Otherwise if he went back, they would definitely put him in prison for more than 20 years."

In the days and weeks following the accident, I witnessed Nancy Osborne becoming Jinpa and Lobsang's compassionate caregiver. It was a spiritual calling. She used her skills as a researcher and public servant – from 35 years of working in Kentucky state government, including 25 with the Legislative Research Commission before her 2009 retirement. She combined that with genuine compassion, respect, kindness, generosity and love for all beings to make sure Jinpa's accident had a silver lining and joyful ending.

She went to the hospital and rehab center almost every day and became the intelligent and common sense cheerleader and spokeswoman for the monks. She talked respectfully to doctors, nurses, therapists, financial directors and staff members. She told them he had no medical insurance and wouldn't qualify for Medicaid because he is a Tibetan monk with no personal income and resides at a refugee monastery in India.

Nancy said it "really helped" being able to show all the medical personnel a copy of The State Journal's May 2019 FRANK magazine story on the Tashi Kyil monks, which revealed through photos and words their beautiful sacred art and important tour work for world peace and compassion.

She was instrumental in helping Lobsang and Jinpa complete the necessary paperwork with the happy result that all expenses were eventually waived at the three medical facilities where he received treatment and care.

The only bill that couldn't be waived was the $1,400 expense for being transported by ambulance from Danville to Lexington. To help defray half of that expense, The Light Clinic in Frankfort held a fundraiser. Many friends of the Tashi Kyil monks gathered at The Light Clinic on a Sunday to attend Buddhist teachings led by Lobsang and Jinpa. The other half was raised through solicited donations.

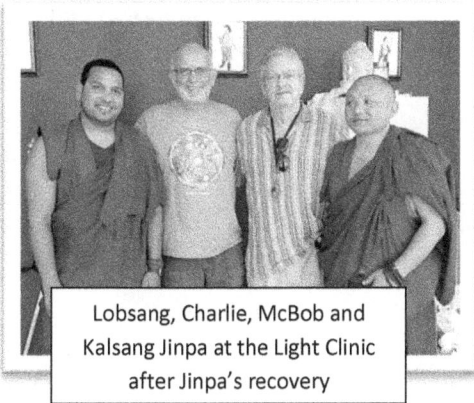

Lobsang, Charlie, McBob and Kalsang Jinpa at the Light Clinic after Jinpa's recovery

Earlier, while Jinpa was recovering in Lexington, Nancy frequently brought the two monks Indian food or any other food they wanted. She washed and dried their clothes. And when the day came for Jinpa to be released from Cardinal Hill, Nancy welcomed them into her home for seven days on Shadrick Ferry Road near Frankfort. It was their request to stay there. They had done a house blessing at her residence in February and loved the quiet setting.

Nancy even restored her old ping-pong table so Lobsang could practice his skills and defeat everybody who challenged him in matches during their stay at her house in the woods. Going outside on the deck or sitting in the screened-in room near the kitchen helped tremendously with Jinpa's healing.

In November 2019, a time of Thanksgiving in the U.S., Nancy received a letter from the Tashi Kyil Monastery.

It said:

Dear Nancy: All of us at Tashi Kyil Monastery send you a very sincere "Thank you" for all your help with Kalsang Jinpa's hospital stay, working on our behalf to eliminate his medical bills.

Your generosity and kindness at this difficult time is so very appreciated. Without your assistance our Monastery would have incurred much debt and that would have taken away from our much-needed fundraising.

215

We feel truly blessed to have a good friend such as you and to have your support.

Thank you again from Tashi Kyil Monastic Sangha members. Much blessings.

Nancy said when she was at the accident site, she had no idea what was ahead.

"I feel you trust what's going to happen and you do the right things with the right behavior. With divine help, you stay strong. There were many lessons I learned from the whole experience, and I am so happy it all worked out. I'm sorry it happened, but on the other hand, many good things happened after the accident."

"Kalsang Jinpa was so neutral from the get-go. He healed so well. He drank a lot of hot water and breathed and prayed. That's what I've been doing a lot of lately."

One of the greatest things the Tashi Kyil Tibetan Buddhist monks have done for me, and I feel for many others, is to connect all of us as a spiritual family. Their love is, and has been, felt by not just a few Buddhists in Frankfort and Lebanon, but also by Baptists, Catholics, Episcopalians, Methodists, Presbyterians, Muslims, Baha'is, Hindus, Jews, Sufis, agnostics and atheists. Everybody belongs.

I've met hundreds of beautiful souls since 2013 through the Tashi Kyil U.S. tours. One of those souls is Shih-In Ma from Pennsylvania. Nancy and Angela and I first met her at an appreciation luncheon in Bloomington, Indiana. The monks wanted to thank all the tour coordinators in various states.

Probably the most successful tour, as far as fundraising during nine months of 2018 and 2019, was at Penn State University where Shih-In Ma first met the monks. We knew from our visit with her in Bloomington that she has a beautiful presence and amazing energy.

We got to know her much better when she drove to Kentucky after hearing about Kalsang Jinpa's injuries. She stayed at Nancy Osborne's house for a few days while Jinpa and Lobsang were there. She joined us at Don and Sylvia Coffey's Dancing Meadow Farm home when Jinpa and Lobsang and Nancy returned for a thanksgiving meal in May. Also attending were two young men from Indonesia and Myanmar, environmental professionals who had been working briefly with the city of Frankfort through an International City Managers Association exchange program.

After dinner, along with the monks and Nancy, Shih-In Ma did a walking meditation at the Coffeys' impressive prayer labyrinth, dedicated to their late friend Jules Delambre.

The next day, Shih-In Ma joined Nancy, Jinpa and Lobsang in a trip to Louisville's Churchill Downs, the historic horseracing track of the famous Kentucky Derby. While Jinpa was still recuperating at Cardinal Hill on the first Saturday in May, Nancy had made sure the Tibetan patient and Lobsang watched horse races on TV in Jinpa's room. They loved the festivities and asked if they could go to the race track. Nancy had promised them before they left Kentucky she would accompany them to a day of racing at Churchill Downs.

After the monks returned to their monastery in India, Shih-In Ma stayed in touch with them. Before 2019 ended, she traveled to India and in the company of Kalsang Jinpa and other Tashi Kyil monks, Shih-in Ma had a private audience with His Holiness the Dalai Lama at his home in Dharamshala.

Chapter 33

A visit to The Light Clinic founders' home

On the morning of November 4, 2019, I sat on the living room floor with Joseph Fiala and Emaline Gray at their home in South Frankfort near the Kentucky River and floodwall. Our breakfast was smoothies with beet, celery, carrot, kale, banana, berries, coconut water and a little liquid chlorophyll.

"I haven't tried it yet," Emaline said. "It could taste weird."

It tasted amazingly healthy, and good. A candle was burning and I felt wonderful energy in the room like the healing energy that greets you when you enter The Light Clinic.

They were training for a 3.1 mile Turkey Trot in Lexington on Thanksgiving Day.

Emaline said she hadn't run much in the last 20 years until they started training for the Turkey Trot.

"I used to run and had a few years of rebellious running, continuing after I had injured my knee. Then I gave it up for a long time."

When asked if she still had a desire to run competitively, she answered, "Yes and no. I do have an athletic, competitive nature. But I've cultivated the last 20 years of not being that way. So I haven't flipped that switch on in me, but I could. Maybe if I got better, it would start to come out more. But I'm not interested in it coming out. It doesn't feel healthy and I run to be healthy."

Joseph says he's a happy exerciser.

"I want to enjoy it and I want that to be my intention. Every time I'm thinking and it starts to get a little bit hard or stressful, I remember I'm a happy exerciser. That's who I am and I bring up that happiness. It's like trying to activate parts of your DNA at different times. So you can activate certain things that bring out certain traits, and it works. Setting that intention, you start to grow toward it."

He said professional athletes are good at setting intentions, "but it often gets into things like, 'I'm the best and nobody can beat me.' When you get into that zone, you can feel the ego come up, and it actually works against you. You start to feel more tension and stress.

"Whenever your body is tight, tense, you're going to have constriction, a lack of blood flow, and you're going to have injuries. But with a relaxed intention and thinking of it as an inner practice – like I just want to be this awesome, best version of myself – then you don't have the ego component. There's room for other people to be physically powerful. Everybody's physically powerful and everybody feels better. That zone of being is a lot more productive."

Emaline says they're both working on getting a doctorate now, "and we've been working a lot on the mindset thing. I did a paper on positive thinking in terms of health. Basically across the board, no matter what, if people think more positively about themselves or their health, then they do better. It's amazing. So that's got us rolling with this positive thinking."

I asked them how Frankfort has evolved spiritually in the last two decades since they were teenagers here.

Joe said that timeframe "obviously correlates with a lot of spiritual changes in ourselves." Before their high school years, Joseph and Emaline went to Good Shepherd (Catholic) School.

"When we were teenagers here in the mid-1990s, Christianity was very predominant," Emaline said. "I went to Good Shepherd but I wasn't Catholic. My mom studies Sufism so I've had that influence my whole life. I was baptized Episcopalian when I was 12 in my grandparents' church in Maryland.

"It's really hard for me to say how spirituality has changed in Frankfort."

Joseph said by the eighth grade, he was no longer going to Good Shepherd School.

"I was trying to go through confirmation and was taking some of the extra classes but I wasn't resonating with it as much. So I stopped and didn't go through confirmation."

He said when he started hearing questions like, 'Do you believe in the Immaculate Conception?' – for me, hearing someone phrase that question that way made me think for the first time that it was an option whether I could believe in it or not."

His father, who had grown up Catholic, became interested in Buddhism in college and is now a practicing Buddhist and Buddhism

219

teacher. When younger Joseph was a high school senior, he began reading books on Buddhism that his father recommended.

Buddhism seemed to resonate more with him. He said he has spent a lot of time healing his relationship with God. "My relationship was really messed up. I think a lot of the injury came from the presentation of it as a religion that couldn't be questioned. That made it dead, not alive. You couldn't interact with it. It wasn't something you could have a relationship with. There was no feeling in it. For me, I started to resent that and I started getting into spirituality.

"A lot of people in spirituality would tend to pose things against God. They would oppose using the word God and organized religion. But that's changing now. There's a great thread of people that are all about integration and that's where I am now. But it took a while to get out of that zone of being injured by the use of the word God.

"It took me a couple of years of dream training in a Christian tradition and being around a bunch of open-minded, open-hearted Christians, and being able to express and be a valuable member of that community without being necessarily a practicing Christian. They influenced me big time, absolutely."

When asked what the word God means to him, Joseph said, "God to me is the whole, the whole of that which is, and that which isn't, together, like the oneness. But it's not just the oneness of creation or the oneness of existence and consciousness. It precedes the oneness.

"In Chinese it's called the Tao, which is the creation of the universe – and maybe there are infinite numbers of these universes. From the Big Bang, literally in quantum physics, something came out of nothing. The Something and the Nothing is the idea of God for me."

Does Emaline think about God?

"Sure, I do or I don't," she said. "I majored in religious studies in college. Part of that came from going to Good Shepherd School and not being Catholic but being surrounded by religion. People were saying, 'If you're not Catholic, what are you?' And I remember thinking as a kid, I don't know what I am; I guess I need to study everything. So I studied everything in college.

"I don't like religion very much because it's very human-focused. So what I got into are the original spiritual texts and they are pretty divine. And so much of those are going toward the same thing, the same truth. So I don't specifically think about all the minutiae of all the religions anymore after studying it for so long. I think about experiencing the universe now."

Emaline said she never had an injured relationship with church.

"I always loved it. But I wasn't a part of it so that was great. I didn't have any of the baggage. Today, Buddhism and Taoism are what I resonate with the most, and a little Paganism. Mother Nature is pretty great."

Their interest in dream work has grown tremendously since returning to Frankfort.

Emaline said it was easy for her to become interested in dream work.

"Everybody dreams, and I know for me, I've had really strong dreams my whole life. So it's been a forced theme for me. Even if I wanted to ignore my dreams, they won't let me."

She says she remembers most of her dreams. "I've been looking at dreams since high school and college days. And talk about synchronicity, we moved back to Frankfort the year after Joyce Hudson moved to Frankfort."

Joyce Rockford Hudson is the author of "Natural Spirituality: A Handbook for Jungian Inner Work in Spiritual Community." She has taught the principles of Jungian inner work to church and community dream groups for three decades. "Natural Spirituality" has been a handbook for dream groups across the U.S. and abroad.

The back cover of the revised edition, published in 2016, says Hudson "moves Jungian dream work from the professional world of the analyst's office into the everyday world of spiritual seekers in local community, both inside and outside the institutions of traditional religion.

"For those willing to meet the divine in the natural flow of life, this book offers an opportunity to embark upon the spiritual path of individuation, whether traveling alone or with the support of a group. With clarity and simplicity Joyce Hudson puts into her reader's hands the tools for inner work that Carl Jung offered to spiritual seekers everywhere."

Joyce is on the faculty of the Haden Institute, where she teaches in the Dream Leader Training Program and helps oversee the annual Summer Dream and Spirituality Conference.

"So all of a sudden having Joyce, an expert Jungian dream mentor, basically in our yard launched our whole formal journey," Emaline said. "She helped us go down to the Haden Institute in North Carolina and we separately did a two-year training and certification. Mary Frank (Emaline's mother) did that as well.

"Like anything, you need to learn its language a little and how to understand it. That's what the work with Joyce at the Haden Institute is about."

Fonda McWilliams does formal dream work sessions at The Light Clinic. A local dream group has been meeting weekly at The Light Clinic for seven years. Emaline and Joseph also meet Joyce once every two weeks to get mentorship. "It's one of the most important parts of our life, I think," Emaline said.

"Joseph and I are physicians, who pick up all these tools and use them in treatments," Emaline said.

Joseph said, "I ask people if they remember any dreams, and if any themes are happening."

"Because it's all symbolic and Chinese medicine is symbolic," Emaline said. "So it's all speaking in this archetypal symbolic language, and it all affects our spirit in who we are and how we grow and heal."

Joseph said, "If you can start to remember your dreams, if you can access that, I really think that's one of the most important things we can do because it is an objective mirror of what's happening inside your mind, heart, soul and body, your psyche.

"It's what's happening. It's not just you but also what's happening in all these currents outside yourself, like in the collective consciousness and also the collective unconsciousness stuff we're not aware of. All of it is forming into these representations in story form that play through our mind and as soon as you start to pierce the veil, you start to crack this whole egg open that has the most rich stuff inside. It's the gold. It's the stuff that life is all about. It's unfolding that inner work journey.

"That's why dreams are so huge in the Bible. Almost every giant thing in the Bible came from a dream. It's been culturally with us forever, but it's not as talked about openly. It's not at the surface as much right now but it's growing."

Emaline said dream work "has the ability to be one of the greatest teachers of our life."

When you wake up from a dream, it helps to write down what the dream was about, they say. However, Emaline said she never documents her dreams in the middle of the night.

"The thing is, if you don't remember your dream or write it down, still there's a message for you and it will come back again," Emaline said.

"Even little snippets of dreams, images you remember are absolutely valuable," Joseph said. "You can get tons out of little pieces of dreams. I've heard neuroscientists talk about dreams and the way the brain functions and how your memory works. They say you will remember the most important things the longest. So as your dreams start to fade away, even if you remember one piece, you're remembering the piece that you probably need to know the most. The least important things will fade away first."

Joseph said he writes down his dreams on his phone, "and I have them saved. Then, for example, it can tell me how many times I've dreamt about guitars. I can type in guitar and it will search and pop up 10 dreams that had a guitar in it. That's incredibly helpful, when you start referencing back over a time period, (in telling you) what your psyche has been working on. You see the change in evolution."

The Light Clinic evolves

They were asked how The Light Clinic, in other ways, has evolved since it opened in 2010.

Emaline said, "In some ways to me, it's exactly the same, and in most ways it's incredibly different. We're in the same space and seeing patients. Because we came in with such a strong focus of what our intention was, that has stayed true. We're very grounded in the medicine. We try to provide the highest-quality care. We have compassion and we're incredibly present. All of that is the same."

The Light Clinic has grown a lot, Joseph said.

"I think there was a lot happening, kind of an energetic cloud over Frankfort for wanting some sort of spiritual outlet," he said. "I think The Light Clinic opening did provide one vent for that to release and express through. That has continued as those rushing energies come through it and inevitably start to churn it and change it.

"We started real early on with education and classes, and doing free meditation. That has continued to evolve to where we're talking about a meditation, spiritual and holistic health center. We're getting to a stage where we're going to start moving that forward a lot more. That's something that can endure whether it's us or not."

"So you're content here and you're not going to leave?" I asked.

Joseph answered, saying, "There's a part of us that feels completely free to be able to move and enjoy life and experience new things; and a part of us that feels very rooted here, very connected to the community. We have so much love for Kentucky and Frankfort, and for our home here and all the people we have connected with.

"That's never going to get tossed to the side. But we have to make sure we're feeding our soul because we love to learn. We're lifelong learners.

We love to have new experiences and travel. It's always going to be a balance."

They love returning to Portland, Oregon, to visit friends and their teachers, and they've fallen in love with Hawaii.

"Yes, Hawaii is a special place," Joseph said. "It's so deeply rooted into the care of nature. The culture is set up differently. They value love – Aloha, the spirit of love and connection, peace and compassion. They value that culturally, and when you come in and you're not bringing that, it gets pointed out sometimes.

"The ocean is so powerful there. Every beach is sacred. All water is sacred. The clouds are so low your eyes have to adjust. The clouds are almost hitting the ground. It's like you're literally up in the clouds, which is a special feeling."

Emaline has a cousin living in Hawaii. "And my mom lived in Hawaii a few times when she was young because her father was in the military," she said. "We had family from my grandparents' time who lived there. This past summer was our second time to go there, and when we arrived it felt like home."

Emaline's mother, a craniosacral therapist at The Light Clinic, "is a special healer. She's intuitive and has always been tapped into other flows and streams of life," Joseph said.

Emaline agrees. "She is most definitely one of the best practitioners I've ever met."

"A lot of times she just talks to you and listens, and the way she mirrors for people is powerful," Joseph said. "They have healing reactions. Her ability to do that is special. We're super lucky to have her in our life, especially for our four-year-old daughter, Olivia Grayce, in her prime development years."

Since the opening of the Light Clinic, Emaline and Joseph have evolved by having Olivia in their lives.

"The surprising thing about Olivia is, I didn't know how much you would be beaten up by your own child – just running at you full force and kicking your head," Emaline says. "It's so rough the way kids play and they don't know their own body strength. I've had serious face injuries – not on purpose but through her playing. It's profound.

"Just being a parent is profound and every day I'm in awe of it, watching and witnessing her progress as a human being. She meditates already . . . for about 10 seconds, and she'll do yoga."

Sponsoring Tibetan monks visit

The Light Clinic has been a major sponsor for the Tashi Kyil Tibetan monks on their three visits to downtown Frankfort to create a beautiful World Peace mandala over four days. Mary Frank Slaughter, and Joseph's parents, Joe Fiala and Stephanie Cramer, have also been major financial contributors to help the monks on their Frankfort tours.

The monks – in 2013, 2015 and 2019 – were on U.S. tours to educate the public about the Buddhist culture and religion; to raise funds for their refugee monastery in Dehra Dun, India; and to promote peace, compassion and interfaith understanding. Donations from the first two tours helped build a classroom for young student monks, and a library.

Before moving back to Frankfort, Emaline and Joseph went to India and studied Buddhism.

"Coming back to Frankfort, it was easy not to focus on that part of our lives," because there wasn't a large Buddhist presence in Kentucky's capital city, Emaline said. "But when the Tibetan monks came to town, it brought up that part in me again, which has been really wonderful. It's an honor to witness their complete love and generosity, and amazing work ethic without any quips about anything.

"I love how much the community has embraced them. That's my favorite thing. It has put out this little ripple effect over Frankfort in such a positive way. I'm so grateful to be able to help them be here."

Joseph said, "They're so dedicated and so truly authentic and expressive of themselves. The battery, the energy source that allows them to continue going through all the ups and downs – and to continue to be in a compassionate, open, perceptive place – is inspiring."

Bourbon on Main

The Light Clinic also has played a major role in opening Bourbon on Main, a popular downtown restaurant by the Kentucky River. Joseph and his father, Joe Fiala, are partners with others in the locally-owned business.

How does a bourbon restaurant fit into spirituality other than the fact that bourbon is a spirit that people seem to love more and more these days?" I asked.

Joseph smiled and said, "I'll start talking and see if it does. It's been quite a journey."

He said when he and Emaline were going to Chinese Medicine School in Portland, they enjoyed going to cocktail bars.

"It's a hip city and fun and we really liked that experience of being in cocktail bars. For us, bourbon was even more special because it connected us with Kentucky. Bourbon was getting popular and it's made in our hometown and state. We could connect with people that way.

"And when we came home, we wanted to be here and bring Chinese medicine here and get things moving. But we also had creative comfort things that were missing here. There weren't an abundance of good places to go out to and eat or have a drink in the evening. So it came from a cultural need too – being here and wanting to make this the best place and community possible for us to live, which makes it better for other people to live."

When Joseph's longtime friend Taylor Marshall listed the Dragon Bar & Grill property, Taylor knew Joseph had been talking about the need for a downtown bourbon bar.

"So he tried to sell it to me and I said, 'That's crazy.' And then I said, 'Maybe it's not, but I don't want to do it without you.' And Taylor said, 'There's no way I want to do it.'"

Joseph eventually talked Taylor into becoming a partner in Bourbon on Main and they both knew who they wanted to manage the upscale bar and restaurant. They said his name at the same time – Kelly May, and right after saying it, synchronicity happened and "Kelly walks in front of the window at Capital Cellars where we were eating." A knock on the window brings Kelly inside, and when they shared their idea with him, Kelly said, "'Yes, that's been my dream for a long time,'" according to Joseph.

"Kelly had already thought about people he wanted to have involved in it. So the whole thing unfolded smoothly. It has already done so much for our community. It needed to happen and it helped a lot of talented people to shine. Kelly is amazing and is pretty big in the bourbon world now."

In addition to great food and drinks inside Bourbon on Main, a beautiful mural has been added to the west wall on the outside. Chicago-based artist Anna Murphy, a 2007 Frankfort High School graduate, painted the 1,200-square-foot mural in blue and white on a glistening gold background – with help from her mother, Paula Murphy, a Frankfort artist.

The mural is titled "Beautiful and Brave." It features a young woman with a tear on her face and her head covered in intricately-detailed lace. A tiger and a fox are with her and they're surrounded by flowers, honey bees and angels.

A description posted beside the mural says:

"How beautiful and brave we are. Brave in love, in kindness, and in peace. Learning from the wisdom of the natural world and the animal kingdom, we are one with all things.

"This mural is a representation of a unified love, between all. Every being of life connected by the divine love of the universe. Surrounded by a glowing gold background, reflecting the riches and beauty of the world. Symbols of resourcefulness (fox), courage (tiger), community (bees) and new beginnings, we look to a bright future, where love is all around.

"This is the message of the mural and our hope for this community, and the world. – Anna and Paula Murphy.

"Special thanks to FrankArts, Josephine Sculpture Park, Richard Rosen, Expree Credit Union, Bourbon On Main, Riverside Development Group and Goodwood Brewing Co. Frankfort."

Anna earned a bachelor's degree in art from the University of Louisville before moving to Chicago.

Anna is Angela Mitchell's niece. Paula and Angela are sisters. Paula also has a large mural of Frankfort landmarks and scenes displayed above the entrance doors at Kroger East in Frankfort. Angela and I are depicted riding our bicycles on the Singing Bridge.

Emaline says Bourbon on Main is in one of the oldest buildings in Frankfort. Major renovations were done before BOM opened.

"Saving buildings like that – historic preservation – there's nothing more spiritual," Emaline says.

Shortly after my visit to Emaline and Joseph's home, the one-Sunday-a-month meditation hour at The Light Clinic changed to a meditation hour every Monday evening, starting at 5:30. Attendance has increased tremendously and it feels as if we have a true spiritual community sangha in downtown Frankfort.

Joseph, who leads most of the meditation sessions, is wonderful in guiding us into being present and surrendering and looking inside ourselves and feeling compassion and love and interconnections with all beings.

Besides sitting in silence for 20 minutes, we chant, do shaking exercises, walking meditation and loving kindness practice. People from any faith or no faith are welcome.

It's a beautiful way to start the week.

Chapter 34

A follow-up with Rich Green in 2019

After our monthly Frankfort Interfaith Council meeting in the community room of the downtown WesBanco building, Rich Green and I took a short two-block hike and sat down at a picnic table at the corner of West Main and St. Clair. In October 2002 when I was assigned to write a cover story on autumn hiking in the Red River Gorge, I asked Rich if he would like to join me. Of course he said "yes."

We had so much fun we decided to go on a monthly hike together, and did that for more than a decade. We went on several hikes to the Abbey of Gethsemani, Natural Bridge State Resort Park and the Red River Gorge of eastern Kentucky.

We also hiked at Ten Thousand Buddhas Summit Monastery near Corydon, Indiana; the Tibetan Mongolian Buddhist Cultural Center in Bloomington, Indiana; Brown County State Park near Nashville, Indiana; Furnace Mountain Zen Retreat Center in the Red River Gorge region; Yuko-En on the Elkhorn – The Kentucky-Japan Friendship Garden in Georgetown; and Buckley Wildlife Sanctuary. Many of our hikes were on splendid trails in Frankfort: Cove Spring Park and Nature Preserve; Kentucky Department of Fish and Wildlife Resources Game Farm; Fort Hill; and Buffalo Trace Distillery.

Rich turned 75 in 2019 and I celebrated my 71st birthday. One of the best things I've done on the interfaith council was to recommend Rich Green as the Catholic representative on the board several years ago when there was an opening. The council has board members from the Christian, Islamic, Jewish, Hindu, Buddhist, Baha'i and Unitarian Universalist religions.

I thought I knew Rich well from having shared many Lebanon, Frankfort and life stories with him on our hikes and travel time together getting to trails. I knew he came from a well-to-do Catholic family and that his father and uncle provided dental care for Trappist monks from the

Abbey of Gethsemani including the noted writer and social activist Thomas Merton.

I assumed Rich had an idyllic life growing up in Lebanon. But what I heard on the night he shared his "Faith Journey" with the interfaith council – not long after he joined the group – surprised me. All humans, all beings, have suffering in their lives. Suffering and joy are two sides of the same coin. We can't have one without the other.

Rich courageously shared his Faith Journey with new friends on the council, and with his permission, most of it is being shared here:

I am a "Cradle Catholic" – born and raised fully immersed in the Catholic religion.

My family life had a lot of pain and turmoil. This was due to our parents having drug and alcohol addictions. Those addictions resulted in physical and verbal abuse.

In spite of a chaotic home life, I did have sources of stability. Possibly the most important was my family's Sunday morning participation in the ritual we Catholics often refer to as "the Mass." All eight of us – parents and six children – would get into the car every Sunday morning (and sometimes during the week) and participate in what is considered the most important ceremony of our church – the Holy Sacrifice of the Mass.

I like Richard Rohr's meditations that our own John Paul Broderson shared with us in the handouts presented at the end of our last meeting. In his meditation on Buddhism, Father Rohr makes the statement that all great religions are about what you do with your pain.

My family took our pain – along with our confusions, failings, joys and sorrows – and placed them on the altar each Sunday. That is what I learned to do with pain.

Christians are taught to unite our own pain and the sufferings of the world with the eternally perfect and supreme Being who shows us how to suffer; who shows us how to be at peace with suffering; who shows us he can transform suffering.

We believe that Yahweh became a man called Jesus to show us how to live and die. And that he chose a cruel death on a cross to show us that we don't have to be afraid of suffering. We believe his tortured, bruised and beaten body was transformed – resurrected as a glorious, ever-living body. So he showed us that good things can come from bad; and that Infinite Bliss and Supreme Peace will prevail.

Christian communities ritualize these beliefs in an offering, sacrifice, and meal. These take place at an altar that is the focus in most of our churches. We bring three things to the altar: 1. bread and wine; 2. money offerings to be shared with

229

those in need; and 3. our own selves – our pains, our joys, all we are, all we do, all we hope for – all placed as offerings on the altar of sacrifice.

Catholics and many Christians believe Jesus, as a sacrificial offering on our altars, also becomes our meal. Catholics believe the bread becomes what we call "the living Bread of Life." The wine becomes what we call "a living Cup of Salvation." And we participate in the sacrificial offering of our lives and of Yahweh by consuming him in that transformed Bread and Wine. If religion helps unite us with our Creator, you certainly get fully united by consuming him!

In the late 1960s, I spent the better part of a year living like a hippie, although I was maybe more a "flower bud" than an actual "flower child." I hitchhiked from coast to coast. I often fellowshipped with the Hare Krishnas. I embraced and chanted with Siddah Yogis. But I always attended the Holy Sacrifice of the Mass whenever I could. During my travels, I spent four and a half months at a monastery in Vina, California. It was home to a group of monks known as the Trappists – maybe the best known of whom is the writer Thomas Merton. For the Trappists, as well as for any Catholic, the Holy Sacrifice of the Mass is the supreme ritual of a loving feasting with our Almighty.

Eventually I ended up back in Kentucky where I married and raised a family. I still attend other religious ceremonies. I love the traditions and nobility of the Buddhists that our own Charlie Pearl has introduced me to. I like the teachings and chanting and practices of Zen Master Thich Nhat Hanh. I am eager to learn about the magnificent faiths of the Baha'is, the Hindus, the Universalists, the Mormons, the Christian Scientists and the Muslims. Every now and then, I even try to twirl in prayer like the Whirling Dervishes – but I keep falling down! So much for my ecstasy!

But, bottom line, I am a confirmed Catholic. I know there is plenty that is wrong with my church. But I place all those wrongs on the altar of the cross – along with my own wrongs and the wrongs of the world. I remain a Catholic because the Catholic ritual of the Holy Sacrifice of the Mass is in my DNA. And the Catholic ritual of The Mass is my source of ecstasy.

In closing Rich Green said, "Let me make an apology based on the beautiful 'Charter for Compassion' this interfaith council promotes on Facebook. I want to acknowledge that my Catholic church often fails to live compassionately and that it often increases what the charter calls 'the sum of human misery.' For my church's self-absorption, blatant offenses and for any negligence of the needs of others, I want to apologize and ask forgiveness."

Rich retired from state government in 2001 and wife Nora retired in 2004. They are volunteers on Monday afternoons at the Frankfort Regional Medical Center.

"I get to visit the patients and their families in their rooms and I love that," Rich said. "You really see a lot of drama and a lot of need. A lot of times I pray with them. If I can tell it's going to mean something to the patient, we will pray. Sometimes I know it's not appropriate and that's really not what I'm supposed to be doing. But nevertheless, if you know somebody will benefit, it's wonderful."

Rich said he's a happier person today than he was in 1997 when I first wrote about him because he's retired now. "Benefits are great and I'm in awe of having the luxury of being able to plan out what I want to do each day. It has helped calm me. The tension of work is gone. What a blessing it is to live long enough to do it, and to live with a retirement system that allows me to do it."

Daughters Karen Green and Jennifer Barbee are teachers at Bondurant Middle School. Karen teaches art and Jennifer works with special education students. Jennifer has two children, Bryce, 16, and Kaylee, 11. Rich loves being with his family and one highlight from the summer of 2019 was grandson Bryce agreeing to go with him on a two-day retreat to the Abbey of Gethsemani.

"He wasn't as enthused as I was, of course, because he didn't know what Gethsemani is," Rich said. "His life is his phone and Snapchat – all day long.

"We got there and he seemed interested. I was happy for a few minutes. Then they put us in old rooms without air conditioning. But I did bring extra fans with us. They didn't have Internet except at the library so Bryce spent a lot of time in the library. I told him he could Snapchat with God and he thought that was the strangest notion. Maybe it made a little sense to him, but I'm not sure," Rich said, laughing.

Rich said he loves the chanting and singing at the eight services throughout the day, starting with 3:15 a.m. Vigils. "I thought Bryce might go with me to Vigils. But I went to his room and knocked on his door and he wasn't there. I think it was too hot, too uncomfortable for him."

But Bryce had gone to 7:30 p.m. Compline the night before, the service of dismissal for the night.

After breakfast the second day, they went to Bardstown and his grandson seemed to enjoy their visit – perhaps because he had Internet service again. On their way back to Gethsemani, Rich gave Bryce the option of staying another night at the monastery or returning to Frankfort.

"I always enjoy being at Gethsemani but this trip was all about him as far as I was concerned, and he politely let me know he was ready to go home."

The former Trappist monk-in-training didn't get to stay at Thomas Merton's monastery in 2019 as long as he had planned. Of course it wasn't the first time he came home early from a Catholic monastery. And getting to spend one-on-one time with his teenage grandson made it all worthwhile and a retreat to remember.

Chapter 35

Surprise: BuddhaLand is in Kentucky

It's always a joy going to Poor Richard's Books on Broadway in downtown Frankfort, especially when a new Buddhist magazine has arrived on the wooden rack in the front of the store. Most of my Buddhist teachings come from magazines and books.

One afternoon at the bookstore when I opened the new Spring 2019 issue of "Tricycle: The Buddhist Review," I saw a story with a "BuddhaLand" headline. Accompanying the story were colorful illustrations of a Chanting Temple with four Buddhist monks in the foreground, a Stupa of Enlightenment, a Mindful Forest Monastery, a Deer Mountain Retreat Center, and in the center of it all a pleasant looking Asian man with his arms open in a welcoming gesture.

The subhead shocked me: "A Buddhist haven emerges in rural Kentucky, thanks to a generous retiree."

I walked a few steps to the checkout counter where friend Mark Roberts was standing and said, "Mark, you've got to see this." We were both elated and stunned, even more so when we found out the 200-acre BuddhaLand is less than an hour drive from Frankfort.

The property owner is Nam Do, a 72-year-old retired mechanical and computer engineer from Kentucky Truck Plant in Louisville, owned by Ford Motor Company.

A native of Vietnam, Do arrived in Kentucky in 1975 after fleeing Vietnam on a U.S. Navy helicopter at the Saigon airport, one day before communists took over the country.

I bought the magazine and read the article as soon as I got home.

Nam Do (pronounced Doe as in female deer) has turned his property in Carroll County at the edge of Henry County into an offering to the Buddha and his teachings.

According to the Tricycle magazine story, written by freelance journalist Carolyn Gregoire, Do – since buying the property in 2002 – "has been offering free land that Buddhist organizations and individuals can build upon with their own funds. His mission is to nurture the American Buddhist community by providing more dedicated spaces to practice in areas where they can connect with nature."

The next day I found the phone number for BuddhaLand online and called. Nam Do answered and was delighted that I had read the story in Tricycle. He has a kind voice, and he invited me to come visit him. Two weeks later I arrived in mid-morning.

We met at the Stupa of Enlightenment, built out of respect for Tibetan Buddhists even though BuddhaLand was created especially for groups associated with the lineage of Do's lifelong teacher, Vietnamese Zen master Thich Nhat Hanh.

Thich Nhat Hanh is a global spiritual leader, poet and peace activist, revered around the world for his pioneering teachings on mindfulness, Engaged Buddhism, global ethics and peace.

A stupa is a dome-shaped monument, which often contains sacred objects such as Buddhist scriptures. A large, concrete walkway, circling the stupa at BuddhaLand, is built in the shape of the Wheel of Dharma. The eight-spoked wheel represents the Noble Eightfold Path, which Buddha described as the path leading to the cessation of suffering: right view, right aspiration, right speech, right action, right livelihood, right effort, right mindfulness, and right concentration.

Do plans to have flower gardens planted in the spaces between the concrete spokes, and Angela Mitchell has volunteered to help with that project.

The Stupa of Enlightenment is 25 feet tall and contains 100 volumes of Buddhist scriptures and 400 Buddha statues.

After walking once around the stupa, I got in my car and followed Do in his dusty maroon Ford pickup to the retreat center. After going upstairs to see a long meditation room with a cedar floor, walls and ceiling, we went back downstairs and he showed me a large map of the property with six projects in various stages of development.

In the proposed Mindful Living Village, about 30 acres have been reserved for three villages. There are 20 lots on which cabins can be built for monks; 18 lots for lay people; and an area where at least four caves will be built into the side of a hill for those wanting a three-month solitary meditation retreat. There will be no city water, electricity or heat at the caves. The year-round temperature inside will range from 50 to 60 degrees.

One of the caves with a cedar interior was ready to be used on my first visit there.

Next, Do invited me to ride with him along the gravel road to see the projects underway. We went in a cave and I loved the scent of cedar inside. We also went in the chanting hall, the log-house monastery, and then stopped at the edge of the road and walked a short distance to the scenic overlook and meditation deck. In the early morning hours, there's an enchanting view in the distance of a thick white mist rising from the Kentucky River, Do said. I felt an amazing energy on the deck, being there with Nam Do on a beautiful spring day.

I asked him if there had ever been a time since he arrived in the U.S. when he forgot about his Buddhist religion.

"No, never," he answered. "The reason – my family in Vietnam were very strong Buddhists."

Do comes from a family of temple builders. "We have four in Vietnam," he said.

The Tricycle magazine article says, "In 1920, his grandfather built the 10,000-square-foot Buu Thanh Temple, which today continues to serve more than a thousand families in two villages in southern Vietnam. His uncle and great-uncle both constructed temples in a neighboring village, and two monks and one nun in his family serve as abbots in temples elsewhere in the country."

He told me he used to sleep inside a temple when he was three or four years old.

"My mom and sister would take me with them at night and go to the temple and do the chanting. I was too small to do chanting, so I would go underneath the Buddha table and sleep there. They would practice until 10 or 11 at night, and when they were leaving they would wake me up to go home. So a temple for me is like a house in Vietnam."

Do visited Vietnam three years ago, and his niece had arranged for the construction of "a room for me and full facility with air conditioning inside her temple. Maybe in two years – in the winter when there's not too much activity here – I will go back there. And when groups here start to run by themselves, I may go back to Vietnam more often and stay in the temple."

In 1975, just before leaving Vietnam, Do was a 27-year-old high school principal and math teacher. He had bachelor's degrees in math and physics. His wife, Mai Pham, and 18-month-old daughter, Nhien, left on the

235

last flight of a commercial airplane one day before him. He said he took all of his Vietnamese money and exchanged it for American money and it amounted to $200, which he gave to Mai for her trip out of their home country.

He said he kept two ounces of gold, "just in case I need to give it under the table to help me get out of the country. Luckily I left Vietnam without having to pay anything. He said he was in a group of about a thousand people that left in American helicopters on the last day. Because his name was not on a list, he had to wait for the final pick up.

"They said, 'don't worry, everybody will leave.' About 10 helicopters would come in at a time. They would drop down and each helicopter could take about 30 people to a U.S. Navy ship in the ocean and then come back to where we were. When there were about a hundred people left, they said, 'ok, everybody go.' There were three or four helicopters waiting for us. So we got on and that was it, no more flights out."

He said he heard a lot of gunfire when the helicopter lifted off, and was thankful to be on his way out of Vietnam, headed toward a new life in the United States.

He was reunited with his wife and daughter on a U.S. Navy ship, and they traveled to Guam, a small island east of the Philippines in the Pacific Ocean. From there they flew to Arkansas and lived temporarily at a refugee camp.

Do and his family ended up in Louisville because a younger brother-in-law and sister-in-law had started studying engineering at the University of Louisville two years earlier. Through a refugee program, they had found a large Catholic church in Middletown in Jefferson County that would sponsor the Do family.

One of the church members, whom Nam Do met not long after arriving in Louisville, was an engineer. Do told him that he would love to return to college to study engineering. "He said he would love to help me but I think it sounded scary to everybody in the church because I had no money and didn't know but a few words in English. So how could I go to engineering school? He said it would be very tough."

After realizing that Do had the intelligence, confidence and determination to succeed at U of L, "he supported me to do it."

The church connected the Do family with a teacher who offered a two-month class in English as a second language.

"And then I taught myself at night," Nam Do said. "The only reason I could go back to college was because I knew French, not English. I had studied French in Vietnam but I wasn't an expert in it. I knew maybe a thousand words in French, and just 300 to 400 words in English. It was tough for me. But when I read English, I could figure out half of the words from knowing French because most technical words are almost the same. So I could understand what they were trying to say. That helped me a lot at U of L."

He enrolled at U of L in 1976 and graduated in May 1979 in three-and-one-half years.

"I graduated at a high level, an honor level. That's why Ford hired me right away. It's not easy to get a job at Ford. They can interview 20 or 30 engineers and hire only one. Somehow they hired me. In fact, they continued to hire an English teacher to teach me at work for a couple of hours a week for almost a year."

Do said he loved working at Ford.

"I had a very good job because I had degrees in both mechanical and computer engineering. After working 10 years as a mechanical expert, I moved to the computer side, and used the computer as a tool to design the job to make it easier and more efficient."

He started at Ford in 1979 and worked 25 years, and through "a special offer, retired with 30 years seniority."

Do dedicated his retirement to serving others as a part of his spiritual practice. He was grateful to the country and state that supported him and his family. He wanted to create a welcoming, peaceful place in the gently rolling hills and forestland of Kentucky where people, usually in a hurry, could visit and slow down, relax and appreciate being in nature.

Then after he bought the 200-acre farm for about $360,000, he realized he needed to go back to work to pay off the debt. He returned to Ford as a consultant, "and they paid very good because they didn't have to take care of my insurance or other benefits. So I worked five more years, and paid off the 200 acres."

In addition to the buildings at BuddhaLand, he's also designed and built a gravel road around the property and installed water lines. "Altogether I've already spent almost $1 million."

Nam Do and wife Mai Pham have moved from Louisville to Florence in Northern Kentucky to live near their daughter and son-in-law, Nhien and Tim Lange, both of whom are computer engineers. "She wanted us to live near her so she can help us when we get old." Nhien and Tim have two children, Emily and Charlie Lange.

Nam and Mai's son, Kiet Do, who was born in Louisville in 1978, lives in Lexington and works in computer technology. His wife, Ana Ruzic Do, is a pediatrician in Lexington.

Nam and Mai also have a residence at BuddhaLand, where they stay a great deal of the time except in winter months.

When I asked him what his wife and children thought about his dream of creating BuddhaLand in rural Kentucky, Nam said, "At first, they are thinking I am so unusual because nobody thinks like me. I kept telling them to not worry, I could do everything, even though I wasn't sure I could."

Did they believe him?

"Now they do," he says, laughing. "They're very pleased. My daughter designed the BuddhaLand website for me. When you read it, it looks like American writing because it's her doing it.

"My children know the Vietnamese language but they talked it only with my late mother-in-law because she helped take care of them when they were little. The language is tough for them so they talk English with us all the time, and that's OK."

When Nam Do worked at Ford Motor Company, he said his "engineering group would say, 'Nam, we understand you except when you get excited and talk too fast.'"

He laughs, but then says seriously, "I feel the United States is my home country. I left Vietnam when I was 27, and I've lived 45 years in Kentucky. That's why I wanted to build BuddhaLand here."

Nam Do hopes BuddhaLand becomes a "Plum Village for the United States." Plum Village is a mindfulness practice center in the South of France founded by Thich Nhat Hanh. It is home to an international community with practice centers in Europe, Asia, the United States and Australia, and hundreds of sanghas around the world.

Nam Do says there are approximately 500 groups in the United States connected to the lineage of Thich Nhat Hanh.

Two group retreats were planned at BuddhaLand for 2019, "and we will try to have three or four in 2020. If the demand becomes greater, we would maybe get up to 10 retreats a year," Do said.

He believes BuddhaLand will be developed to his satisfaction in 10 years. "My plans should be complete by then." He knows that everything is impermanent and life is unpredictable, but he tells me, "I plan to be alive up to 100 years old, and still be productive. There are some secrets on how to live long. I'll talk to you about that later."

If he doesn't reach the centenarian mark, he's confident his children will keep BuddhaLand alive and well.

Before leaving BuddhaLand that afternoon on my first visit in March 2019, Nam Do said, "Come back anytime, and any friends who want to come with you, they are welcomed too." He needed to go work on a gravel road extension.

Before driving back to Frankfort, I took a short walk from his residence to the Stupa of Enlightenment and did several circumambulations, chanting "Om Mani Padme Hum."

Several days later I called Nam Do, telling him I would like to bring seven Tibetan monks from Tashi Kyil Monastery in India, and several other friends to visit Buddhaland in April. He was elated and said if the weather permitted, they could take a hayride, touring the property on a wagon pulled by a tractor.

It happened. Joining the monks and myself on the April BuddhaLand tour were Angela Mitchell and Nancy Osborne from Frankfort; Mary Batt and her mother-in-law, Eleanor Batt, from Lebanon; and Scott Garrett from Springfield. They were all major supporters and hosts for the Tibetan monks when they came to Kentucky on three U.S. tours.

Getting out of the van in front of the retreat center, Lobsang Manjushri, the main translator for the Tashi Kyil monks on their U.S. tour, was in a joyful mood, saying, "We're here – in BuddhaLand. We've arrived. We've arrived. BuddhaLand!"

As soon as they saw Nam Do, the monks and Nam Do realized that they had met before in Chicago. Nam Do told the visitors about various projects underway on the property. Then we headed for Carrollton where Nam and Mai treated the monks to a lunch buffet at Hometown Pizza.

After lunch we took a hayride to the stupa, the cave area, the monastery, and the scenic overlook and meditation deck. At the monastery, Nam Do told the group about his life in Vietnam and Louisville before his retirement as an engineer at Ford.

He invited the monks to come back to BuddhaLand on their next U.S. tour, and to stay there for a retreat if their schedule permits.

Angela was happy she had the opportunity to ride as a front-seat passenger in the van with the monks from Frankfort to BuddhaLand and back to Frankfort. Their kindness and joyfulness brightens your day.

On their nine-month U.S. tour, the monks had very few days when they could just relax and not work. Today was one of those times – no sand painting to work on, no cooking class and Tibetan dinner to prepare, no children's art workshop, no yoga or meditation classes, no house blessings. The fund-raising was basically over.

They had earned a couple of weeks of rest and relaxation before flying back to India to their monastery, and they wanted to spend part of that time in central Kentucky – about three hours from their U.S. base in Bloomington, Indiana – where they felt deeply loved and appreciated by down-to-earth people who were mostly non-Buddhist.

Tibetan monks and sponsors visit the stupa
in BuddhaLand in Kentucky

Chapter 36

Gambia native forging her own path

This feature on Sigga Jagne, a native of The Gambia and a Kentucky State University graduate, was the cover story for the February 2020 edition of FRANK magazine. I met Sigga when I attended a 2018 fundraising dinner for Starfish International at Bridgeport Christian Church. Starfish is an educational mentorship program for girls in The Gambia in West Africa. Since 2015, Frankfort Interfaith Council members Julia and David Rome have spent about half of their retirement years working as volunteer English teachers at Starfish. Sigga, a native of The Gambia, was one of the sponsors for the Starfish dinner in Franklin County. In addition to providing financial support for the dinner, Sigga helped prepare the food and participated in a panel discussion after dinner. She shared her story of how difficult it was for young girls, who loved learning, to get a good education in The Gambia when she was a young girl. After listening to her, I knew I wanted to meet her and hear more about her life story. In 2019, Sigga invited the Romes and me to her home and we stayed much longer than I had planned. After we arrived, Sigga spent several hours preparing a delicious Gambian dinner for us. Her hospitality was amazing, which is typical for Gambian people, the Romes told me. We stayed until almost midnight, and I had to return to her home on another day to do the interview which led to this story.

Sigga Jagne was the 24th child born to a well-respected educator in The Gambia in West Africa. Her father, Alhaji Mamour Jagne, who died at age 84 in 1993, had five wives during his lifetime including three at the same time.

Sigga's mother, his last wife, is younger than some of Sigga's siblings.

Sigga Jagne: Photo by Hannah Brown

"Dad was a gentle soul," Sigga said. "He was one of the first black principals of a recognized high school. He had a huge orchard with all kinds of fruit trees in a forest and would spend much time there in solitude, prayer, reading and writing. He was very much into nature and had all these stray cats and pigeons he would feed. They would always follow him. He was a practicing Muslim his entire life.

"He spoiled me a lot because I was his last child. I was the only one allowed to sit with him when he was praying."

Although Sigga earned a full academic scholarship to Kentucky State University in 1994, she admits it wasn't easy for girls who loved learning to get a good education in The Gambia when she lived there.

In the winter of 2018, Sigga talked about growing up in The Gambia at a fundraising dinner for Starfish International at Bridgeport Christian Church. Starfish is an educational mentorship program for girls in Lamin, a village of 25,000 in The Gambia, where a third of the population lives below the international poverty line of $1.25 a day.

Yassin Sarr co-founded Starfish in 2007 with her husband, David Fox, originally from Syracuse, New York.

Yassin and Sigga grew up in Lamin during the same time period but didn't realize they knew each other until meeting at the dinner in Bridgeport.

Sigga – founder and CEO of Signara Global Solutions Inc., an international consulting firm – was one of the major sponsors of the dinner.

Yassin went to Berea College in Kentucky and met Frankfort's Nathan Rome when he was a student there in the 1990s. While at Berea, Yassin had the vision of returning to her home country and starting an after-school program for girls, Nathan said.

Since 2015, Nathan's parents, David and Julia Rome, of Frankfort, have traveled to The Gambia five times, staying five to 10 months and working primarily as volunteer English teachers at Starfish.

Today, Sigga and Yassin "communicate all the time. We call each other twin souls," Sigga says. "We're very different in some ways. Yassin is much calmer, more centered. We went to rival high schools and were the head girl prefects at our schools. We would see each other at the same places, over and over, but we never became close growing up."

In 1993, the late Anthony Woods, a KSU professor, came to Sigga's high school to give a lecture. He was doing volunteer work through a program called Teachers for Africa.

"Being the head girl prefect at my school, I gave the word of thanks to Dr. Woods after his lecture. He told me I was very articulate and asked about my future plans.

"I said, 'I'm definitely going to a university. I don't know how because I don't have the money. But I know I'm going.'"

Woods advised her to take the SAT, an academic exam she hadn't heard of. But she took it, "and had a real good score. I earned a full presidential scholarship."

At KSU, she majored in biology and chemistry, and was graduated with high honors. Her family wanted her to go to medical school, "but it was not the calling of my heart to go into medicine."

She also earned a master's in public administration from KSU, and an associate degree in public health at the University of Tennessee.

She worked 14 years in Kentucky state government and was a director overseeing the state Department of Health's HIV-AIDs program.

"I had a good job. I was traveling all over and sitting on national boards. I was going to Congress and having press conferences with the governor. But I got to the point where I literally had to drag myself to work. I knew it was time to leave."

Sigga said 10 years ago she started learning about meditation and it triggered a lot of changes in her life. Her meditation practice helped her find the courage to leave state government and work fulltime at Signara, a small sideline business she had started in 2010.

Her childhood struggles

When Sigga was 12, she went to evening classes to prepare for an important exam that would determine which high school she would get to attend.

"I would get a beating from an uncle when I got home because his wife complained to him that I was supposed to stay home and help her. But I kept going to the classes because I loved learning." She said her uncle "was very remorseful later in life for giving me whippings. He's a different person now."

Sigga also remembers a brother checking out books at the library, and reading those because she wasn't allowed to go to the library. That way of thinking has changed a lot now, thanks to girls' mentoring programs like Starfish, she says.

"In my generation, what was emphasized was a woman growing up and finding a good husband to marry," Sigga says. "A part of me resented that. Why can't I be the right person to do the things I need to do?

"I've always had this inkling of rebelliousness, not doing what everybody else does. So you can imagine growing up in that environment and having that attitude. I got a lot of beatings because I questioned things. I was the hard-headed difficult one."

She said if someone was getting bullied at school, she would "jump in to make sure the fight got stopped."

Today, Sigga owns a nice home overlooking Duckers Lake on Village Drive in Frankfort. While preparing to buy it in 2004, a friend in the U.S. with a master's degree, originally from The Gambia, advised her to wait until she got married to buy a house.

"She wasn't doing it from a place of hate," Sigga said. "But she was saying because I'm young and not married yet, 'If you build your whole life and get everything you want, what is a man going to bring to the table? He would feel intimidated.'

"And I said, 'The man who is going to get intimidated because I'm living my life the way I want is exactly the man I don't want.'

"It used to irritate me. But I've settled into realizing that we see the world differently. For me, it's not a get married for the sake of getting married; it's get married for the right reason with the right person, at the time that is right for me."

More spiritual than religious

Sigga grew up Islamic in a country where 90 percent of its people are Muslim. She still considers herself a Muslim "because I was born a Muslim. But I am more spiritual than religious."

Her mother, Yassin Jobe, 74, who lived with Sigga in Frankfort from 2007 to 2016, didn't have a formal education. "But she valued my education and was happy I came to KSU. She saw the difference it could make." She's witnessed her daughter's generosity, empathy, kindness and compassion for others.

"She respects that," Sigga says. "But she would rather have me pray five times a day and be very religious so God would definitely take me into heaven."

Sigga still feels "absolutely comfortable" when she goes to the Islamic Center of Frankfort. "I'm comfortable no matter what the religious environment is. I know there's a level of truth in each religion. But as human beings, we sometimes take the message and twist it."

Now that meditation is part of her spiritual practice, she realizes she was meditating as a Muslim child in Gambia when she would sit down for her five daily prayers "and communicate with God. I would take forever because I was praying from my heart. And mom would say, 'Get up, that's enough.' But I couldn't hear anything around me. It was like I was transformed and one with God."

The experience was similar when she read books as a child.

"I would get into the story and people would pass by and talk to me and I couldn't hear them. I was not only reading the story, I was in the story as it was unfolding. I got into a lot of trouble for that because people thought I was ignoring them."

Family tragedy

Today, Sigga says she's as happy as she's ever been. But life's road to joy also brought overwhelming grief.

One of her brothers, Njaga Jagne, a captain in the Kentucky National Guard, was killed in a December 30, 2014 attempted coup that failed to topple the government of then-Gambian President Yahya Jammeh. Sigga's brother was one of four plotters killed at Jammeh's headquarters.

He had moved to the U.S. in 1993, and joined the National Guard in 2005 at age 34, a few years after earning a degree in criminal justice from KSU. He was deployed to Iraq twice, in 2006 and 2010.

A January 2015 story in Business Insider, an online newspaper, said the decision Njaga Jagne made to participate in the coup attempt "is almost incomprehensible: He left a family and a stable life in the U.S. to foment regime change in a country he had been born in but hadn't visited in over 20 years, joining a far-flung group of plotters that he may never have even met before."

Sigga was quoted in the story, saying, "He was willing to risk his life to help people where it didn't directly affect him." She believes her brother died in a heroic struggle against tyranny. "His legacy is that he stood up for people who had nobody to stand up for them . . . people who were daily being abused and tortured and abducted and killed. It was worth it for him," she said.

In 1994 Jammeh led a bloodless coup that overthrew the government of Dawda Jawara. Jammeh was elected president of Gambia in 1996 and was re-elected three times. But he lost to Adama Barrow in 2016.

Jammeh is accused of having stolen billions of dollars from the country's coffers to fund a life of luxury, Sigga says. After leaving office, his assets were frozen by many countries and he went into exile. In addition to charges of corruption and human rights violations, he is accused of having raped a number of young women.

In 2000, one of Sigga's brothers, Assan Suwareh, was shot in the stomach and arm at a student demonstration in The Gambia while peacefully protesting against the Jammeh regime.

"Innocent civilians and children were demonstrating in broad daylight and the military turned their guns on them," Sigga said. "He was in a coma and in a hospital for a long time. I brought him to Kentucky in 2002 to get better medical care. He's very gentle, giving and caring. He has an associate degree from KSU, lives in Lexington and is finishing his engineering degree at the University of Kentucky."

War and exile

Family tragedy and time have sparked a renewed interest in genealogy for Sigga.

"Through research we've developed an extensive family tree of thousands of people, extending multiple generations," she said – including royalty on both sides of her family.

Sigga's family history includes a 19th century alliance formed between her paternal ancestor, a warrior ruler, and her maternal ancestor, a king, which defeated the invading French army in a battle led by another maternal ancestor. The alliance rulers were later killed in separate battles, and the surviving members of these great families were driven by the French from Senegal into The Gambia, where many remain today.

Change is coming

Sigga says she's always had a passion for helping others. That's why she started her own business.

She and her small staff do grant writing, problem-solving for small and medium-sized businesses and non-government organizations, project management and program designs. Signara provides worldwide services

246

through an expansive network of professional experts around the globe, according to the company's website.

"We have about 20 experts we contract with," Sigga says. "We've developed a lot of mentorship programs. We've helped young women – who have a skill, a business idea and a passion, but no funding – to get the resources so they can thrive and be independent."

Signara's agribusiness division, called Green Love, focuses on organic farming.

Sigga says Africa has about a million young people turning 18 every month and the majority doesn't find work, she said. She thinks organic farming is the solution.

"Africa imports more than a trillion dollars of food a year, and most of it is over-processed and poor quality. Our ancestors used to eat from the land and science has proven the best food you can eat is organic from local land, which optimizes your immune system.

"Now people go to the supermarket and buy canned stuff, over-processed products that haven't been stored right. Chemical fertilizers have damaged the soil. In The Gambia, a very high percentage of people have diabetes and high blood pressure. We have a sick culture because of what we're putting in our bodies, and we don't have a good public healthcare system."

But there's hope, she says, because of Gambia's young labor force, arable land, a river in the middle of the country and a lot of superfoods.

Green Love has created a cashew farm with 2,000 trees in Gambia and a moringa farm. Moringa is a native tropical plant in The Gambia, which has been used for centuries due to its medicinal properties and health benefits.

"We are also expanding into rice farming because we have a local rice that is the most nutritious in the world and tastes amazing," Sigga says. "It's called Carolina Gold. We've also secured the rights to an organic fertilizer, all natural, to distribute in all of West Africa."

She says getting people to eat better is a slow process. "There's a gradual awareness that's happening but it's nowhere near the levels we want it to be."

Today at age 46, Sigga has lived longer in Kentucky than in The Gambia. She says Kentucky has become her home away from home. She's renovating her house and getting ready for "the next phase in my life.

"The next five years I want to travel the world. I want a mobile, nomadic lifestyle. I can be anywhere with a laptop and do my work. Gambia is going to be the base. Everything I've learned along this life journey, I want to give back. I want to use my talents where it's needed even more.

"For a long time I couldn't do as much work in The Gambia because of the dictator there. I was very vocal against him, publicly and in the media. I'm sure he would have been happy to get his hands on me. But he's no longer there. I've been doing a lot of work, both behind the scenes in some projects and from a distance. But now it's time to be there and do hands-on work.

"No matter where I am, I'll always travel back to Kentucky because I have family here, a brother and nephews. My brother who died, his sons are in Frankfort and Lexington. I've developed a lot of ties here as well, and I have a home here."

The two years following her brother's death were the darkest of times for her.

"But coming out of that makes me appreciate things more, makes me see much clearer. I feel I've come through this fire, and out of it I'm forged in ways I never would have been without that experience. Now there is a knowing there's something greater that can hold me through the worst of times. There's a level of courage, a level of inner calm, a level of wealth that money can't buy. There's a knowing that no matter what, everything is going to be OK."

This Prayer Labyrinth has been created to send
love, joy, happiness, compassion, kindness,
healing and good health; generosity; personal
wealth used for the highest good; forgiveness,
inner peace which ripples out to world peace; and
wisdom and a shift to higher consciousness to
those that enter and walk it. May you find it to be
an inspirational journey in your life.

Charlie and Angela
Dedicated 11-11-11 at 11:11am

PART FIVE

Finding Joy in Dance

"Dance as though no one is watching. Love as though you've never been hurt. Sing as though no one can hear you. Live as though heaven is on earth."
--John Philip Souza

Chapter 37

GABRAKY with son-in-law Jamie Garrett

When we arm wrestled in Angela Mitchell's living room one Friday night six years ago, I never dreamed my future son-in-law Jamie Garrett would want to participate in the Grand Autumn Bicycle Ride Across Kentucky (GABRAKY).

But when I first heard in 2013 that Jamie was serious about doing GABRAKY, I knew he could. He's strong physically. I was no competition for him in arm wrestling. He's a hard worker – on the job for the Lebanon Water Company, and on the farm in Gravel Switch.

He loves a challenge and pedaling a bicycle 243 miles for four days over hilly terrain isn't easy.

Angela and son Kevin Pearl and I, who have done multiple GABRAKYs, knew Jamie would complete the journey. But we were surprised at how well he did all four days. We underestimated his strength and determination.

GABRAKY isn't a race. It's a fun ride. If you do your homework and put in the training miles before the final exam, you'll do fine and enjoy the outing.

It's also a fundraiser for Frankfort's downtown Grand Theatre, an intimate performing arts center, and WalkBike Frankfort, a group dedicated to building safe pedestrian and bicycle paths in the capital city.

Angela and Kevin trained for the "A." Jamie and I were hoping for a "B." My only concern for Jamie was, he didn't log many miles in the last two weeks of training. He was too busy on the job and with farm work.

But that little bit of rest obviously paid off. Jamie made Day 1 from Carrollton to Frankfort look easy.

Several days before the start, Jamie said, "Somebody's got to finish last, somebody's gotta be the fattest." He thought Jamie Garrett would take both categories. Wrong.

OK, we both need to work on slowly reducing the basketballs in our bellies in 2014. But Jamie looks more like a solid linebacker than an obese cyclist. And he didn't come close to finishing last as I did in my first GABRAKY in 2005.

He didn't suffer through GABRAKY 2013. He conquered Peaks Mill Hill, Devil's Hollow Hill, Pea Ridge Hill, Scott's Ridge, Heart Break Hill in Cumberland County about 10 miles from the finish line, and hundreds of other hills with a smile.

I have special memories of the last nine GABRAKYs. My favorite GABRAKY until this year was 2006 when I met Angela Mitchell and felt an immediate spiritual connection, and rode with son Kevin on his first ride across the Bluegrass.

Angela, Kevin, Joanna Hay and I rode in the back of the Kentucky State University bus on the "Twilight Zone" trip back to Frankfort. I remember Angela telling me later one of her special memories that year was seeing Kevin, sitting behind me on the bus, gently putting his hand on my head. Without speaking he was saying thanks for inspiring him to bicycle across the state.

The 2013 GABRAKY was definitely my favorite. Why? Jamie and daughter Charlsie, driver of our support-and-gear vehicle, joined Angela, Kevin and me on the ride. But actually our GABRAKY family is larger than that now.

Other adopted members include:

•Frankfort's Nathan Rome, who was in Charlsie's class at Frankfort High School, and cycled with Angela, Jamie and me all four days.

•Jennifer and Julie Crossen, breast cancer survivors who have now completed five GABRAKYs each, and Julie's husband, Mark Jensen, an art instructor and librarian at Miami University in Ohio. Jennifer lives in Anderson County, and Julie and Mark reside in Cincinnati.

•Bob McClain, whom I met while training for GABRAKY in 2006, the same year I met Angela. Bob is best known for miraculously surviving an accident on a treacherous downhill after he and his bicycle soared over a guardrail and down a steep embankment. That place on the route is now named McBob Hill. McBob recovered and participated in the 2007 GABRAKY, and has been a valuable volunteer for the event in recent years.

•Tim Stout, a Georgetown resident who is a close friend of Kevin. Together, they have a bicycling website, Ramcycling.com.

•Ed Stodola, the founder of GABRAKY, returned after missing the 2012 ride because of cycling overseas to celebrate his 70th birthday. This was his ninth GABRAKY, and he cycled across the U.S. several years ago.

•Chris Schmidt, dean of students at Lindsey Wilson College in Columbia, Kentucky. His college is a major sponsor of GABRAKY every year. Chris, 42, says what he remembers most about previous GABRAKYs are the friendships made before the rides, at every rest stop and afterwards.

"The hardest hill and the scariest descent become the fondest memories," he says.

Chris has completed the "Louisville Ironman" the last two years, finishing two hours faster in 2013 than in 2012 when he swam 2.4 miles, biked 112 miles and ran a 26.2-mile marathon in 17 hours and 15 minutes.

Riding with Kevin, Chris also completed numerous "century rides" in 2013, covering 100 miles in a day.

So after an Ironman and multiple century rides, is GABRAKY easy?

"No," Chris says. "It's challenging. Traveling Kentucky by bicycle, especially along the GABRAKY route, you learn there's not a lot of flat land in our state. The course has many short climbs and some fairly long, sustained climbs."

If you don't plan and train for GABRAKY, "you could still suffer through it," Chris says. "But the ride shouldn't be about suffering. It should be about enjoying the experience."

I think everybody in the family enjoyed GABRAKY 10. Most of us had a few moments of suffering every day, but we knew it was temporary. The entire journey was pure joy, even when the rain arrived at breakfast under the shelter at Green River Lake State Park. Before we arrived at Dale Hollow Lake on the Tennessee border, we rode through rain, high winds, ominous black clouds, thunderstorms and lightning.

And sopping wet, we kept pedaling and completed the journey, injury-free and thankful. On the ride home, Jamie was already talking enthusiastically about riding in his second consecutive Redbud Ride the very next spring in London, Kentucky. And when the time came, Kevin, Angela, Charlsie and I joined Jamie in doing it.

Chapter 38

California dreaming with Angela

This feature story on taking a vacation to California with Angela Mitchell's family is similar to one published in the October 2017 issue of FRANK magazine.

An early 69th birthday gift to myself was an eight-day trip to California this summer. Going there had been in the back of my mind since I fell in love with The Mamas and the Papas version of "California Dreamin" in 1966 as a high school senior.

The Giant Sequoias and Redwoods have been calling me for decades, especially since moving to Frankfort in 1988 to work as a communications officer for the state Natural Resources and Environmental Protection Cabinet.

For four years I worked with brilliant Kentuckians who put their heart into protecting and improving our water, land and air quality – Art Williams, Russ Barnett, Don and Kay Harker, Valerie Timmons, Bill Eddins, Ken Cooke, Ed Councill, Vicki Pettus, Betty Beshoar, Hannah Helm, Annette Hayden, Van Fritts, Lily Cox, Lou Martin, Jack Wilson, Bob Logan, Pat Haight, Susan Bush, Tom Bennett, Karen Armstrong-Cummings, Charlie Peters, Rich Green, Brian Baker, Scott Hankla, Don Dott, Dara Carlisle, Eddie Riddle, Alex Barber, Leah McSwords and others.

Their enthusiasm and passion for seeing the big picture, all the interconnections, inspired me, and there's no going back once the Earth spirituality thing clicks. And thanks to the late State Journal Editor Carl West who hired me in 2001, I wrote about environmental issues for 12 years.

In late 2016 I knew the California procrastination was over. A long bicycle ride 10 years earlier and a longer 2017 hike led to Yosemite, Santa Cruz and San Francisco.

On a fall Sunday morning in 2006, I met Angela Mitchell on a narrow street behind Ed and Sue Stodola's Frank Lloyd Wright house. A small group had gathered for a training ride for the Grand Autumn Bicycle Ride Across Kentucky (GABRAKY), a three-day 225-mile journey from the Ohio River at Carrollton to Dale Hollow Lake at the Kentucky-Tennessee border.

GABRAKY – a fundraiser for the Grand Theatre – brought us together. Angela and I realized we were kindred spirits in wanting to enjoy, protect and honor our Mother Earth.

Ten years later Angela's older daughter Sarah was preparing for a 2,650-mile backpacking trip on the Pacific Crest Trail from Mexico to Canada.

An Eastern Kentucky University graduate who majored in art, Sarah and her boyfriend, Joseph Merchant, saved enough money working as servers at Bourbon on Main to take a year off from work to do the West Coast hike.

Sarah's 26th birthday was June 22 and Angela wanted to be in California that week with Sarah and her brother and sister, Nathan, 23, and Katie, almost 21, to celebrate. She figured Sarah and Joseph wouldn't mind a short break from the Pacific Crest Trail. I was invited to join them and quickly accepted.

I had read President Trump was considering eliminating or downsizing several of the country's most famous national monuments. One of those is the Giant Sequoia National Monument, where 328,000 acres of preserved forest are home to some of the world's biggest and oldest trees.

I felt a little better in September when I read California's protected forests, deserts and mountain ranges would be spared from Trump's plan under new recommendations from Interior Secretary Ryan Zinke.

Our first vacation day was mostly spent in airports and in the air, leaving Lexington in early morning and traveling to Chicago, Los Angeles and then Fresno, where we picked up our rental car and met Sarah and Joseph.

Several weeks earlier their hike took a disappointing turn at mile 600 when Sarah ran out of energy. A week of rest didn't help. She finally went to a medical clinic and test results revealed she had mononucleosis.

They went to Bakersfield to pick up their car at Joseph's uncle's house, and Joseph drove them back to Kentucky.

It didn't take nearly that long, however, to get Sarah back to California. The thought of her mother and siblings celebrating her birthday in California without her was not one she wanted to dwell on while recovering.

Two days before we left, Sarah booked flights for Joseph and her – from Louisville to Dallas to Fresno – for the same day as our flights.

The temperature was 104 when we met in Fresno in mid-afternoon. Angela drove the van 48 miles to the Best Western Plus Yosemite Gateway Inn in Oakhurst, 14 miles from the south entrance to Yosemite National Park. We stayed four nights in Oakhurst, a small town in the foothills of the Sierra Nevada mountain range.

Lodging with five who liked to sleep late, I enjoyed two-hour solo walks beginning at dawn each morning, after 45 minutes of sitting meditation.

On a town mural – by a walking trail alongside a flowing creek – was a familiar John Muir quote: "In every walk with nature one receives far more than one seeks."

Finally meeting the Giant Sequoias

Our first full day in California, Joseph drove to Nelder Grove, a Giant Sequoia grove in the Sierra National Forest.

Before seeing the giant trees, we stopped by a sparkling waterfall. Nathan and Katie climbed on rocks beside the rushing water.

Later, from the Nelder Grove parking lot, we walked only two-tenths of a mile before seeing our first living Giant Sequoia, 2,400-year-old Big Ed. Joseph, Sarah, Katie, Nathan and I formed a line and joined hands in front of the stately cinnamon-barked evergreen and we barely stretched beyond its diameter as Angela took a photo.

We hugged it and I could have stayed there the rest of the day. But we moved on and soon 2,700-year-old Bull Buck came into view. Bull Buck reaches a height of 246 feet and has a ground-level circumference of 100 feet.

A tour guide, who had driven a van from San Francisco and was leading a small group through the grove, said this is his favorite place to see the Giant Sequoias because there's far fewer tourists here than in Yosemite National Park.

When he heard we were from Kentucky and the Giant Sequoias and Redwoods had been calling me for decades, he asked, "How did they get your number?" We laughed.

Seeing photographs and documentaries and reading about the ancient trees in National Geographic, Orion and Sierra magazines helped connect us. Reading Julia Butterfly Hill's book in 2000, "The Legacy of Luna:

The Story of a Tree, a Woman and the Struggle to Save the Redwoods," touched my soul . . . and broke my heart.

Hill lived in a 180-foot tall, 1,500-year-old California Redwood tree, affectionately known as Luna, for 738 days from December 1997 until late 1999. She went through all kinds of hell to prevent Pacific Lumber Company loggers from cutting Luna down.

I can't fathom anyone wanting to clear-cut magnificent trees that have been living on Earth so long, some of them since the time of Jesus and Siddhartha Gautama (Buddha). They're our living, breathing cathedrals and temples.

Sitting in silence in front of Bull Buck for a short time, feeling the amazing energy of this ancient being, I knew if we had returned to Kentucky that night, the California vacation would have been wonderful.

But we still had outdoor adventures to enjoy.

Rock climbing in Sierra National Forest

The next day was Sarah's birthday and her mother's gift was a visit to Cloud Nine Massage in Oakhurst. Afterward, she relaxed in her motel room while everybody else headed back into the Sierra National Forest for a sizzling afternoon of rock-climbing.

We met our guide, Riley West, a friendly young man who grew up in Philadelphia and earned a degree in outdoor leadership from Warren Wilson College near Asheville, North Carolina.

I went along for the scenic hike up to the granite wall, but was a spectator while the others took turns climbing in 105 degree weather. I had been rock climbing only once – in the Red River Gorge with Angela and her family 10 years ago – and it was the most physically challenging sport I've done. I wasn't up to the task this year.

But I admired the strength, agility and determination of Nathan, Joseph, Angela, and especially Katie in successfully scaling to the top. A Type 1 diabetic since age 10, Katie knows strenuous exercise often causes her to feel bad later, but she's courageous and insisted on climbing first.

Angela, 58, went last and struggled initially to find small indentions for her hands and feet. After several minutes, she said, "I don't think I can do it."

We all knew then she would. She has more inner strength than anybody I've ever met. The next minute she moved up, up, and up, and soon made it look easy getting to the top. We cheered. She loved the splendid panoramic view at the top and felt Mother Nature's embrace.

That night we ate at an outstanding Mexican restaurant for Sarah's birthday, and had Ben & Jerry's non-dairy ice cream at our motel for dessert. Sarah and Joseph are vegans and they inspired me in the spring to go from being a vegetarian to vegan.

It's much easier being vegan in California than Kentucky. All restaurants we visited had many vegan options and everything we tried was delicious.

A day in magical Yosemite

The entire crew got up earlier than usual the next morning because we wanted to see as much as possible in Yosemite National Park. Sarah and Joseph had purchased a family pass to all national parks in California earlier in the year, so our admission was free.

Finding a parking place was no problem at our first stop, Glacier Point. At 3,000 feet above the valley floor, the overlooks offer a sweeping bird's-eye view of Yosemite Valley, massive granite peaks including the famed Half Dome, and Yosemite Falls, Vernal Fall and Nevada Fall.

The air was pure and peaks in the distance were snow-covered. Looking through a telescope, hikers on top of Half Dome looked like ants.

Later in Yosemite Valley we saw Bridalveil Fall, which drops 620 feet to the valley floor.

Afternoon traffic was heavy and it took a long time to find parking. On a short hike in the valley, we saw several rock climbers scaling El Capitan, a massive granite sculpture of nature standing 3,593 feet from base to summit. From spring to fall, climbers come from all over the world to scale El Capitan. A 2011 National Geographic said 23 people have died trying.

I wouldn't be surprised if lean and quiet Nathan returns to California before his 35th birthday to climb El Cap or Half Dome. He's a natural when it comes to climbing anything and has unbelievable balance, calmness, patience and passion for scaling rock walls.

The next day Nathan drove us 175 miles to the Pacific Ocean and Santa Cruz, where we stayed one afternoon and night before heading north on scenic Highway 1 to San Francisco. I loved sitting in the back of the van and watching the lay of the land change to gentle rolling hills of yellow and beige, dotted with green trees and blue lakes.

259

In the fertile coastal region, we were in awe of the number of massive vegetable and fruit farms, and numerous roadside stands selling produce at low prices.

Watching outstanding surfers

In Santa Cruz, Nathan did an excellent job in bumper-to-bumper traffic getting us to our motel near the Monterey Bay.

After checking in Fireside Inn By the Beach, I picked up a free tourist magazine. The intro said, "The people who make up the Santa Cruz community are its greatest asset. We come from all walks of life, and form an eclectic mix of '60s hippie idealism, surf culture, cutting edge technology, and one of the largest per capita arts communities in the country."

We walked several blocks to Saturn Café and everybody loved it. The sidewalk sign at the entrance said, "Breakfast, Brunch, Dinner, Burgers, Shakes, Soups & Salad … 100% Vegetarian."

After our mid-afternoon meal, Katie and Nathan headed to the boardwalk, Angela and I went looking for surfers and Sarah and Joseph slowly returned to the motel. Besides having mono, Sarah sustained a back injury and was in pain the entire trip. It was sad seeing this young woman, a yoga instructor who's so dedicated to health and fitness, being unable to participate in outdoor activities she loves.

She's backpacked 1,300 miles on the Appalachian Trail, hiking in every state along the way except Maine, the last one going north. It's on her to-do list, and she'll get there. She's good at rock climbing, caving, kayaking and anything she attempts.

Wandering toward the beach, Angela and I saw a young man and asked him where the popular surfing area was. He pointed us in the right direction and then said, "It's such a beautiful day, I'll walk you there." Along the way, he pointed out four Redwood trees.

We had never seen good surfing and this was a great place to start. Steamer Lane is a famous surfing location off a point on the side of cliffs near downtown. There are railings near the edge of the cliffs and spectators have wonderfully close views of the numerous surfers in wetsuits.

The Santa Cruz Surfing Museum is housed in a lighthouse at Steamer Lane. We watched expert surfers for almost two hours and saw numerous intermediate to beginning surfers on smaller waves as we walked back to our motel.

Shortly before dusk, we walked to the boardwalk, which has a seaside amusement park with more than 34 rides and attractions including the Giant Dipper wooden rollercoaster.

We both like rollercoasters, although I haven't ridden one since undergoing spinal surgery in 1999. The lines were too long so I didn't have to get nervous thinking about riding one again. We enjoyed watching others have fun and late Saturday Angela, laughing, said, "You might be the oldest person here." For a half-hour, I joined her in looking for other potential candidates and spotted two. But we didn't ask for IDs.

It was still crowded and loud when we left. Walking back to the motel, I said, "This was fun for one night but if I had to choose between being in this noisy crowd every night and dying, I'll take death."

I looked forward to my Sunday morning solo walk back to Steamer Lane. I got there at daylight. It was cold and overcast but plenty of surfers were already there. I talked to a man, in his mid-60s, who rode there on an old bicycle. He said he's surfed all his life and never plans to quit. Slender and muscular, he said he rests on weekends because it's too crowded on the waves.

A tall, slender woman with long blonde hair was busy taking action photos of her two college-aged sons with a Nikon camera and long zoom lens. They've grown up surfing and her husband, a medical doctor, was out in the bay as well, moving smoothly through smaller waves on a paddle board.

She said Jack O'Neill, "a great man and surfing legend," died June 2 of this year at age 94. He lived on beachfront property in Santa Cruz and helped invent the wetsuit. He was the founder of O'Neill brand, one of the world's best-known surf brands.

I walked down a stairway to the beach to feel the cold water and sand and get a closer look at a congregation of sea lions on a large rock out in the bay.

At mid-morning my Kentucky family arrived at Lighthouse Point and watched the surfers. Katie climbed over the railing and walked to the end of a cliff farther out in the bay.

Before noon we all gathered at the van and Joseph volunteered to drive us 75 miles to San Francisco. Not long after leaving Santa Cruz we stopped briefly at Big Basin Redwoods State Park and Waddell Beach to watch kite surfers.

Loving SF and Pride Parade

In downtown San Francisco, traffic was insane and Joseph did an incredible job getting us into a parking garage several blocks from Hotel Union Square where we would stay for two nights.

We couldn't get to the parking garage by our hotel because the 47th annual Pride Parade was underway. It was crazy. We loved it.

This is how the San Francisco Chronicle newspaper described it the next morning: "Hundreds of thousands of revelers descended on Market Street like a rainbow-colored river Sunday to join the explosion of wildly painted floats and chest-thumping music as the Pride Parade took over downtown San Francisco.

"People from all over the world jammed sidewalks – five deep in spots – for the chaos of costumes, camaraderie and celebration as they watched more than 200 floats, musical acts and groups of marchers pour down the 1.3-mile parade route."

The parade began long before we arrived but we still saw the last 90 minutes. It was wonderful standing in this massive celebration of human diversity, seeing people feeling free to laugh and love and be themselves. I felt a kinship to all of them. This is the compassionate America I cherish.

Not long after the parade, Sarah, Joseph, Katie, Angela and I walked to nearby Westfield San Francisco Centre on Market Street for dinner. The nine-story shopping mall features Nordstrom, Bloomingdale's and 200 shops and restaurants. Nathan chose to take a nap before eating.

The Loving Hut, a vegan cuisine chain with an Asian-accented menu was an easy choice since Katie, Angela and I had never eaten at an all-vegan restaurant. The food was heavenly.

A short time later, however, the joyful atmosphere inside Westfield Centre turned chaotic. We briefly returned to our hotel and Nathan was up and ready to eat. So Angela, Katie and I returned to the Westfield food court with him. Katie went shopping on an upper level, and Angela and I sat at a table by Panda Express where Nathan got his dinner.

Two minutes after he started eating, a large brawl erupted in the food court and spread to other areas. Dozens of police officers arrived quickly. An employee of Panda Express shouted they were closing the metal gate to their business and invited us to come inside. We declined since we weren't sure where Katie was. Calm Nathan continued eating his shrimp, chicken and rice – oblivious to the pandemonium coming in waves around us.

The mall was forced to close its doors early because of the violence and the number of innocent bystanders. Nathan finished his meal, Katie was found, and soon, like everybody else, we were escorted out of the building by police.

One police officer suffered minor injuries after being pepper sprayed, a juvenile was taken into custody and several others were detained.

The next day Angela recognized one of the officers from the night before because he brought his bicycle into the mall with him. He said it would have been stolen if left outside. He told her the fight was between two local gangs and had no connection to the Pride Parade.

When he heard it was our first trip to San Francisco from Kentucky, he said he hoped we wouldn't think San Francisco was a terrible place because of the incident. Angela assured him we "absolutely love this city."

We didn't let the brawl stop us from enjoying the city of love Sunday night. In the cool air with a ubiquitous scent of marijuana (it's sort of legal) we walked for blocks, watched historic cable cars pass by, and listened to street musicians. On one corner Angela and I danced to a female vocalist's beautiful soulful performance of "Stand By Me."

A large Walgreen's store across from our hotel stayed open all night, and I loved going there in the early morning on Monday and Tuesday to buy a Chronicle newspaper. We returned to Westfield Centre for lunch Monday and ate again at the Loving Hut. Everything was calm.

Cable car operator Gerald is a gem

Angela bought cable car tickets for everybody. Lines were long in the afternoon so we waited until after 5 p.m. to ride. A friendly hotel desk clerk encouraged us to take the winding route to Fisherman's Wharf.

It was crowded when we boarded but we got good seats in the front. On the wharf we watched the sun go down over the bay with the Golden Gate Bridge in the background. I walked to the water's edge and felt the frigid water.

Fifty yards out we saw two swimmers without wetsuits moving swiftly through the water.

We went in a clothing shop and I bought a black fleece San Francisco jacket.

We waited in line 45 minutes to board a cable car back to Market Street. We were the last ones to get on so we stood near the back, holding on to leather straps for stability. Several blocks after starting, a man and his granddaughter in the very back with the operator got off.

I asked the friendly operator, Gerald, if I could join him back there and he said "sure." I held on to a rail, but noticed as soon as we started my new fleece jacket slid out of the plastic bag and fell on the street.

I told him what happened but he couldn't hear me. At the next stop a couple of blocks down, he understood what I had said. I told him I wanted to get off so I could go back and try to find it, and would walk back to the hotel.

He said, "No, stay here. I'll go back and try to get it." Angela said she thought she saw a car run over it. Gerald ran two blocks uphill in the dark and came back smiling, handing it to me. The car must have straddled it because it looked perfect.

I offered him a $10 tip but he said he isn't allowed to accept tips.

The next night we were flying back to Kentucky, by way of Salt Lake City and Atlanta. But Gerald and his cool gray city of love and his charming California will stay forever in our hearts and dreams.

Charlie and Angela and her family
visiting Yosemite

Chapter 39

Gerry Faust: favorite football coach

This feature on former Notre Dame Football Coach Gerry Faust is similar to the cover story for the November 2019 issue of FRANK magazine.

My first memory of feeling a divine presence was at the University of Notre Dame. It was an early Saturday morning in July 1967. I was 18. A lifelong friend, Carl Crews, and I had been up all night driving in heavy rain through Michigan on our way back to Lebanon, Kentucky, our hometown, a predominately Catholic community. The rain had stopped when we arrived in South Bend but we had a two-hour wait before the bookstore opened to get Notre Dame football t-shirts.

So we walked across campus, past the Golden Dome administration building, to the Grotto of Our Lady of Lourdes, by the twin lakes, inside Sacred Heart Church, by Theodore Hesburgh Library with the Touchdown Jesus mosaic mural facing Notre Dame Stadium. We pretty much had the campus to ourselves at that hour. I felt a calm inner peace and was thankful we had survived the night before when we had to change a flat tire on a busy highway in a pouring rain.

We walked around the locked football stadium and I wondered what it would be like to walk across the grass where Coach Ara Parseghian's national championship team played last year. Wouldn't it be great, I thought, to sit in the stadium and watch huge players in their glistening gold helmets and blue and gold uniforms running from the tunnel onto the field. I never dreamed it would happen. But it did three years later.

While going to Western Kentucky University, I met Karen Lanz from Elizabethtown, Kentucky, on spring break at Daytona Beach, Florida in 1970. She was a student at Eastern Kentucky University. What I remember most about some of our first conversations was that her parents had four season tickets to Notre Dame football games.

Six months later I was invited to go with them to a game. Notre Dame crushed Army 51-10, finished 10-1 and defeated No. 1 Texas in the Cotton Bowl on Jan. 1, 1971. Twenty-nine days later, Karen and I married in St. James Catholic Church in Elizabethtown.

We are no longer married but for decades we saw the Fighting Irish win many football games in South Bend. Our four children – Charlsie, Kevin, Kennedy and Kathryn – and most grandchildren are Notre Dame fans too.

Gerry Faust fan for life

During those years, there was a five-year span when the Irish record was mediocre (30-26-1) by ND standards. Ironically, the Coach Gerry Faust Era from 1981 through 1985 became my all-time favorite and most-miserable years at the same time.

Even today at age 71 – going beyond Notre Dame and taking into consideration all football coaches I've ever known, watched or read about – Gerry Faust is still my favorite.

I became a Faust fan after reading a Sports Illustrated article on him before his first season at Notre Dame. He had taken one giant step from coaching a high school football team to what I thought was the College Football Capital.

His 18-year-record at Cincinnati Moeller, an all-boys Catholic high school, was unbelievable: 174-17-2. There were five state championships and four mythical national titles following unbeaten seasons.

When he left for Notre Dame, the Moeller Crusaders had a 33-game winning streak and had won 70 of their last 71 games, 90 of their last 93.

College football scholarships went to approximately 250 Moeller players while Faust was there, and 20 players moved on to play at Notre Dame.

But Gerry Faust, the person, was what impressed me most about the Sports Illustrated story.

Under Faust, the creed for the Moeller player was: "No matter how great you are, you better never curse; you better never play dirty football; and if you burp, you better say excuse me."

Faust has always attended daily Mass, and while at Notre Dame, he visited the campus Grotto twice daily to pray.

The 1985 ND football season would be the last of Faust's five-year contract. I knew it was a long shot that he would survive beyond that. I knew it was now or never to try to meet this coach I admired. I wanted to find out if he was the same decent person – after experiencing defeat way too often – as he was when his teams always won.

Requesting an interview

I was a small-town editor of a weekly newspaper in the Lake Cumberland region, The Times Journal of Russell Springs. I wrote him a letter in early summer asking if I could come visit him. It would have been easy for him to say "no" because he was way too busy.

But a week after sending the letter, he called, asking if I could come to his office on August 9. "If you get here at 11 a.m., we could spend a couple of hours together," he said in his familiar hoarse voice.

When I arrived at the football office, a television crew, taping a commercial against drunken driving, had just left. His schedule was crammed with interviews from major TV and newspaper reporters. But first Coach Faust took time to hand out autographed blue and gold Nerf footballs to Charlsie, Kevin and Kennedy, who were with their mother and hoping to get to see him for a few seconds before I interviewed him. He gave them an extra football for Kathryn, their baby sister back home, and invited them to see his office.

Kevin, 9, asked him what he had to do to become a Notre Dame football player.

"First of all Kevin, you've got to be a great athlete. It wouldn't be fair to bring someone in here who couldn't play. So it's really important to develop yourself physically as far as weight training and quickness. You can develop quickness by skipping rope and playing tennis.

"The second thing, and equally important, is you've got to have 14 college prep classes. And the third thing is, you've got to be a top-quality person because I'm not going to take anybody who doesn't have good values, doesn't believe in the right things."

Any athlete on the Notre Dame or major college level has to have some natural ability, Faust said. "But most athletes who succeed have done it through hard work. And to be honest with you, I would rather have an athlete that is not as gifted but gets the job done by hard work than a guy who is gifted but never works at it and doesn't have the right attitude."

Few nine-year-olds become Joe Montana or Tim Brown caliber, and few high school football players earn a free college education. But football goes way beyond the game, and those who give it their best effort – whether they play or not – will be better off, Faust said in that 1985 interview. So all the sweat, bruises and sacrifice are worth it.

"High school football is the closest thing to reality as far as what life is all about," Faust said. "I found out when I coached high school football that young men had to give up a lot and work hard. We're in a society now where we have it too easy, and a sport like football, where you have to sacrifice a lot, drill a lot and work hard, really develops a young person into a more self-disciplined person. And I really think it will help later on in life."

After that first visit to Coach Faust's office in South Bend, I began praying Notre Dame would win games, even though I felt God doesn't care who wins athletic events. I was really just praying for Coach Faust to get to stay at Notre Dame. That meant eight wins.

It didn't happen.

I went to the Southern Cal game after the maximum three losses had already occurred and the Irish breezed to a 37-3 win. After two more home wins, it was on the road to face undefeated and top-ranked Penn State. My prayers picked up. But in the rain and mud, the dream ended. John Shaffer, a former Cincinnati Moeller player, quarterbacked the Nittany Lions to a 36-6 win.

Our family tickets to the LSU game weren't available. That didn't matter. Kevin, Kennedy and I were going to the final home game of the season and Faust's final game on the sideline at Notre Dame.

Thanks to Coach Faust, we sat high in the stadium on the 50-yard line. Our feet rested on snow and ice. It looked and felt as if a new layer of snow may cover the field before halftime. The Golden Dome, visible from our seats, brightened a dark gray sky.

Faust's first game as coach at Notre Dame had been against LSU, and an 18-point victory at home vaulted the Irish to a No. 1 ranking. It lasted one week . . . and never returned. It didn't take long for sports writers to put embattled in front of his name. After his first season many ND fans began crying "Oust Faust."

In his final game at ND Stadium, the Irish scored early and for most of the afternoon it looked as if his farewell game there would be a win. But LSU, which managed a field goal just before halftime, added a touchdown late in the game and won 10-7.

Most of the crowd were long gone when Faust exited the brick stadium for the final time. Several partying LSU fans, wearing purple and gold, walked by as he came out of the dressing room. They asked if he would pose for a picture with them. He found a smile and obliged. After the coach signed a few game programs and ticket stubs, Kennedy, Kevin and I walked with him to his football office. I told him we would see him next year.

"But I won't be here," he said.

"It doesn't matter," I said. "We'll go wherever you are."

Three days later, he resigned.

He had one game left, at Miami. In the closing minutes of that one, CBS-TV's Ara Parseghian, a former successful coach at ND, predicted that Notre Dame will rise again. "From these ashes will come a winning Notre Dame team," he said.

When it was finally over, the ups and downs of Gerry Faust's five-year career at Notre Dame were highlighted while the audio was lyrics to the pop song, "Just Once," by Quincy Jones: *I gave my all, but I think my all may have been too much, Lord knows we're not getting anywhere. It seems we're always blowing whatever we've got going . . .*

"Just once, can't we figure out what we keep doing wrong, why the good times never last too long . . . Just once, can we find a way to finally make it right? Make the magic last more than just one night . . . Just once . . ."

"He's an awfully nice man," said TV's Brent Musburger. "He was just in the wrong place at the wrong time. And it ended unhappily here in the Orange Bowl this afternoon, losing to Miami 58-7. It was a sad one, indeed, to witness. The Gerry Faust Era is over now."

University of Akron years

In the autumn of 1986, my 8:02 a.m. knock on the door of Room 116 at the Holiday Inn in Murfreesboro, Tennessee, woke Gerry Faust, the new University of Akron head football coach. It was homecoming Saturday at Middle Tennessee State University.

But first there was Mass at 8:30 in Father Clyde Foster's room. Then in a private dining room, spaghetti, lasagna and pizza were served to the players for breakfast. After breakfast, an interdenominational church service was conducted in the dining room. Around 20 Akron players, several assistant coaches, Faust and his older son, Gerry III, a student then at the University of Dayton, attended.

Akron's road uniforms were gold, white and navy, like Notre Dame's. Helmets were gold with a blue A on both sides.

It was a close game but Akron lost.

Several weeks later, Akron played at Tennessee Tech and our entire family, plus the Rev. Dave Stoltz, pastor of Holy Spirit Catholic Church in Jamestown, attended the game. Akron scored 28 points in the final quarter to win.

In the dressing room after the game, just before the Lord's Prayer, Faust told the players that punter Mike Knapp just learned of his grandfather's death. Mike's eyes were red. He told the team his grandfather was "85 and just worn out."

Then Faust spoke. "He's with God now, Mike. That's the important thing. That's one thing you've always got to remember men. I'm not trying to be sentimental or anything like that, but we're here for a trial in life. How you approach life is how you're going to be rewarded afterwards. That's important.

"And you know what? I forget about it and so do you. We get hung up in this game of football and other things. But we need to be good neighbors and try to be good persons. Someday we're all going to have to answer to the Almighty. Let's say a prayer . . ."

Akron finished 7-4 his first year. We continued to follow him through the years – in road games at the University of Louisville, University of Tennessee, East Carolina University and Ball State University.

After home games, the Pearls were always invited to the Faust home for conversation and food. On our first visit to Akron, we arrived at the football office early on a Saturday morning of a night game. He was alone, watching game films of his opponent. He stopped what he was doing, took us to his car and gave us a tour of the campus. That's Gerry Faust.

He drove down one street the wrong way, where construction was underway, and got yelled at by a frowning worker. Faust smiled, waved and said, "They don't have any idea who I am."

Akron fans didn't usually fill the stands of the 35,202-seat Rubber Bowl. It was a humbling experience going from Notre Dame to Akron. But Faust worked just as hard as he did at Notre Dame, and was just as energetic, enthusiastic and optimistic.

"He has boundless energy," said priest Clyde Foster. "He can't sit still longer than 20 seconds."

Steve Love, a writer at the Akron Beacon Journal, said Faust, an organized man, at times seems disorganized because he schedules himself for 28-hour days and expects others to keep pace. Love later co-authored Faust's autobiography, "The Golden Dream," first published in 1997, three years after Faust's coaching career ended.

In nine years at Akron, his best season record was 7-3-1 in 1992. After his 1994 team finished 1-10, Faust was fired.

The late Ray Meyo, a businessman who became a Faust fan at Notre Dame and remained a friend at Akron, said, "It's very easy to show class and dignity when you are on top and everything is going well. But how you judge a guy is by what he does when things aren't going well. In my life, I've come across a lot of people with character, but I've never come across anyone with more character than Gerry Faust."

Father Foster said Faust is a man of integrity, commitment and dedication. "He's very deeply a family man and his faith is the center of who he is. Coaching for him is much more than a job. It is very much in the light of a calling."

Quite a few of his Akron players were inner-city kids from poor backgrounds, Foster said. "He realizes their physical talent is a gift, an instrument to get them out. [For a Faust player], getting an education, a degree, to grow as a person, is first and foremost. His players are not animals. They're not treated like animals and they don't act that way."

Faust friendship rekindled

Daughter Charlsie (Pearl) Garrett – a 1991 Frankfort High graduate who earned a bachelor's degree at Centre College in Danville, Kentucky, and played basketball there – called in June 2019, asking if I had kept old stories I had written on Coach Faust.

"I was talking today with a Notre Dame fan, Jon Nebriaga, and telling him about getting to meet a Notre Dame football coach when we were kids, and that you had written stories about him. He wants to read about Coach Faust."

Charlsie's call brought back good memories and I wanted to talk to him. I was pretty sure he still lived in Akron. I tried his old cell phone number, guessing it wasn't going to be his number today.

But he surprised me. The familiar hoarse voice answered. He's 84 and it took a minute for him to remember me. He's touched the lives of thousands in his lifetime and has many close friends. We hadn't talked in eight years. That was when son Kennedy was in South Bend for a game and saw Faust signing his "Golden Dream" books before the game. He asked about me, and Kennedy called me and put him on the phone for a brief conversation. The call made my day much better.

271

Coach Faust has that good compassionate energy that's contagious. He uplifts everyone in his presence.

Life after coaching is good, he said. "The good thing about now is I have more time to spend with my grandchildren, my kids and wife, which I didn't have before."

Faust said when Father Edmund P. Joyce – Notre Dame's then-executive vice president and head of the faculty board in control of athletics – offered him the job, Joyce said, "Before you say 'yes,' I'll tell you that you will never be home."

"And I said, 'I'm never home now, being athletic director and football coach at Moeller High School.'"

Then Joyce said, "It's the toughest job in America."

He was speaking the truth, Faust said.

Now Faust enjoys going with wife Marlene to St. Vincent-St. Mary High School football games on Friday nights in Akron. That's where a granddaughter goes to school.

When Moeller plays a game in Cleveland, Faust goes to those. "It's been a couple of years since I've seen them play in Cincinnati. I try to go to one Notre Dame game a year now in South Bend, and I try to watch most of their other games on TV.

"When I'm at home, I go to University of Akron games. They're great to me. I go to a lot of Akron's home basketball games too. I'm really close to the basketball coaches."

Faust still goes to Catholic Mass every morning. He said he doesn't do much to stay physically fit other than playing golf once a week with friends from church. "I'm not very good at it. In fact, I'm terrible." Most of the men play 18 holes, "but I'm so busy, I don't have time to play 18. I play because it's good exercise and it's good friendship."

His breakfast every morning is cereal with milk, a doughnut, and a diet Coke.

He said Marlene loves reading and finishes a book about every four or five days. "I haven't read a book in 30 years," he said, laughing. "I can't sit still that long. I did, however, have to read my book, 'The Golden Dream,' before it was published to verify everything."

The Fausts have three children: Gerry III, a businessman in the Cincinnati area; Steve, a Notre Dame graduate who is a doctor of veterinary medicine near Akron; and Julie Marie, an elementary teacher at an inner-city public school in Akron; and six grandchildren.

Faust has undergone successful heart surgery. "My surgeon was a Notre Dame graduate," he said. "The first thing I told him when I went to his office was, 'My record at Notre Dame wasn't the best. You're not going to take that out on me, are you?' He laughed and said he wouldn't, and he did a great job."

Now that he's in his mid-80s, "I have my aches and pains. But I look around and see all the people who are really hurting. I just offer my aches and pains up to the good Lord for my mistakes I've made in life."

I told him a lot of people today in Frankfort are trying to make our state capital a more compassionate community, and asked what his suggestions would be.

He said, "Three things I do in life are: I never judge a person. I treat people the way I want to be treated. And if someone starts talking about another person and it isn't congratulatory or positive, I walk away and don't say anything. I don't want to be involved in that stuff."

I mentioned that it's been more than a decade since I talked to him last and was wondering if he had ever said that first curse word, since the first story I read about him in the early 1980s mentioned that he never had.

"No, I never have," he answered. "I think when you get upset, you have to learn to control yourself and your words."

I had asked him the same question on my first interview with him in 1985. He had said, "No, I never have. I'm personally against abusive language. I think it shows a lack of intelligence. If I say Jiminy Cricket or doggone it, people know I'm upset."

In 2019 I had several brief follow-up phone conversations with Coach Faust after the first one in June. I told him I was including him in a magazine article I was working on for November and that he would also be included in an interfaith spirituality book I was hoping to get published in 2020. When I would ask him what would be a good time to call him back, he laughed, meaning he's always busy so just keep trying.

Once when I called he was in a urologist's office waiting for an annual exam. Later that day when I tried again, he was at a University of Akron preseason football practice. Another time he was on the golf course.

My all-time favorite football coach doesn't text or send emails. He doesn't have a phone with a camera. I don't know that I'll ever see him again.

But I do know every Thanksgiving I'm grateful that in 1985, on an extremely busy day when the pressure to win football games was at an all-time high for him, Gerry Faust welcomed me into his office and life for a couple of hours at Notre Dame. His kindness and compassion have been etched in my heart and mind ever since.

Pearl family gathers before cheering on Notre Dame

PART SIX

Dance with the Animals

"The greatness of a nation and its moral progress can be judged by the way its animals are treated."
--Mahatma Gandhi

Lily sits outside the entrance to the Labyrinth

Chapter 40

Love the Universal Christ

If I could have read Richard Rohr's book "The Universal Christ" in the 1960s, I might have never wandered away from being a Baptist. Since the book wasn't published until 2019, that would have been impossible.

Although my main spiritual practice now is Buddhism, I still feel at home in Immanuel Baptist Church of Frankfort where Chuck Queen is senior pastor. And if I asked him, Chuck would probably be able to name a few other progressive Baptist ministers I would enjoy listening to. I feel fortunate Kentucky's small capital city has a great one in Chuck Queen. Interestingly, a Baha'i woman, Julia Rome, was the person in Frankfort who told me I needed to go listen to one of his sermons. "He's amazing," she said. I went and she was right.

Richard Rohr is a globally recognized ecumenical teacher whose work is grounded in Christian mysticism, practices of contemplation, and compassion for the marginalized. He's a Franciscan priest of the New Mexico province and founder of the Center for Action and Contemplation in Albuquerque, where he also serves as academic dean of the Living School for Action and Contemplation.

Rohr is the author of many books, including the bestsellers "Falling Upward," "The Naked Now," "Breathing Under Water," and "The Divine Dance." His work has been featured on Oprah's "SuperSoul Sunday and Krista Tippett's "On Being" and in the New York Times.

I had bought several of his paperback books over the years at the Abbey of Gethsemani gift shop in Kentucky and loved all of them. But when I saw a hardback copy of "The Universal Christ: How A Forgotten Reality Can Change Everything We See, Hope For, and Believe" on a front-window shelf of Poor Richard's Books, and opened it, I knew I couldn't wait a year for the paperback edition.

The first thing I read was, "I dedicate this book to my beloved fifteen-year-old black Lab, Venus, whom I had to release to God while beginning to write this book. Without any apology, lightweight theology, or fear of heresy, I can appropriately say that Venus was also Christ for me."

WOW! I was hooked.

On page 52, Rohr says, "When you look your dog in the face, for example, as I often looked at my black Labrador, Venus, I truly believe you are seeing another incarnation of the Divine Presence, the Christ. When you look at any other person, a flower, a honeybee, a mountain – anything – you are seeing the incarnation of God's love for you and the universe you call home."

On page 132 – which I've shared with all of my dog-loving children and grandchildren – is another reference to Venus.

Rohr wrote, "Honestly, and without any stretch, my dog Venus taught me more about 'real presence' over a fifteen-year period than any theological manual ever did. Venus taught me how to be present to people and let them be present to me through the way she always sought out and fully enjoyed my company for its own sake. She was always so eager to be with me, even if I interrupted her in the middle of the night to go with me on a sick call. She literally modeled for me how to be present to God and how God must be present to me: "Like the eyes of a handmaid fixed on the hand of her mistress (Psalm 123:2), Venus's eyes were always fixed on me. If only I could always have been as loyal, eager, and subservient to her. But she taught me how.

"Presence is always reciprocal, or it is not presence at all."

Rohr's black Lab had to be put down because she was suffering from an inoperable cancer.

On page 150, he writes, "Venus had been giving me a knowing and profoundly accepting look for weeks, but I did not know how to read it. Deep down, I did not want to know. After her diagnosis, every time I looked at her, she gazed up at me with those same soft and fully permissive eyes, as if to say, 'It is okay, you can let me go. I know it is my time.' But she patiently waited until I too was ready.

"I cried off and on for a month after Venus's death, especially when I saw another dog, or pronounced her name. But in those weeks before she died, Venus *somehow* communicated to me that all sadness, whether cosmic, human, or canine, is one and the same. Somehow, her eyes were all eyes, even God's eyes, and the sadness she expressed was a divine and universal sadness. I wondered if God might have an easier time using animals to communicate who God is, since they do not seem as willful and devious as we are."

I read Rohr's words about Venus to daughter Charlsie Garrett in July 2019 after her and husband Jamie's beloved 7-year-old boxer, Jake, died of cancer on July 7. All the Pearls were heartbroken because Jake was such a full-of-life, lovable boy who kept you laughing nonstop when you were in his presence. He loved snuggling up to you on sofas or beds.

Charlsie said Rohr's words were soothing and helped ease the pain somewhat.

For me, what Richard Rohr says throughout "The Universal Christ" feels right, deeply touches my heart, and gives me hope for the survival of humanity and all beings.

Not long before his death in October 2018, the late Dr. John Paul Broderson, who served with me on the Frankfort Interfaith Council, talked to our council about Richard Rohr's daily meditations that are free and available online from the Center for Action and Contemplation. Broderson read them every day and put them into practice.

His recommendation inspired me to start reading Rohr's meditations as a part of my daily spiritual practice. Each morning, I thank John Paul and the Franciscan monk for reminding me to see God in everyone and everything.

Chapter 41

Tucky taught us a lot about life and love

This column is similar to one published in The State Journal on September 19, 2004.

In his younger years, his name occasionally made it into print in my weekly newspaper columns in several small towns. There is nothing I enjoy more than hiking, and Tucky was a faithful hiking partner.

Here's an excerpt from a feature on the Cecil Gorley Nature Trail in Marion County:

If Tucky Tarheel, our 5-year-old black Lab, could talk, he would tell you the finest day of his life was December 27, 1995. That was the first day he hiked "the trail loop," which winds magnificently around the 135-acre Lebanon Reservoir through the forest, by the water's edge, up and down, for 3.2 miles.

It was cold and cloudy. Patches of snow were on the ground. The air pumped new life into our veins. We took our time. Tucky led the way, but stayed close. Occasionally after he ran over a hill and around a bend, I would stop and be still. He would quickly return to make certain his partner stayed on the path, near him. He did the polar bear plunge into the icy-cold water several times.

Tucky and I went on to hike the Gorley Trail more than a hundred times over the years, plus many other Kentucky nature trails. We always saw small wonders on the trail – Canada geese and ducks on the water, usually a great blue heron, sometimes a red-tailed hawk, wild turkeys, white-tailed deer and various wildflowers.

Tucky was more than a hiking partner. On work days when it seemed the whole world was mad and complaining, Tucky was always standing at the door greeting me when I arrived home, wagging his tail, jumping up and licking me in the face.

After I underwent spinal surgery in the summer of 1999, I wrote this, titled "Dogs Life," in my personal journal in Frankfort on July 3:

Black Lab Tucky, thinks I've turned into a dog. I live his lifestyle now, lying around on the bed most of the day. Turning occasionally. Getting up occasionally and moving slowly around the house. Waiting for somebody to feed me, and take me out three times a day for a short walk. We're both 50 now and have gray whiskers around our mouths. Tucky reads my mind. He feels my love as we share the same bed. His eyes tell me he senses my pain. He's helping me heal, and he knows it.

Slowing down

After I recovered from surgery, Tucky and I continued to go on occasional hikes. We both realized slowing down has its advantages. Sitting on a bench by a lake with Tucky resting beside me one autumn afternoon, I learned one oak leaf, falling and ricocheting through a tall tree's bare branches, makes beautiful music floating to earth.

Then one Saturday in September 2001, a new black Lab puppy arrived at our house. Ebony was adopted from the Franklin County Humane Society's animal shelter. Tucky was 10 then. At first, he wasn't excited to have a little one running around all the time, climbing over him, biting his ears, wanting to play. But he never growled at her, and soon liked having her around.

As he continued to slow down and Ebony matured some, they became best buddies. Tucky always forgave her for chewing the tags and some of the heads off their mother Karen's beanie babies and placing them next to him on the sofa as if he had done the damage.

He always forgave me for taking Ebony on long Sunday morning walks and leaving him at home. We both knew he could no longer do the long walks. I dreaded the day Tucky would no longer be with us, and tried to push it out of my mind.

But that day came in his 13th year, on Saturday of Labor Day weekend. For three days, I prayed Tucky would die in his sleep, on his mattress beside our bed. In the last year of his life, he could no longer jump up on our bed and he was too heavy for Karen and me to lift.

The Pearls had a family reunion scheduled for Sunday and all of Tucky's family came to see him Saturday: our children, Kevin, Kennedy, Charlsie and Kathryn; Kevin's wife, Maria, a compassionate nurse; our grandsons, Charles III and Preston; Kristi Buffenmyer, Kathryn's friend and dog lover; and Laila, Charlsie's young tan boxer. We huddled around him all day, hugging him and talking. For most of the day, Ebony curled up on the sofa next to him with her back being his pillow.

We had hand-fed him his dog food the three preceding days. But on Saturday he wanted no food or water. He wouldn't even take his favorite vanilla wafers, the first people food he ever sampled when he was 6 months old at his first home in eastern North Carolina. Early Saturday evening, he finally licked part of an orange Popsicle and drank a little water.

Maria placed Carolina blue pads under him on the sofa in the living room, but he refused to go to the bathroom in the house. Every few hours, Charlsie, Kevin and Kennedy would turn him over and carry him outside and hold him up while he relieved himself. Then he would collapse.

A Saint Who Was No Saint

Several years ago, we canonized Tucky as a saint. But Tucky was no saint. He was just a wonderful dog, who happened to be ours. He loved anybody who came to our house. The kids recalled a lot of Tucky stories over Labor Day weekend.

"He chewed up mattresses, box springs and head boards," said Kevin, who selected Tucky as a puppy before he opened his eyes. He carried him home for the first time in a blue, white and gold Notre Dame stocking cap. "He chewed up baseballs, tennis shoes, flip-flops, a thousand socks and 50 pairs of underwear."

In his hometown of Plymouth, North Carolina, Tucky and his running partners, Blue and Big Liz, a bluetick hound and black Lab, never knew about leash laws. They roamed the neighborhood and swam in and shared the wetlands behind our house with the water moccasins, herons and egrets.

On the move to Kentucky, soon after exiting West Virginia we made a fast food stop. When we returned 10 minutes later, Tucky had eaten half of the large planter the Pearls had received as a going-away gift.

In his last years, Tucky, in his quiet, laid-back way, passed along wisdom to family members. Tucky and all beloved dogs are peace makers. In his youth, our family visited the Outer Banks nearly every weekend and we spent most of our hours walking the beaches and climbing tall sand dunes. Everybody who passed Tucky wanted to pat him, and Tucky loved all the affection and attention. He quickly learned, or instinctively knew, kindness creates kindness. Through Tucky, we met many nice people.

At the same time, Tucky was a competitor and loved to give you a big head start on the beaches and breeze past you easily in a foot race to any finish line. He finished his first cross-country season undefeated and his numerous trophies were big ol' long-lasting hugs.

All Beds Were Tucky's

In several homes through the years, Tucky never had his own bed. All of the beds in the house were his, and he would make the rounds, nightly. He would move you over, find his spot, and stay there until he chose to move on. Trying to get him to return the favor, and move over slightly, was hopeless.

"He was a wonderful sleeping companion for many years," said Kennedy, who filled in as his daddy when Kevin headed for Marine Corps' boot camp one September. Tucky grieved some when Kevin left, and took up closet meditation. But he learned patience pays off. When Kevin returned, he was thrilled.

Now we're grieving. We have his ashes in our bedroom in a large navy and gold velvet bag with an orange leather dream catcher and miniature wind chimes attached to the draw string. Kristi gave us the dream catcher as Kevin, Kennedy, Karen, Maria and I transported him to the Frankfort Animal Clinic.

Kevin, Kennedy and I finally saw the simple prayer for help in his weary eyes and face that other family members saw weeks earlier. Tucky had become a pro at deep sleeping in his last years. We held him in our arms as Dr. Stephanie Kennedy gently and quickly sent Tucky on his peaceful hiking journey to the pure lands at 9:10 p.m.

Karen and I miss his sweet face, companionship and unconditional love. He taught us we never want to live a day without a dog in our home. Tucky taught a grieving Ebony that closet meditation helps turn life's temporary wounds into wonder.

"Tucky taught me that love and family and family time are more important than anything," Kevin said. "He taught me that I want to die and come back as a Pearl dog someday. He had good food, good beds and a loving family. He went hiking but never had to go shopping. He never had to get up early and go to work or pay any bills. And like everybody else in the family, he always received plenty of Christmas gifts."

And Tucky taught Kathryn on September 4, 2004 that U.S. Marines do cry sometimes. And it's OK.

Chapter 42

Jenny Neat balances pet rescues and artwork

This front-page feature story on animal rescuer Jenny Neat was published in the October 28, 2013 issue of The State Journal. In early 2020, Jenny was still keeping the roads hot in Kentucky saving dogs and cats.

She's always had a big heart for animals and art. And for Jenny Neat, finding time to work as a stained-glass artist and iconographer – painting religious icons – has gotten more difficult this year.

The reason? Dogs and cats.

Since March, she's saved hundreds of them by being a volunteer transporter for The Way Home Rescue Alliance in Midway, which networks with more than 300 animal rescue groups in the U.S. The alliance is "a part of what's considered the Underground Railroad for Dogs and Cats," Jenny says.

Several times a week, Jenny drives to an Estill County regional shelter to save animals from being euthanized. She transports them to a veterinary clinic in Georgetown, All 4 Paws, before they're relayed by others to foster or adopted homes.

In early September, Jenny – wife of the Rev. William Jessee Neat, rector at Church of the Ascension – had a new experience while transporting nine dogs and a cat.

"It miraculously turned into 14 dogs," Jenny said. "One of the dogs had puppies while in my car. Four were born while I was driving and a fifth arrived while I was parked at All 4 Paws.

"I was shocked. Miss Macy was so emaciated no one knew she was pregnant."

Jenny says most of the dogs she takes from Kentucky animal shelters "go to northern states, which have very effective spay/neuter laws. Kentucky does not.

"It's a constant battle, but I'm making a difference for those I transport, and they're most appreciative, unlike some humans.

"This is one of the most fulfilling volunteer jobs I've ever had. I hope to make people aware of the millions of animals thrown away and euthanized each year, and work to get effective spay/neuter laws and programs into place."

In her Governors' Place home, Jenny has a large "gratitude jar" with names of all the dogs she's saved since March on slips of paper. It's filling up fast. She rescued 90 in August and 75 in July.

She's always felt an interconnection with all of God's creatures.

"When I was in seventh grade, I refused to dissect a frog and was sent to the principal's office," Jenny recalls. "My mother was called in and she supported me, asking why my compassion for a living creature should be punished. It was agreed I could do an alternate assignment."

Her love for animals is the main reason she's been a vegetarian for 20 years.

She's thankful to her late mother "for making me aware of all the beauty in life – just being outside looking at clouds, bugs, everything. She was a great photographer and I learned from her."

Art runs in Jenny's family. Her father and both grandfathers were artists, as is her son, Will, 35, a Morgantown, West Virginia resident.

"My dad was a sign painter in Lexington and started his own business in the 1940s, Sherrod Sign Company, which still exists."

Jenny took only one art class at Lafayette High School and won the Senior Art Award.

One of her icons, "The Korsun Mother of God," won third place this year in a National American Heritage Art Contest sponsored by Daughters of the American Revolution.

After high school graduation in 1971, Jenny figured she would go to college, get married and live the rest of her life in Kentucky in her "dream log house. I couldn't have imagined anything further from the truth."

Jenny majored in law enforcement and social work at Eastern Kentucky University. In her junior year she married Jessee Neat, from Adair County, who served 21 years in the military and retired as an Army lieutenant colonel in 1996. Then he studied three years at General Theological Seminary of the Episcopal Church in New York City.

Before moving to Frankfort in 2011, they lived in South Korea as well as nine states – Alabama, Louisiana, Kansas, Indiana, Massachusetts, Virginia, Pennsylvania, New York and Maryland.

"Over the years I had a few paid positions. But mostly, because my husband was in the military, we moved a lot and most businesses were reluctant to hire for such a short time. Thus, I became a professional volunteer while raising our son and becoming an artist."

Thirty years ago, she took a stained-glass art class in Indianapolis, "and fell in love with it. I'm like a kid in a candy store with glass."

While her husband studied in NYC, Jenny worked almost 70 hours a week managing the Episcopal seminary bookstore. She met an iconographer who got her started in creating icons.

Later she attended an iconography workshop at an Episcopal Retreat Center in Hendersonville, North Carolina. She's gone there eight straight years for a week in February, completing an icon each time.

"We work eight hours a day for five days and the instructor is mixing the paints. When I'm doing one at home and have to mix the paints, that really adds to the time.

"You have recipes to mix the pigments with egg yolk. You can't let egg white into the paint because it will crack."

The complex process requires numerous layers of paint on wood.

"It's a process of trust, and it's fascinating. I absolutely love doing them, especially when a face starts emerging.

"You're putting intense light in certain areas, especially in faces. That's why in icons you're drawn to the eyes and they seem to glow because you've built that light in."

She's completed 15 icons and is currently painting "Do Not Touch Me," in which Mary Magdalene sees Jesus in the garden after he's risen from the dead.

Now at 60, Jenny is "on the go constantly," singing in her church choir, caring for her father, attending DAR meetings, taking photos for various events, saving animals, caring for two rescue cats at home, enjoying granddaughters, and "trying to find time to work on art."

The only reason she would like to sell more of her artwork is "to have more money to give away" to good causes like saving animals and the earth.

Chapter 43

Good Acres Sanctuary for farm animals

This feature was the cover story for the March 2018 issue of FRANK magazine. When a friend, Franklin County environmental and animal rights activist Ceci Mitchell, told me about the amazing things going on at Good Acres Sanctuary, it sounded too good to be true. Ceci wanted me to write a story about the animal sanctuary for FRANK magazine. I felt that I needed to visit the farm and meet the owners and animals before I asked the State Journal editors for permission to write the story. I did that, and my heart was filled with so much love and joy that day that it hurt. And I'm pretty sure that when State Journal photographer and now FRANK

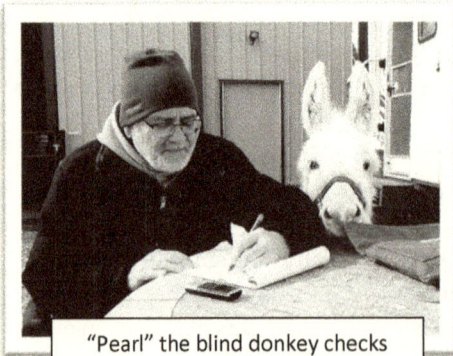

"Pearl" the blind donkey checks out Charlie as he takes notes

Editor Hannah Brown joined me on my third trip to Good Acres, her heart felt the same way. I am so grateful that Diana and George Shaffner decided to move from Texas to Kentucky, near Frankfort. Their farm, home and loving commitment to a small group of previously unwanted animals are a testimony to what is good about humanity.

A young, white blind donkey named Pearl gently bumps into a visitor sitting at an outdoor table on a cool February morning at Good Acres Sanctuary in Anderson County. Then she nudges his arm and nibbles at his notepad.

The 50-acre farm – just south of the Franklin County line on Graefenburg Road (Ky. 151) – is "a little slice of heaven" for rescued horses and farm animals. The current census is six horses, two donkeys, two pigs, two cows, three dogs and seven cats. A few chickens may arrive before summer.

The owners of Good Acres – Diana and George Shaffner – moved to Kentucky in 2014 from Abilene, Texas, where they had a small ranch for rescued horses. Diana says they loved the farm. "But because we were so far from town, Diana really felt isolated," George adds. "I can deal with isolation but she can't. She's more herself when she has people she can visit and talk to."

Everybody knows how great Kentucky is for horses, Diana says, so that was an attraction.

"We had no roots to Kentucky other than thinking this might be a good place. It's very beautiful and the cost of living and property taxes are extremely far less here."

Diana, 47, a native of Munich, Germany, has worked in horse rescue many years. She met George, originally from Los Angeles, in 1998 and they married in 1999. He worked in information technology for oil and gas companies in Houston, Texas.

At Good Acres, George handles maintenance, mowing, building fences and stalls, and he does meticulous carpentry. He likes creative work and doing things for the animals. The farm had no buildings on the property before they purchased it. Now there are four metal buildings, including a large stable for the donkeys, horses and pigs; a smaller stable for the cows; a machinery and maintenance facility; and their office and three-bedroom house, which they share with the dogs and cats.

"My obligation to the animals is to make sure they always get what they need," he says. "What I'm hoping to see is that what we've got here gets finished, and everything gets prettied-up. I want more time to spend with the animals instead of building and working and mowing and fence-fixing all the time. I love getting to know the animals and their feelings."

He says Good Acres Sanctuary will be his final home. "I like that Kentucky is green and rolling, and that we're close to Frankfort and Lawrenceburg. Everybody here seems to be nice. It's a comfortable place to be."

Diana's longtime German friend living in Austria, Michael Aufhauser -- who founded Gut Aiderbichl, a network of sanctuaries for hundreds of farm and rescued animals – was inspirational in Diana deciding to take in a few farm animals at Good Acres.

"Michael, George and I incorporated together and formed the nonprofit, 'GA Sanctuaries – US Aiderbichl Foundation Inc.'," Diana says.

"However, due to a near fatal heart incident, following a coma and strokes, Michael was unable to move forward with our plans of making the Kentucky organization into the U.S. branch of Gut Aiderbichl."

But the Shaffners retained the nonprofit name and now the GA letters stand for Good Acres Sanctuary, which is funded solely through donations and sponsorships.

Aufhauser's compassionate work led Diana to thinking about saving animals other than horses. An animal lover as far back as she can remember, Diana became a vegetarian as a teenager and a vegan 10 years ago.

"I wanted to create a place where people can come and experience animals that were typically getting zero compassion or consideration before they arrived here," Diana says. "I think it needs to be rethought how we pick out some animals like dogs and cats and do almost anything for them. We spend billions of dollars on them and call ourselves animal lovers.

"And we put other animals to unbelievable torture. It's not just that they get killed. The life they live is beyond torturous in many cases. And we don't even think about this."

Educational and healing center

Diana wants Good Acres to be a tranquil educational center where adults and children – "without being judged for whatever they eat or buy – can meet cows, pigs and donkeys and see what loving creatures they are. We have a lot of misconceptions about them – that they are dumb or smell bad. Those are ideas that help us shut them out of our idea of kindness.

"The farm is not so much a petting zoo but a place where people can visit during events. We're not open regularly like a store would be."

The Shaffners don't want a lot of animals because they want to give the ones they have enough one-on-one attention that they become familiar and calm around visitors.

"However, I would like to add chickens because they're probably the most abused animals of all in the food system," Diana says.

One pig at Good Acres is Lex, who made TV news while running around Lexington last summer.

"We think he was in somebody's back yard," and was probably intended to be killed and served at a July 4 barbecue, but he broke loose and saved himself, Diana said. "That's illegal in Fayette County, which is probably why no one came forward and claimed him."

Good Acres had a vegan potluck lunch on July 3 and a Lexington woman, hearing about the runaway pig, was determined to go back and catch him. She purchased a "humane wire trap" and accomplished her goal.

With TV coverage, Lex arrived at Good Acres on July 5, "and has been happy ever since," Diana says. "When he got here he was little. He since has grown into a big boy. But he's one of the sweetest guys. He's such a survivor. He was seen a couple of times in a McDonald's parking lot, just standing there."

Lex's companion is a Vietnamese pot-bellied pig named Charlie. "It was a case of being cute and little and then he grew big." After two years the owner wanted to get rid of him.

"He was lonely here and then Lex materialized. It was perfect timing. Everybody told me they will fight and I would have to be careful socializing them. I put them in opposite horse stalls so they could see each other. Then I let Charlie out to walk over to Lex's gate and sniff through the rails, and they loved each other from the start."

Since moving to Kentucky, Diana – who has college degrees in education and business – has become involved in counseling programs for recovering addicts, traumatized children and abused women. She's the board chair for Anderson County's Agency for Substance Abuse Policy.

"Addiction is not something I had ever experienced from my own background or family. But when I moved here I met people who told me how severe a problem this is here. I thought I could somehow incorporate healing work with the farm.

"The pigs are such characters. I love it when people come out – maybe suffering with depression and other things – and gather around the pigs or cows. The animals will do something funny, which they do frequently, and people laugh and have a relaxing, peaceful time."

Handsome Hank

Hank, a palomino horse, is becoming famous at the sanctuary for his flamboyant personality, and his stunning yellow coat and white mane and tail.

"He was given to me by the Kentucky Equine Humane Center in Nicholasville," Diana says. "They had him for over two years. His behavior was such that they didn't want to adopt him out to a private person, so they asked me if I would take him."

She said yes before seeing him, even though she had heard about his behavioral problems.

"We hit it right off. He's one of the best horses I have ever had. He has such a funny, outgoing personality, he gets even severely-depressed people to laugh. If he were a human and had a career, he would be a standup comedian because he can't be serious for very long. He has to do something goofy."

Diana has a calming presence and animals sense her love, kindness and understanding. She says horses with problematic or dangerous behavior all tell her what they need from her as a trainer.

"I don't shove a preconceived set of training methods down their throat. I feel their upset behavior is a sign of not being well, psychologically speaking. I know they want to feel balanced and well. So I just allow them to tell me what they need from me, and who they need me to be for them to grow.

"I then change my personality, communication style and training method according to the individual horse's needs. Things usually fall into place from there within a few days. It's really not difficult. It's about being willing to listen and leaving one's big trainer ego at the door."

Mystical love story

Bridgette, a Holstein dairy cow, and Lucky, a red angus calf, came to Good Acres from Indiana.

Not long before their arrival, Diana decided to add cows to the farm but didn't quite know how to go about it.

Then one day while standing in line at Panera Bread sandwich shop in Frankfort – waiting to order coffee – a silent voice inside told her to look at Craigslist Farm and Garden.

"I was thinking about coffee, not cows. And I don't do Internet on my phone because of the little screen. I thought I would look on my computer when I get home." Then the inner voice said, 'Not later…Now.' I realized a sense of urgency."

She got her coffee, sat down at a table and reluctantly took out her phone and pulled up Craigslist Farm and Garden. The first ad on top was from someone needing to get rid of two cows.

"I instantly knew it was a listing I was supposed to see, so I didn't scroll down further."

She replied to the ad and soon Jennifer Jackson called, saying she was trying to find a place where a calf and a mother cow could go together. Jennifer asked Diana what she needed.

Diana said she wasn't necessarily looking for cows, but has a sanctuary and wants to eventually add them. She said a strange feeling came over her at a café and she felt compelled to reply to her ad.

"Then Jennifer became so emotional, almost in tears, saying she had prayed for two days and nights straight and was so exhausted trying to find a home where the two cows could go and stay together the rest of their lives."

Jennifer got the angus calf free from a neighbor. She was bottle feeding it, and soon realized it would be nice to have a cow nurse him. She visited a nearby dairy farm and found a mother cow in distress because her first calf, very young, had been taken away from her.

"She screamed and screamed for three days and refused all nourishment," Diana said. "She was dehydrated and her weight declined drastically. Jennifer agreed to take her for a few dollars to keep her from being butchered."

Jennifer named her Bridgette. When they got to Jennifer's farm, Bridgette had stopped screaming but was still depressed. She was put in a stall next to the new calf named Lucky. They could see each other and Lucky was excited. But Bridgette didn't react to him.

"But within 48 hours, she began to pay attention to him and sniff him, and ate and drank a little," Diana said. "Then Jennifer introduced them in one big stall and all of a sudden Bridgette made up her mind this is going to be my baby, and I'm going to take care of him. She ate and drank up a storm, and her milk production kicked back up and she has been a fierce protector of him."

Good Acres Sanctuary answered Jennifer's prayer, and she and her husband transported Bridgette and Lucky to Good Acres in December 2016. Then last April they returned to the sanctuary the Saturday before Easter to attend a "Blessing of the Animals" ceremony and vegan potluck dinner.

Special day at the sanctuary

The Blessing of the Animals and vegan potluck is an annual event and the public is invited. Michelle Redmon, founder and pastor of Emerge Ministries of Frankfort, has officiated.

"I love blessing the animals because when we bless something, we are acknowledging the perfection God put into it when he created it," Redmon says. "We are expressing our gratitude and thanking him for his creation and its purpose."

Redmon says the animals at Good Acres are a blessing to many people who are suffering and struggling to relate to other people. "The animals have a rescue story of their own, which is inspirational, and they provide therapeutic relief to those who interact with them," she says.

Curious, always-busy and a little-sassy, Pearl, the blind donkey, and her companion, Rosie, a brown crippled donkey, would get their blessings. So would Hank – the handsome palomino and standup comedian – and other beautiful horses, cows, pigs, dogs and cats, who together, somehow, have mystically found a safe and loving home.

Contact Good Acres: For information on special events at Good Acres Sanctuary, go to the website GoodAcres.us or send an email to farmoffice@goodacres.us.

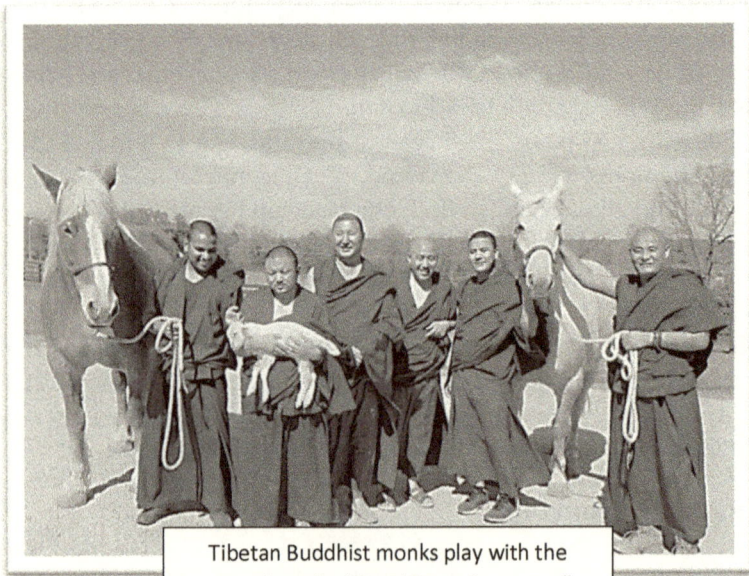

Tibetan Buddhist monks play with the animals at the "Good Acres Sanctuary"

Chapter 44

Finding peace for Lily

This guest column to The State Journal was published on July 9, 2017.

L ily is fortunate. She has many homes in Kentucky and loves visiting all of them. We also have a passion for finding places of silence.

In our first year together, we traveled to 14 states. We took long walks at daybreak on the dog-friendly beach at Cape San Blas, Florida.

We hiked on the Continental Divide Trail in New Mexico, seeing red rock cliffs, mesa tops and canyon lands, the Chama River and adobe architecture. One morning in the stillness, we stood in awe as a raven flew over us, hearing for the first time the rhythmic, mystical whoosh-whoosh sound of wings flapping in the air. I've never forgotten that moment.

In Kentucky, we usually go to 35-acre Garrett Ranch on the outskirts of Gravel Switch in early July because Lily is terrified of fireworks and that's the quietest place we've found. But we're always searching for a quieter one.

Charlie and Lily overlooking downtown Frankfort

When we get to Perryville, Lily, wearing her peace collar and standing up in the back seat, gets excited because she knows we're almost there.

Daughter Charlsie and Jamie Garrett and their 20-year-old son Jordan live on sparsely-populated Craintown Road, not far from Poor House Road in Boyle County, three-tenths of a mile from Marion County. They have two energetic tan boxers, Jake and Ella, a brother and sister who will turn six in August.

Everybody loves big ol' sweet Jake. Ella isn't as friendly but she tolerates Lily and leaves her alone.

I've had dogs all of my adult life and Lily is my third consecutive black Lab. She's a friendly nine-year-old, 85-pound Lab/Doberman Pinscher mix with brindle legs, who came from the Franklin County Humane Society's animal shelter in 2008. She rescued me from a deep depression several weeks after seven-year-old Ebony died tragically on U.S. 60 when she was struck by a vehicle.

Lily is my first dog to be terribly frightened of thunderstorms and fireworks.

She has a thundershirt – a swaddling garment designed for dogs, which is supposed to help provide a calm and comforting feeling during thunderstorms and fireworks. For Lily, it helps slightly. What helps most, however, is a mild sedative prescribed by Dr. Denis G. King at Frankfort Animal Clinic. He recommended it a couple of years ago when Lily was getting her annual check-up and shots after I told him about her anxiety.

Well, it looks as if Lily has survived another Fourth of July holiday, although as I write this on July 6 I'm sure more fireworks are ahead, unfortunately.

There were Friday night thunderstorms at Lily's main residence in Arlington Heights near downtown Frankfort, and she spent most of the night in the bathtub, her favorite hideout.

We spent Saturday, Sunday and Monday nights at the Gravel Switch farm. She worked her way into a small space between Charlsie's recliner and the living room sofa on Saturday when she heard a little thunder in the distance.

She did the same thing on Sunday and Monday evenings when she heard the faint noise of fireworks. Jake and Ella aren't one bit afraid of thunder or fireworks.

On the morning of July 4 in a drizzling rain, I decided we would return to Franklin County and stay at Angela Mitchell's house in Bridgeport that evening. In Lawrenceburg on U.S. 127, as we approached the Walmart shopping center, I saw a big fireworks tent with a sign saying, "Buy one, get six free."

Lily heard me cuss. The sign one day later would probably say, "Buy one, get 25 free," or "100 free."

I felt nauseated. I don't hate community fireworks celebrations on July 4. But two weeks of noisy nights around the 4th is pathetic and takes away from the specialness of our country's birthday.

Angela and I have a yurt – a one-room circular structure with a skylight – and an adjacent walking meditation labyrinth that we built on a 33-acre farm owned by Angela's mother, Mary Mahoney.

A round, metal sign hanging on a walnut tree at the entrance to the yurt and labyrinth says The Pearl Center for World Peace. But Lily will testify there's no peace at the yurt around July 4. And Lily has it great, even though she doesn't think so.

She gets to be inside on noisy days and nights, unlike many dogs and cats and deer, birds and other wild animals.

I thought perhaps it would be quiet in Bridgeport on Tuesday night since Frankfort was to have its big Independence Day fireworks show at Capitol View Park that night and local folks would want to go there.

Wrong. Bridgeport neighbors had spectacular Happy Birthday USA shows of their own that went on for hours.

Lily had an early supper and got her second half-pill of the day to calm her. She retreated to Angela's bathroom and Angela turned on the dehumidifier to drown out some of the noise. I turned up the television.

We checked on her frequently. Her eyes were open but she wasn't panting. She was lethargic, in a deep meditation. Lily felt our love, and I felt grateful to have this adorable creature in my life, to have her around-the-clock unconditional love. I brushed her gently for a long time until we both fell asleep in the floor.

Wednesday, Lily and I went for an early-morning walk on the Mahoney farm. We stopped by the pond and Lily went swimming briefly. Then we walked the mowed path to the yurt. In the center of the labyrinth, I did a 30-minute sitting meditation in silence. Lily stayed close. It's a daily ritual for us. Sometimes you have to experience noisy nights to fully appreciate the sacred beauty of silence.

PART SEVEN

Dance with Death

"The existence of ours is as transient as autumn clouds. To watch the birth and death of beings is like looking at the movements of a dance"

--Gautama Buddha

Chapter 45

Death experiences and the great blue heron

This newspaper column was published in The State Journal on January 20, 2008. The story was accompanied by this large drawing of three young men in a canoe going down a turbulent river, and a great blue heron watching over them, created by State Journal illustrator Linda Boileau.

Almost every time I go home to Marion County, Kentucky now, I see a great blue heron. Surely they were there when we were growing up. But I don't ever remember seeing one.

The first time a great blue heron touched my heart was in the spring of 1968 on the Pierre Marquette River in Michigan. Mike Fenwick was with me. He was one of my best friends through high school and college, and helped me survive the most traumatic experience of my life.

Our sophomore year of college had just ended, and we were in Michigan to work for the Kalamazoo YMCA as counselors at Camp Aharah near Lake Michigan. Mike and I arrived three weeks before the camp would open.

We were getting paid a little extra to get the facilities and grounds ready for another camping season. We had the lake to ourselves with two sailboats, a skiing boat and a pontoon.

Michigan and America were in turmoil – with race riots and the Vietnam War and assassinations. Peace activist and civil rights leader Martin Luther King Jr. had been killed two months earlier. And now Robert F. Kennedy, our Democratic presidential hopeful, was dead.

The tragic news of Kennedy being shot came from Los Angeles to us on a transistor radio as we were on the pontoon boat listening to Motown's Marvin Gaye and Tammi Terrell singing "Ain't No Mountain High Enough."

When the news of his death came the next day, we decided to retreat ever farther into the wilderness. We took a two-day canoe trip on the scenic Pierre Marquette River. The first night we camped near rushing yet peaceful ripples.

We were thankful we didn't have a TV and didn't have to watch every painful moment the way we did in 1963, our sophomore year of high school, after President John F. Kennedy's assassination.

The light and the warmth from the campfire, and the sound of water running over rocks soothed our souls. We didn't try to solve all the problems of the world that night. Just listening to nature's orchestra brought contentment.

Not long after daylight the next morning, we saw a great blue heron at the water's edge. Our hearts soared when it lifted off so gracefully.

Two weeks later on another canoe trip, I almost died. Mike and Billy Harmon, another counselor from Kentucky, saved my life.

The final day of a one-week counselor training session was a canoeing journey down the Pine River, a much swifter river than the Pierre Marquette. In the last hour of the trip, all I had to do was ride in the middle of the canoe and let Mike handle the stern and Billy the bow.

Rain was pouring. We were singing "My Old Kentucky Home," heading into the Dead Man's Curve rapids.

Then the canoe struck a tree branch in the water and we began to rock. We overturned and I was trapped. My legs were crossed and lodged underneath the middle bar of the canoe. I had on a lifejacket, but couldn't work my way free from underneath.

I kept fighting but the canoe and the rapids were winning. At age 19, I was swallowing water, drowning, and a long way from home. I had always imagined drowning would be the worst way to die. And now I'm thinking the worst is happening, and it's not so bad.

I saw a long tunnel with a dim light shining in the distance. I was rushing through the tunnel, with walls of continuous doors and windows on each side. I saw an elderly Indian woman calmly watching me through one of the windows. I relaxed, thinking this is it, and it's OK.

Then suddenly Mike and Billy were there. They had somehow managed to get the canoe off of me. Perhaps it was because I finally gave up and relaxed. I vomited water and was dazed at first. Then the water felt icy. But it didn't matter. Before long we were jumping up and down in the water, laughing and yelling. It was great to be alive in Michigan with friends from my Kentucky home.

On a cool, breezy Friday afternoon in December 2007, at my mother's urging, I retold the 1968 drowning story under a small dark green tent in Old Liberty Cemetery in Marion County. Mike's parents, his younger brother and sister, and an uncle smiled, knowing how deeply Mike was loved. He had died of cancer at age 59 just before Thanksgiving.

There were plenty of other good memories I could have shared, like the snowy night we did the polar bear plunge in the Rolling Fork River, or the nights Tina Turner dripped sweat on us while performing on stage with her then-husband Ike at Club 68 in our hometown.

Thirty-five gathered in the little cemetery – surrounded by rolling farmland – for his memorial service. His ashes were in a reddish-brown wooden box resembling an old radio.

After college we lost touch for decades until 2006 when I received an e-mail from him. We exchanged a few e-mails, and then one weekend when he was visiting his parents in Louisville, we decided to meet on a Sunday for breakfast at Cracker Barrel in Shelbyville.

For 10 minutes, he had stood on the porch while I sat nearby in a rocking chair, waiting, before he took a chance and asked, "Are you Charlie?" We laughed.

After talking for two minutes at the breakfast table, I thought: of course you're Mike. How could I not have known? We had so much fun reminiscing, we left the restaurant, went to downtown Shelbyville and sat at a picnic table and talked two more hours.

I told him I had been working on a book of fiction for 12 years, and the opening chapters are in Michigan, where we had been in 1968. To sharpen scenes, I wanted to go back. Mike and I planned to return there and go canoeing, camping and hiking.

I was going to visit him in Indianapolis. Mike worked at WFYI Public Radio, where he produced "The Art of the Matter," providing listeners an overview of arts and cultural events. He was the station's announcer for NPR's "Morning Edition."

Before going to Indianapolis, Mike had been an Emmy-winning TV news anchor, having worked in the Cincinnati, St. Louis, Denver and Greensboro, North Carolina, markets.

A creative soul, Mike had a wild idea that in our senior years we would work together on documentaries. But that dream and our plans for more reunions in Indy, Michigan and God knows where else never happened. We got busy with everyday life again. And I figured Mike would be here forever.

I wish I could have seen him one more time. I wish I could have saved *his* life. Anna Laura Evans Davenport, his closest friend in high school, and I had planned to go visit him on Thanksgiving weekend. But he couldn't wait for us.

One week after his memorial service, Anna Laura and I attended the funeral of another classmate and close friend in Lebanon, Billy Gordon. After the service, we decided to ride to the nearby Abbey of Gethsemani monastery to find some comfort in the silence.

On the way, soaring over the highway in front of Anna Laura's convertible was a great blue heron. We knew Mike's spirit was with us, and always will be.

Chapter 46

Black Lab Ebony struck and killed

Early Tuesday morning, December 2, 2008, was one of the saddest days of my life. My black Labrador, Ebony, 7, who was born at the Franklin County Humane Society's animal shelter, died when she was struck by a vehicle on U.S. 60 (Louisville Road) in front of Angela Mitchell's residence in Bridgeport, about seven miles from Frankfort.

I let her out of Angela's house early to go to the bathroom, as I always did, and she hadn't come back by the time I had to leave for work in Frankfort. That wasn't too unusual since she liked being out in the early morning. Angela's front yard is about a quarter-mile from U.S. 60 and Ebony's territory was behind Angela's house, where our yurt is, a half-mile from the road.

The only thing I can figure is she must have seen a deer and went chasing after it. Right before pulling out of the driveway to turn left to go to town, I looked right and saw what looked like something in the middle of the highway. It wasn't light yet so it was difficult to see. But I thought I should check to make sure it wasn't her. It was her, and it was horrible picking up her mangled, limp body out of the middle of the road. At that moment, I honestly didn't care if a vehicle ran over me.

I carried her to the car and took her back to Angela's house, got her out, and then lay down beside her on the paved driveway, hugging her for a long time in the cold. A light snow was on the ground. The sun was rising and it created a mystical golden glow across the white lawn.

We buried her about two hours later by the yurt. I had planned to grow old with her in our yurt. I couldn't believe she was gone. My heart was torn apart. I had never hurt this bad, not even when Tucky, our 13-year-old black Lab, died a few years earlier . . . because I still had Ebony then. And that was a terrible loss. Ebony and I had a wonderful short time together in the yurt (construction was finished in October 2008). She meditated with friend Bob McClain (known as McBob) and me for three hours Monday night and loved lying between us and listening to the calming music of Robert Gass and his renowned choral group, On Wings of Song, from their CD titled "Enchanted."

I couldn't help but wonder in the next few weeks – and even now, almost 12 years later – if her listening to that beautiful meditative music for hours that Monday night somehow lifted her consciousness to a level where the spirit world was calling her home Tuesday morning.

A phone call brought McBob back to the yurt Tuesday morning and he helped Angela and my son, Kevin, and me dig her grave. Maria Pearl, Kevin's wife, also came with him from Georgetown, where they lived at the time. We said prayers and had spiritual readings.

Kevin, a master plumber, asked if it was OK to put a cross, which he had assembled from PVC pipe, at her gravesite. "Of course it's OK," I said. Ebony loved watching the yurt being built, and living inside it. She loved being on the farm, swimming in the pond and chasing the frogs.

I sent an email to a few close friends, who knew Ebony well, later in the week, telling them of her tragic death.

I concluded the message by saying, "I feel like I want to die right now. But I wanted you to know about her death because she loved you and I know you loved her. I want you to come and see the yurt soon. I think you will feel her spirit alive there in our little home. Peace and Love Always!"

Two days later, I received this reply from Gene Coverston, a friend and former next-door-neighbor in South Frankfort:

"Oh Charlie – my heart breaks. It is hard for me to imagine that Ebony, so full of life, vim and vigor was run over. I know how much you loved her and she was easy for others of us to love too – her ever eager spirit, so glad to greet!! She left her mark on Fourth Street for sure – as did you of course.

"Though her death was tragic and untimely, I am glad her last days were so gleeful, enjoying country life and the yurt as she shared her life with her beloved Charlie.

"I am glad you had family and friends with you as you committed her body to the earth. Her spirit will live on in our hearts and memories. Please consider yourself HUGGED. I know you are shattered right now, but many of us love you and with the love of family and friends your heart will slowly mend. Though I know there will always be a spot in your heart that will ache for Ebony, you are of us and with us. My thoughts and prayers are with you and with Ebony's spirit . . . Much Love, Gene"

I didn't go to work at The State Journal on the day of Ebony's death. I had planned to go in for part of the day, and then I had a doctor's appointment scheduled in Louisville that afternoon. When I called Editor Carl West, a dog lover, he was so kind and understanding, and told me to definitely take the day off.

McBob said he would drive me to Louisville so I decided to not cancel the doctor's appointment to undergo routine tests. Angela spent hours while I was gone, cleaning Ebony's blood out of the back seat and floorboard of my car, and washing the blood out of my clothes.

The next day when I went to work, I closed the door to Carl West's office, sat down across from his desk, and broke down crying, and apologized for not being stronger. Carl could be a tough, hard-nosed editor. But there was another compassionate side to him that those in the newsroom saw occasionally.

"I understand what you're going through," he said. "It's awful. I've been there. You don't need to be here today. Take off as long as you need."

I went back to work the next day because I needed to be there to help keep my mind off the pain I felt inside. Sheri Bunker, who worked in composition in the newsroom, lived in a subdivision near Bridgeport, and her little dog, Lucky, was struck and killed on Louisville Road, the same day as Ebony.

I remember going to the Frankfort Christmas parade on a Saturday evening, and standing on Capital Avenue with Angela and other friends, and feeling so empty and unhappy. I remembered the only Christmas parade I ever took Ebony to when she was little, and she was so frightened from the loud music of the bands I had to take her home, one block away on Logan Street.

Soon after her death, I remember going to Georgetown to spend a Friday night with Kevin and Maria and young grandsons, Charles III, Preston and Dawson, and their mixed black Lab, Molly, the same age as Ebony. Early Saturday morning I took Molly on her leash for a walk in the neighborhood. The first thing we saw outside were four Canadian geese flying low over the house and honking. I knew somehow it was Ebony and Tucky and Terry Ward and Clay Thomas Pearl's energy letting me know they were all enjoying life in the spirit world.

Terry, a very close friend and former next-door neighbor in Lebanon, and Clay Thomas, my second stepfather and first cousin (it's OK to go on and laugh "because *it is* Kentucky," as we say) died just before my 60th birthday in the summer of 2008, the same year as Ebony's death. Clay

Thomas was a wonderful, loving father and all my children and grandchildren loved their Papa Clay. Clay Thomas had also been my biological father's best friend growing up and as adults in Louisville. And through Clay Thomas, I learned a lot about my dad, many years after his death. That helped me love dad much more than I ever had.

A few days later, in the afternoon, I went alone to the yurt and lay down on the floor in the center, looking up through the domed skylight. Soon I saw a red-tailed hawk fly over, and it continued to circle over and over and over. I felt again that it was Ebony letting me know we were still connected, and always would be.

Angela was kind and compassionate, as always, in the two weeks after Ebony's death and tried to cheer me up. I had told her plenty of times in the two years we had known each other that Ebony would be my last dog. And I was being honest each time I said it. But now Ebony was gone . . . at least five years sooner than I expected.

That Buddhist teaching of impermanence hadn't really sunk in. It should have. In my long career of community journalism, I had been at the scene of way too many horrible, tragic events – vehicle crashes, fires, drownings, a helicopter crash, fatal shootings. I had witnessed how young and old people's lives had been snuffed out in a second, causing tremendous suffering and grief to those who loved them.

Buddhist master Anam Thubten's book, "Choosing Compassion: How to Be of Benefit in a World that Needs Our Love," wouldn't be in my hands for another eleven years. But when it finally was, it helped immensely in healing my heart.

Thubten, my main spiritual teacher now, in the final chapter titled "The Ultimate Awakening," says, one method for experiencing very profound liberation is through surrendering to the way things are. "We surrender to all situations. This is not about being totally passive. It's about knowing deep down inside that we actually have very little control over our own existence.

". . . Everything that happens in our life is part of the cosmic dance, the divine play."

I don't think my children – Charlsie, Kevin, Kennedy and Kathryn – had ever seen me in such a deep state of depression. They and a couple of other close friends suggested I go visit the local Humane Society's animal shelter, which had been Ebony's only home until we adopted her.

That didn't feel right. In my mind, it seemed disrespectful to Ebony that I would quickly go out shopping for another dog to replace her. And I had made a commitment to Angela that Ebony would be my last dog.

But I went to the animal shelter three times in one week. On the first visit I saw two black Labs. Both were beautiful but one was obviously happier to see me. It was like she was waiting for my arrival. But unlike the other one – and Ebony and Tucky – she had brindle legs. She was beautiful but I wasn't ready to commit. I tried to get Angela's blessing but her reaction was, "I don't want another dog in my life."

I waited two days, thinking that if the black Labs are gone when I go back, it wasn't meant to be. Both were still there when I returned after my oldest child, Charlsie, who had a tan boxer named Laila, encouraged me to do what felt right. "I think you need a dog in your life," she said.

Lily, the six-month-old one with the orange legs, seemed happier than ever to see me. We were allowed to go in a little room and have some one-on-one time. She was adorable. I was told she was scheduled to be spayed the next day, and I could take her home with me on Saturday if I wanted to adopt her.

I said "yes," I want her and completed the adoption application. I would be back in two days to get her and pay the adoption fee. Charlsie and her husband, Jamie Garrett, went with me early Saturday afternoon and they immediately loved her. And Charlsie and her siblings went together to pay the adoption fee as my Christmas gift.

Christmas gift Lily

It was my Saturday afternoon and evening to work at the newspaper office and I transported Lily to Buddhist friend Kathleen Moffitt's house to stay temporarily until I got off work. Lily got along well with Kathleen's dog, which was nice to know.

Angela had gone to bed when we arrived at the farm, so Lily and I went to the yurt to spend the night. She seemed happy to be with me in her new home. I built a fire in the woodstove to keep us warm. Sunday morning I called Angela and left her a message that I had gotten a new dog from the animal shelter.

Not too long after the call, Angela walked to the yurt to see us. She was nice to Lily and said she was cute. But my heart told me Lily and I needed to get away from Angela's home and family farm for a while. That afternoon, I left with Lily and headed to Lebanon to spend the night at my mother's house. She was surprised to see us, but happy.

The news traveled fast in my family that Lily and I were in Lebanon. Ex-wife Karen Pearl called later and said Lily could stay at her house while I was at work on Monday. Lily and I left for Frankfort very early Monday morning. I remember it started raining hard when we reached the Franklin County line on KY 151 and I had bad windshield wipers and could barely see. There was a long line of traffic behind us, and when the road briefly widened to two lanes, drivers were blowing their horns at me for not getting over quick enough. I was a nervous wreck, but we survived.

I bought new windshield wipers that day and it was a good thing because it was snowing the next morning when Lily and I were traveling from Georgetown to Frankfort. We had spent the night with son Kevin and his family Monday and when I merged onto I-64 west the car slid slightly as a tractor-trailer whizzed by us on the left, making our lane slushy. But again we survived.

Lily and I slept on the sofa at Karen's house the next two nights and I knew I needed to quickly find another place for us to stay.

Downtown on Wednesday afternoon, Angela and I ran into each other on Broadway while she was doing last minute Christmas shopping for her three children. We went into Kentucky Coffeetree Café and talked briefly. She invited me to bring Lily back to the farm to live.

We soon returned but it didn't take long for me to realize that Angela and her children needed their own space, just as Lily and I needed ours. I don't think Lily cared. She was happy wherever I was.

I called Joel Schrader, a staunch Republican friend who lives in Bridgeport and owned a four-plex residence on Fourth Street in Frankfort. Ebony and I had lived in one of his downstairs apartments a year or so earlier and when I called this time, an upstairs apartment was available. I took it.

Angela wasn't happy initially when I moved out. But I think we both realize now – 12 years later – that it was the best thing for all of us. We both love our time together and we love days when we're not together.

Angela loves Lily and has always been kind, compassionate and loving to her. The only rule at Angela's – which doesn't apply at my residence or any of my children's residences – is that Lily cannot lay on a sofa or bed. It's always been the rule and Lily, a smart girl, understood it early on and never complained. That's what I love about dogs.

Chapter 47

Remembering Lucy Pearl

Lucy Pearl

The morning after Cinco de Mayo, Tuesday, May 6, 2014, was a day of turmoil. All kinds of emotions came rushing in, starting early when I went to the bathroom shortly before 6 a.m.

Blood was on the floor, on the toilet, on the sink, on the wall. Blood-soaked paper towels were in the trash container. A paper-towel roll, smudged with dried blood, lay on the cabinet top by the sink.

My first thought was my 88-year-old mother had gotten bitten in the night by Clay, her short, obese, caramel and white Jack Russell dog. He had bitten her several times through the years. She either rolled over on him in their king-size bed in the night, or had tried to lift him from the floor to the bed and touched a sore spot.

Deciding not to go in her bedroom and wake her, I went to the den and meditated, and then read from Shambhala Sun magazine until I heard her get up. After leaving the bathroom, she walked through the kitchen to the den and opened the door to the garage, holding a plastic trash bag in one hand.

A couple of minutes later when she returned to the den, she said, "Good morning."

And I responded, "Tell me about the blood in the bathroom, mom."

"I don't know what's happening," she answered softly. "It's like I'm having my period again."

"So Clay didn't bite you?"

"No. Oh, no. Clay didn't bite me."

Then I immediately remembered Agreement Number Three: Don't Make Assumptions. I had forgotten or ignored that one in my thoughts this morning. Ever since reading Don Miguel Ruiz's best-selling book, "The Four Agreements," more than 15 years ago, I try to make it a point to remember them each morning, and through the day. The other three are: Be Impeccable With Your Word, Don't Take Anything Personally, and Always Do Your Best.

"The Fifth Agreement" a later book by Ruiz and his son, Don Jose Ruiz, offered a new teaching in Toltec Wisdom: Be Skeptical, But Learn To Listen.

I didn't have a clue as to what was going on, but I knew it was a day to do my best and listen closely.

The first thing I did was apologize to Clay and pat him gently.

Then I called Mary Batt, a friend who lives five houses down Bruce Street from where mom resides. Mary is a nurse and massage therapist. She said to call the office of mom's family physician, Dr. Brian Scott, and get her there as soon as possible.

I called my sister, Beverly, who lives in Marion County, and told her what had happened. She said she would come over and go with us to Dr. Scott's.

While waiting for mom to bathe and Beverly to arrive, I went into the garage, opened the trash bag and my heart sunk. In addition to all the bloody paper towels, mom's underwear and gown were saturated with blood. I took photos of every bloody item with my iPhone to show Dr. Scott.

Mom enjoyed riding to Dr. Scott's office in Beverly's new red Camaro convertible, which will never have the top down, Beverly said.

Mom loves Dr. Scott, and after taking her to his office several times in the last year for checkups relating to her diabetes and declining memory, I understood why. He seems to be a gentle soul with an abundance of compassion and patience.

I show him the photos I took earlier. Then after several routine tests and being examined, mom hears Dr. Scott say he wants her to go to Spring View Hospital today for additional tests and to receive blood, since her blood volume has dropped considerably.

The hospital is in the same medical complex, and mom chose to walk to Spring View rather than be transported by car to the front door. After filling out admissions paperwork, mom learned that her room would be in the Women's Center where babies are born.

"Oh, good Lord, I hope I'm not going to have another baby," she said, laughing.

"We need to call The Lebanon Enterprise (newspaper) if you do," I said.

The news that Lucy Pearl was in the hospital traveled fast. Soon granddaughter Charlsie Garrett, director of the Lebanon Aquatic Center, arrived. So did Mary Batt and longtime Spring View nurse and friend Georgiana "Jody" Mattingly. Dr. David Whitlock, pastor of Lebanon Baptist Church, and his wife, Lori, also came to see Lucy and say prayers.

In mid-afternoon, we learned mom had two tumors, one on her uterus and the other on her bladder, which was blocking a kidney. Dr. Mark Ackermann, a gynecologist, and Dr. Sam Kriegler, a urologist, said biopsies would be taken Friday and the results wouldn't 't be known for several days.

"But don't get your hopes built up that this isn't cancer," Dr. Ackermann said.

We liked his honesty. And he was right.

Neither doctor recommended radiation, chemotherapy or other treatments because of her advanced age. And mom wasn't interested in any of that.

"All I want to do is go home and be with my doggie," she said repeatedly.

When we asked Ackermann how long she could live, he said, "Six months will be pushing it."

Kriegler agreed.

She stayed in the hospital Tuesday night, and after receiving two units of blood, was released Wednesday afternoon.

That night, Mom ate dinner with Charlsie and her husband and son, Jamie and Jordan Garrett, nurse and family friend Jody Mattingly and me at Ragetti's Italian Restaurant in downtown Lebanon. As usual, mom had a good appetite.

I had only one brief, emotional moment. Mom still looked healthy and just imagining this smiling, happy woman not being with us at Christmas made me sad. I had to stop eating because I couldn't swallow.

Mother's Day was four days away, May 11, and would this really be the last one that Mary Lucy Pearl would be in a human body?

I always thought mom would live to be at least 100. I think she thought that too.

Her mother, Julia Irene Webb Crowdus, lived to be 92, and mom took better care of herself than Mamaw Crowdus.

Both were tough women, and I thought mom, because of her deep love for life, would stay with us longer than the six-month estimate.

I was wrong again.

She lived only 46 days after Dr. Ackermann told us her large tumors would be cancerous.

On May 14, the day we received the official biopsy results, I called all family members and close friends and shared the news. Mom sat next to me on the sofa, and I turned on the speaker phone so she could talk to everybody.

It was a sunny day and when I asked her what she would like to do today, she responded, "I think I would like to go walk the Gorley Trail barefooted."

She was joking. She always had a sense of humor.

But she had walked the beautiful 3.2-mile wooded, hilly trail that loops around the Lebanon reservoir probably a dozen times.

We would do several short walks in the neighborhood and at Graham Memorial Park in Lebanon in the next month, but Mom wouldn't hike the Gorley Trail again.

Perhaps the fact that mom's memory was failing was a blessing. In the next three weeks she would ask me often what her illness was.

"Did the doctors say I have cancer?"

"Yes," I would say.

"How long do they think I can live?"

"Maybe six months. But I think it's up to you and God, mom."

"I want you to know I'm not afraid to die," she would say. "I know I'm going to heaven. But I'll miss all of my family here, and my doggies, Clay and Lily."

While the two units of blood she got in the hospital gave her a boost of energy and seemed to help sharpen her mind for a few days, when Mother's Day arrived mom said she didn't feel like going to church or out to eat.

Going to church and eating out were two of her greatest joys in life. I knew she was going downhill fast. But I also had hopes for a turnaround, a miracle.

She wasn't in pain as far as I could tell, but her energy level was extremely low.

In 2011, I moved out of my duplex apartment in Frankfort and stored my furniture and belongings in mom's garage and lived part-time at her residence and part-time at Angela's home and our yurt.

313

Mom loved having Lily and me live with her, and we enjoyed being there. At first she seemed capable of taking care of herself without much supervision.

But her confusion and memory loss had become much more noticeable about a year before cancer was detected. Mom was never a complainer, but whenever I would ask her how she felt, the answer was always the same: "I just feel tired all the time. I guess that's how an 88-year-old woman is supposed to feel."

I believed much of her confusion was caused by being on too many prescription drugs: for high blood pressure and cholesterol, and aching, burning feet. She also was a Type 2 diabetic and taking insulin.

Angela and I both felt if mom would eat healthier, she could probably get off some of her medicine, and that would improve her memory.

First Mother's Day without Mom

My mother died on Friday morning, June 20, 2014.

This is the first Mother's Day that I can't get a hug from her, or talk to her on the phone.

I'm trying not to feel sad. But I am. I feel greedy feeling sad, because I had her in my life for 66 years.

I wish I hadn't volunteered to write a Mother's Day column for the newspaper because putting your heart on paper can be painful. But I know it can also help with the healing.

Several years before she died, I remember driving her home from a family funeral in Louisville. At a stop light in Bardstown I pointed out a bumper sticker on the car in front of us. It said: "Be kind to your children. They decide which nursing home you go to."

Mom laughed, saying, "I'm not going to a nursing home. I'm going to die at home. I'm just going to sleep one night and not wake up."

She was serious.

I wondered if it could possibly happen that way. Both of her parents had Alzheimer's and died in nursing homes.

Although mom had memory problems and was a diabetic, she refused to give up desserts or high-carbohydrate foods. She had good hiding places in her house for her Oreo cookies and Little Debbie's cakes so I wouldn't throw them away.

My mother outlived three husbands. The first one, my father, broke her heart.

314

But she had two good marriages. After her third husband, Clay Thomas Pearl, died in 2008, I called her every night for several years. Then in the last year of her life, I spent more time in Lebanon than I did in Frankfort, trying to be her caregiver.

She loved hearing the story about me getting stopped by a deputy sheriff and having to take a Breathalyzer test one Friday night because I had stopped to call her. After attending a Grand Theatre concert, I remembered I hadn't called her and it was getting late. I didn't see any car behind me so I stopped on the Singing Bridge for a minute to call her number.

Then I drove several blocks to my apartment and blue lights came on. Since I had given up alcohol several years earlier, I scored a zero on my test.

Lucy Pearl was a Democrat and I'm pretty certain she voted for only one Republican in her life, state Senator Jimmy Higdon.

She was a longtime working mother who loved her job at the Lebanon Water Company until retirement. She was a member of Lebanon Baptist Church, longer than any other member, as well as a Sunday school teacher. She loved Dr. Chuck Queen at Immanuel Baptist Church in Frankfort.

She was concerned about her son's interest in Buddhism. But when seven Tibetan monks visited Lebanon for a week in 2013, she fell in love with them in 30 seconds. The morning they left Lebanon, two of the monks visited mom's home and gave her a colorful spiritual banner. They had tears in their eyes when they left, and so did she.

Her last two weeks were a time of discomfort. Pressure from the tumors caused almost nonstop bathroom trips. But she never complained.

The last 14 days were also a time of great joy. She knew she was loved by grandchildren, great-grandchildren and many others. She wasn't afraid to die. She looked forward to her family reunion in heaven.

Mary Lucy Pearl opened my heart in a million little ways in the 66 years I had her in my life. And her final teachings were:
- Be kind.
- Smile.
- Material things aren't important.
- When you give to others, you get so much more back in return.
- Forgive.
- Love everybody, even your enemies. If she had one, she didn't tell me about it.

• Life is beautiful, even in death. She died just as she said she would – at home, in her sleep, peacefully.

Chapter 48

Infant granddaughter Lucie dies

Written March 4, 2015, three days after granddaughter Lucie Nicole Pearl died at birth.

Those who know me well know I love life, every single breath. But Saturday night I wanted to die. I wanted God to take me instead of 17-week granddaughter, Lucie Nicole Pearl. Oh, how I wanted that.

When you live 67 years, plenty of heart-breaking experiences come . . . along with innumerable happy times. Saturday was the most painful yet. The night before was pure joy. I had never been to a baby-naming celebration before Friday. Andrea and Kennedy Pearl were so excited about having their first baby, they wanted to have a party to announce the gender. About 50 family members and friends gathered at Andi's parents' home in Lexington. A large cake was uncovered by Andi and Kennedy to reveal in white and pink icing: "It's a Girl! Lucie. Coming in August." Shouts of Joy rang through the house.

. . . Around 2 a.m. Sunday in Lexington's Central Baptist Hospital, Andi asked me if I would like to hold Lucie. Wrapped in a white cloth garment, Lucie felt lighter than a feather. Her little fingers and legs were perfect. Looking into her face, I knew I was seeing Divine Wisdom. Lucie told me, "This is what is. I'm perfect, and I'm with you and my family always." . . . She is!

Earlier Saturday night, my older son, Kevin, in his USMC sweatshirt, held Kennedy in his arms and promised, "Somehow, we will get through this together."

Sleep never came Saturday night. Light seemed to come earlier than usual Sunday morning. The first thing I saw on Facebook was an Ekhart

Tolle quote: "Acceptance of the unacceptable is the greatest source of grace in this world."

In a drizzling rain, I drove Kennedy to the hospital. Andi was eating pancakes when we walked in her room. She held a strip of bacon in her hand and asked her vegetarian father-in-law, "Do you want this?" She smiled, and I knew then I wanted to continue living. In the last nine hours, Andi and Kennedy had shown me a strength, courage and compassion I had never witnessed.

I can't trade places with Lucie, named in honor of my mother, Lucy Pearl, who died June 20, 2014 at age 88. And Mom, I'm sure, loves the new spelling. I know Lucie Nicole Pearl is in Divine company. Her shining light will be in my heart forever. And I look forward to the day when she greets me in the Spirit World.

Chapter 49

A life well lived, but too short

L isa Morrison was a very busy young woman but she always took the time to help me when I needed to know something about upcoming Tibetan Buddhism events in Indiana and Kentucky. She had a kind voice, a beautiful smile, and a compassionate, generous heart.

She understood that most community journalists aren't blessed with an abundance of money. When she wanted me to attend a two-day writers' conference in Bloomington, Indiana, in 2011, she arranged for me to have a complimentary room at a bed-and-breakfast inn for two nights.

When I went on my first retreat at the Tibetan Mongolian Buddhist Cultural Center (TMBCC) in 2012, she helped me get a substantial discount so I could stay in a small cottage for a little more than a month. At least once a week while I was on retreat, she would drop by to visit my black Lab, Lily, and me, making sure everything was going well. She would always ask if we needed anything. She loved Lily and Lisa's visits always excited Lily.

Lisa loved the cultural center and I'll never forget her telling me about the time she attended the cremation ceremony for the center's founder, Thubten J. Norbu, the Dalai Lama's oldest brother. The cremation took place on the grounds of TMBCC and Lisa said the energy from the fire was "so powerful it became overwhelming. I had to go inside the temple and sit down. But not long after I sat down, Mr. Norbu's energy came into the temple. It was incredible."

In 2016, Lisa Morrison, also known as Lisa K. Lewis, died at 12 a.m. Sunday, January 24, at Indianapolis Methodist Hospital from injuries suffered a week earlier in a vehicle accident on a slick, snow-covered road in Bloomington, Indiana. She was 47.

Lisa was on her way to the Tibetan Mongolian Buddhist Cultural Center to help at a wedding ceremony when the wreck happened in a sharp curve. Cultural center director Arjia Rinpoche's nephew, Chenli Rejie, was getting married and Lisa was a philanthropist, publicist, florist and wedding planner.

Since 2003 Lisa had donated thousands of hours of her time managing all media, organizing events, and planning fundraising endeavors for Buddhist centers, causes related to His Holiness the 14th Dalai Lama and his visits to the Midwest.

She was born in Terre Haute, Indiana, on December 30, 1968, and raised in Bloomington where she resided most of her life. She attended Franklin College.

Lisa's contribution to the arts and the city of Bloomington began with her debut on local radio when she was only a teenager. In the 1990s as a single mother, she dedicated her early career to promoting and supporting artists both local and international.

There were numerous tributes to Lisa following her death and one that really touched my heart was by Bloomington's outstanding press photographer Jeremy Hogan, whom I met in 2003.

Hogan said on Facebook, "It's been a sad week here. I learned a couple of days ago that my friend Lisa Morrison passed away. I worked with her often over the years when she did publicity work for the Dalai Lama and the Tibetan Mongolian Buddhist Cultural Center. But I would also see her around town and she was a friend.

"She always had a smile, and was always positive, even in some times when a lot of people would have folded from stress. I've watched her deal with some chaotic situations. Most of all, she always was kind, and had something nice to say, and I am learning now, seeing people's tributes, this is who she was, and that she did much more to help people than most realized.

"She was involved with nonprofits and arts events on many levels. She will be missed immensely, people like her are actually rare, and I'm well aware it's a huge loss for our community.

"I hope wherever she is now in the spectrum of existence, somewhere in the beyond, that she is in peace. I'll miss seeing her around town and talking to her. Please meditate, say prayers, or send out some supporting thoughts for her son, Jeremy Gotwals, and her husband, Jeff Lewis. The loss for them has to be unimaginable."

Her son Jeremy wrote her obituary and he concluded it by saying, "Lisa had the most beautiful smile, voice, and energy that lit up every room she entered while being engaging, compassionate and kind to all. Her family couldn't be more proud. Lisa will be missed greatly by her family, friends, and loved ones.

"Bloomington has lost a true independent icon and champion for local music and the arts. She was truly one of a kind and her like shall never come again. God bless Lisa."

The Tashi Kyil Tibetan monks, on tour in Kentucky after Lisa's death, canceled their last day of cultural programs to return to Bloomington for her memorial services.

On Saturday, January 30, an interfaith funeral service was held in her honor at the First Christian Church with Buddhist Lama Arjia Rinpoche and Christian Minister Helen Hempfling officiating. Burial was in Valhalla Memory Gardens.

That night a celebration of life took place at The Lodge on Bloomington Square.

Sunday morning, January 31, prayers were offered at the Tibetan Mongolian Buddhist Cultural Center.

I was unable to attend her funeral but went to Bloomington in February 2016 specifically to meditate and say prayers in the TMBCC temple for my dear friend Lisa. I felt her beautiful presence there that day, and still do every time I return to the temple. I still miss her and wonder why she had to leave us so young.

Chapter 50

Farewell to peacemaker Ruby Layson

This guest column was published in The State Journal on June 16, 2017.

My last phone conversation with Ruby Layson was an odd one. Ruby was a retired journalist, educator, environmentalist, world traveler and tireless worker for peace and equality.

She was a kindred spirit. We were on the Frankfort Interfaith Council together, and I loved listening to Ruby's compassionate wisdom and just being with her.

Late on the night of May 27, I opened an email saying Ruby Layson had died and her memorial service would be held later at the Unitarian Universalist Church of Lexington. Survivors also were listed.

All of Ruby's close friends knew she was dying of cancer. But it was still a shock that she had passed so quickly after seeing her sitting in the Paul Sawyier Public Library's community room, on the front row, at our interfaith council's "Celebration of Diverse Faiths" on April 23.

The next morning after receiving the obit email, I forwarded it to all Frankfort Interfaith Council members. Then I called Linda Boileau, Ruby's neighbor and friend and State Journal illustrator, to see if she knew more details of Ruby's death. Boileau wasn't aware of her death, and said she had just talked to her a day or two before. She said she would call Ruby's son, Randy Sexton in Versailles.

Meanwhile I sent another group email to our interfaith council saying, "I'm really confused. Ruby might still be living. I'm thinking she sent me that (email I forwarded) so I would have it when she died. But I'm not sure."

Soon Boileau called me and said Ruby is still living. "Great," I said.

Then I quickly sent a third email to the interfaith council saying, "I apologize for the confusion, and I'm happy to report that Ruby is alive, according to her neighbor, who just checked. I'll be quiet now."

I called Ruby and asked her if she had read any emails that morning. She said "no." I said "good."

Then I told her what happened – my fake news report of her death to the council. She laughed.

I told her it was wonderful to hear her voice. She talked about her declining health, saying she felt much worse than at the interfaith gathering in April.

We had ridden together last year to attend a memorial service in Lexington for our journalist friend Carl West, longtime editor of The State Journal.

"Since then it seems as if I've lost at least one good friend a month," I said. "It makes me sad, and now I have to think about you leaving us."

Ruby said, "It's just a part of life, Charlie. I've had a great, interesting, long life."

After our conversation, she continued reading and watching TV – keeping up with local, state, national and world news. On Facebook, Ruby continued as long as she could her activism for world peace, protection for refugees, and fairness for LGBT friends.

She was a woman of strength, courage, compassion, kindness and generosity. I'll never forget her beautiful smile and her heavenly brownies she baked for interfaith gatherings.

Ruby Lee Layson, 89, died Saturday, June 10.

Aejaz Shaik, a Muslim and interfaith council member, had earlier transported Ruby to the April 23 Celebration of Diverse Faiths.

"Ruby was very committed to helping immigrants, Muslims and other marginalized people," Shaik said, after her passing. "She strived to build bridges between communities through meaningful dialogue.

"I always felt comfortable talking to her on various subjects including religion and politics. I was impressed by her passion in what she believes."

After initially planning to attend the April interfaith community event, Ruby notified Shaik she would be unable to attend because of her declining health and the lack of handicap access at the library during ongoing construction.

Shaik, knowing she would love to attend, offered to give her a ride and assist her in getting into the library. She accepted.

"When I arrived to pick her up, she was already waiting at the door with a book in hand. It was a gift for Afeef, my 14-year-old son, and was titled, 'Muhammad – the Story of a Prophet and Reformer.'

"As a Muslim I was pleasantly surprised to receive a book on Muhammad from a devout Unitarian Universalist Christian."

He said it wasn't a surprise, however, that her encouragement had led to the formation of the Frankfort Interfaith Council several years earlier. "As a humanitarian she personally knew several Muslims in Frankfort and around the country."

Knowing people of faiths at a personal level "is surely a way to overcome fear of others," Shaik said.

While driving Ruby back home that day, she told Shaik she was "very old and ill. I'm not sure if cancer is going to get me first or old age." She smiled.

"I helped her get into her house and bid goodbye to her," Shaik said. "That was the last time I saw her.

"Ruby has inspired me to become a better person and to care about people around me."

Ashiq Zaman, president of the Islamic Center of Frankfort, knew Ruby for more than 10 years. She invited him to speak about Islam in a study group at her church.

"After that our paths crossed many times, which led to cooperation on common issues," he said.

The last five years they worked together on the Frankfort Interfaith Council.

"I cannot say I have come across many people like her in my life," Zaman said. "Ruby was well-educated, well-read, and a well-traveled individual always willing to listen and learn. I cannot remember any conversation completely foreign to her regardless of the topic.

"I have seen her, from my personal experience, not to judge people based on their background or external appearance, but first and foremost as a fellow human being."

Zaman said faith was important to Ruby. "She was deeply devoted to her Unitarian Universalist Church. She actively participated in so many causes for promoting love and peace. She took every opportunity in helping marginalized folks, seeking fairness for everybody and building bridges between people of different backgrounds. In recent times, her ill health limited her physical participation on the council. But she was always there for us, guiding us.

"She was an example of a true humanitarian. I will miss the soft-spoken and full-of-spirit Ruby in all of our future initiatives."

Jim Jackson, a Methodist and interfaith council member, met Ruby five years ago while attending a monthly meeting of the Lexington Christian-Muslim Dialogue, an interfaith group. She was the only other Frankfort person at the meeting, Jackson said.

"I introduced myself to her and asked if she might be interested in starting an interfaith group in Frankfort. She immediately and enthusiastically said 'yes.'

"What I was most impressed with after getting to know Ruby was just how committed and passionate she was for peace, compassion for all and respect for diversity. I never saw her waiver from her commitment to these beliefs."

Jackson said she was providing email input into interfaith activities just three or four days prior to her death.

Don and Sylvia Coffey were friends of Ruby at the Unitarian Universalist Church in Frankfort.

"We shall always remember Ruby as a quiet, genteel friend whose great determination to confront injustice stood above the crowd by orders of magnitude," Don Coffey said. "The towering integrity housed in her small body was of a quality attained by few, and she leaves lasting inspiration for us all."

A native Kentuckian, she was born in Henderson on October 1, 1927 but resided in Harlan through her high school years. Later she was inducted into the Harlan High School Hall of Fame.

She graduated summa cum laude from Wesleyan College in Macon, Georgia in 1949 with a major in English. She earned a master's in journalism in 1952 at Indiana University, and studied education at California State University in Los Angeles.

Ruby was a teacher, a newspaper reporter and editor, and a writer and planner for the Kentucky Department of Education.

After retiring she taught English as a Second Language part time to Spanish-speaking students at Anderson County Schools.

She spent her final years in Frankfort, living close to her many friends and family.

She was a longtime member of the Frankfort Chapter of United Nations Association-USA and a board member about 12 years. She helped organize and observe International Day of Peace in the state Capitol for several years.

Ruby took part in archeological and environmental projects in New Mexico, Utah, New Hampshire, Spain, Peru and Australia. She also traveled in Russia, China, Canada, Central America, Mexico, South America, Kenya, Greece, Israel, Jordan, Egypt, Western Europe, Eastern Europe, Puerto Rico and most U.S. states. She took train trips across Canada and through Copper Canyon, Mexico.

She began playing the dulcimer in 1978 and from then on was a member of the Frankfort Dulcimer Group and Lexington Folksingers, performing at churches, civic clubs and cultural events. She also taught dulcimer in community education.

Her neighbor Linda Boileau said, "When I think of Ruby I think of her huge heart. She was a brilliant woman but her kindness was what really shined about her.

"I locked myself out of my house early one winter morning and Ruby let me right in to use her phone. She always made me feel welcome, always."

After learning of her death last weekend, Zaman said, "We are all a part of God's creation and we all have to return to God. It was the time for Ruby. But it is hard to accept that she is gone."

Amen.

PART EIGHT

And Now Rest

"Inner rest is the sacred ground on which we meet the light of enlightenment"

--Anam Thubten

Chapter 51

Love letter to grandson on his first birthday

M ay 11, 2018

Dear Luke:

Your daddy told me twice in the last month you don't need anything for your first birthday. He meant material things, like toys and books. After looking in your bedroom, and seeing all the animals, gadgets and clothes, I believe him.

So instead of going shopping, which I don't enjoy unless I'm going to a bookstore, I'll try to string together a few words on paper for your birthday. It may sound easy but it rarely is. Writing for newspapers has been my job for more than 40 years. It requires you to be around a lot of different people but then you must get away from the crowds, be alone with only your thoughts, to finish your work.

I love writing, even though the monetary pay has never been great. Perhaps long before you graduate from high school, newspapers that you hold in your hand will be ancient history. And that's OK. I may be ancient history too. And that's OK.

I absolutely love the mystery of life and I'm going to do my best to stay here as long as possible – to be with you and watch you grow up into a young man. We'll go to Lexington Legends games together. We've already done that once and now it's a new season. I like going there because they're close to your home and Lily can housesit with Maggie and Jeter. Maybe we'll travel not too far up I-75 to watch the Cincinnati Reds play, or maybe you would just prefer going to the zoo to connect with all the amazing animals. That's fine. Bicycle rides on the Legacy Trail and hikes at the Red River Gorge or Cove Spring Park sound like fun too. Or we can just sit around a campfire, roasting marshmallows, and talk and listen to the magical night symphony of crickets and frogs and owls and coyotes.

The only certainty in life is that we can't stay here forever.

I've heard it said that Life is 10,000 joys and 10,000 sorrows. It's an unlimited mixture of pleasant and unpleasant experiences. Luke David, every one of your family members – especially your mommy and daddy – felt overwhelming grief the night your older sister, Lucie Nicole, died. We will never forget her or that rainy, winter Saturday night in 2015 when we learned only her spirit would live with us.

Somehow we survived, and then you arrived and filled our hearts with love and joy and gratefulness.

Going to the hospital baby window to see a miracle, to see pure innocence, never gets old. Thank you Luke for coming into our lives. I love your perpetual smile, those incredible blue eyes, your long toes and fingers, and your wild spiky hair. I love watching you laugh and play in the dogs' water bowls.

I love knowing when I'm gone from this earth, you're still going to have a lot of cousins and kinfolks who love you unconditionally. That's comforting. Keep being you, grandson.

All My Love!
Papaw Pearl

Chapter 52

Working on becoming a minimalist

A bumper sticker affixed to one side of my bedroom dresser says Less is More. Yes, I believe it. I'm always fascinated with film documentaries or magazine articles featuring tiny houses. I've never had an abundance of money. Today, at age 71, I'm thankful to still earn a little extra money by freelance writing. Perhaps I'm satisfied with less because I've never been close to monetary wealth. I can't imagine what it would be like to have a million dollars.

Occasionally, maybe once every two years, I go in with family members or friends to buy a lottery ticket when the prize money gets extremely high. If we won, how would we change and what would we buy? I think I know. I would want to share it with family and friends and those in the world who need it the most. I hope that's what I would do.

I used to want a job at a major daily newspaper where you could hop on a plane and travel anywhere in the world to write a feature story.

Today, I'm content for the most part staying in Frankfort, bicycling on backroads with Angela, kayaking on the Kentucky River or Elkhorn Creek with Angela, dancing with the Glitterbugs, going to Frankfort Interfaith Council meetings and being with council members, whom I consider family; walking on mowed paths on the Mary Mahoney family farm where our yurt and labyrinth are located; going to concerts, plays and movies at our downtown Grand Theatre, where we've had season tickets since the intimate 428-seat facility reopened in 2009 after a major renovation; and taking afternoon naps.

I haven't had a TV since 2006. But I still enjoy watching college football games at my children's homes, especially when Notre Dame, Louisville or Kentucky is playing. I like college basketball games when

March Madness tournaments begin. College and professional baseball games are fun to watch, especially at World Series time.

In the winter of 2015 I bought a small five-room house in Arlington Heights subdivision, off East Main Street between downtown and Kentucky State University, thanks to a small inheritance from my mother's estate after the sale of her home in Lebanon. One of the two bedrooms on Lindsey Avenue is a meditation room. My mother died in 2014 and I had stored a lot of newspapers, books, magazines, photos, and other memorabilia in her attic, garage and a bedroom closet.

It was time to get rid of a lot of stuff from the past. I wrapped up the only sports trophy I ever won – the 1965 Most Valuable Back award from Lebanon High School's football team – and took it to a lifelong friend, Anna Laura (Evans) Davenport, who has always been like a sister to me. I asked her to give the package to her brother, James "Butch" Evans, the next time he visited Lebanon from his home, now in Bloomington, Indiana. Anna Laura, a retired educator in the Marion County public school system, promised me she would.

Accompanying the trophy was a thank-you card. It said: *"I've wanted to give this to you for a long time. You were the Most Valuable Back and the Most Valuable Player (he received neither) for Lebanon High School's 1965 football season. Coach (Robert "Buck") Hourigan gave the MVB award to me because I was a senior. Coach was young and intelligent then, but not as wise as we've all become with almost 50 years of additional living experiences.*

"It was an honor playing high school football with you, while your father, Curtis Evans, was always there watching us from the bleachers, never missing a game or practice, offering us his coaching advice and even designing a trick play or two. Congratulations on going on to play on winning teams at Eastern Kentucky University and earning All-Ohio Valley Conference recognition. Good luck in the Lebanon Labor Day golf tournament. Tell Coach Hourigan hi. Thanks for your friendship.

"I apologize for the one broken hand on the trophy. The many moves over the years have taken its toll. Be well."

Sincerely,

Charlie Pearl

In letting go of things – and I've still got a long way to go – I've tried to recycle as much as possible by donating to St. Vincent De Paul Society Thrift Store; New Leash On Life, a volunteer thrift store in downtown Frankfort that benefits animals; and Goodwill.

I've donated hundreds of books to the Paul Sawyier Public Library bookstore, and I need to donate a few hundred more. I'm working on it, every week, slowly letting go. It's a joy. The rule today is, if I buy a book, I have to give away two. I don't buy more than five books a year now, and almost all of them have a spirituality theme.

In September 2019, I called my four children – Charlsie, Kevin, Kennedy and Kathryn – and asked permission to not participate in the family gift exchange at Christmas. I said I wanted to be with them at the traditional family potluck lunch, but for quite a few years I had felt very uncomfortable with the excessive gift buying. I don't like to ever use the word hate, but I did hate shopping when I had no idea what I could get for each person in our large family that would be meaningful. I felt bad because I didn't want to be remembered as Papaw Scrooge either.

I asked them to please not get me anything for Christmas this year, because there was nothing I needed, and to pass along the word to other family members. I had all of the baseball caps, T-shirts and sweatshirts I needed to get me through this lifetime.

All four were kind and understanding and honored my request. And it was one of my all-time favorite Christmases.

On a Sunday afternoon in December, I took grandchildren Kamdyn and Kalleigh Johnson to the Grand Theatre to watch the "Polar Express" movie. They wore their pajamas and got popcorn, candy and drinks. Kamdyn wanted to sit in the front row, so we did. Kamdyn loved the movie and Kalleigh slept through most of it. When the movie ended, they met Santa Claus and he gave them a little bell.

After leaving the Grand, we walked to Hoggy's Ice Cream shop for another treat.

Grandson Luke Pearl will join us at the Grand Theatre in December 2020 but I've already told Kamdyn we're sitting at least four rows back from the front.

Becoming Minimalist

One of my favorite Facebook sites is Becoming Minimalist. There's great information on the benefits of freeing yourself from material possessions, and numerous common-sense tips on getting started and enjoying the changes.

In addition to reading about minimalism, I'm fortunate to have two young minimalist masters in my family – Sarah Mitchell and her boyfriend

Joseph Merchant. They've done much more than talk about it. They're living it. I always love being with them, listening to them, and seeing and being in their living space. They're an inspiration in many ways, including their commitment to being vegan for better health and reducing their carbon footprints to try to help heal an ailing Mother Earth.

A book that has helped me along the path to minimalism and buying less is titled "Hooked! – Buddhist Writings on Greed, Desire, and the Urge to Consume," edited by Stephanie Kaza. She is professor emeritus in the Rubenstein School of Environment and Natural Resources at the University of Vermont, and has taught religion and ecology, ecofeminism, and unlearning consumerism.

In the book, 17 well-respected Buddhist teachers explore our seemingly endless drive to acquire. They offer practical ways to combat consumerism on a personal and global level.

Paul Hawken – an environmentalist, entrepreneur, journalist and author – says in the foreword, "It is tempting to see the problem of consumption as something other people do. People with SUVs should cut back and buy smaller cars, get more exercise, and use a bicycle. But this wonderfully edited volume shows us that it is more relevant and poignant to look at our own lives. A Buddhist perspective on consumption offers understanding of oneself."

Hawken said he has a friend who has 600 objects in his home.

"That includes everything, even teaspoons. At one time he was an officer of one of the world's largest banks. When he wants to buy something, or receives a gift, he selects something to give away. This is not a zero sum game. As the years have gone by, his home has become more nuanced and lovely. Every object has meaning; nothing is retained unnecessarily. His home is like a small temple. He needs very little money to live on, which means he spends most of his time helping others. He is utterly alive, elfish, bright-eyed and present.

"We are human. We will always consume. The big question is how."

Another Stephanie Kaza book I recommend is titled "Green Buddhism: Practice and Compassionate Action in Uncertain Times," published in 2019.

Five days before Ash Wednesday 2020, I received two compliments on how clean and uncluttered my little house looked. Daughter Charlsie and Angela both said, at different times of the day, "I've never seen it look this nice."

334

I loved hearing that because I was feeling it.

It saddens me, however, that the city of Frankfort's curbside recycling program isn't nearly as good in the winter of 2020 as it was a year ago because the demand and markets for recycled materials aren't available anymore. It hurts my soul to have to put newspapers and magazines and other paper products and all glass and many plastic containers in the garbage container now. I hope it's a temporary setback.

It's a joy to walk downtown and to many other nearby places in our little capital instead of driving. It's a joy to ride my bicycle to grandchildren's soccer games. It's a joy to mow my little yard and adjoining vacant lot on East Main with an old hand-me-down push mower.

Before my 72nd birthday on August 3, 2020, I want to return to an alcohol-free life again. I know I can do it because I did for nine years.

I'm addicted to all kinds of junk foods too: chips, crackers, cookies, M&Ms, ice cream, pies, cakes -- you name it and I love it. I'm living proof you can be an overweight vegetarian or vegan.

I know my good friends, Don and Sylvia Coffey, and Angela – the guru of "all things in moderation," will be excellent, inspirational coaches, as will the Becoming Minimalist writers on Facebook.

Chapter 53

Coronavirus stops the world

The last chapter was originally the final one in this book. Then our planet, our nation, our state, and our capital city of Kentucky, where I live, changed drastically. It has become the biggest worldwide change, the biggest news story, in my lifetime.

When it really hit home for me was at 3:20 p.m. on Tuesday, March 10, 2020, when I arrived for our weekly Glitterbugs' dance practice at the Capital City Activity Center for senior citizens.

We were told that the center was now officially closed until further notice because of the coronavirus (COVID-19). Our next dance performance was scheduled for the following Tuesday, St. Patrick's Day, at a nursing home in Versailles, Kentucky. This was supposed to be our last practice before we got to wear our new glittery green vests.

Before we exited the front door to the center, we heard that Kentucky nursing homes were also closed to the public, so our St. Patrick's Day dance would be canceled.

But we still planned to dance on St. Patrick's Day. Sylvia Coffey, our dance teacher, told us we could have a dance party at her and husband Don's Dancing Meadow Farm home. Sylvia, one very busy woman, is always eager to host a celebration in her home.

Five days later Sylvia sent the Glitterbugs an email titled "Raincheck for St. Patrick's Day." She wrote, "With everything locked down at this time, it seems the right thing to do and **NOT** gather at our house Tuesday for supper. I'd rather be too cautious at this time. So we'll try our gathering at a later date. Take care and be safe."

But the seriousness of COVID-19 really hit home for most of us in Basketball-Crazy Kentucky when the announcements came that NCAA basketball tournaments were canceled, as were the boys' and girls' state basketball tournaments. Are you kidding me – No March Madness? That's insane! All NCAA spring sports were canceled.

Each day, it seemed, from that point on, brought big changes. Restaurants closed except for those offering carry-outs or deliveries. Businesses, except for those providing essential services, closed. Toilet paper, paper towels, hand sanitizers disappeared from the shelves of groceries and pharmacies. Schools, colleges and universities closed and students did their classwork at home. Most government employees did their work from home. Many people lost their jobs. Most churches closed and had TV or online services during the Lenten and Easter season, and beyond. People were getting sick and dying every day, especially in the major cities. Nurses, doctors, medical staffs, all employees of medical facilities and nursing homes put their lives at risk treating the sick, and many medical people contracted the coronavirus. Police officers, firefighters, grocery store and pharmacy employees, liquor store employees, jail and prison staffs, public service workers – and the list goes on and on – also put their lives on the line serving others. Social distancing became the new norm. Hugs and handshakes were out.

As I write this in late April 2020, I have no idea what the future holds for our Commonwealth of Kentucky, our United States, our World Family, and our Planet Earth. I'm guessing it's going to get much worse before it gets better.

I'm grateful a good spiritual friend, Taylor Marshall of Frankfort, is recovering from the coronavirus. I'm thankful my daughter-in-law Andrea Pearl's sister, Christine Dudley of Pulaski County, Kentucky, has recovered from the virus. I'm sad that Mary Nickles – a good friend in our Light Clinic meditation group – lost a dear friend and former teacher in California, Russ Abraham, to the coronavirus. Mary shared with several of us a heart-warming video and story about Russ from a Sacramento TV station. Many of his former students and medical staff at the hospital gathered in the hospital parking lot to pay tribute to him in his final hours.

"Russ was a true humanitarian, with a wicked sense of humor," Mary told us. "We had great conversations, floating in the pool, and drinking whatever craft beer he recommended. He was a music teacher and played the guitar every day."

Angela and I had never heard of country music singer Joe Diffie until 2019 when we went to watch a summer preview film of the upcoming 2019-20 Grand Theatre season. The entertainment brochure said Diffie was a Grammy winner, had 12 #1 singles, and had sold over six million records with his beloved songwriting and vocals. We love the intimate 428-seat Grand Theatre and have purchased season tickets every year since the season opener in 2009. We loved the Joe Diffie Band's performance on November 22, 2019 too. He had all kinds of fun and energy on stage that night. And now, he is gone. He died on March 29, 2020 in Nashville, Tennessee, at the age of 61 from complications of COVID-19.

On April 30, 2020 the total number of COVID-19 cases reported by the New York Times were: 3.25 million worldwide; 1.08 million in the United States; 4,539 in Kentucky; and 16 cases in Franklin County. The death toll from COVID-19 was: 231,000 worldwide, 62,444 in the United States; and 235 in Kentucky. I'm thankful that the Frankfort and Franklin County community has been spared any deaths at this time.

While it breaks my heart to see the worldwide death toll from COVID-19, I realize this pandemic is sending us a wake-up message. This is the biggest spiritual teaching so far in my lifetime. The new normal cannot be the old normal.

It's our opportunity to save Mother Earth. What am I doing right now? And what little things can I do to help heal our country and planet?

I had called Hannah Brown, editor of FRANK magazine, on the day before Easter to talk to her about two stories I had planned to write for upcoming issues of The State Journal's monthly magazine.

She told me in a kind way the Frankfort newspaper is no longer using paid contributing writers during this pandemic. I understood. The State Journal office had closed and employees were working from home. Longtime sports writer Linda Younkin, was writing mostly news and feature stories. The print edition of the newspaper had been reduced from five days a week to two.

Life seemed like the Twilight Zone. But then I always liked that TV show when I was growing up in Lebanon in the 1950s and '60s. I retired as a State Journal staff writer in 2011 but continued to freelance, so this was the first time in my long career as a journalist (since the early 1970s) that I was officially unemployed.

It felt weird. But I took it as a message that I was supposed to be spending additional time getting my first book ready for publication. I've always loved going on small retreats, and this was an opportunity for another one.

Instead of going to a cottage at the Tibetan Mongolian Buddhist Cultural Center in Indiana, as I did in 2012 when I started writing this book, my retreat place would be my small home near downtown Frankfort, or at our yurt on Angela's family farm.

I haven't been bored for a second since social distancing arrived. What I miss most are hugs from family and close friends. I'm still writing, researching, and reading more than ever. I'm currently reading Normandi Ellis' new spiritual book, "Hieroglyphic: Words of Power." Normandi, a friend and former Franklin County resident, is an award-winning writer, workshop facilitator and archpriestess of the Fellowship of Isis. She has authored and coauthored several books, leads tours to Egypt, and lives in a spiritual community in Chesterfield, Indiana.

Since meeting Brother Paul Quenon – a monk, poet, and author at the Abbey of Gethsemani – I try to write at least one haiku a day. That's one of the things he does daily. I love a book he coauthored titled "The Art of Pausing: Meditations for the Overworked and Overwhelmed." He signed it for me in 2013, saying, "May you too pause with 17 syllables." I also have taken up journal writing again.

Another book I'm rereading is "In Praise of Slowness: How a Worldwide Movement Is Challenging the Cult of Speed" by Carl Honoré. When I read it more than a decade ago, I circled a paragraph near the end of the last chapter. He said, "The great benefit of slowing down is reclaiming the time and tranquility to make meaningful connections – with people, with culture, with work, with nature, with our own bodies and minds. Some call that living better. Others would describe it as spiritual."

Another meaningful book I'm reading is titled "Ecology, Ethics, and Interdependence" by The Dalai Lama in conversation with leading thinkers on climate change.

I try to go for an hour walk each day. Occasionally Angela joins me in town for walking. Some days I join her in Bridgeport to walk on the mowed paths around her family farm. We've been on one 15-mile bicycle ride together since the pandemic hit, and we plan to do more frequent rides on the backroads when I'm finished with this book writing. Soon! It's easy for us to do social distancing while walking or bicycling because Angela goes at a faster pace.

I'm hoping we buy used kayaks this summer to paddle on the beautiful Kentucky River that runs through downtown Frankfort, so close to my residence.

Creative Angela has found a new project for us on her family farm – clearing away brush from a grove of tall, white pine trees. She and her siblings and late father, Lloyd Mahoney, planted the pine seedlings 48 years ago when Angela was 13 years old. It has been a mindful-meditation practice, working slowly, three or four hours a day, usually one or two days a week. That's my work schedule. Angela has put in considerably more time at the pines.

There's a good reason we're doing the work. Adjacent our yurt is a labyrinth for walking meditation, centering prayer or contemplation. The labyrinth is built from nearby field stones and the path is lined with pine needles. Each fall or early winter, we put down a new layer of pine needles. In 2019, we lost our major source of needles when the person, who kindly allowed us to annually rake them up from his front yard in Shelby County, sold his house. The new property owner said 'no' to our request.

I drove to Marion County and brought back a carload of white pine needles from Graham Memorial Park where my daughter, Charlsie, is director of the Lebanon Aquatic Center. Several more bags of pine needles came from friends' lawns in Frankfort, and Angela purchased two large boxes of dried needles from Lowe's to finish the 2019 replenishment project. The path isn't as spongy this season, "but we should have our own source of pine needles from now on," said innovative Angela, smiling, when she announced our new work project in early 2020.

It's been a joy working under the tall pine trees on the Mahoney farm. Angela's brother-in-law and sister, Kenny and Linda Winkle, and their 6-year-old grandson, Austin Parker, have been a big help. Austin has enthusiastically marked little pine seedlings that we've found while clearing the land. My black Lab, Lily, and Angela's black-and-white Maine Coon cat, Xander, love to be there in the shade, watching and supervising. The sloped land by a little creek under the pine trees is being transformed into a natural cathedral. The tall pines are alive and happy. We feel their happiness. Angela has a new source of mulch for her vegetable gardens and flowers. It's a perfect social-distancing project. Thank you, Angela.

In the last six weeks, I've started making more frequent phone calls to longtime friends in my age range to make sure they're doing well. Tuck Kerr, a friend since elementary school days, moved this year from a large old house in South Frankfort to a small, fairly-new duplex in Springfield, Kentucky. He's been working on letting go of material possessions for several years and is one of my main advisors on minimalizing.

About a week ago, Tuck sent me an online story with photos and charts showing how the natural world is thriving now that humans are staying indoors. The photos brought joy to my heart. I thanked him for sharing such uplifting news and told him my favorite part was a video of a black bear climbing a big tree in Yosemite National Park, which was closed to the public. It was fascinating. After watching the video over and over, I sent Tuck a text saying being present watching the bear in its Yosemite home, mindfully climbing a tree, "probably gets me about as close to enlightenment as I may ever get in this lifetime."

On the day before Earth Day, I called longtime friend Barney Bush, a Shawnee Indian living in the Shawnee National Forest in southern Illinois, not far from Paducah, Kentucky. Barney is a 75-year-old writing teacher, environmentalist and author of several books of poetry, essays and novels. A diabetic, he's recovering slowly from prostate surgery, and needs to undergo right knee replacement surgery.

He said he's thankful to still be here on this earth, "but I feel I need more energy to accomplish things, to get some writing done, to deal with the politics of colonialism that goes on around here."

We talked about recent changes that have come following the coronavirus outbreak. Regarding the necessity of social distancing, Barney said, "People ask me if I'm staying inside, and if I'm getting bored sitting at home. And I tell them, 'The things we're being told to do to combat this virus – that's the exact way that I live day to day anyway.' Other than the illnesses that are trying to take over my body, nothing has changed. I have never made a lot of trips to the grocery store anyway. I try to keep a list and go in and knock it all out in one fell swoop."

I asked him if he feels the coronavirus is a major teaching from Mother Earth. He talked about World War I and the 1918-1919 influenza pandemic that killed somewhere between 20 and 40 million people, including an estimated 675,000 Americans. More people died during the 1918 flu pandemic than in all of World War I, with the majority of deaths occurring during the deadly second wave of the influenza outbreak. Generally speaking, there was an increase in influenza cases where social distancing rules were ignored, I had read. Several million died in the first bout, and then the second round killed many millions more, when people started relaxing and wanting to go back to the way things were, Barney said.

I asked him, "As a longtime teacher, what would you say to people who might now want to change the way they live their lives for the good of humanity and the planet?"

He answered, saying, "The reality of something spiritual is happening in the earth, and it's not playing games with people." In our lifetime, he said COVID-19 "is the biggest condition in which humans are no longer in control of their own day-to-day lives. If they take control of it, there's a good chance they will die from their own arrogance. You've got to follow the prescription, whatever it is that prevents this outbreak from affecting you, and you have to follow it right down to the T.

"You can't play that game – 'I'm an upper-middle-class white boy, and I want to go out and get a haircut.' In other words, they want life to return to the normal that they knew. That's not going to happen with this, not right away. We don't know yet what might happen with this. The evidence in the world for these kinds of pandemics has never been good. It has always been disastrous. That's the clear route or clear evidence of what happens when you mess with nature."

He talked about gas being cheap right now, and laughed, saying, "but most people don't have anywhere to go. That cramps the style of people. There's nowhere to gather. You can't go to movie theaters and sit in the crowd. You can't go to sports events. As far as I'm concerned, I don't care about any of that, other than how it affects people in their relationship with the earth. If it affects them in a bad way toward the earth, then I care. But if they have to sit at home and practice civility, I'm all for that. I think you ought to have to do that. You don't know where this coronavirus is going to go. The advance of it coming across this country is very ominous. It could actually go on for several years.

"But don't suffer with it so heavily. Just get down to the real business of being associated with life and spirit, and wake up to being present to all the natural beauty that surrounds you."

My solo morning walk on the day before Earth Day was up East Main to Martin Luther King Jr. Boulevard, then left on Cold Harbor Drive, and on up to the Kentucky State University's Athletic Drive. Taking the uphill pedestrian path that runs behind the KSU president's house, I bowed to several deer in the woods. It was a breezy morning and the grasses, the dandelions, the trees danced and swayed in the wind. I felt so alive.

On my Earth Day mid-afternoon walk through Frankfort Cemetery, a five-minute walk from my house, I always think of granddaughter Lucie Nicole Pearl when I see the signs directing me to the Kentucky Memorial for the Unborn. Lucie was buried in Lexington Cemetery in 2015, but I carry her in my heart everywhere I go. I want to get her name etched in a brick at the memorial in Frankfort. I feel her presence every time I see a cardinal and hear its beautiful song. It was sunny and warm, and pink and white dogwoods were in bloom, along with a few redbud trees.

I usually stop and rest a moment at the gravesite bench of Jacob Andrew Coulter who died August 28, 2018 at the age of 22, way too young.

But several people were walking in that area, so I took another route out of the cemetery that day. Jacob's mother, Gayle Coulter Deaton, is a close friend and former journalist who shared a cubicle with me at The State Journal more than 15 years ago. I can't begin to imagine the pain and emptiness in her heart from the loss of a son. I keep her and her younger son, Max, in my prayers every morning. Their names are on my meditation altar at home.

On my way out of the cemetery I noticed a large gravestone with a soccer player in action etched on one side. I walked across the grass to get a closer look. It's a memorial for Bradley Austin Camic, a young Frankfort High School soccer player who died from a sudden illness in 2015 at the age of 16. His death brought such loving unity to the entire community. My grandson, Preston Pearl, was one of Bradley's many close friends. Bradley's mother, Julie Camic, is a friend who lived in my neighborhood.

Buried next to Bradley is Timothy Neil Tincher. When I read the message on the back of his gravestone, I got cold chills: "Dance As If No One Is Watching, Sing As If No One Is Listening, Live Every Day As If It Were Your Last."

The Divine Dance of Life – Amen!

Occasionally now, I do a late night walk around the Capitol and by the Governor's Mansion. On most nights, green lights are glowing on the Capitol dome and Governor's Mansion to show compassion for the victims of the coronavirus who died that particular day. I'm thankful we have a compassionate, progressive, wise and courageous governor in Andy Beshear, who has worked tirelessly in his first year of office to educate and protect all Kentuckians and citizens outside the Commonwealth. We're all interconnected, and COVID-19 has no respect for borders.

Epilogue

Someone once asked me, "If the Buddha and Jesus Christ were to meet today, what would they have to say to each other?" And my answer is, the Buddha and Jesus Christ are already meeting every day, everywhere. Because Buddhists are the continuation of the Buddha, and Christians are the continuation of Jesus, and they are meeting today everywhere. We should help make their meeting successful.
                                                                      –Thich Nhat Hanh

I love being in Dr. Chuck Queen's office at Immanuel Baptist Church and listening to him answer my questions. He has never said, "Off the record," or "I don't feel comfortable giving you my honest answer about that." He just speaks from the heart.

I returned to his office in February 2020, to ask him a follow-up question from the 2016 Q & A interview. I had asked him in 2016 if he loved Donald Trump. His partial response was, "I can't say that I do. . . . I wish I did, and I would pray that I would. But I'm not there yet. But maybe I can be." (His complete response and the entire interview are in Chapter 7.)

We both were surprised and sad that Trump had won the presidential election – through the Electoral College. Since the progressive Baptist pastor had had four years to work on it, I felt I needed to ask him again if he now loves Trump.

Chuck laughed saying, "I haven't mastered it yet. It is more of a struggle now than it was then because you have to deal with his destructiveness, contempt, his demeaning and dehumanizing of people and institutions and democracy that we all realize help constitute who we are. You face it every single day and what we see is our democracy changing. I do wonder if he is elected again, if he gets four more years, what will our democracy look like?

"It is a constant struggle. It is a struggle not to return the anger and the hate and the contempt that is flowing out of the White House every day. How do you absorb it, deflect it, so that it doesn't become you, so you don't become what you are hating? That is a deep spiritual question and issue. I have not mastered it."

Then I asked if Donald Trump walked alone into his office right now, do you think you could have a meaningful conversation with him?

"I would like to think so. Yeah. I would like to think I could be calm, hold my emotions in check to ask some penetrating questions, and listen to his response. The moment that I lose it is the moment that any constructive or positive outcome of that conversation would be eliminated, lost. So I would like to think I've grown enough to have enough maturity that I could very calmly set aside those emotions and feelings and be able to have a conversation, and try to find out why he wants to do what he's doing."

We both were aware that we have friends and family members who like or love Donald Trump and his actions, and as much as we don't understand it, we have to live with it . . . for now. He's one of our main teachers in the practice of patience. Having one day a week of solitude, fishing in a kayak on a lake, in all seasons, helps Chuck keep his blood pressure under control. I like to dance at the yurt or sit under the skylight and read writings of spiritual masters.

Everything is Impermanent.

The late Anthony de Mello – a Jesuit priest, spiritual writer and teacher – popped into my mind while I was in Chuck's office. In the opening paragraph of de Mello's wonderful wake-up book, "Awareness: The Perils and Opportunities of Reality," he writes, "all mystics – Catholic, Christian, non-Christian, no matter what their theology, no matter what their religion – are unanimous on one thing: that all is well, all is well. Though everything is a mess, all is well. Strange paradox, to be sure. But, tragically, most people never get to see that all is well because they are asleep. They are having a nightmare."

He mixes Christian spirituality, Buddhist parables, Hindu breathing exercises and psychological insight.

Sister Margaret Gallagher, pastoral administrator at little St. Joan of Arc Catholic Church in Plymouth, North Carolina, gave me a copy of de Mello's "Awareness" book in 1991, one year after it was first published. He died of a heart attack in 1987 at age 55.

She loved his writings and teachings and felt I would too, knowing my feelings about the oneness of humanity and passion for finding common

345

ground between Eastern and Western religions. She was right and I still have a deep appreciation and love for Sister Margaret, three years after her death in March 2017 at the age of 83. Whenever I think of her, the "Awareness" book by Anthony de Mello comes to mind.

I'm glad I introduced de Mello's writings to Chuck Queen in February 2020. Several weeks after being in his office, he sent me a text saying, "I'm loving Anthony de Mello." He said it again the next time we met on the Capital Bridge in Frankfort on March 1 while attending a peaceful march marking the 55th anniversary of the "Bloody Sunday" civil rights march over the Edmund Pettus Bridge in Selma, Alabama in 1965.

His enthusiasm led me to start re-reading a few pages of de Mello's "Awareness" every morning after sitting meditation, and it is good medicine for the soul.

In 1998, 11 years after de Mello's death, the Congregation for the Doctrine of the Faith, under the leadership of its Cardinal-Prefect, Joseph Ratzinger (who later became Pope Benedict XVI) conducted a review of de Mello's work and released a lengthy comment expressing appreciation but also theological concern that, while there was no explicit heresy, some might be misled into seeing Jesus not as the Son of God but as simply one who came to teach that all are children of God.

Ok, thanks for the warning.

Rabbouni man

Another book that has become a part of my 2020 daily life is titled "Rabbouni: The First 100 Homilies"　by Father Lawman Chibundi. I read one homily each day, sometimes two because, like Chuck Queen and Richard Rohr, Father Chibundi brings God and Jesus "alive in the present moment" for me in the third decade of the 21st century.

Rabbouni is an Aramaic word meaning teacher, and his faithful followers believe Father Chibundi excels as a teacher.

"I love the way he explains the scripture," my daughter Charlsie Garrett says. "I had gone to church all my life and I would wake up on Sundays and think, oh, no, I've got to go to church. It was a chore. Now on Sundays I wake up early and can't wait to get there. I love the simplicity of it all and that he and Father Kevin are so very welcoming to everybody.

"You don't have to be Catholic to go there and receive Jesus, and really feel his presence. I like that they don't have to serve wine out of a gold chalice. It can be out of a glass cup. I like that it's not about the money, that it's more about the teaching, sharing and welcoming. He gave great sermons at St. Augustine, but I think he feels freer now to speak from the heart and like Jesus, he has an all-inclusive heart."

Chibundi was born in the village of Chibombo in Zambia, Africa. When he was an infant his family moved to Livingston and he grew up by the famed Victoria Falls in southern Africa. The misty falls plunges 354 feet, roughly twice the height of North America's Niagara Falls. Zambia is a landlocked country of rugged terrain and diverse wildlife, with many parks and safari areas.

At age 13, he felt called to the priesthood and at 16 was enrolled in the minor seminary in Choma, Zambia. After completing high school there, he joined the Passionist priests in Botswana and lived with them for seven years, making his first profession.

He left the Passionists and immigrated to the United States in 2001 to study for the Roman Catholic Archdiocese of Louisville. He was ordained a priest by Archbishop Thomas Kelly in 2004 and began a ministry of preaching and celebrating the sacraments. He left the Archdiocese of Louisville on December 31, 2008.

Three weeks later he created the independent Rabbouni Catholic Community, which retains the basic Catholic beliefs of faith and love, spirituality and community, prayer and sacramentality.

On the front of Sunday bulletins is a statement saying the mission of Rabbouni "is to provide an understanding of the connection with liturgy and everyday life. Rabbouni offers spiritual support for those seeking a deep and personal relationship with Christ, in a respectful, non-judging community."

I thank daughter Charlsie for insisting that I go to 9 a.m. Catholic Mass with her in November 2019 when I wanted to stay on the farm, relax and watch CBS Sunday Morning on TV. The last time I had seen Father Chibundi was on June 5, 2010 in the back yard of Garrett Ranch in Gravel Switch, when he married Charlsie and Jamie Garrett.

More than a decade ago, I had heard maybe two of his homilies at St. Augustine Catholic Church in Lebanon and liked them. I enjoyed the few brief one-on-one conversations we had. I knew he was intelligent, kind and compassionate, but I was older now and tired. My mind was focused on editing an interfaith book I had started in 2012, and I was determined to not add another word, just subtract.

I went with Charlsie to my first Rabbouni Catholic Community Mass and Father Chibundi was not there. Father Kevin Przybylski, associate

347

pastor and music director, was officiating. I was disappointed at first, but not for long.

I was happy to be back in Lebanon at United Presbyterian Church for a Catholic Mass with mostly African Americans.

"We are nesting, paying rent at welcoming Presbyterian churches in Lebanon and Louisville, because we are a small church community and don't currently have the financial resources to have our own church buildings," says Father Chibundi. I felt at home. The same Presbyterian church congregation in Lebanon opened their hearts, minds and doors to the Tashi Kyil Tibetan Buddhist monks in 2016 and February 2019 to create, over four days each time, a World Peace mandala in the front of the sanctuary.

Inside the sanctuary with a large radiant stained-glass window of Jesus, I had spent many hours watching the monks build their beautiful interfaith sand paintings, and loved every sacred second of it.

Now, nine months later, I was back in the church and I heard angelic voices from the small choir gathered with Father Kevin at the piano. I loved the compassionate homily and hearing that everyone was welcomed to take communion. I had taken communion a few times at Church of the Ascension – the downtown Episcopal church, and Immanuel Baptist Church, both in Frankfort. But it was the first time since 2006 that I had taken the bread and wine at a Catholic Mass.

I loved taking the wine from Ann Peterson, a longtime friend who I hadn't seen in probably 20 years. And I was happy that Charlsie was a lector.

Charlsie didn't have to beg me to return to church with her and Jamie on Christmas Eve. It had been a wonderful day in Marion County, getting to spend several hours with my sister and brother-in-law, Beverly and Tom Harmon, and nephew Kelly Harmon and his wife, Marla, and their two sons, Cameron and Chase.

Father Kevin and the choir were amazing again. Father Chibundi was there in his white, red and gold robe, being energetic, funny, entertaining, loving and

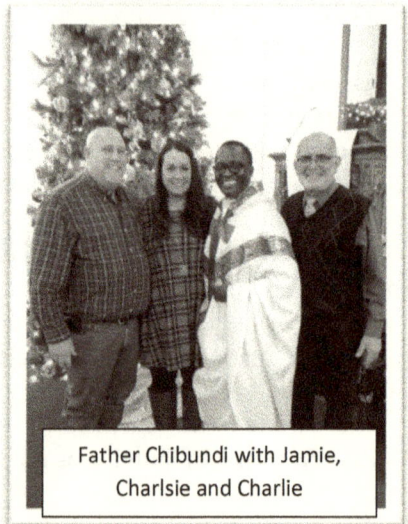

Father Chibundi with Jamie, Charlsie and Charlie

348

happy in giving the homily; and serious in joyfully celebrating the Eucharist.

Father Chibundi opened his Christmas Eve homily with a side note by recalling the first time in his life he had a panic attack. When he left the archdiocese, he knew he would need a job to financially support himself. Today he is an officer with Louisville Metro Police, working a night shift. While in training at the police academy, he was at the shooting range, and firing a weapon was something new to him.

"I know my way around a prayer book, but the shooting range, I was hopeless," he said. "I had never shot a gun before. So when I was firing rounds, one of the casings got stuck in the barrel and nothing was happening. The instructor saw me struggling and came and stood right next to me and began yelling in my ear, 'FIX IT! FIX IT!' The other instructors heard him and they came over. It was Full Metal Jacket. And they were all screaming, 'FIX IT!'

"And I asked, 'How?' And they said, 'Just tap and clear the chamber.' I panicked, and if you panic, you lose the gunfight. I fell to my knee and tapped it and cleared the chamber and got up and finished the rounds. That episode of the instructors all around me screaming 'FIX IT' was so very present."

Then he said to his congregation, "I don't know what you are going through in life, but Fix It. There is not one scenario that ends perfectly. Something will always happen. So Fix It. If it's that important, you will find a way to fix it. Sometimes we fix it alone but sometimes we gather as a church family to help each other fix whatever is broken. It will not fix itself. Amen!"

He then went into his prepared remarks.

Later when I was talking to him, he said, "I think the 'fix it' comment was a distracting thought that kept coming into my mind as I was preparing the homily. I usually take those as a message that somebody needs to hear.

"However, Joseph and Mary had to fix it when they could not find a room in the inn. They did not sit around and cry. Sometimes we have to make do when our best plans fail. And there is God, and grace in making do."

After 9 a.m. Mass in Lebanon at United Presbyterian Church, 157 East Main Street, Rabbouni has 12:30 p.m. and 5:30 p.m. Masses every Sunday in Louisville at Springdale Presbyterian Church, 7812 Brownsboro Road.

In January 2020, I attended another Mass in Lebanon with Charlsie and Trish Nebriaga, of Springfield. Trish works with Charlsie at the Lebanon Aquatic Center and was overjoyed with the hospitality and love she felt the first time she met and listened to Father Chibundi. She was Charlsie's inspiration to try Rabbouni Catholic Community.

Father Chibundi, at the January service, invited all Lebanon parishioners to attend Rabbouni's 11th anniversary celebration in Louisville on Sunday, February 9, and a potluck meal after Mass.

Daughter Kathryn Pearl, of Frankfort, invited me to ride with her and her young children, Kamdyn and Kalleigh, to Louisville for the celebration. Louisville has been recognized four times as an "International City of Compassion" and we certainly felt an abundance of compassion at Rabbouni Catholic Community. Being in a major city, church attendance is much higher there and you could feel a loving kinship between the two congregations. The music from the combined choirs was heavenly.

In one of the daily homilies in his book, Father Chibundi said, "I am very grateful to this God who chooses to come to me in very ordinary ways. I am not one who looks for miracles or extraordinary events that should speak of God's presence and power. I see God in a flower, in my dogs, Tazi and Bourgeois, in the people who have been generous to me, and in the people who challenge me."

In another homily he talked about being grateful for the different forms of prayer he was introduced to in his early years of priest training – the Psalms, the love of the rosary and other Marian devotions, eastern religions and charismatics. Novices would begin the day with yoga and then do sitting meditation. Sometimes they would chant Om or J-e-s-u-s.

"We did pranayama, the breathing exercises," he said. "It was beautiful. You should try it sometime. People do not know how to breathe and that is why we always seem to be tired. Deep breaths are the way to go. Concentrate on your breathing and you might breathe pain and stress away."

Then, he said, they would go from silent prayer to prayer "with those crazy charismatics. . . . Talk about coming from quiet prayer to a joyful noise for the Lord! We were jumping up and down, praising the Lord. We were slain in the spirit, we spoke in tongues.

"I am so grateful for this wonderful experience because it makes me, today, a priest who can connect with those who love the Psalms, those who love the rosary, those who love silence, and those who love making a joyful noise for the Lord."

Amen Father Chibundi!

In his book, Chibundi also wrote a message to his Lebanon congregation in response to negative statements said about him and the Rabbouni Catholic Community.

"My dear friends, you were told this past weekend that I am not in right standing with the Church and living in sin because I have decided to continue my ministry without the blessings of the powers that be. You were also told that if you came to Rabbouni, or encouraged anyone to come to Rabbouni, you too will be committing sin.

"I have steered clear of responding to any negative comments that have come from the powers, but it would be out of my character if I did not have at least one response to the many things that have been said.

"Tell me this: In your opinion, which is the greater sin – coming to a church where you feel spiritually fed or covering up sexual abuse? If coming to Rabbouni is a sin and excluding people from communion because they left a terrible relationship and got married without getting an annulment is not, then I would rather sin and welcome them to the table. If coming to Rabbouni is a sin and calling our gay and lesbian brothers and sisters disordered is not a sin, I would rather live in sin and welcome them to the table of the Lord. If going to any church other than the Roman Catholic Archdiocese of Louisville is a sin, then sign me up for a sinful life."

Chibundi said this is not the time to throw stones at those who choose another path. "That is so juvenile and below the belt. I believe people these days go where they are fed and not where an institution makes them go using fear and guilt. Those days have come and gone."

Regarding his second job to financially support himself, Officer Chibundi said police officers, in a way, do the same work as priests, "even though emotions are rawer in police work." In a recent Sunday homily he asked, "What does the voice of God sound like?"

And he answered, "Sometimes the voice of God sounds like handcuffs clicking behind your back, saying you're going in the wrong direction. There was one young lady I was arresting one time in a domestic incident. I said, 'This will be horrible when I put cuffs on you and take you to jail. I hope this will be the moment when you stop this and have a new beginning.'"

He said he doesn't mention God in his police work when he is trying to reason with people, "but it's the same kind of job."

When he started his independent Catholic church, he didn't know what the future held. He had heard that a Roman Catholic priest stood up in

351

his church and said this Rabbouni church thing won't last three months. "That Rabbouni Catholic Community has been around for 11 years now is a great, great miracle," says Father Chibundi.

Now as a Catholic priest, he is a husband and father. His wife, Mary Ann Schaffer Chibundi, has a master's in occupational therapy from Spalding University. They have a son, Grayson, age 7. Mary Ann's mother is a former nun and her father is a former Dominican brother.

Father Chibundi, who will be 46 on June 28, said he met Mary Ann at a salsa dancing class and a friend of hers introduced them. He said dancing is a big part of his African culture.

"We had dance at Mass in church. I had always been fascinated by dance, and I could dance, but I didn't know salsa or any Latin dances. I had never heard of salsa dancing. But I went to the class and I absolutely loved it. I was terrible at it at first, but I loved the dance community in Louisville. It's very strong."

In addition to salsa, Father Chibundi has also learned bachata and merengue dancing in Louisville. "Now I want to learn how to tango dance." Earlier this year, he went to a birthday party and there was dancing. After he danced with a woman from Bulgaria, someone asked him if they had ever danced together before, "because we danced so well together and the connection was absolutely unbelievable," Chibundi said. "It was the first time we had danced together. But she's from a dance culture and I'm from a dance culture, and we spoke the same dance language. We were mixing. We did some merengue, some salsa, and some bachata. Whatever music was playing we would find a rhythm and go with it, and move from one form to the other."

I talked with Father Chibundi by phone on Saturday afternoon following Easter and he said he and Mary Ann had danced in the kitchen that morning. "In dance there's a leader and a follower, and sometimes the man doesn't do a lot of movement," he said. "The man stands for stability while the woman is the flower. And from that point, Mary Ann is a much better dancer than me."

The divine dance of life – I Absolutely Love It! My hope is that before 2020 ends Father Chibundi and Mary Ann will visit our yurt and show us some salsa, bachata, merengue and tango dancing. They'll meet the Glitterbugs and other kindred spirits, I promise. And bring Grayson to play with my grandchildren Kamdyn, Kalleigh, who loves dancing at age five, Luke, and Angela's granddaughter Sunnie Mae.

About the Author

Charles Pearl

...is a retired journalist, who has won numerous awards for writing and photography. He continues to do freelance writing, mostly for The State Journal newspaper and FRANK magazine in Frankfort, the capital city of Kentucky. He was born in Jeffersonville, Indiana, in the summer of 1948, just across the Ohio River from Louisville, and grew up in Lebanon, Kentucky. He has a bachelor's degree in business administration from Western Kentucky University. He lives near downtown Frankfort with his 12-year-old black Lab, Lily, and serves on the Frankfort Interfaith Council. "Dancing at the Yurt: An Interfaith Spiritual Journey" is his first book.

Writing the book began in 2012 when I met fascinating people in Bloomington, Indiana, at a Tibetan Mongolian Buddhist Cultural Center retreat. I write about their spiritual journeys, and then include many others of diverse faiths who have inspired me on a winding path of being Baptist, Catholic and Buddhist.

www.ingramcontent.com/pod-product-compliance
Lightning Source LLC
Chambersburg PA
CBHW022113080426
42734CB00006B/109